Knowledge Production in the Arab World

T0298719

Over recent decades we have witnessed the globalization of research. However, this has yet to translate into a worldwide scientific network across which competencies and resources can flow freely. Arab countries have strived to join this globalized world and become a "knowledge economy," yet little time has been invested in the region's fragmented scientific institutions; institutions that should provide opportunities for individuals to step out on the global stage.

Knowledge Production in the Arab World investigates research practices in the Arab world using multiple case studies from the region, with particular focus on Lebanon and Jordan. It depicts the Janus-like face of Arab research, poised between the negative and the positive and faced with two potentially opposing strands: local relevance alongside its internationalization. The book critically assesses the role and dynamics of research and poses questions that are crucial to furthering our understanding of the very particular case of knowledge production in the Arab region. The book explores research's relevance and whom it serves, as well as the methodological flaws behind academic rankings and the meaning and application of key concepts such as knowledge society/economy.

Providing a detailed and comprehensive examination of knowledge production in the Arab world, this book is of interest to students, scholars and policymakers working on the issues of research practices and status of science in contemporary developing countries.

Sari Hanafi is Professor of Sociology and Chair of the Department of Sociology, Anthropology and Media Studies at the American University of Beirut. He is also the editor of *Idafat: The Arab Journal of Sociology* and the Vice President of the International Sociological Association and the Arab Council of Social Science.

Rigas Arvanitis is Sociologist and Senior Researcher at the Institut de Recherche pour le Développement (IRD), specializing in the sociology of science and innovation, and research policy. He is also Director of the French consortium on research, innovation and society (IFRIS).

Routledge Advances in Middle East and Islamic Studies

Knowledge Production in the Arab World

The impossible promise

Sari Hanafi and Rigas Arvanitis

LONDON AND NEW YORK

First published 2016 by Routledge

2 Park Square, Milton Park, Abingdon, Oxfordshire OX14 4RN
52 Vanderbilt Avenue, New York, NY 10017

Routledge is an imprint of the Taylor & Francis Group, an informa business

First issued in paperback 2019

British Library Cataloguing-in-Publication Data
A catalogue record for this book is available from the British Library

Library of Congress Cataloging-in-Publication Data
Names: Hanafi, Sari, author. | Arvanitis, Rigas, author.
Title: Knowledge production in the Arab world : the impossible promise / Sari Hanafi and Rigas Arvanitis.
Description: New York, NY : Routledge, 2016. | Series: Routledge advances in Middle East and Islamic studies ; 25 | Includes bibliographical references.
Identifiers: LCCN 2015029523| ISBN 9781138948815 (hardback) | ISBN 9781315669434 (ebook)
Subjects: LCSH: Research–Arab countries. | Learning and scholarship–Arab countries. | Education and globalization–Arab countries.
Classification: LCC Q180.A65 H36 2016 | DDC 303.48/309174927–dc23
LC record available at http://lccn.loc.gov/2015029523

ISBN: 978-1-138-94881-5 (hbk)
ISBN: 978-0-367-87430-8 (pbk)

Typeset in Times New Roman
by Wearset Ltd, Boldon, Tyne and Wear

Contents

Figures

Tables

Acknowledgments

The authors would like to thank all colleagues who contributed in different ways to this book, data collection and fieldwork, mainly Abdelhakim al-Husban, Nada Maghlouth, Claude Tayoun and Ola Hanafi. Our most grateful thanks are extended to all those who commented on earlier versions or chapters of this manuscript, in particular our colleagues from CNRS Lebanon – Mouïn Hamzé, Fouad Mrad, Hassan Charif, Fawaz Fawaz, Rula Atweh – but also in many more institutions in Lebanon and elsewhere: Jacques Gaillard, Lokman Meho, Christophe Varin, Toufic Rizk, Elisabeth Longuenesse, Rita Yazigi and Fadia Homeidan. Additionally, special thanks go to our workmates Rafael Rodriguez, Aurélie Pancera, Chiara Morini, Kyriaki Papageorgiou, Hatem M'henni, Rachid Ghrir, Yasemin Koç, Said Jabbouri, Bruce Currie-Adler and David O'Brien, as well as Anaïd Donabedian and Nicolas Puig and others that we certainly missed here and to whom we apologize. This book has been a collective endeavor; many of our students of the "Social production of knowledge" course at AUB participated in the debates, and we are grateful to them.

This book was made possible by support received from the Lebanese National Council for Scientific Research (CNRS), the Institut de recherche pour le développement (IRD) and the American University of Beirut. Some of the material we include in Chapter 1 is drawn from a study we performed in 2013–2014, funded by IDRC Canada.

Special thanks to all our interviewees who took time out of their busy schedules to sit with us and discuss their research experiences. Many persons have participated in the creation of this book since we have partly published some of the material and have been intensively discussing its content for three years. We are grateful to them, and to all our friends who may not recognize the discussions we had. Lastly, we thank our wives, Maha and Chantal, for their patience as they put up with our mood swings and stress during the last years of fieldwork and writings.

Introduction

> Science is a sort of metaphor for politics, because its ostensible rationality covers up any messy conflicting interests and is also the purest expression of development and modernization.
>
> (Siino 2004: 73)

In June 2014, our university department organized a tribute to Samir Khalaf, who is a professor of sociology at the American University of Beirut (AUB). When we sent this invitation to our mailing list, we received seven phone calls and emails asking us when Samir passed away, and four other emails asking when he retired. This anecdote alludes to the lack of tradition in the Arab world of giving a tribute to someone who is still alive or still has a professional life. It indicates the absence of a "scientific community" in Lebanon that acknowledges the contribution of its members. Of course, traditions are the result of an active re-enactment of our history. Scientific, academic and disciplinary communities are fond of these small rituals that revive the intellectual standing of its members and permit us to gauge our own position as a group within the "community." What is at stake, in any of these informal evaluations, is where we stand, and at the same time to which group we belong. Institutions make some of these boundaries,[1] and an important motive for our book has been to understand the institutionalization process that has taken place in the Arab world, and particularly in Lebanon. We will ask ourselves why it was so late, why the scientists waited so long to create an active scientific community.

In March 2014, the Lebanese Association for the Advancement of Science held its twentieth annual conference. It was an opportunity to present more than 400 posters and presentations in the natural and exact sciences. For a small community, in a small country, these numbers are relatively high; it is not so much a question of the mere size of the scientific community, but rather a question of proportion. The researchers are there, but is there a community? "In this country, you can find a specialist in any specialty, but you will never find two persons in the same domain" was the witty remark of a research director who we interviewed last year. Maybe it appears to be an exaggeration, but certainly it reflects a widely felt reality. This lack of "community" appears so strange in a country where the notion of community is so present, referring to the religious and social "communities" that are recognized in the political life of the country. And maybe a part of the answer lies, precisely, in the division of the country into its many competing fragments. The particular context of Lebanon is a nuance of a phenomenon evident throughout the Arab world.

The first issue we would like to tackle in this book are the reasons the scientific community is so little recognized in Arab countries, despite them being rich with universities and hospitals, and having some level of scientific production. On some level, we question whether the problem stems from institutions or whether it is a result of political matters, in which Arab countries are comparatively less active than other regions, like Latin America. Is it possible that the problem is grounded in deeper social and political problems that influence the production of scientific knowledge?

1 Identifying the local engines of globalization in research

We were not initially guided by this questioning about the scientific community. Rather, we arrived at this issue, and as we will see it will relate to one of our main conclusions. As we know, since the seminal book of Roland Waast and his colleagues (Gaillard *et al.* 1997a: 12), scientific communities were born in the age of *national science*, after colonial rule withdrew:

> For almost three decades or so after the War, national mode of scientific development promoted the strategies of import-substitution and self-reliance in the overall economic policies, also governed the organization of science and the goal orientations of scientific communities.

But this new era of "national science" has been short-lived: we can date this period from the independence or liberation wars, when the nation states were set-up against colonial rule, until the 1980s, when globalization became the new name of the game.

At that time, until approximately the 1980s, research was essentially equated to science. Nation states were creating new institutions, among them universities and public research centers. The debates on development always mentioned economic growth, and science was just a background activity useful for technological development. All that counted was technology and, for those who recognize the unequal exchanges between developing and rich countries, technological transfers. The endless debates on technological development translated the frustration of those newcomer countries that lacked access to up-to-date technology. This debate, as Ruffier (1991) claimed, was terminated when it was found out, in the process, that technology cannot be bought: it has to be developed, it has to be incorporated locally and mastered in-house, it has to rely on previous knowledge, it has, also, to rely on research. Technological developments do not depend on research exclusively; they relate to the technological experiences of companies, among which R&D and public research are, indeed, vital inputs.

Since the 1980s, a second fundamental change has taken place: globalization has profoundly affected research. Research is no more an exclusively national endeavor. The divided world in the aftermath of World War II gave rise to a hierarchical world where centers and peripheries are more widely distributed. Scientific collaborations are all about how to link this "national" science (that is, the local scientific community) with the available international competencies, as we will see later.

As a result of this globalization process, science has grown very rapidly. Estimates[2] of the world expenses in R&D show a figure around €1,113 billion, which represents 2.15 percent of estimated world GDP; this figure has grown 77 percent in seven years, from a low of €640 billion in 2000 to today's €1.2 trillion. Over the same period, world GDP grew at a slightly slower pace (72 percent in seven years).

Not only has the scale of science changed in large proportions; its geographic distribution has also changed. The world production, in terms of publications (excluding social and human sciences) is no longer entirely bound to North America and Europe. The geographical distribution is as follows: 38.6 percent of publications come from Europe, followed by North America (28.4 percent) and Asia (24.3 percent). China represents around 11 percent of the world share of publications. New players in world scientific production have appeared since the early years of our new era: China, India, Brazil, Turkey, South Africa. The club of countries that give priority to research has grown, and now includes countries such as Mexico, Thailand and Chile, for instance. Later, we will examine in more depth these important, yet limited, changes.

This increase in the size of science also reflects a larger scope of activity and a stronger interest in the results of research. This was the impetus for the increasing importance of PhD programs created in every country and, as a result, flows of students worldwide have soared. The information and telecommunication technologies created a global information infrastructure, which has triggered further collaborative activities within research networks and for users of scientific knowledge.

The governance and predominance of science in political debates (think of climate change, genetically modified organisms [GMOs], international property rights, negotiations on drugs, biodiversity and the like) has changed. Scientific questions have become global. Scientists of the natural and social realms have become accustomed to thinking about issues at the global level. Of the two scientific fields, this phenomenon possibly occurs more with natural scientists. Objects are global; communities of specialists are global; training specialists has become a question of feeding an international distribution of competences, making every new PhD candidate a future emigrant. Caroline Wagner (2008), among many other authors, has quite brightly defended the idea that international scientific networks are essentially made of individuals who seek collaboration with peers having mutual interests and complementary skills around the world. In this globalized world, international collaboration functions as a global self-organizing system through collective action at the level of researchers themselves (Leydesdorff and Wagner 2008).

According to this view, in this global era, the individual researcher becomes the hero of international collaborations, by taking decisions where individual interests are the main driver; the basis of this explanation is the idea that the individual recognizes potentially interesting collaborators and is able to evaluate and seize the expected outcomes of the planned collaborations. Leaving aside many flaws[3] in the argument, we believe this view of a sort of gigantic, world-wide network of scientists, in which competences and resources circulate easily, does not correspond to reality. Individual scientists, even the best among the best, need to be able to objectively "choose" their collaborations, a judgment that relates to her/his insertion in their local environment, institutionally, politically and economically. The existence of a local scientific community as well as the institutionalization of scientific activity plays a very important role here. It is through the participation in local training and scientific teams that the young, individual scientist can become increasingly involved in international collaborations and, consequently, be involved in the global scene. This is because, locally, policy instruments have been used to consolidate research activities, doctoral programs and research units, making research a recognized item in policy, budgets and organizations. Personal decisions are important, but choices are also influenced by other factors that go far beyond what we are usually ready to accept when assuming that research (and international scientific collaboration) is beneficial.

We will insist on this aspect, since international collaboration will be an important part of our book. However, for clarity, we want to follow this simple idea that globalization is also a matter of locating the actual places where globalization is based (Sassen 2007). The particular networking that scientists produce through their movements (for training and research), their travels in order to participate in international conferences and meetings, the broad and pervasive movements by the scientific diasporas in foreign countries to study and occupy post-doc positions or work abroad in order to acquire a specialty that will permit a better return home – all these more or less permanent migrations – are in fact dependent upon some local engines of globalization.

Two processes apparently build these engines of globalizations. First, there is an institutionalization process (Vessuri 1994) in which "capacity building" is the first step toward creating research institutions. In most countries where research was not a sizable activity, through a period that can be named "national science," scientific research has been closely linked to universities, instead of national public research organizations. The creation of these particular social institutions goes well beyond the objectives of this book. Nonetheless, the establishment and consolidation of research activities inside the universities has become a crucial aspect of the institutionalization process. The evolution of research, the acceptance of science as a legitimate source of knowledge, is not a mere question of "development": it is a question of political willingness and of its embodiment inside the national institutions. We would like to trigger a discussion, in the Arab world, on these aspects inside the universities, inside the local scientific communities.

The second process at work is the building of the scientific community – we could add the "national" scientific community – and this process, as explained above, is dependent on the historical momentum, and the resources available based on whether the political system is willing to pay for research. In the case of Lebanon, the apparent lack of a scientific community is also a reflection that is valid for a large majority of countries in the Arab world. As proof, very few, if any, Arab scientists are involved in any of the international scientific debates we have been discussing in these pages.

Since the 1990s, policies have moved away from the import-substitution model to the neoliberal dogma (the "Washington Consensus" and "post-Washington Consensus") that oblige us to think about socio-economic issues only as market issues. The institutionalization process that was slowly taking place was shattered by the lack of resources of public institutions, which directly impacted universities and public research organizations. Thus, science policies also changed.

All these processes (institutionalization, community building and internationalization) were driven by certain ways of understanding the economy and its relation to knowledge. Since the end of the 1990s, the emerging *knowledge economy* became the concept of the day. At the start of the new century, the world appeared increasingly multipolar, with "knowledge" playing many different vital roles. The (once known as) developing countries seemed to have disappeared from the radar within the new knowledge economy. A new concept was needed for what Alice Amsden rightfully called "the Rest," in contrast to "the West" (Amsden 2001). If "developing" is no longer the right word for these economies, what should it be? Have the modes of producing, using and diffusing knowledge changed so much that development itself became an obsolete concept? Are we all living in a "flat world" (Friedman 2005) without borders, where power structures have disappeared? Whether one views globalization as beneficial or harmful, there is a tightly interconnected economic structure with science and technology, as stressed by the Arab Knowledge Report (Al Maktoum Foundation and UNDP 2009).

Multipolarity, indeed, does not indicate the disappearance of hegemony; on the contrary, it is a clear indication that several large centers of research and innovation will exercise hegemony over the field, in a far more aggressive competition than had existed in the divided world of centers and peripheries. If we look at the geographical distribution of the number of articles over time (1978 to 2008), the distribution has not changed for most countries, although absolute numbers have grown immensely. China, Brazil, South Korea and Taiwan are still exceptions (see Figures 2.7–2.10). The next to come seem to be South Africa, Turkey, Thailand, Malaysia, Chile, Argentina, etc. It is not so much a question of more numbers of publications, but rather a changing position that these countries are acquiring. Losego and Arvanitis (2008) have proposed to call the countries that belong neither to the old center nor the new emerging economies as "non-hegemonic countries."

The notion of a non-hegemonic country relates to two essential dimensions: the position of the country in the international division of scientific work, and the fact that these countries do not have financial instruments capable of influencing the broader goals of knowledge production, unlike the United States, the European Union and a small number of Asian countries. The research "agenda," as it is usually named, is still set by research groups that belong to a very few large countries, mostly those belonging to the OECD. Knowledge and research seems even more unequally distributed than commercial goods and economic wealth, and strangely enough seems to be very much tied to locational advantages, rather static over time, situated geographically and linked to age-old institutions. This translates into the fact that research policies have been stressing the importance of the public sector, of strong locational advantages – which means rooting the research activities in a specific country because of some advantage you can only find in that specific space. This determination of the research agenda by some very specific places, in some very precise institutions and by some very particular research groups is confirmed by the fact that contrary to our usual thinking (reinforced by the triumphal statements one finds in newspapers), emerging countries have still not been very much able to modify the main flows of investments in R&D (Larédo 2003). Even if growth of scientific production in intermediate urban localities can be observed, rather than a concentration in very large cities (Grossetti *et al.* 2013), the main places of production of scientific research have not changed a lot since the end of World War II. Numerous literature have been written to show the changing ranking of countries and the contribution of research to their wealth. Most, invariably, end up at more or less the same ranking, an issue we will tackle in Chapter 1. This issue of the position of a country within the world circulation of knowledge is probably different for innovation, as opposed to research, since not all innovation is research-based, and since innovation can be more multifaceted than research. Nonetheless, non-hegemonic countries have usually adopted an incremental development model, based on strategies of technological catching up. The experience of the Asian Tigers is precisely one of catching up, learning and adopting technologies, until they become key tools of economic development.

In brief, we need to examine the local roots of globalization, or rather how "globalization" functions locally. The large globalization process of research that we have mentioned above is something rather different from an extension of international activities in research that can be qualified as the "internationalization of research." Rather, we need to identify the changing nature of the research activities in a multipolar world that is not just the outgrowth of a quantitative increase of research. In other words, there is a change of paradigm in the way research is undertaken; it is no more a by-product of extending the research activity into an international arena, adding up more resources (more money, more human resources and also more institutions); rather, it is a definition of the research activity since its very beginning, when research programs are defined from a worldwide point of view rather than a national point of view, which is apparently a paradox; the more globalized activities thus seem to be the more locally rooted. By way of consequence, the more deeply rooted the research activity locally, the more far-reaching it could be. Or, at least this is our claim.

We titled this book *Knowledge Production in the Arab World: The Impossible Promise* because local activities often reflect global and international activities, as if the later were an impossible target to attain. Research activities are demanding, not solely because of the resources needed for their performance, but also because of their connection to scientific and extra-scientific interests. The mandate to attain a "knowledge economy" is implicitly a mandate to forget about the societal problems and challenges and make the activity visible internationally, no matter the cost. Here, we will shed some light on the status of the research in the Arab world. In the absence of some rooting of the research locally, it can just become the door for more "exits": pure and simple brain-drain, and poor research performance in universities and research centers. Research locally will be, under these conditions, an impossible promise.

2 Knowledge society/economy: the impossible promise

We began this research as a regional project, and Egypt was one of the countries we initially wanted to examine in-depth. "We are not in modernity," was the statement of an Egyptian colleague some four years before the 2011 revolution when talking about research. He was expressing, in this way, the fact that research was absent from any policy consideration. The country had left aside all reflexive work on how and why it should produce scientific knowledge. This commonly made statement was also accompanied by a reproach: "why are Egyptian researchers not taken seriously?" Was it that the country in fact impeded developing research? One can see that is largely not the case, but the research system had come to a halt in these years (Bond *et al.* 2012). An example can be read in the work of Kyriaki Papageorgiou (2007) on the development of biotechnology in Egypt, where she shows political difficulties that impeded the development of European scientific collaboration in Egypt, although US cooperation had forced changes in the legal intellectual property regime more convenient to enterprises. The Mubarak reign left feelings of discomfort among fellow academic colleagues at the University of Cairo. The stress on the university system was enormous: lack of funds, inappropriate structures and bad management. All that made the public research institutions almost paralyzed. Egypt seemed like a showcase of the disastrous situation we mentioned above. While some research fields were finding their way, as we show in the ESTIME project,[4] a revolution happened in the meantime. We cannot but be convinced that some of the dry tinder that fed the revolution can be found among the frustrated academics and students. And, when we began a second project in 2012, based on the same ambition to describe the state of knowledge production, this time in Lebanon and (to lesser extent) Jordan, our aim was to understand the dynamic of research, as we will explain later, and not only its institutional setting.

In recent years, research and analysis on knowledge production and innovation in the Arab region has grown. Probably, this was triggered by the first Arab Human Development Report of the UNDP (UNDP 2004 & 2005), which stressed the need for better education, freedom of thought and more adequate jobs in Arab countries. Thus, the production of knowledge was put on the agenda, and joined, not unexpectedly, the interests of enterprises, promoters of a more competitive economy and the World Bank in the promotion of a knowledge economy. Thus, the issue was no longer only that of expanding awareness of the importance of knowledge in society, but that of competitiveness of the Arab economies, through the promotion of a knowledge economy. Research appeared to be one among other "pillars" that needed to be constructed in order to accompany the entry of Arab countries into the knowledge economy. These claims are so broad because they are based on macro-economic assessments, themselves "empirically" founded on broad indicators with little to no understanding of the research dynamic. Essentially, they are grounded on a thin theory of development – a theory that is basically void of political forces, with a vision of a consensual and uniform society, where competition is an individual contest on a single ladder that goes to the top. Rankings and knowledge economy go hand in hand, and the knowledge economy could thus grow under authoritarian regimes that seemed to do quite well on this part. Tunisia had to follow the example of Finland; the Gulf countries were showing the way by growing rapidly in terms of the knowledge economy and the index of competitiveness. Unfortunately, this view is to be found in practically all recent reports on research in the Arab countries. They include a *promise* for development based on a sort of miraculous inclusion into the knowledge economy. But then Nokia fell, and Finland was no longer a good example; the Arab countries had the curious idea to perform revolutions instead of seeking the competitive advantages they were told to pursue. Ben Ali flew to Saudi Arabia, and a long process of reform and revolution (what Asef Bayat calls "refolution") seized the Arab world (we examine the discourse about this fundamental change in Chapter 8). Quite conscious of this extraordinary political change, the World Bank repeated, practically unchanged, this *impossible promise* by publishing the report "Transforming Arab Economies: Travelling the Knowledge and Innovation Road" (Center for Mediterranean Integration 2013). The only thing that changed in this report was its milder tone! Again it is a clear proposition to enter the knowledge economy, and again the real revolution that had occurred just two years before this publication is absent.

Perhaps prematurely, Arab countries – or rather some actors inside the Arab countries, mainly government officials – have wanted to be called "knowledge societies."[5] Every country appears driven by the need to become a "knowledge economy,"[6] a title that became popular since the 1999 World Bank report (1999), and that was actively promoted by the knowledge assessment methodology designed by the World Bank, and specifically targeted to the MENA region (Reiffers and Aubert 2002). Building a knowledge economy became a policy objective alongside, and sometimes in contradiction with, the goal of establishing national innovation systems. The concept of a knowledge economy was formulated by focusing on some aspects of the developed economies that enjoy a dense network of research institutions, a high degree of investment in research and development (R&D) in both public and private institutions and a strong infrastructure, known, since the rise of the digital age, as "knowledge infrastructure" (Bowker 2001). This is sufficiently true for the United States and other G8 countries with the importance of what Richard Florida (2014) calls *the rise of a creative class*. Knowledge is about using information, not about mere exchanges of information; it is a practice rather than a possession. Knowledge infrastructures and knowledge circulation would then need to have previously constituted the social and economic conditions that would favor knowledge creation, a task that goes beyond promoting more exchanges of information, or inducing more young people to join creative companies.

Curiously enough, the "knowledge economy" was proposed by the World Bank (1999) on the basis of a comparison of the trends in Asia and Latin America, which was under the direction of a Bank official based in Mexico City. Probably one of the very first authors who wrote about the "knowledge society" was Nico Stehr (1994). He noted that, as a result of the remarkable growth of science and technology in modern society, it had undergone a fundamental shift and become an immediately productive force. Technology was no longer a "cultural" product, but a basic ingredient of any sustainable, long-term economic strategy. The closeness of science and technology that research has uncovered is here to stay, and will run ever deeper in social and political decisions. As many scholars from different regions have shown, a new set of institutional capabilities is deployed everywhere (Valenti *et al.* 2008). Yet, beyond glorifying the word "knowledge," there has been little reflection of these changes in the Arab region (Arvanitis and M'henni 2010).[7]

We could summarize how the knowledge society discourse has been projected in the Arab world as follows: the UN/World Bank ring alarm bells concerning the situation of knowledge production, but at the same time they adopt a methodology and indexes that cannot help the Arab world in how to create knowledge that is useful to their political and socio-economic status. This methodology is based on four pillars of the knowledge economy framework: first, an economic and institutional regime to provide incentives for the efficient use of existing and new knowledge and the flourishing of entrepreneurship (this is often based on the leaders' opinions); second, an educated and skilled population to create, share, and use knowledge well; third, an efficient innovation system of firms, research centers, universities, consultants and other organizations to tap into the growing stock of global knowledge, assimilate and adapt it to local needs and create new technology; and fourth, information and communication technology (ICT) to facilitate the effective creation, dissemination and processing of information (see Figure I.1).[8]

As Tremblay (2011) reminds us, Arab countries have rarely developed typical knowledge economy industries, such as production or assembly of electronic components, biotechnology or pharmaceutical industries. Ali Kadri (2014) talks even of policies of deindustrialization that have laid to waste the production of knowledge." The indexes used for post-industrial society (Bayat 2010) do not fit the reality of many Arab countries.[9] Two examples may show methodological and/or data collection problems. The ICT indicators for Tunisia showed positive

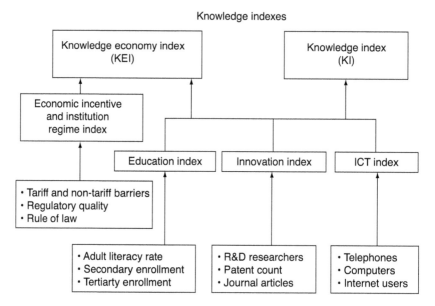

Figure I.1 Knowledge indexes (source: World Bank http://siteresources.worldbank.org/ INTUNIKAM/Resources/2012.pdf).

progress in the early 2000s. During that time, Ben Ali took over the internet from the very prestigious research center the Regional Institute for Computer Sciences and Telecommunications (IRSIT). ICT ranking is not sensitive to the state repression, surveillance and filtering; it even tends to favor countries that apply these repressive technologies. The second example is related to the innovation leaders' opinion surveys and ICT; these surveys conclude an advancement in many Gulf countries ranked better than Lebanon. This claim is wrong, as we will show in Chapter 4 (see also Kumar and Welsum 2013), mainly because it equates development to the opinions of some leaders in enterprises more interested in getting access to world markets than in the local economies' growth. Finally, one of the major effects of the "knowledge society" discourse is to legitimate policies, as was the case with the promotion of the concept of good governance by the World Bank, when it was used as a word that permitted avoiding the use of the word *democracy*, seen as politicized. So far we don't know if the knowledge society discourse is just a mask without real effect, or if it will, somehow, trigger some unintended effects. It is not anecdotal to mention that in Saudi Arabia, the Center for Strategic Studies of King Abdul Aziz University launched a series of e-books[10] on the knowledge society, in which we were positively surprised to find that while writing on the contribution of Saudi women in research, the author alludes to the violation of women's rights in this country. It is too early to see how society will benefit from such discourse to "reform" society and produce a critical thinking-based research.

We have tried, as have others, to keep an optimistic view about the future. But hiding the situation by the ritual invocation of the "knowledge economy" or the "knowledge society" as a solution to the problem of research is nothing but a rhetorical tool. We, as social scientists, cannot but convey this permanent feeling of unfulfillment that our colleagues express in their own words when they blame a "brain-dead country" (!), the inadequate procedures and the short-sighted policies. Although not unanimous, these negative judgments are quite common and contrast strongly with the positive and political platitudes served by governments concerning research: that we should triumphantly enter into the new knowledge economy, leaving behind us under-development, and embracing willingly globalization and its benefits! (See such discourse in Center for Mediterranean Integration 2013). Beyond the resources issues, engineers and economists are challenged to accompany this change while political challenges are still very important, including the democratic ideal that was behind the nahda (Arab renaissance).

Even worse, social sciences have no part in that; national councils and ministries are very cautious in dripping resources by small amounts such as to justify support for social sciences and thus not be accused of barring the research support against social scientists, and simultaneously pretend social sciences are not "of the same nature" and thus do not "really" participate in the research environment. Social scientists themselves have done little to overcome this state of affairs. Social sciences are still very fragmented (with interdisciplinarity not yet to enter into the Arab world), while the scientists publish too little, reject the collective and teamwork and are seeking simply to survive in the university system. To our knowledge, the Arab Council for the Social Sciences is one of the very few initiatives that seeks to overcome all these issues and create a funding scheme that can appropriately benefit the social sciences. The diagnosis concerning the social sciences is rather worse than those of the natural sciences: it often relates excessively to the political engagement of its members at the expense of the content of their research (and sometimes the opposite: technical social science with no political soul). It relates to the way social sciences are barred from being a research domain and is still very much thought about as "intellectual work" of some kind (presumably different from that of an ecologist or a physicist) or as a political and ideological activity.

Strangely, as we will show, research (even in the social sciences) may still be a marginalized activity in the Arab world, but scientists in the Arab world today are more likely to be equivalent in training and social profile to their European or American counterparts. In retrospect, from 20 years ago this is an extraordinary change, as compared to the situation in the mid-1990s (Gaillard and Schlemmer 1996; Gaillard 1994). Thus we have a paradox well-illustrated by a Syrian professor, an engineer in material sciences, who told us back in 2007, after having spent 12 years in Japan: "I have produced 12 high-level peered articles in twelve years in Japan; today, I am closing twelve years in Aleppo since I came back and I have not been able to publish even one paper!" So the environment is what makes the difference. And the research environment is the most important subject of this book.

3 Understanding the practice of research

Research as a social activity needs to be recognized politically, since most of it is public or publicly funded. Before going any further, it is essential to remind readers that this is not a default proper to "poor" countries as is hinted in some international reports that underline with a suspicious insistence the low level of private funding. A majority of research has always been public, whereas development (or R&D) in firms is usually privately funded. In Europe, the share of publicly funded research is higher than in the United States. However, the extent of this varies from country to country. In the rest of the world, large variations also exist, but research is mainly funded and performed by public institutions. This is also the case in the Arab world.

Most of the original and breakthrough research is public: infrastructural work and the surveillance economy that is needed to monitor local resources require levels of investment that no private firm is willing to fund (but will gladly share). Even the most profitable and commercial private firms developed new technologies that come directly as a result of public programs (Mazzucato 2013). These reminders are necessary because many voices call for a strong participation of the private sector; however, it is also necessary to keep in mind that the private sector will never fund the so-called basic research.[11] Thus, politics, plain and common as they are, play an important role in the game. Jean-Jacques Salomon (2001) points out that it is not because it concerns science that science policy is any more "scientific" than other public policies. Indeed, science (and technology) policy is as messy as any other policy: it relies on political work, political alliances and the use of scientific activities as political resources. Failing to recognize this political nature of science policy comes from a bureaucratic vision on what science is about.

There are two aspects that deserve our attention on this front: the political standing of science inside the state, and the relevance of the activity itself.

Roland Waast (2006) urges us to examine the political position of science when he mentions the need for a "pact" that elites can establish between them and with the political personnel in order to develop research – a rather strange and remote activity that seems to be far away from everyday life. The political forces and the institutional structures within a country should reach an agreement. A country where internal disagreement is strong will be less prone to develop this inside-the-walls obscure activity that serves no immediate and visible purpose. Marcel Antonorsi-Blanco and Ignacio Avalos (1980) wrote some famous pages 35 years ago mentioning that science is interesting only when it allows one to inaugurate some libraries. Most importantly, Mouton and Waast (2009) have shown that the reasons why some middle-income countries actually give priority to research does not rely on GDP, investment or any other resource; rather, it depends upon a political choice. When research becomes part of the arsenal of wealth and power, then it is given some attention. Of course, that is an indication of which research areas will be favored by state policy, areas that will be shown in Chapter 2 when we study the development of specialization patterns for each Arabic country.

So, what is research useful for? This question relates to another one: Whom does it serve? We would rather tackle this second issue here, by focusing on the particular question of the *relevance of scientific knowledge*. It appears to us that this is an issue at the very heart of the relatively marginal interest for research in Lebanon, Jordan and more generally in the Arab world. It is the issue of the relevance of scientific activity that crystallizes all discontents: everyone has a solution for science and why and how it should be, and how it should be useful to development, modernization, integration of the world economy, whatever you name as grand national objectives.

We follow the tracks of Antoine Zahlan, who is a long-time observer of scientific development, and his recently published book (2012) that not only underscores a general move toward more scientific activities, as we all do, but also carries out a reflection on why scientific research should be developed. Zahlan's book, like many assessments, calls for more research and innovation. This is based on a diagnosis of the low intensity of research, and is accompanied by a wish that science and/or innovation will ultimately become a matter of priority for the Arab states. Zahlan quite bluntly states that not one Arab country has ever given science and technology a chance, despite the rhetoric about the necessity for science. He also states that the issue is related to the fact that science does not serve any strategic objective like defense, feeding the people, guaranteeing their security or supporting their economic activities. He insists that science and technology should be recognized or the sovereignty of the country could be undermined. While he is interested to understand why the research has been marginalized so strongly, he fails to investigate why it happened this way.

In this book, we make a claim not only about the necessity of research, but of research that has neither direct economic objectives nor "strategic" objectives. Research that is curiosity-driven is a major ingredient for the future. It can lead to fundamental breakthroughs and indirect economic advantages. It can lead to unexpected results, or to a dead-end, but failure, in this case, can be a major breakthrough since it obliges us to re-open other basic avenues. We seem to repeat an old song here, and in reading it young researchers might find these old-style and démodé claims of university professors that just defend their corporation. However, in the Arab world there is a sort of mantra of pragmatic usefulness that has also fed the idea that the future will be "engineered," that translates also into a good deal of useless research, not unlike many other countries in the world, that does not favor creativity and a critical stance. Our claim is that the research we have been seeing in most of our interviews relates rarely to path-breaking work not because of a lack of resources, but because of lack of audacity, lack of organization and lack of independence. As Louis Pasteur said, chance only favors prepared minds. Alexander Fleming would never have found penicillin if he had not been actively engaged in searching for an antiseptic. His cultures were contaminated by pure chance, but the identification Fleming did later of the anti-bacterial effect of this specific substance was anything but chance. It was systematic research and openness that guided the researcher in a path paved by previous similar discoveries. Serendipity, this curious phenomenon that produces simultaneous inventions, unexpected results and amazing innovations, produces immense social and cultural benefits (see the beautiful book of chemist Jean Jacques (1990) called *L'imprévu ou la science des objets trouvés*). Some of these benefits, although difficult to measure, are quite straightforward: the first and foremost result is attracting young people to research, increasing the awareness about the fact that not everything can be bought outside our frontiers, and that genuine and original research is ground for powerful economic, political and cultural independence. There is also a strange, often implicit, belief that research that is not useful should be left aside: urgent tasks for the development of the country should lead the way. Why is it that non-hegemonic countries shouldn't enter into these areas of research that have no immediate relation to development? And, since all this is about judgment, who is the authority that decides what is useful or not?

We believe this last question is the crux of the matter: funding decisions, recruitment, publication, awareness and technology transfers are activities that relate distant interests and different social worlds. The power of research is the fact that it creates linkages between socially different worlds: different social classes, different locations, different places, different interests and different objects. This is a very powerful tool and not only does it create bridges among different sides, it also invites us to think differently about development itself. None of these aspects can be observed other than by focusing on research practice.

And it is exactly what this book intends: to investigate some of the research practices in the Arab world through the case of Lebanon. We are also particularly aware of the situation in Jordan, where we have had many interviews, particularly in the social sciences. We have also examined the institutional situation of the Arab countries. The objective here is not to focus on success or failures, but to depict the Janus-like face of Arab research, poised between the negative and the positive, faced with two potentially opposing strands: the local relevance and its internationalization. We would like to critically assess the role and dynamics of research, not perform an evaluation.

In the Arab world, most, if not all, countries failed to undergo the policy changes we are mentioning here. Neither the institutionalization of research, nor the scientific community formation seemed to have been taking place. Social and political issues have often not revolved around scientific research; worse, research has often not really integrated any of the local social and political issues. Even if we exaggerate a bit (as we will show, mainly in the second part of the book), most, if not all, of the "hot" issues in science, be it natural or social sciences, were developed outside the frontiers of the Arab nations. Known for their originality, few scholars, including European descendants and the European immigrants to the Arab world, were recognized for their interest in the local conditions. If a bright young Arab PhD student finishes his studies in France, the best choice is either to stay in France or change profession and get out of academia. The mostly authoritarian regimes applied a continuous process of reinforcing heightened pro-development policies, were blinded to the university environment, restricted themselves to short-term policy objectives, under-funded public laboratories and repressed reflexive thought and freedom of expression. Sparse cohorts of highly trained personnel engaged in public organizations as a unique means for research. Most of the universities were never seen as the locus for research either. And, meanwhile, there was no construction of a scientific community, which was neither socially nor politically recognized. When these groups were created, it was always along disciplinary lines, with weak internal social exchange mechanisms (journals, meetings), haphazard international collaborations and sometimes even lack of recognition of research practices inside the training institutions (schools and universities). The effect of all these phenomena has been devastating; most Arab countries have become blind to the circumstances occurring around them and even inside their own societies and their own natural environments.

As mere reflections of the Arab revolution, universities and research centers have also heard urgent demands, such as employment, more freedom of speech and an increased scope for practice. To commit to such, we repeatedly hear demands about the need for better governance of the research systems. Slow administrative processes, heavy bureaucratic burdens, corruption, unclear methods of management and opaque decision-making processes are part of the institutional structure of the research-performing units that are manifested in the university systems. They translate into inadequate management procedures that affect directly research, especially inside universities.

4 Some interrogations and choices

The time is right to understand why this absence of reflexivity. Research – or rather the absence of research – has left a profound wound that will take many years to heal. Our proposed remedy is to trigger a wider reflection on the status of research in the Arab countries, beginning with Lebanon. We do not focus on "science," nor "innovation" nor "knowledge economy," but only on how research is working.

We adopt a national perspective (we will sometimes refer to the research systems of the Arab countries),[12] although the dynamic of research and innovation is not only related to national policies and national frontiers, it is a dynamic dependent on many social actors directly or indirectly involved in the development of scientific activities that work at the global or national level, according to their own needs, perceptions and objectives. Their logics of action may thus be different, divergent, or in direct opposition to one another and are observable at the local (and national) level where programs effectively translate into actual work.

We are also interested in scientific collaborations, an instrument through which research has grown locally; also, through which the training of future researchers is done. Research has always been an international endeavor based upon international collaborations. They play a structuring role in countries with scarce resources, less historical experience, or less diversified research systems. Collaborations seem to be a founding element of a local scientific community, along with a more localized effort to structure disciplinary fora, publications and management of resources. It is thus always by seeking to maintain this tension between what is recognized internationally as a valid interrogation and what is the more localized need that research is constructed. Institutions play an important role because they maintain a certain continuity as they guarantee sufficient resources to permanently feed labs and teams, whereas a project-base science tends to be always "on the go" by seeking funding opportunities. Academics and scientists thus act as geo-strategists in their respective disciplines by identifying main actors and possible collaborations. In addition, they act as entrepreneurs of research by managing permanent resources which include personnel, PhDs and post-docs, money and information.

In the scope of public health, manufacturing innovation, biological and other natural resource management, or pollution, there is not one issue that is clearly not global. Questions which include access to anti-retroviral medicines, or intellectual property disputes over global technologies, or disputes over the management of local knowledge systems (e.g., in natural products with pharmaceutical action) or biodiversity resources are fundamental issues involving human security, energy, food security, environmental degradation and desertification, and demand local solutions draw upon global knowledge resources. To do so, these resources are all developed and accessed through research. Therefore, a non-existent research structure misses the ability to manage the issues. Research also plays a key role in international fora where standards defining legal codes, security, health and trade regulations are debated and established. Membership in the exclusive club of those proposing norms and regulations at the global level is determined by research. All these reasons make really urgent the development of research in the Arab world.

Non-hegemonic countries, as mentioned before, have a very minor role in the global "agenda" setting for research. It is important to keep in mind that there inherently exists an agenda for research, which is always political; ultimately, influencing how knowledge is created, used, and disseminated, a process that is still not well understood in the Arab region. Because of the globalized nature of scientific knowledge, an active research structure requires the development of multilateral linkages, involving centers in different countries. Until now, various new institutions, for example those mentioned by the Arab Knowledge Report, have been national endeavors with little multilateral cooperation. This relative isolation is a symptom of lack of sufficient confidence, in all senses of the word, and from all actors involved.

To understand how the issues can be turned into a research and innovation agenda, we focus on the conditions of knowledge production, dissemination and use, by looking at the nature of existing problems in academic life inside universities and research centers of the region. When it comes to innovation, it is even less understood because of the scarcity of studies on what effectively happens inside private and public economic sectors.

In order to understand that, we will rarely use the word "*science*" as our interest lies in *research*. We are indeed interested in the study of research in the making. As Hebe Vessuri *et al.* (2013) reminded us, we need to frame the discussion in terms of a transition from the culture of "science" to the culture of "research." For Vessuri, research and society today are entangled to the point where they cannot be separated any longer. For this reason, we opt to study the research practice in Lebanon and not Lebanese science, which is the practical activity of doing scientific research and not how its results become stable "as a science." As Bruno Latour (1987) pointed out, "science" is cold, straight and detached, whereas "research" is warm, involving and risky. Science puts an end to the vagaries of human disputes, research creates controversies; science produces objectivity by trying to escape the shackles of ideology, passion and emotions. Ghassan Hage (2013) adds that Latour sees research to "capture" and to "extract" knowledge as part and parcel of the very apparatus of capture and extraction that constitutes modern capitalism. He, therefore, invites us to think more carefully about the kind of reality in which research is enmeshed and about the possibility of writing and even performing research differently.

With these choices, we also would like to insist that opportunities for increased research activity will never be the outcome of research "on its own," "for its own sake," just because of the mere increasing of numbers of academics, or through the organic growth of the academic sector or simply increasing entrepreneurial activity. Mouton and Waast (Mouton and Waast 2009) show that many reasons explain this development of research activities, such as historical precedent, the role of the state, the relation of the state to its scientists and to the use of knowledge in the state apparatus, the type of development strategies (and to what extent national development becomes an objective) and trust in science. As we also mentioned above, it is also related to how elites view science. Investment in research and innovation is a policy choice, and in non-hegemonic countries the active decisions of the state influence more profoundly these choices than countries with multiple actors engaged in research and innovation and broader historical commitment to research.

5 Sources and methodology

This book is the outcome of a long reflection on the status of knowledge production in the Arab world by the use of not only empirical observations, but also historical-structural analyses. In addition of bibliometric, empirical and desk research, we have longstanding experience in this field as a researcher and participant observers.

Rigas Arvanitis has developed programs on the dynamic of research, the links between research and production, the rise of scientific communities in the developing world, the international collaborations in science, the study of technological learning and innovation in firms. He has worked in France, Venezuela, Mexico, China and the Arab Mediterranean countries (17 years permanently outside Europe). Sari Hanafi, as editor of *Idafat: The Arab Journal of Sociology* (Arabic) and a member of the editorial board for many Arab and international academic journals,[13] has overseen a large number of social science manuscripts.

Also, by being a faculty member at AUB, he draws on many arguments grounded in his experience and by doing so this university is considered for this book a special case study. Also, as director of a research center – Center for Palestinian Refugees and Diaspora (Shaml) – he was exposed to policy and public social research. Being vice president and a prior member of the Executive Committee of both the International Sociological Association and the Arab Council of Social Science familiarized him with issues related to the formation and institutionalization of the scientific community. We should admit that this native familiarity with the universe that we analyze was thus an asset, but could also be an obstacle that we had to overcome.

In preparing this book we relied on a long desk review of existing country studies in research and innovation in the Arab region (Hanafi and Arvanitis 2013a) and a strengths, weaknesses, opportunities and challenges (SWOC) analysis (Hanafi and Arvanitis 2013b). In this manner, we systematically reviewed most information on research policies and research institutions. We also reviewed available science and technology indicators and we examined the question of data in the region.

In addition, we conducted the following surveys, whose methodology will be detailed at the beginning of each chapter:

- In-depth interviews in 2009–2010 in the Arab East (Egypt, Syria, the Palestinian territory, Jordan and Lebanon) with 23 social scientists about their authorship practices and their participation in the evaluation of colleagues with regard to promotion.[14] Interviews were organized around accounts of personal stories of research and publication, the importance of writing, the different tasks undertaken in the research process and the decision-making processes of journals.
- We underwent a complete analysis of the policy framework in Euro-Mediterranean cooperation. We examined all documentation provided through international negotiations that R. Arvanitis had participated in and were publicly made available. Moreover, as head of the ESTIME project, Arvanitis has reviewed a series of research policies in the whole Arab region (Arvanitis 2007).
- 203 CVs of scholars from Egypt, Jordan, Syria, Lebanon and the Palestinian territory were broadly studied in 2009–2010. These CVs were collected over the last four years through research on university websites, together with consultants' CVs provided by the UN human resource department, as well as from those who submitted manuscripts for publication in the journal *Idafat: The Arab Journal of Sociology*. We use these CVs only to look at the language of publication, the outlet of publication, the ratio between published articles, newspaper articles and unpublished reports, and finally at participation in conferences, workshops, public and academic talks. This "sample" cannot be considered in any way representative of the Arab East social scholarly community, and therefore we do not use percentages in this analysis.

- Online survey by questionnaire that serves the purpose of organizing the issues at stake. The 27-item questionnaire survey concerned the use of references in PhD and Master's these, and was answered by 165 people who hold a Master's or PhD degree from a university in the Arab world, regardless of discipline.

- The syllabi of 30 social science courses taught in Université Saint-Joseph of Beirut (USJ), the Lebanese American University (LAU) and the American University of Beirut (AUB) were analyzed.

- A systematic random sample of 225 op-eds in 2010–2011 to determine the importance of the contribution of academics to editorials, compared to other categories of authors. Three Lebanese newspapers were chosen based on a combination of high circulation rates and robust national and regional coverage (*Al-Akbar*, *Al-Nahar* and the *Daily Star*). In addition, we increased the number of analyzed op-eds published in Lebanese newspapers by targeting academics appearing in the last three years (2011–2013) in the same three newspapers, as well as four additional newspapers. In total, 147 op-eds authored by Lebanese scholars were studied.

- Survey based on semi-structured in-depth interviews focusing on the biographies of a sample of 125 professors/researchers in Lebanon (respectively 50, 42, 23 and 5 from AUB, LU, USJ and CNRS) and 80 professors/ researchers in Jordan (the three biggest public universities: University of Jordan in Amman; Yarmouk University in Irbid; and Jordan University of Science and Technology).[15] Multistage cluster sampling was used. The questions revolved around the conformation of the scientific community, scientific pressures, role of institutions, influence of academic mechanisms (evaluation, promotion, etc.), role of gatekeepers in the publication system and social, including family, factors that directly affected the biographies of the scientists.

- Bibliometric studies on Arab publications in general and Lebanese and Jordanian publications in particular, based on Web of Science (WoS), Scopus for English production and E-Marefa. We created a publication database using available databases as well as the annual reports of faculties in various universities.

- Specific bibliometric analysis of academic articles written on the Arab uprisings, in Arabic, English and French, yielding 519 results. English references were primarily derived from WoS and Scopus; Arabic references were scarcer, primarily due to the limited availability of Arabic databases. E-Marefa, the only reliable Arabic database, yielded only 15 results, while the rest of the articles were only available in hard copies.[16] Concerning the French articles, they were derived from the CAIRN platform.

- A large survey by questionnaire within the framework of a European project called MIRA (www.miraproject.eu), answered by 4,340 researchers from 38 countries (27 in Europe and 11 Mediterranean country partners of the EU). More than 100 Lebanese scientists were included in this survey.[17]

6 The organization of the book

Combining statistical profiles, ethnographic vignettes and prosopographic detail, this book is organized into two parts. The first part is about research dynamics, Arab research systems and knowledge produced in all disciplines; the second part focuses particularly on the social sciences.

In Chapter 1 we present a descriptive analysis of research, innovation systems in the Arab region and research funding. It tests the significance of indicators commonly used in most publications about science and technology in the Arab region and provides a critical assessment. Chapter 2 delves into one of the outputs of the research – the publication – and analyzes the size, authorship and different impact factors. This chapter also has a special focus on different levels of collaboration: local, regional and international. However, as research cannot be understood without investigating both locus of research (institutions) and the researchers themselves, Chapter 3 investigates universities and national and diasporic researchers. We end this part by studying the research practice in Lebanon as a case study and partially compare it to the Jordanian case (Chapter 4).

The second part tries to locate the size and place of production of the social sciences in the Arab world and attempts to highlight the different forms of compartmentalization (Chapter 5). Then we examine the Arab sociological production through *Idafat: The Arab Journal of Sociology* (Chapter 6). This case will show the marginalization of the Arabic language, a topic we examine in more depth in Chapter 7. Chapter 8 is an opportunity to examine the interactions between scholars in the Arab world and abroad through the case of academic journal productions on the Arab uprisings. However, research is not only limited to academic production (articles in refereed journals and specialized books), but also exists in the realms of knowledge translation in policy advice or public activities. To examine the "public" social sciences, we unfold the writing op-eds in Lebanese newspapers (Chapter 9). In the concluding chapter, we draw the arguments together and consider the implications of our analysis for different stakeholders (the scientific community, policy-makers and the public).

Notes

1 For the concept of boundary work, see Gieryn (1995).
2 Sources: expenses of R&D and world publications are from observatoire des sciences et de technologies (OST) reports of 2008 and 2010. (www.ost.uqam.ca/en-us/data. aspx). GDP current prices are from World Economic Outlook (IMF) series.
3 We have delved extensively on this issue in Gaillard and Arvanitis (2013: 2) and Arvanitis (2011b).
4 www.estime.ird.fr.
5 See the first chapter of the Arab Knowledge Report (UNDP 2009), which stresses the different meanings and visions that the term entails.
6 A knowledge economy is an economy in which growth is dependent on the quantity, quality and accessibility of the information available, rather than the means of production. It is thus primarily defined by ensuring access for all to computers and the internet (World Bank 2002).

7 Antoine Zahlan, with a different wording, insists on the need to integrate more reflection in the development of knowledge organizations:

> Today the Arab countries could easily mobilize thousands of leading scholars – scientists, engineers, and doctors – to initiate high quality universities. Surprisingly, there are no tendencies toward improving higher education by utilizing national intellectual resources.... Scholarship, quality, research, and knowledge are still not prime considerations.
>
> (Zahlan 2012: 165; see chapter 10, pp. 157–175)

On Emiratis knowledge society, see Dumortier (2008: 195).

8 See the Knowledge for Development website of the World Bank. There are two indicators for performance (average annual GDP growth [percent] and Human Development Index); three for the economic incentive and institutional regime (tariff and non-tariff barriers, regulatory quality and rule of law); three for education and human resources (adult literacy rate [percent aged 15 and above], secondary enrolment and tertiary enrolment); three for innovation system (researchers in R&D, per million population, patent applications granted by the USPTO, per million population and scientific and technical journal articles, per million population); and, finally, three for information infrastructure (telephones per 1,000 persons [telephone mainlines + mobile phones], computers per 1,000 persons and internet users per 10,000 persons). For more details about KAM, see Chen and Dahlman (2005) Note that, because countries are ranked on an ordinal scale, the KAM illustrates the relative performance of a country as compared to other countries in the KAM database. As such, when a country's performance in a specific variable is indicated to have declined, it could have occurred for two reasons. First, the country's performance in that variable declined, resulting in lower values in absolute terms. Alternatively, the country's performance could have improved and resulted in large absolute values, but other countries experienced even larger improvements, leading to the country's ordinal ranking falling and resulting in a lower value in relative terms.

9 Countries such as Tunisia, Egypt and Morocco have an industry whose bulk specializes in international sub-contracting, requiring an upgrading process which is different from that prescribed by the recipe of the knowledge economy.

10 Curiously, all these books are publications without authors.

11 Counter-arguments usually come from historians of technology and from the chemical sector. DuPont's labs were seen, in the 1950s, as similar to a certain extent to academic labs. Today, no R&D unit of a good size would exist in the same form; with the changing paradigm of the 1980s came also the change of orientation of R&D units in firms (see Dennis 1987).

12 This was briefly presented in our report titled "The broken cycle between research, university and society in Arab countries" (Hanafi and Arvanitis 2013a).

13 *Al-Mustaqbal al-Arabi* (an Arabic refereed journal in the social sciences targeting specialized and non-specialized audiences), *International Sociology, International Journal of Contemporary Iraqi Studies, Global Sociology, Journal of Iranian Social Studies, South African Review of Sociology, Istanbul Journal of Sociological Studies* and *International Sociology Review of Books* (ISRB).

14 The time spans of interviews fluctuated between one-and-a-half hours and two hours.

15 The time spans of interviews fluctuated between one and two hours.

16 In the following journals: *Idafat, Al-Mustaqbal Al-Arabi, Majalet al-Dirasat al-Falastiniya, Majalat el 'Ouloum el Siyasiya* and *Omran.*

17 More details on the MIRA Survey can be found in Gaillard *et al.* (2013).

Part I

Arab research dynamics

1 Decisive impact of the national research and innovation systems

In many ways, the reference model for the study of research systems is the existence of a national system that includes research institutions, universities, agencies funding research, technical centers, private R&D units, "intermediate" actors such as brokers in technology and providers. Over the years, notably so because of the multiplication of studies in a large variety of countries, the complexity of the systems appeared much greater than could have been predicted on the basis of a simplistic, although systemic, view. Arab countries are also complex in their organization of research institutions and policies. Nonetheless, some constants can be drawn and this chapter presents an empirical descriptive analysis of research systems in Arab countries, with the aim to reveal these constants. We have long wanted to test the significance of indicators commonly used in most publications about science and technology in the Arab region. These indicators are employed here to develop a typology of research systems that, hopefully, can help understand the riddle of underinvestment in scientific research in Arab countries. The purpose of the exercise is to relate patterns of publication, aspects relating to the governance and organization of the research system, the role of universities, and other factors. This empirical approach is not so much interested in each country's ranking in a unique scale of values than on the characterization of their profiles, highlighting what makes similarities and differences between one profile and another.

1 Indicators and data in the Arab research system

1.1 Absence of indicators

Before describing the research systems and the factors affecting the dynamics of science and technology in the Arab region, the authors explored the indicators commonly available to public scrutiny. The sources here are less numerous. Most of the statistical information has been compiled by the United Nations Educational, Scientific and Cultural Organization (UNESCO)[1] and the Organisation for Economic Cooperation and Development (OECD)[2] and contain data for member states of those organizations. These organizations follow recognized standards for manpower and financial resources. Countries of the Organisation of Islamic Cooperation's Standing Committee on Scientific and Technological Cooperation (COMSTECH)[3] have also gathered some of these data without employing any recognized definition for manpower and financial statistics. All of these organizations necessarily rely on reporting by public authorities, but most of them do not follow the international standards or, more simply, do not really have the ability to effectively count the resources dedicated to research. Moreover, national authorities in most Arab countries have not given special attention to science and technology as part of their statistical administration.

In short, after many years of recommendations by all possible international organizations, in the Arab countries there are still no reliable input statistics; that is, data gathered according to the international standards that are defined in the "Frascati Manual," the document that contains all the internationally recognized definitions for science and technology statistics. It should be emphasized that these statistical standards have been the product of a professionalization of statistical data on science and technology. Even if they have their own drawbacks (Godin 2005), they were designed to respond to the need of a global view of science and technology and to identify the competitive status of OECD countries. The statistical infrastructure was created for this specific purpose after World War II, but most Arab countries have not been involved in this techno-economic competition that affected OECD countries. Thus, they have lacked the incentive to promote statistics of the same nature; a lack that is usually underlined by international organizations, which press them to produce uniform data. In brief, most Arab countries have had the same debate on the necessity and uses of scientific research as OECD countries, but unlike the OECD countries this occurred later in time, and competitiveness was not their main interest. It is of course difficult to make generalizations on all Arab countries, but those lacking oil, as did many countries that acquired their independence in the dawn of the twentieth century, intended to consolidate the academic institutions performing research – apart from teaching. This capacity building required crude data on the number of professors and students; as a result, more complex questions were left unattended. The richer, oil-producing countries were usually less interested in competitiveness, with the very notable exceptions of Iraq and Algeria, which were the sole oil-producing countries that defined a scientific capacity building strategy as part of their political project of independence (El-Kenz and Waast 1997). Thus, it appears that Arab countries have not had a strategic understanding of the role of research. Most recently, the debates on science and technology in society were mainly triggered by international organizations, in particular after the 2005 Arab Human Development Report of the United Nations Development Program (UNDP), which stressed the idea that research was hindered in the Arab region due to lack of freedom (UNDP 2005),[4] and triggered a very intense debate on the gaps in research in the region.

Since no reliable statistics exist on research and innovation in the Arab region, and no statistical infrastructures or institutions have been designed to produce them, it can be particularly problematic to establish international comparisons. This situation is not unique to the Arab region. Beyond Europe and

North America, only Latin America has developed a good network of observatories, called the Network for Science and Technology Indicators (RICYT), which receives regular support from UNESCO. No such network exists in either Asia or Africa, although some organizations, like Globelics,[5] have promoted linkages between units working for policy-making bodies in technology, innovation and economic development. In the Mediterranean region, because of its strategic importance for the EU, a number of networks have been promoted.[6] Nonetheless, these statistical indicators are available only in those countries that have demonstrated a political interest in science and technology at the national level, which is by itself an indicator of their focus on research and innovation (Mouton and Waast 2009).

1.2 Science and technology observatories in the Arab region

It would be unfair to say that no effort has been made to establish a reliable statistical basis for the development of science and technology in the Arab region. The Evaluation of Scientific and Technological Capacities in Mediterranean Countries (ESTIME), funded by the European Union (EU) between 2004 and 2007, was one such attempt; the 2007–2012 Mediterranean Innovation and Research Coordination Action (MIRA) included the creation of an observatory as part of its objectives. In three workshops, MIRA produced a white paper outlining plans for the observatory.[7] Experience has shown that a science and technology indicators unit would have to manage a variety of data: input data on resources (money, human resources, other resources); output data on results of research and innovation (publications, innovation, patents); and relational data, showing networks and collaborations or connections (Barré 2001). No entity of this sort has ever been created in the Arab region, capable of managing these different kinds of data. To be fair, few countries have been able to create such a unit, able to manage all of this diversity of data. What is striking in the case of Arab countries is the expressed need for such a unit by officials and the simultaneous fear to really have it. Moreover, all experts agree that such a unit should be independent from the political authorities, something unimaginable in most of these countries, where statistics and all things related to "information" are high-profile security issues. At best, they can accept including them as an office closely linked to the head of a research council, but none of the Arab governments is willing to see any such unit appear as an independent public structure; worse, the simple idea of having a non-official unit for science and technology indicators appears as absurd and senseless, since officials can only think of statistics (of any sort) as a public, that is governmental, venture.

Some countries, like Tunisia, Lebanon and Jordan, have actively sought to create observatories. Their fates are still unclear. The Jordanian project was more or less halted, and in no case could be imagined as independent of the council of science and technology. Tunisia created its national observatory and then, one year later, after a change of minister, the Ben Ali regime just decided that this was no longer necessary, relegating the unit to a simple service of the ministry;

the project has not yet been revived, although formally the observatory has been maintained as an office inside the Ministry of Research and will probably remain there. Lebanon has announced the need to create an observatory in its science and technology plan; the National Council for Scientific Research (CNRS) has launched the Lebanese Observatory on Research, Development and Innovation – and alongside it, the first feasibility study, funded by ESCWA. The Lebanese Observatory's first initiatives, including an innovation survey, science and technology survey and the establishment of indicators, are currently underway. But it couldn't create a Frascati-compatible statistic of human resources, and the figures on R&D investments are still a guess, as far as public investment is concerned, and a dated first statistical estimate concerning private R&D investments. The activities of the unit, still inside the CNRS, are also linked to political willingness. Morocco has tried on various occasions to create a structure, either inside the Ministry of Research, or the Ministry of Commerce and Industry, or inside the National Research Center (CNRST) or the Academy of Sciences Hassan II. The last attempt to date was a proposal inside a large Morocco–EU "twinning" project, that again was not followed by any results, as with all previous attempts. An ongoing private initiative might rise, finally, and this in itself should be a clear indication of the diversification of the national research system.

In the Arab region, the ESCWA has repeatedly proposed to include an indicators observatory as a support for policy-making, and it has periodically published data on science and technology. The newly created ESCWA Technology Center, based in Amman, includes an indicators unit that is focused more on specific studies than indicators of production and maintenance. At some point in the last ten years, many countries have mentioned a similar effort, but alas this was rarely translated into concrete action. When figures are (miraculously) produced at the national level, it is usually in some conference, presented by an official authority on science and technology, and one can only wonder on the light-speed efficiency of such public civil servants.

Looking at the successful experiences of countries that have developed an indicators unit for science and technology – for example in Latin America – we find that in all cases the unit has been supported by an academic team, or at least a policy-making "think tank" that is composed of academics with backgrounds in various social sciences, as well as natural and exact sciences. There is, moreover, a virtuous cycle established between (a) the fulfillment of policy objectives; (b) the provision of adequate information, processed in an intelligent way and responsive to policy needs; and (c) the production of "basic" knowledge on the science and technology community, the interaction of different scientific areas, and the productive and service sectors. The Latin American experience demonstrates the value of this close connection between academic work and the development of science and technology policy (Arellano *et al.* 2012). A similar development exists in Thailand, centered on the concept of regional innovation systems: indicators appeared as a result of the development of regional clusters of production and technology, and the governments' desire to understand and promote this economic phenomenon. Thus, in Malaysia, Thailand and China, indicators appeared from offices responsible for industrial policy-making.[8] This example illustrates that indicators can emerge as a by-product of intellectual effort to understand science and technology in the particular context of each country. That none of this has happened so far in the Arab countries is also the result of a lack of academic research on the research activities, or scarce studies on all the aspects related to the science, technology and society linkages.[9]

1.3 Composite indicators and rankings

In the absence of reliable and robust indicators, two strategies are normally employed: the first is opinion surveys or polls; the second is rankings based on composite indicators that can compensate for the diversity of sources.

Policy-makers and the literature that is aimed at business people prefer to rely on indicators drawn from opinion polls. This method relies on a survey of persons considered "knowledgeable informants," that is, professionals with particular knowledge and insight of research and innovation activities. Academics, entrepreneurs and policy-makers are asked to grade a series of variables related to different aspects of research and innovation. This mitigates the risk of false or incomplete data; nevertheless, the view of the field is reduced by the mean of opinions expressed by this collection of informed persons. Since no one can claim to have a global view of the sector, this is considered as an acceptable way to show the state-of-play. The identity of the persons responding to this kind of survey is as important as the points of view they express. Moreover, the answers obtained are measured using some ranking method which produces a "mean" opinion not necessary reflected by any real social actor (Leresche *et al.* 2009).[10] This average opinion becomes a social norm by itself; it could well be said that it reflects the demise of our capacity to modify this social norm.

A second strategy, employed by the World Bank and INSEAD's Global Innovation Index, relies on more general indicators, producing indexes and transforming the variables either into rankings or marks. This strategy also enables the creation of somewhat more robust (though less detailed) indicators. The rationale behind these complex indicators is their ability to reflect the various factors contributing to a country's competitiveness, level of innovation and so on. In its knowledge assessment methodology, the World Bank (2012) used a four-pillar set of indicators. They are: (1) economic incentives and the institutional regime; (2) innovation and technological adoption; (3) education and training; and (4) infrastructure in information and communications technologies (ICTs).

This strategy is thought to be suitable for complex issues. A similar methodology has been proposed to measure the Europe 2020 strategy for smart, sustainable and inclusive growth within the European Union, which was launched by the European Commission in March 2010 and approved by the heads of states and governments of the 27 member states of the European Union in June 2010 (Pasimeni 2011; 2012). The Europe 2020 strategy, known as the "Lisbon

Strategy," can be reduced in this way to eight indicators. Dreher uses the same method for measuring "globalization" in three dimensions: social, political and economic (Dreher *et al.* 2008; Dreher 2006). But, without any doubt, the well-known index employing this kind of methodology is the Global Competitiveness Index developed for the World Economic Forum, composed of 12 pillars, which ranks 133 economies. Technological readiness and innovation are two of its 12 pillars (Schwab and Sala-i-Martín 2012).

Finally, the European Institute for Business Administration (INSEAD) has developed a Global Innovation Index covering 141 countries.[11] This index relies on a series of indicators grouped into five input pillars of innovation: (1) institutions, (2) human capital and research, (3) infrastructure, (4) market sophistication and (5) business sophistication. Two output pillars capture actual evidence of innovation: knowledge and technology outputs and creative outputs (Figure 1.1). The Global Innovation Index is fairly consistent and we use it in our statistical analysis (see the next section).

The success of these composite indicators needs to be understood, and this would drive us very far away from our subject. In the Arab countries, it is important to remember that the very notion of a "knowledge economy" has been supported by this kind of ranking. The tacit model that is supporting this analysis in terms of composite indicators is a model of competition, since the very nature of the rankings produces comparative scales and sets the arena of the competition. The knowledge economy, as the difference of the concept from the innovation system, relies on this competitive view of the economy. Proponents of the knowledge economy will favor such a type of indicator.

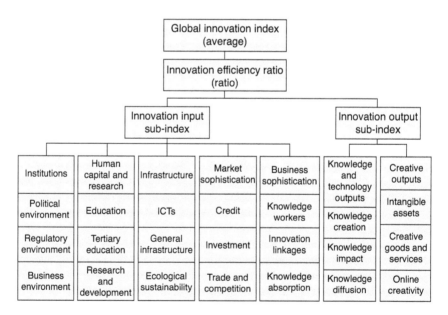

Figure 1.1 Global Innovation Index (GII) framework (INSEAD).

1.4 Bibliometric indicators and impact factors

Usually, two sources of research output are used to measure science and technology innovation: publications and patents. Both of these sources, however, rely on the existence of databases which are, in turn, dependent upon a specific social and economic system: the publication system in science, on one hand, and the patenting system, on the other hand. In the case of scientific publications, scientific and financial considerations compete for primacy in the relationship between authors and publishers. The network of scientists that evaluate the quality of scientific articles (usually anonymously) and control the circulation of ideas and scientific results has been referred to as an "invisible college," a term that recently re-appeared in the literature under the pen of Caroline Wagner (2008), where journal editors are acting as "gatekeepers." Today, this social organization is becoming increasingly complex, with the hierarchy of journals, disciplines, institutions and countries ever more difficult to disentangle. The social system of publications is further complicated by the fact that scientific publishers are, mainly, commercial ventures. Part of the debate on the validity of the impact factor stems from this discussion: it is because the structuring of the scientific community has become so diverse that no specific system or institution can claim primacy.

With regards to patents, national economic and research policies, as well as strategies developed by firms, organize the patenting system. Japan and South Korea, for instance, are very high-patenting countries in part because the patenting strategy of their firms is to register multiple patents for a single product, rather than one patent covering most aspects of an invention. Complex strategies are elaborated that take into account the cost of patenting and expanding patent protection to other countries, alongside the risk of revealing information. After all, patenting is very much more than a legal tool (Bowker 1992); it is also a way of publishing, and as such it discloses information about the technology in question. Both forms of publication, whether in academic journals or through patents, are not "objective" indicators: they depend upon strategies and social organization. Thus publications and patents do not simply reflect performance (or impact); they indicate how a society validates these outputs that are an integral part of a social system. By way of consequence, we should be careful regarding the existence or not of these "publication markets."

Bibliometrics (statistical indicators of publications) is still considered the most reliable source on scientific production, mainly because it is independent of national authorities. Only two large multidisciplinary databases of citations exist, produced by two major publishing entities. Thomson produces the Web of Science (WoS), and Elsevier produces Scopus. Both databases are also commercial activities as much as they are sources of information. While they are not the only two sources available for bibliometric analysis (Arvanitis and Gaillard 1992), they share the aim of being multidisciplinary and independent, and of providing information on author affiliations and citations. Scopus covers more journals and other publications than WoS. While these databases don't cover

Arabic references, there is a newly established database, E-Marefa[12] that includes academic material that covers full texts of academic and statistical journals as well as theses and dissertations.[13] However, it is still not fully operational as the author affiliations and citations index are not available in the search engine of this database (see our use of E-Marefa in Chapters 4 and 8). In addition there is Dar Al-mondouma in Saudi Arabia, which produces a quite extensive coverage of journals in Arabic language (1,249 titles, out of which Egypt accounts for 237 and Saudi Arabia for 211). It remains to examine the exact content and the uses of these new repositories.

It should be noted that new methods have been proposed for bibliometrics, focusing more on strategy than evaluation, and engaging in analytical assessment and mapping analysis (Lepori *et al.* 2008). This new way would rather insist on positioning the entities that produce the measured items. It is derived from what can be called "relational analysis," based either on words or citations, that permits depicting the relations between these items. Linkages can be rather complex[14] and a whole new field is emerging that can also be mobilized for use in the Arab region. The metrics of science, as it is called sometimes, has unfortunately too often been limited to simple indicators of a rather crude and simple type. Curiously enough, a fair amount of reflection has been given to improve *input indicators* (inputs to research being usually limited to funding and personnel dedicated to research) and to adapt them to the specific conditions of research in non-hegemonic countries, much less so for output indicators (in particular publications and patents). Jacques Gaillard (2010a) has described the general characteristics that have been changing in science and technology in the developing world and that should be taken into account by the Frascati Manual, the international reference manual that guides the collection of these indicators: increasing international collaborations, increasing international circulation of scientists and engineers, high concentration of scientific activities in some countries, profound crisis in the scientific and academic institutions and difficulties in evaluating national budgets dedicated to R&D data. But, bibliometrics, limited to the statistical analysis of publications, have been much less "adaptable," based on the assumption that, contrary to inputs used in research, publication works in the same way for all. In fact, it is largely not the case, even in the frame of one country, when comparing different disciplines. Not all disciplines publish in the same way and not all institutions promote publications in the same way. By way of consequence, not all countries support or favor scientific publication in the same way. It is not the right place here to delve into all of these aspects,[15] which have been quite often studied in Latin America. As an outcome, a society for the study of science in Latin America (ESOCITE) has been created. Here again, we can see how closely related are the academic reflection on the role and dynamic of science in a given society and the indicators that can be used to describe the scientific activity. Developing indicators in the Arab countries will require much more that simple training and stable employment of information engineers.

1.5 Measuring the impact of research

Another issue related to indicators is the measurement of the impact of research. By impact, we don't mean citation counts, but the effects of the scientific activity on society. Impact measures are becoming a pervasive topic in research policy because governments want to construct a coherent discourse on the reasons why they finance scientific activities and academic institutions. In periods of economic and budgetary constraints, parliaments and the population in general require an explanation on the expenses of the state. While after World War II the relation that existed between the state, citizens and researchers was based on an undisputed linkage, related to sovereignty and power, today this relation needs to be renewed and justified again and again.[16] The underlying political objective is neither unique nor solely defended by the state. A multiplicity of objectives and actors participate actively in both the funding and performance of research. Public research organizations need to take into account this diversity and adapt their strategies in a context of reduced public budgets.

But none of the public research organizations have any standard method to report on the benefits or effects of research on society, although the issue has been on the agenda for many years. For the Mediterranean countries, in 2011 the MIRA project issued a white paper (Arvanitis *et al.* 2013b) showing that the impact of scientific research can be measured relatively accurately at the level of a project, but this accuracy diminishes as the level is increased; thus disciplinary studies are less accurate than project studies, and country studies are less accurate than disciplinary studies.[17] The MIRA white paper concludes that impact measurement should better concern a program (that is, a collection of projects defined by the policy instruments that support it) than a discipline (since the definition of the frontiers of a discipline is always a matter of interpretation) or a country (since the scope of a policy is not necessarily national). Moreover, it showed that none of the countries that were involved as partners of the European Union had developed any public methodology or public report assessing the effects of the scientific research on society and the economy.[18]

Before entering into the analysis, we should underline that the impact of research is a complex concept that must take into account not only the disciplines being measured, but also the structuring of the scientific community that occurs by consolidating research teams, research networks and research organizations, as well as its capacity to generate new and original research projects. Measuring how new teams are set-up, consolidated and how they collaborate worldwide is the only possible impact assessment that would take into account the social dynamic engaged by the researchers and their institutions. Certainly, this kind of measurement would be more meaningful than one based on the number of citations received by a journal (wrongly called "impact measurement").

It is very strange how policy-makers, either in Europe or in the Arab countries, have resisted strongly this simple idea that it makes more sense to evaluate a public policy directed at research by looking at how teams and resources are used in a more efficient way, rather than simply counting beans – that is, numbers of papers or citations that depend so much upon both the publication system, a social organization by itself, and the existence of large, multidisciplinary databases that include citations, of which two exist today: WoS and Scopus. Policy-makers and science program managers, as well as promotion committees, selection committees and other evaluation entities, in most Arab countries seek the easy-to-apply figure that permits the university or the research organization to appear in the international rankings.[19] Moreover, the relation of the research community with society is even more difficult to appraise. The structuring of research itself is certainly not a sufficient objective and the factors that trigger a closer relation of the research with the economy and society are rarely explicitly measured, although they usually are a central motive for the research community and the public funding agencies.

So far, the Arab region has not benefited from such an exercise in measuring the impact of research activities, either in terms of the structure of the scientific capabilities or in terms of the relation of the research activities with the wider social and economic environment. Part of the difficulty relates to the fact that, although program managers are, at least nominally, interested in measuring the impact of research on the ground, they have little information on the process involved in the performance of the scientific research. Given that very few of the indicators that could measure the nurturing and mobilization of research capacities are available in the Arab countries, as we already mentioned above, it is not a surprise that "impact" has been reduced (in the best case) to scoreboards based on publications or, in the worst case, to counting "impact factors."[20] The recently published "Leiden Manifesto" (Hicks *et al.* 2015) shows that this abuse of bibliometrics instead of sound evaluation practices is becoming very challenging and undermines research.

Moreover, as we know the funding framework in Arab countries is changing profoundly, new programs are only recently defined independently of the academic institutions that host the research potential.[21] Policies to support research inside universities have been usually limited to supporting the academic institutions themselves, not any specific research through programs, calls for projects or specific scientific orientation. Universities were supposed to support research on their own, something that has rarely happened. There is some change in this regard with the appearance of independent funding agencies or funding programs among most Arab countries. Evaluation could be attached to measuring at least the impact of these new funding programs or agencies. Nonetheless, this change is still very recent and only time will tell if the change in the policy framework will induce a more permanent monitoring.

2 Mobilizing the data for a factor analysis

After reviewing the available data, we had to use most of the standard data meaningful at the national level. These macro-indicators, even if not very accurate, point in a certain direction, and show some interesting tendencies useful for our understanding of the research system. There were 114 indicators found in the literature, from a large variety of sources, and many of these were redundant. Table 1.1 provides the final list of those variables used in the factorial analysis and shows the different types of data:

- *indicators of size*, such as the number of professors, students, researchers, volumes of production (in number of articles), shares of global scientific production and gross expenditures in R&D (GERD);
- *proportional indicators* that relate science production and the number of researchers to the size of the population;
- *indicators of changes*, such as the growth rates of scientific production;
- *complex indicators* based on the General Innovation Index (INSEAD), or the assessment of R&D business investment (Competitiveness Report of the World Economic Forum), as indicated above. Their ranking (rather, the score of the composite indicator they produce) is used to complement the lack of data that exist on these activities.

Principal component factor analysis was conducted[22] to assess the underlying structure for the statistical items gathered. Before performing the factor analysis, the data were "reduced" to percentile groups in order to eliminate the distortions that could be introduced by the mere size effect, due to the large variety of scales across the data. The first five extracted factors represented 80 percent of the total variance (as reported in Table 1.2), which can be considered a very satisfactory result. Each factor is a component of the analysis that needs to be explained by the variables that are best "loaded" in this factor. The variables' representation (or "loading") in each component allow interpretation of the factors which are otherwise mere statistical constructions. Table 1.3 displays the variables and components loadings, that is, the statistical weight of each variable on the extracted factors.

2.1 Interpreting the data

Each factor can be depicted graphically. It is usual to limit the graphical representations to the two main factors, factor one being represented as the horizontal axis and factor two as the vertical axis, as in Figure 1.2, which displays the projection of variables on the plane formed by two main axes (or main components).

The horizontal axis represents the first component (31.6 percent of the total variance) and is relatively easy to interpret in both statistical and substantive terms. The component collects the variables that are *indicators of size*. It identifies, on the left side, the paramount importance given to international collaborations, as measured by co-authorships; and on the right side, indicators of scale (i.e., mass indicators, such as the number of students and teachers, shares of world scientific production, etc.). There is a direct relation between the size of a country's scientific community and the level of international collaboration, with smaller countries showing usually higher rates of co-authorship than larger ones.

Table 1.1 General list of variables used in the characterization of research in Arab countries

Gross domestic product (GDP) (in billion US$) (2010)
GDP per capita US$ (2010)
GDP per capita US$ PPP
Rank HDI (2007)
Total population 2010
Growth (%) (2010)
PPP gross national income/per capita US$ (2010)
Manufacturing, value added (% of GDP) (2010)
Value chain presence (2007)
Personal computers per 1,000 people (2009)
Internet users per 1,000 population (2009)
Knowledge Economy Index 2012 (out of 145)
EFA Development Index (EDI) (2008 ranking) out of 127
Literacy level
Percentage of literate adults
Percentage of literate young (15–24)
Percentage of students/pop that can attend
Total enrolment (2004)
Secondary enrolment (%)
Tertiary enrolment (%)
Public expenditure per student as a percentage of GDP per capita 2004
Public expenditure on education as a percentage of GDP
Public expenditure on education as a percentage of total government expenditure
Teaching staff
Total number of graduates
Gross domestic expenditure on R&D (GERD; as a percentage of GDP)
Private sector spending on R&D (rank)
GERD financed by abroad
Percentage GERD financed by abroad
Business enterprise expenditure on R&D (BERD)
BERD financed by foreign-owned companies and percentage
R&D budget/GDP percentage
Technology balance of payments
Specialized government research center
Centers at universities
Laboratories
Branch research units
Technological research cities
Global Innovation Index (GII) ranking 2012 (out of 141 countries)
PCT patent applications per million population
USPTO patents granted to residents of Arab countries 2008
Number of patents in 2005–2006
Average annual number of patents (2002–2006)
Trademarks
Academic ranking of world universities (ARWU) 2010
Expenditure on higher education (budget of the Ministry of Higher Education)
Expenditure on higher education (percentage of GDP)
Expenditure on higher education per student
Number of universities
Number of students
Number undergraduates
MSc students (2006)

PhD students (2006)
Number of faculty
Number of researchers (2005)
Local collaboration
Regional collaboration (with the Arab region)
International collaboration (2005)
Researchers per one million inhabitants
Estimates on full-time equivalents (FTEs) (2008)
Estimates on full-time equivalents (FTEs) per million population
Number of scientists and engineers in refereed journals (2010)
Number of scientists and engineers established in the United States
Number of publications in basic sciences, natural, and applied sciences 2005
Share of Arab publications (2005)
Scientific publications per 1,000 publications
Number of articles per million inhabitants (2005)
Scientific articles per million inhabitants (2008)
Co-publications (2008)
Regional co-publications (2005)
Publications in WoS/Scopus
Language of publication
Specialization index
Percentage of world shares (2004)
Growth of publications (2001–2006) in world shares
Government bodies responsible for R&D policies and coordination in the Arab region
Existence of organization of Ministry of Research, or Ministry of S&T
Coordination/funding agencies, other funding mechanisms
Document that defines the national research strategy
Type of governance in S&T
Expenses on scientific research (2005)
S&T policy document
Brain drain and rank out of 142 countries
Company spending on R&D
Quality of scientific research institutions
University–industry research collaboration
Local availability of specialized research and training services
Firm-level technology absorption
Value chain presence
FDI and technology transfer
Capacity for innovation
Quality of management schools
Availability of scientists and engineers
Laws relating to ICT
Intellectual property protection
Efficiency of legal system in settling disputes
Quality of math and science education
Internet access in school
FDI (in millions US$)

Table 1.2 Total variance explained by each component

Component	Percentage	Cumulated percentage
1	31.6	31.6
2	18.6	50.2
3	13.9	64.2
4	9.3	73.5
5	6.9	80.4

Note
We indicate here only the percentage weight of the components in total variance.

Table 1.3 Variables and components

Variables	Components extracted from the analysis				
	1[a]	*2*[a]	*3*[b]	*4*[b]	*5*[b]
International collaboration (co-authorship) in SCI	−0.689	0.2	−0.062	0.463	−0.001
GII (ranking 2012 out of 141 countries)	0.014	−0.445	0.32	0.698	0.278
Growth 2005–2008	0.037	0.303	0.706	−0.505	−0.18
Growth 2001–2004	0.131	0.641	0.421	0.136	0.441
Business R&D expenses (ranking 2008)	0.275	−0.344	0.046	−0.225	0.768
USPTO patents granted to residents of Arab countries 2008	0.282	−0.232	−0.824	0.085	0.008
GERD 2007	0.393	0.041	0.381	0.297	−0.302
Students 2007	0.446	−0.743	0.315	−0.221	0.085
Researchers per one million inhabitants 2007 (UNESCO)	0.528	0.57	−0.119	0.216	0.172
PCT patents applications per million population	0.572	0.522	−0.393	−0.064	−0.035
Teaching staff 2004	0.587	−0.687	0.207	−0.079	−0.116
Number of universities 2006	0.616	0.385	0.415	0.083	−0.071
Scientific articles per one million population 2008	0.644	0.488	−0.207	−0.287	0.169
Researchers 2005	0.805	0.079	0.201	0.405	−0.097
World share (Publications SCI)	0.905	−0.162	−0.13	0.104	−0.177
Publications in Web of Science (2008)	0.918	−0.154	−0.217	0.013	−0.019

Notes
Principal component analysis with no rotation of axis. The table is sorted on the values of the first component.
a Components 1 and 2 as shown as axes in Figures 1.2.
b Components not shown graphically.

But the analysis clearly separates the level of international collaboration: this means that international collaboration is the main variable that allows differentiating most clearly the profiles of the countries; the degree of connection with foreign scientists is thus of great significance.

The second component is represented by the vertical axis (18.6 percent of the total variance). As can be seen, on one side (upper part of the axis) we see the

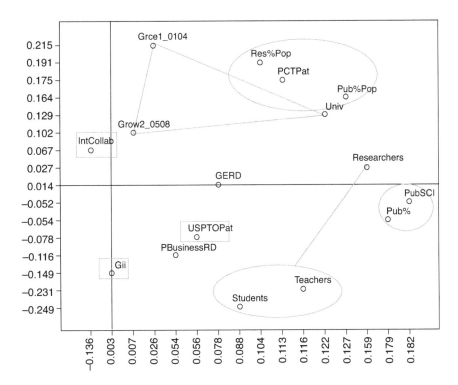

Figure 1.2 Diagram of variables.

importance of growth rates of production and of proportional indicators (researchers per million inhabitants and articles per million inhabitants); on the other side (lower part), we find indicators of the university system (number of students and professors), the composite General Innovation Index (GII) indicator, and an indicator of the involvement of the private sector (research and development business expenses as evaluated by the Competitiveness Report). Variables with less important contribution to this component are patents from the United States Patent and Trademark Office (USPTO). Interestingly, applications for patents from the Patent Cooperation Treaty (PCT), which are easier to obtain than from the USPTO, are represented on the opposite side of this second axis, which can be easily explained by the fact that PCT patents are more closely related to indicators of size than USPTO patents, which result from a deliberate strategy of firms looking for protection of their innovation in the United States. Also, many applicants first begin filing a PCT patent and, if the product and the market are worth it, subsequently file a USPTO or European patent. These indications permit interpretation of this component represented by the second axis of Figure 1.2: it shows the importance of business and innovation, on one side, and the importance of the academic system on the other. In short, the component depicts the opposition inherent in the research system between business-related drivers and academic ones (publications being the main indicator). Most of the weight in the second axis falls upon the size of the university system, larger countries being on the upper part of the second axis and smaller university systems on the lower part. In brief, the axis represents a closer relation to innovation and productive outputs as opposed to variables expressing size and growth.

The third component (14 percent of the total variance), not represented in Figure 1.2, represents the variables in a very different manner. On one side, we find simple (or crude) indicators of output (patents and scientific publications), and on the other side growth rates of publications (which are dynamic indicators of active involvement in research), the indicators or gross expenses for R&D and the GII indicator. This component distinguishes between systems that are heavy producers from those with lighter rates of production, and countries that have a dynamic growth as distinguished with the slower growth rates. For many Arab countries, which make a relatively small contribution to global scientific innovation, this has a very unique meaning: dynamism serves to balance this low production. Any explanation concerning the research system should therefore be able to satisfactorily explain both the low levels of scientific production and the dynamism (here, the Gulf countries play a significant role). Interestingly, on the "dynamic" side of the axis, we find the variable "Number of universities in 2006." Indeed, universities, in particular in the Gulf states, Saudi Arabia and Jordan have played an active role by promoting an aggressive strategy to promote research. We will tackle this issue later in the book, but it is quite clear that universities are a crucial institutional factor to be considered in any analysis of the research systems.

The fourth and fifth components represent a small contribution to the overall variance. With 9.3 percent of the variance, the fourth component compares the growth rate of publications between 2005 and 2008 to the rate between 2001 and 2004, contrasting them against the more complex and fundamental indicators of the research system (GII, international co-authorship, researchers per inhabitant). This component serves to distinguish between newer research systems in Jordan and the Gulf and the more established ones in the Maghreb and Lebanon. Finally, a fifth component (6.9 percent of the variance) opposes resources and results; on one side we find GERD and human resources, and on the other side older growth of publications (2001–2004), GII ranking, and scientific articles per million inhabitants. Interestingly, it also shows private sector involvement in research and development as a result. The validity of this assumption has been confirmed through empirical research in the universities of several Arab countries, and its significance should be emphasized: involvement in research and development does not depend upon the size of the university system. It is the result of an active policy at the university level that may be supported (or not) by the state. In other words, the movement is pushed by the individual institutions (universities in the case of academic research, or firms in the case of innovation as measured by patents). As we will show later, the innovation surveys of firms confirm this strategic orientation.

2.2 The main dimensions of the national research systems

Many messages are delivered by this first analysis. First, size indicators, dynamic indicators, and innovation indicators allow for a typology of Arab countries that we will examine here. Next to size, a research system is very much defined by the importance of co-authorship; international collaboration plays a very important role in the more rapidly growing countries but also in more consolidated research systems. Those countries with high levels of co-authorship (Jordan, Lebanon, Morocco and Tunisia) are countries with rapidly expanding scientific activity, a longer history of academic research than other Arab countries, and a trend toward consolidation of their research system. By examining the publication patterns (Chapter 2), we will reveal a specialization pattern for these countries that is more focused on biology and medicine (mainly Tunisia, Jordan and Lebanon), whereas the dominant discipline in most other Arab countries is engineering. In recent years Egypt has enjoyed a renewal after many years of relatively sluggish scientific production and an exaggerated production in the engineering field. The rate of its international collaborations has also increased, along with new growth in areas that had been largely abandoned, such as health and biological sciences, which are now gaining on chemistry and engineering. Only Algeria remains focused on engineering and material sciences, making its production profile similar to that, for example, of China.

Figure 1.3 represents countries in this same space formed by the first two axes, with each axis representing the first and second component that we just

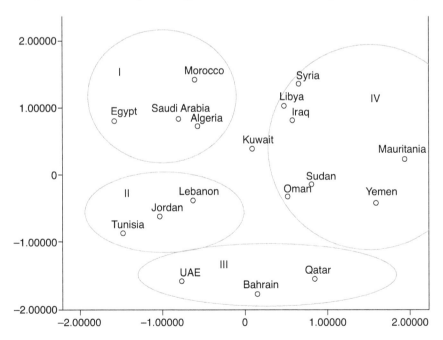

Figure 1.3 Countries represented in the space of two main factors.

interpreted above. The name of the countries is quite revealing: variables related to size (and thus, larger countries) are on the left; smaller countries are on the right; dynamic variables are pulling on the lower part of the first axis; and the size of the university system is on the upper part of this space. Driven by the second component, we see larger and more dynamic countries on the upper-left part of the graph; small and dynamic countries on the lower left part; and less dynamic countries on the right part of the diagram (the scale is not exactly the same for variables and for countries: countries vary on a wider scale than variables). Kuwait has always occupied a relatively central position on this graph, with most of its variables tending toward the middle of the spectrum; probably, its modest size but its relatively old university explains this strange middle position.

Based on these variables, four distinct groups of countries emerge (Figure 1.3).

Group I   Large research systems with slower growth, relative to other Arab countries: Algeria, Egypt, Morocco and Saudi Arabia. These are comparatively large or rich countries. Egypt is unique in this group (or any other), set apart by its lack of natural resources. But the group is basically aggregating larger research systems characterized by a certain amount of inertia, slow growth and consolidation of international collaborations. Morocco has only recently entered a period of sluggish growth following the rapid expansion of its research system in the late 1990s, a phenomenon explained by the return of many Moroccan academics that had been living abroad. It is the most diversified system in the sample. Kuwait, which stands between Groups I and II, could for analytical purposes be integrated into Group I, given its older, more established strategy of research support. Only its small size distinguishes it from the other countries in this group. Egypt and Algeria share a very similar profile of disciplinary specialization, which will be explored in more detail below.

Group II   Small, dynamic and integrated research systems: Jordan, Lebanon and Tunisia. These are the countries with the highest rates of publications and growth of production. They are also small countries with proportionally high numbers of researchers and scientific production. Although their scores in overall innovation are low, these countries tend to have niches of innovative activities. Intriguingly, Tunisia has a very centralized research system, while Jordan and Lebanon do not. Had there been an indicator to measure level of centralization, the categorization of countries would likely have been different; however, recent work has confirmed that Jordan, Lebanon and Tunisia are engaged in an active pursuit of scientific research, and consolidate the evaluation systems inside their universities. Jordan is the country that has changed most recently, with a surge in its scientific production.

Group III   Very small countries with rapidly expanding research systems: Bahrain, Qatar and the United Arab Emirates. These are very small, rich Gulf countries, with an active policy of developing technologies and universities, actively pursuing branding strategies for their universities and seeking to capitalize on their high-level resources.

Group IV   All other Arab countries. It is quite difficult to differentiate between these small and less integrated research systems. Some universities seem to be developed, but scores are low for many variables. Iraq has been placed in this group, in spite of the fact it was before the 1990s one of the large producers of basic and applied science in the region thanks to its national science system (Ghafoor *et al.* 2009; Hammam and alhajaj 2014) but it has yet to engage in the reconstruction of its once well-regarded university system.

2.3 Models of governance of the research systems

Some years back, the ESTIME project intended to describe the state-of-the-art of the research systems in eight Arab countries that are partners of the EU. Among other things, it focused on the type of governance and the main visible characteristics of the research system (Arvanitis 2007), which we reproduce in Table 1.4. Four "models" of governance of research in the Arab region were identified based on the degree of centralization of the system as well as the relation to the economy and society.

This first, intuitive categorization permits introduction of the following discussion on the governance of the research systems that will consider history, centralization, dynamism and performance before proposing a renewed typology, taking into account these characteristics. Before entering into detail we

Table 1.4 Four institutional models in Arab countries based on governance models (ESTIME analysis)

Type	Countries	Main features
The Gulf model	Gulf countries	Trade-oriented governance in performing institutions National funding for research is rather centralized de facto Public and foreign universities open to foreign teachers/researchers Research based on international collaborations and few regional projects Foundations for research
The Middle East model	Syria Egypt Iraq	Centralized type of governance Research in large public research centers and universities Large public universities and few recent private universities
The Machreq model	Lebanon Jordan	Decentralized governance National funding for research is rather centralized de facto. Numerous alternative sources of private funding. Research concentrated mainly in private universities in Lebanon and much less in the public university; main research universities are public in Jordan
The Maghreb model	Algeria Morocco Tunisia	Centralized governance for both funding and management in performing institutions Large public universities Research mainly in universities and mission-oriented public research institutes

would like to compare it to the typology explained above that was drawn from an analysis of the main statistical variables.

We can see some clear differences, mainly because the ESTIME typology does not take into account the *size of the research system*. This explains the fact that Saudi Arabia is not included in Group III above, although all the other countries belong to the ESTIME typology called the "Gulf model." What is common to all these countries in the "Gulf model" is the aggressive strategy to consolidate research by encouraging international institutional cooperation and attracting foreign researchers to the university centers. Also Egypt, a case in itself, is included in Group I above but was included as the "Middle East model" by ESTIME. Again size can explain this difference between the two typologies, and our present statistical typology is probably best fitted to the changes that are promoted since 2007 in Egypt, giving research stronger autonomy and more budgets. Finally, in our Group II above we find a strange mix of rather different, but "small" countries: Jordan, Lebanon and Tunisia. The two first are examples of a decentralized mode of organization (Lebanon and Jordan), while Tunisia is a typical centralized system, molded after the French administrative system. But, looking at the specialization patterns, these three countries are probably better off by being closely linked than the grouping proposed on the basis solely of the centralized mode of governance. Indeed, the three of them focus very much on life sciences and health, when most other Arab countries have distinct preferences for engineering sciences, as we will see in the next chapter.

3 A typology of the Arab national research systems

Synthesizing this discussion based on a comparison of the factor analysis and the more intuitive institutional models presented above, four models for the governance of research systems can be proposed, which combine the results from the statistical analysis and the political vision of the research system.

The comparison of both analyses teaches us to be careful when making generalizations. By looking only at the obvious, in this case the modes of governance, one misses dimensions that are less apparent, namely the specialization and dynamics of the research system, the growth pattern or the size of the research capabilities. Nonetheless, focusing on governance is really meaningful. It permits us to discuss the elements of the research systems that are derived from history, and are observable in today's evolution. Table 1.5 sketches briefly this synthetic typology before examining these structural aspects linked to history and the dynamism of the research system.

1 Large, centralized and dynamic research systems   Size matters in research. Many have sought to identify the "critical mass" at which size begins to result in the under-development of research capacity. After 30 years of searching for this elusive critical mass, it is time to acknowledge the fact that size also translates into a certain diversification of interests and stronger expansion of the research system. When this dynamic process is underway not only because the population is large, but because the growth of the scientific activity is strong and

Table 1.5 A typology of research systems

Type	Main characteristics	Countries
1	Large, centralized and dynamic research systems	Egypt, Morocco, Saudi Arabia, (Algeria)
2	Large, centralized and low-performing research systems	Iraq, Libya, Sudan, Syria
3	Small, dynamic research systems	Tunisia, Lebanon, Jordan, Kuwait
4	Small, flexible and market-oriented research systems	Qatar, United Arab Emirates

consistent, then a dynamic research system can be said to exist. This is the case in Morocco, Saudi Arabia and, more recently, Egypt, which is undergoing a major overhaul of its research system. In Algeria, where the government has recently decided to invest heavily in research, this dynamic process is maybe getting underway, although issues that are known difficulties since long ago are still there. While all of these systems are centralized, they appear able to manage the emergence of competitive funds and favor collaborations with foreign partners. With the (very notable) exception of Egypt, they are rich countries. As was shown in the factor analysis, Morocco is the most diversified system in the sample. The remaining three countries (Algeria, Egypt and Saudi Arabia) share a very similar profile of disciplinary specializations. Nonetheless, Algeria shows signs of a strongly under-performing research system.

2 Large, centralized and low-performing systems   Low levels of research activity, relatively few research centers operating with limited government funding and a lack of diversity in their financial and human resources are the hallmarks of this group, which includes Libya, the Sudan and Syria, as well as Iraq, although the latter's efforts to rebuild its formerly renowned education system are worthy of note. In these countries, public research centers are burdened with the scientific services required by public organizations, while professors have to mainly comply with their teaching responsibilities. Universities generally have poor records of research. As such, the contribution of these countries to the production of original research and patents are limited and does not include all scientific fields. These countries belong to Group IV of the factor analysis. Many international recommendations appear geared towards improving the record of these countries.

3 Small, dynamic research systems   The research centers in this group, which includes Tunisia, Lebanon, Jordan and Kuwait, are characterized by flexibility in their relationship with the public sector and diversity in their sources of funding and human resources. Their most significant research production remains linked to the institutions that are able to draw international support and build partnerships with industry. The institutions within this model show promising dynamism. Universities play an important role and, more importantly, there are many universities with explicit research policies. However, these countries are also characterized by brief tenure of their professors. Most of the countries in this model fall within Group II of the factor analysis. They boast the highest numbers of publications and growth of production. They are also small by any standard, but have proportionally high figures of researchers and citation impact, and proportionally strong scientific production. As was discussed above, Tunisia is quite different in its centralized governance of the research system, which is mainly based on the recognition of university labs.

4 **Small, flexible and market-oriented research systems**   This Group 4 is quite similar to the above Group 3, but distinguished by research centers with flexibility toward, and sometimes independence from, the public sector. They are also characterized by being rich and thus able to have a diversity of funding sources, and the ability to attract specialists from abroad. A significant percentage of their scientific production comes from universities and private centers and they are able to benefit from international cooperation programs, as well as from independent local funds in the cases of Qatar and the United Arab Emirates. The countries of this model correlate to Group III in our factor analysis (UAE, Bahrain, Qatar). They are characterized as very small, rich and rapidly expanding. Nonetheless, being "market-oriented" does not mean the private sector is more active in R&D. These countries have been emblematic of the "knowledge economy" because they have quite strictly applied recommendations concerning the privatization of research funding through the establishment of universities and the adoption of international standards. They have also tried to promote science cities that gather universities, technical centers, incubators of start-ups, etc. According to a study on science cities, these countries tend to be very responsive to policy at the international level and to a large extent have followed the recommendations of global financial institutions (Khodr 2011). This conformity to a perfect model also indicates the difficulty of creating a research community from scratch. Historically, the experience of small countries is limited; for example, Singapore has also undergone this process long ago with some success (Goudineau 1990), but it had to wait for more than 30 years before science of a certain quality could be nurtured locally. Finally, not all small countries are included here (Kuwait, for example, has a rather long experience mainly based in the expansion of universities). Finally, the quite surprising case of Oman is rather more complex, basing its strategy on a smaller local science base. The complexity of turning a policy recommendation, the expansion of a "knowledge economy," into a full-fledged research and innovation system should not be underestimated. We will examine this aspect after revising some of the historical roots of the research institutions.

4 History, structure and evolution of the research systems

History shapes institutions and the research path taken by a country. Arab research centers at first focused on basic sciences and medicine.[23] They subsequently diversified their programs to include applied science and technology specializations. Over the past two decades, human, social and environmental sciences have also been added. More focused centers have been created, usually because of the availability of specific, usually international, funding; for instance, there is a focus on locally significant palm tree research in a number of Gulf countries. It has not always been the case: Tunisia has a quite impressive network of small but industry-oriented research and technical centers, copied from the French model of the technical centers that are partly funded by the state and partly by industry. Traditionally, agricultural research depended on Ministries of Agriculture, which have been quite important in Egypt, Morocco, Syria and the Sudan. International agricultural centers belonging to the network of the Consultative Group for International Agricultural Research,[24] like the International Center for Agricultural Research in the Dry Areas (ICARDA), headquartered in Aleppo until 2012, have also played an important role in structuring the research in this field; desertification, water pollution and management of water resources have been promoted through French bilateral cooperation, mainly with Tunisia and Morocco; linguistic research in the Maghreb grew out of interest in Amazigh language and historical research; the Balka research center in Jordan grew out of international (mainly British) funding of environmental sciences. Many research projects are currently being implemented through partnerships with Western industrial states and the exchange of scientific visits and training. A large series of research observatories has also been created, usually linked to a specific research institute, and these act as platforms for international collaborations and further research programs, centered around specific instruments and issues (health, environment, energy, water, science and technology monitoring, political change, demography).[25] A number of new research units, public or semi-public, are created in this way, based on a mix of availability of funds and expressed needs.

A second aspect that shapes strongly the research systems is this combination of growing number of research units, and of more intense international relations. This has led to both a diversification of research interests as well as a diversification of institutional arrangements. Since for all these countries applied research and development issues are always set at the center of their concern, the increasing academic population has always been a difficult issue for governments. Research in agricultural centers belonging to a Ministry of Agriculture has a clear development objective. Whatever the activity of the research center, its mission will be to serve agricultural development. But as academia grows, and new university research activities emerge, the fundamental mission of research is less clear to the state. And as we already mentioned, research in most Arab countries is academic research. This explains the success of the "networks paradigm," as we called it (Arvanitis *et al.* 2010). Any activity that could show its links to economic entities, either firms or other, is welcomed. The same thing happens for technoparks, technopoles and incubators. When promoting a general economy of links between research and the productive sectors, or NGOs and other social actors, the network paradigm, which is very appreciated by managers and policy officials, in fact hides two structural aspects: a very controlled dynamism and the overarching role of the state.

4.1 Growing and dynamic research systems

The growth of research units is difficult to monitor (again the issue of indic-ators!). Egypt, as expected, has the largest number of research centers (14 specialized government research centers, 219 research centers under the auspices of ministries and 114 centers at universities). Much more interesting is Tunisia: there are 33 research centers comprising 139 laboratories and 643 branch research units (M'henni 2007).[26] Technological research cities are few, limited to Egypt, Saudi Arabia and Tunisia, and they have very different forms and func-tions. The ANIMA Investment Network is an association trying to function as a networking tool among them. There is a general trend toward the promotion of technoparks and science cities. And some new research "cities" are under way in the Gulf countries: they usually link research to an institution of higher educa-tion (such as an engineering school or university) and a hospital or business. Tunisia has had the most ambitious technoparks program, which, although not growing as quickly as intended, has nevertheless been effective in some cases (M'henni and Arvanitis 2012).

The Gulf countries have relied on this idea that research and technology can be entirely fed through the creation of innovation hubs, or specialized areas. For example, there is a Science and Technology Oasis under the umbrella of the Qatar Foundation (UNDP 2009: 188). Jordan launched the El-Hassan Science Park in 2009 (UNESCO 2010b: 256). The Mubarak Administration had created its own Mubarak Science Park (which has since changed its name), but, as we personally witnessed it, was rather a research center than a unit connecting research to the outside world. Very high expectations concerning the "useful research" for development is of course understandable; nonetheless, these efforts usually take for granted that research grows by giving more resources, and because public administrations should obey the desires of their hierarchical tute-lage, namely a minister, prince, king or president. This vertical, top-down approach is the rule, and even research systems with a decentralized governance seem to adopt this rather authoritarian view of the research organization.

Hiba Khodr (2011) studied three specialized "science cities": the Dubai Healthcare City, the Abu Dhabi Masdar City and the Qatar Education City. These institutions are exemplary for the governance style of these entirely new entities that combine a hospital, schools, universities and scientific research. According to Khodr (2011: 7),

> the decision-making process was repeatedly described in all the interviews as a predominantly centralized top-down process. The presence of a vision by the country's leadership is another common denominator to the inter-viewees' answers to the question related to main actors involved in policy development and formulation. [...] These decision makers share the follow-ing common characteristics: they are in the ruler's circle of trust, they have access, they have vested interests, they have "connection with the vastness of the space, otherwise they won't see the need," they have exposure to the

outside world, they are competent people, they are not necessarily consultants, the majority are expatriates, and they are subject matter experts who are well known in their field.

Besides being established as free zones, all the cities in the study are either subsidized by the government, semi-governmental organizations or government-funded projects. They aim to diversify the economy and, in their design and policy objectives, they also target sustainability. For that, the innovation perspective is crucial to understand the implementation process of specialized cities. Khodr (2011: 15) points out that

> A specialized city seeks to be attractive not just for the home country and the region, but also for the whole world. Being the first city to implement the education, health and environment concepts on such a large scale is important and is what is common to these cities; the specialized cities-within-the-city want to become a hub and a global benchmark. They intend to gain the so-called "first mover advantage" [...] where customers tend to have a preference for the pioneers while others copy their innovative concept and buy their acquired expertise. [...] The cities attract internationally well-founded institutions and foreign professors to staff massively the newly founded universities.

The Gulf countries were able to attract many foreign branches thanks to their generous grants of million of dollars to the endowment of their home university. Moreover, the universities are considered to add value to the city. Another common characteristic of these cities is joining education and research under one roof, with the ambitious aim of bridging policy and research. Finally, the pressure to conform to internationally and regionally accepted standards represents yet another policy determinant to the establishment of the three cities. Related to this are elements of national pride and regional prestige. These cities are quite recent and it is too early to see if they will succeed in realizing their declared objectives and expected outcomes. Nevertheless, one can see a clear business orientation prevailing, linked to an authoritarian way of managing and concentrating economic and political power, and finally a certain willingness to control the whole creative process.

These new orientations are linked to a certain dynamism. It should be mentioned that Arab countries are no exception to the world changes affecting research policy. This business orientation, the rather new and consolidating role of universities, the innovation-oriented research activities, the programming through funding agencies and the world competition for competences are affecting the governance of research everywhere and in the Arab countries also. What has been intriguing in the case of most Arab countries, particularly those being dynamic, is the fact that this dynamism, which claims to rely on confidence of private actors, decentralization and closer public–private relations within research programs, triggering higher investments in both education and research, is closely monitored by the state. The factorial analysis shows that differences in growth rates between different countries, as well as performance on the Global Innovation Index, do make an important difference, something that is not only related to money by itself, although it represents the concrete translation of pro-research policy engagement. But it does not underline the pervasive importance of the states, even in the pro-business strategies.

4.2 A policy framework always centered around the state

The relation of research to the state is very central: larger countries usually have a more "centralized" science policy system. Centralization can also, however, operate in smaller countries like Tunisia. Moreover, centralization has no relation to performance. A totally decentralized system like Lebanon, an exception in the Arab region, performs as well as Tunisia, which is highly centralized. Lebanon from this point of view should be the showcase for its permanent support to research by decentralized actors, among which the state is one among others. The concept of a national council (rather than a ministry) as a central coordinating figure for science policy is an indicator of this absence of centralization. This "English" system of councils fits well with decentralized countries. The "French" system of a central state administration for both higher education and research is usual in larger countries. However, caution must be taken with this gross generalization. Egypt is, apparently, in a process of rapid "decentralization" of its science policy, following an original course that has no historical precedent in the country. It has dismantled its Science Academy (modeled on the Soviet Academy of Science) and is now transitioning to a quasi-council and program-based funding. The same goes for Morocco which, within a centralized administration, is undergoing a series of state initiatives from competing government ministries as well as from administration supported by the king's counselors. The motivation in both cases is related to a need for efficiency: the old institutions and the ministry in charge have not been particularly efficient in either of these two large and complex countries; probably this explains the changes one can observe in both of these countries, with the creation of King Abdulaziz City of Science and Technology in Saudi Arabia and the complete change of the funding system in Morocco. This need to trigger new funding mechanisms and boost research is felt even by the most bureaucratic offices. But no one seems really to give space to allow free decision-making at the level of performing teams and performing institutions. Even privately funded budgets are managed by the same controlling state machineries, or the same control-minded personnel either in public offices or private entities. Many researchers in all Arab countries, usually from internationally recognized laboratories, are asking for the creation of new decision-making processes inside the public administration rather than real decentralization. What is at stake is the existence of independent research in publicly funded institutions.

In most Arab countries, research is the responsibility of Ministries of Higher Education and Scientific Research (eight countries), Ministries of Education (three countries), and a Ministry of Planning (one country), in addition to some specialized ministries (agriculture, health, industry). Five Arab countries (Bahrain, Kuwait, Lebanon, Qatar and the United Arab Emirates), all of them small countries, show an exception to this trend, having assigned the task of research and development to relatively independent councils and academies (Salih 2008; UNDP 2009: 188). Table 1.6 depicts, to the best of our knowledge, the various institutions and governance modes in various Arab countries. The diversity is rather larger than expected, something Roland Waast (2008) had already underlined in his regional analysis of Arab countries. Moreover, the very few public entities in charge of research usually cumulated functions (coordinating, performing, funding, etc.). In Lebanon, for example, the National Council for Scientific Research (CNRS), as we will see in Chapter 4, has functioned primarily as a coordinating body but also as an agency distributing research grants on the basis of competitive calls for proposals. The CNRS also has four institutes of its own, but these are relatively small.

In most Arab countries, organizations performing scientific research are mainly attached to higher education institutions rather than being independent public research organizations. Nor is it very common to see research units attached to productive or services firm or other types of organization linked to the economic activity. It has been stated, notably in the *Arab Knowledge Report*, that this contributes to the creation of a wide gap between education and research on the one hand, and research and economic and social needs on the other. The Arab Knowledge Report, as practically all policy reports on research systems that deliver a message in favor of development, advocates for a closer relationship between research organizations and industry, agriculture and other productive sectors. Since most research is public, this would entail the organic connection of research organizations to a different ministry, as is mostly the case of agricultural research; in effect, we find an organization devoted to agriculture that hosts research and development activities, basic research and extension services, and sometimes is linked to specific training schools for the agricultural sector. This very strong specificity of the agricultural sector has been reproduced in French-speaking Maghreb countries, as well as in Lebanon (with the Lebanese Agricultural Research Institute created very early, in 1964). Egypt has also had such a specific public research organization, mainly because this fitted perfectly in the state-controlled view of research for development, where a public institution was assigned to a specific economic sector. It has less been the case in other Arab countries that have experienced more recent creation of research institutions. In the particular case of agriculture, the network of internationally funded research centers (coordinated by the Consultative Group of International Agricultural Research Centers, hosted by the World Bank), has "doubled" the activity of many public research organizations, and promoted seeds and agricultural practices related to the so-called Green Revolution. Arab countries host some of these, but the main agricultural research has relied on the national public research organizations.

In any case, the overall structure of the research in the country has less been the outcome of a unified decision-making process and rather the result of a

Table 1.6 General descriptions of research systems in various Arab countries

Country	S&T policy document	Permanent policy-making bodies with national authority		Funding agencies	Other funding mechanisms	Type of governance	GERD/GDP (percentage)
		Council	Ministry				
Algeria	Yes (National Plan, 1998)	–	Yes	–	National research programs National Fund RTD +	Centralized	0.25*
Morocco	Yes (Vision 2006)	–	Department of a larger ministry (since 2004)	CNRST	Various funds to support innovation: PTI, incubators	Centralized	0.8*
Tunisia	Yes (5th Plan and following Plans since 1977)	–	Yes	National Science Research Foundation (since 1989), among others	Various funds to support innovation: FRP, NPRI, PTI, Techparks	Centralized	1.0*
Egypt	No	Formerly: Academy of Science	Yes	STDF and other funds	Initiatives from various ministries: Agriculture, Industry, Telecom, etc.	Centralized	0.2**
Lebanon	Yes STIP = Vision (2006)	Yes CNRS	–	CNRS since 1962	Performers get contracts from all sorts of sponsors	Decentralized	0.22*

Country							
Jordan	No	Yes HCST	–	HCST since 1987	Performers get contracts from all sorts of sponsors	Decentralized	0.34*
Syria	No	Newly established (2007)	–	No	–	Decentralized	0.12**
Bahrain	–	Higher Education Council	–	BCSR (acting as agency)	–	Trade-oriented	0.04**
Oman	–	The Research Council	–	OCIPED Invest Promo 2002	Sponsors	Trade-oriented	0.07**
Emirates	–	Institutional research and strategic planning	–	–	Sponsors	Trade-oriented	0.2
Qatar	–	–	–	Qatar Foundation	Sponsors	Trade-oriented	0.6**
Kuwait	–	Still in discussion	Yes Ministry of Higher Education and Scientific Research	KFAS funding and coordination since 1988	Sponsors	Trade-oriented	0.2
Saudi Arabia	–	KACST	Ministry of Education	KACST since 1977	–	Centralized	0.14**

Source: ESTIME final report (2007). Kuwait and Saudi Arabia: recent monographs. Data on GERD as a percentage of GDP come from ESTIME project, others from Nour (2005). Some additional information comes from the work done by S. Hanafi for ESCWA on benchmarking research systems.

historical, slow and haphazard process. Thus future attributions to specific ministries and issues such as the management of public research funds are still very much the subject of political decisions. Even if the closeness of research to productive sectors, as well as innovation, are among the main objectives of the new knowledge economy, we will still express some skepticism on the possible outcomes of a voluntary process based on changes of attributions of research from higher education to industry, as is usually proposed. In practically all Arab countries there has been rampant competition between "modernists," usually to be found in "technical ministries" (industry, telecommunications), and representatives of a political personnel that is more preoccupied with issues related to political representation and the power play that affects the state. The technicality of research makes it a weak link, and policy needs political, meaningful objects of attention. As Ignacio Avalos, a former minister of science in Venezuela, has written, the value of science is too often reduced to the value of an inauguration of some library (Antonorsi-Blanco and Avalos 1980). Universities are a "better" political object (at least a more understandable and visible one) than research, but the questions affecting universities are far away from research: the number of rooms of the student dormitories, the management of social services, the availability of cantinees are usually politically more important than the problems affecting scientific research. Moreover, there is no way to prove that improving education (that is, teaching in universities) and research will make things easier. The evidence is that research labs can feed their research activities with researchers by connecting to Masters and doctoral students. But the interaction of the university, as an organization and as a political entity, with research units is not simple in any of these countries.

Education is not only an internal political object, it is also one of the key arenas where competition between countries is focused. Higher education has been profoundly affected by global changes and the pressure placed on universities; the privatization of higher education in most countries and the connection of higher education to markets[27] go well beyond the usual willingness of the state apparatus to control student life and rein in potentially rebellious universities. Research can find its way with difficulty under this very strenuous political pressure. It is a paradox, since international rankings of universities are based mainly on outputs of research rather than teaching or other social dimensions. Finally, the predominance of Ministries of Industry, Agriculture and Telecommunications in innovation policies, as well as hospitals, is becoming a central policy-making locus for research, as they are both a place of useful research and a key employer. Moving slowly away from research to innovation has, in this way, a direct consequence of consolidating the political status of these "technical" ministries: its does entail that research be better considered!

4.3 Organization and performance of the research system

To begin with, it is necessary to mention the Arab Knowledge Report, which made a very severe assessment:

Data related to national income of seventeen Arab countries show that Arab GDP was $1,042 billion in 2006, and yet annual gross expenditure on scientific research did not exceed two billion USD, an average of 0.2 per cent. This expenditure produced only 38 invention patents and 5,000 scientific papers, meaning that the cost of one scientific paper came to around $400,000. This estimated cost for the production of a scientific paper or patent is clearly exorbitant, and weakens the trust of society and its production sectors in Arab research programs and their researchers. In comparison, Malaysia spends on research and development 22.5 per cent of gross Arab expenditure, while Finland spends 1.75 times as much as the Arab region and registers 855 invention patents at the cost of $4.1 million each, equaling 8 per cent of the cost of one patented Arab invention.

(Al Maktoum Foundation and UNDP 2009: 201)

Until now, we have tried to show that the different situation affecting Arab countries makes these generalizations less meaningful. Nonetheless, all international reports insist on the low performance of Arab countries. We would like to qualify the riddle of under-investment in research. One aspect that seems important, performance, seems unrelated to structural aspects such as policy centralization or institutional and organizational choices.

Tunisia, which has been a leading Arab country in research,[28] has a centralized science policy, as do Algeria and Egypt. These two countries have had a much lower performance, at least measured by publications. So centralization is not really a deterrent to performance. Tunisia could be our yardstick into investigating the performance of a research system as a whole, since it is the only country that has seen a spectacular growth in its research output in the last ten years. What happened before and after this growth was the implementation of a labeling policy, a somewhat unimportant administrative measure, in order to have a catalogue of research units inside the various universities and research institutions, regardless of their institutional status. The important decision was not so much the labeling, but the fact that to obtain the label the research units and laboratories needed to write a four-year project, submit a budget and explain their needs and means. This project is evaluated on a two-year basis by a national committee (CNEARS) that respected the terms of scientific excellence and research quality as its paramount criteria. As Rachid Ghrir, former director of research in the ministry explained,[29] the evaluation was totally independent from political pressure, based on evaluation committees with international standards and with foreign and national experts. The National Committee's evaluations have been very much respected, both by researchers and the administration. Although, this might not appear to be a revolution, in the context of the Arab countries it definitely changed the rules for research. The main result is to identify clearly where research is performed. Although it does not solve the riddle of under-investment, or the policy, administrative and management difficulties that are confronted by the research units, the clear identification of the performing actors of research at the "ground level" is a formidable tool. As a result, resources were more efficiently allocated and monitoring was performed both by the laboratories and the administration. This labeling and evaluation scheme has had a permanent effect on research production (see Chapter 2).

It should be mentioned that Morocco tried a somewhat similar exercise by performing a large evaluation and review process of the research system by an international expert team that brought in foreign and national experts, as well as a complete review of the research system (Kleiche and Waast 2008; Waast and Kleiche-Dray 2009). Results were not as spectacular as was the case of Tunisia; after the evaluation process took place, the government didn't sustain its policy in favor of research; for example, the "research" part inside the national accounts disappeared, the labeling of the research units in the universities took more than ten years to be completed and the whole process of reforming the research system took a very long time. Similarly, just before the Arab revolutions, Egypt went through a major overhaul of its research system after a change of minister. The change affected mainly the policy framework and permitted creation of a fairly efficient funding structure.[30] But no other country has experienced such a profound change as did Tunisia. Strangely, Tunisia stands as a paradox, being dynamic and centralized; it is a country showing both a fragile research system, but fundamentally a resilient policy and research administration (M'henni and Arvanitis 2012). Finally, maybe in a more visible manner than other Arab countries, Tunisia demonstrates the extreme difficulty of promoting technological research and innovation from within the research system. This latter aspect, the opposition between research and innovation, between promoting research and promoting technological development, is a difficult issue not only for Arab countries, but in general for research policy.

Numerous studies have tried to decipher the relation between the structure of the research system and the performance of research. None is quite conclusive, and it has to do with the way benchmarking is done: either one looks at policy concerning structural and organizational aspects, or one examines the system as an entity, where one measures inputs and outputs. The "OECD model" had strongly adopted the latter view (Henriques and Larédo 2013), and with it a linear model between inputs and outputs. In this view, one measures the performance independently from the organization. Another view would focus on the relatively complex web of institutions, which makes measurement dependent on the institutions rather than the system itself. The very central issue of funding and performance is thus difficult to examine when one focuses on the actual organization by drawing the organigram of the country. The variety of institutional arrangements does not correspond to any particular policy mix. Algeria is very centralized but demonstrates an abundance of resources, a highly complex organizational arrangement and a rather simple policy mix that does not really give research the policy space it should occupy inside the ministries in charge of research and innovation. Egypt has had a largely under-funded university system and the dominance of a Soviet-style Academy of Science inherited from the Nasserian times, where the national research center has been far less productive than one would have expected from such a large research organization (4,000 researchers). Some universities, like Ain-Shams or Alexandria University, and some hospitals, as well as some rather small but highly efficient research centers (VACSERA, Theodor Bilharz Research Institute and many others), have been performing excellent research to international standards, regardless of the rather sluggish growth of financial resources.

4.4 Foreign funding sources for research and cooperation

Relying on foreign sources as a substitute for too few national resources is a symptom of a weakness. It translates into research that has little impact. For example, a 2009 report from the United Nations Development Program complained that funding projects through foreign capital resulted in projects having a persistently weak impact (UNDP 2009: 187–188). Foreign funding can be worse: it might orient researchers to topics that are not really relevant in their own country. The debate over this opposition between relevant or international science is at the very heart of all the policy debates on research. In a sense, we could say that our own research was guided by this very fundamental question.

On the contrary, co-funding between national and international funding, or additional funding from international cooperation that accompanies a national policy, is the right way to go. In effect, all experiences of co-funding, for example between the EU and Arab countries, have been rather successful when Arab research units are not relegated to a secondary role (Pancera *et al.* 2013). Addressing nationally relevant research topics with local funds and additional international funds is not an easy task, since it includes negotiations on various policy levels. In research policy studies, this issue has only come to attention recently (Gaillard and Arvanitis 2013; Beigel and Sabea 2014; Keim *et al.* 2014), and funding is definitely the most important criteria in defining a non-hegemonic country (Losego and Arvanitis 2008). In the Arab East, Sari Hanafi (2010) has shown that the multiplication of foreign sources has been fragmenting the social sciences, and oriented the research on social issues that could be done in an academic context toward small, non-academic, policy-oriented private consultancies. Nonetheless, overall, the actual impact of external funding on research is still an open question. What is certain is that "academic" research centers in most Arab countries will actively search for external sources of funding.

As the available local funding is insufficient, research centers will tend to seek external funding. In some cases, it affects directly the research orientations of the research units. We just mentioned the case of social sciences in the Arab East (Lebanon, Palestine, Jordan, Syria, and to some degree Egypt) where research has been basically funded by foreign foundations and UN institutions. In the more technological areas, a somewhat similar process of re-orientation of research is taking place. Suffice to mention one very intriguing case, that of the technical centers in Tunisia devoted to technological research for the productive sector. As these centers continue to grow, they are seeking additional funding and, despite their valuable (possible) contribution for national development, this funding is being provided through foreign (primarily European) institutions.

In fact, the technical centers, instead of establishing closer relations with end users outside the research world, participate in research programs, such as those funded by the European Union like Framework Programs (FP6, FP7 and Horizon 2020), exactly as any university laboratory would do it. The lack of funding is not specific to the public sector, as shown by the example from Morocco, where OCP, the largest Moroccan enterprise, capable of funding its own research and development, has nevertheless turned toward foreign sources of funding, again primarily European. In this particular case, it might be a temporary situation, as can be witnessed by the announcement of a new OCP funding program oriented toward sustainable production technologies. It might also be a different motivation than the lack of funds, such as the need to connect to international research networks. Still, even companies that need research for their own products and markets are very reluctant to fund their own research in Morocco. This situation seems mainly to affect large companies in Morocco, and has been documented alongside the fact that small- and medium-sized enterprises (SMEs) have had a steadily growing introduction of new technologies and new products, as a consequence of funding applied research with their own internal capabilities.[31] Moreover, this is largely the case in all Arab countries, as attested by all the innovation surveys that have been performed in the last ten years.[32] The World Bank has ordered a study based on its Climate Assessment Surveys in the MENA region, which also confirms the importance of fast-growing SMEs (CMI 2013: 85).

The EU has shouldered much of the cost of many research projects in the Arab region through participation into European research calls. As an example, during the decade 2001–2010, in Egypt the European Commission accounted for almost half of total science and technology cooperation, mainly through the RDI Program, while the United States accounted for 17 percent, Japan 16 percent and Germany 13 percent. In Tunisia, international cooperation covers approximately 5 percent of GERD and the European funds cover approximately 40 percent of these foreign funds, 90 percent of which come from EU Framework Programs. In the case of Morocco, its specific "Advanced Status" agreed with the EC led to it being a privileged partner of the EU. Lebanon has no agreement signed with the EU, but it participates actively in all EU-sponsored projects; European projects represent around 28–30 percent of the research budget of CNRS in Lebanon (approximately €2 million).

Although the Barcelona Process, triggered by the EU in 1995 after the Barcelona Declaration, has not been a success story in economic and political terms (Moisseron 2005), it appears that scientific cooperation has been rather successful. It should be mentioned that a variety of common funding schemes have been deployed in the last few years between the EU and the Arab countries. For example, for the period 2007–2013 we can mention: a co-funding program (RDI) in Egypt (€11 million in 2007 and €20 million in 2010), a similar programmed in Tunisia (€12 million), in Jordan (€5 million), in Algeria (€38.6 million, co-funded by the EU for €21.5 million), a twinning project with57Morocco (€1.3 million), to which one should add "Erasmus mundus" scholarships and various TEMPUS projects. We estimate that the EU has spent the non-negligible amount of €300 million in the period 2007–2013.

As a result of this intense activity, the European Commission has funded international collaboration platforms supposed to facilitate dialogue between Europe and Mediterranean partner countries of the EU.[33] The EU has also created, following the Barcelona Declaration in 1994, a monitoring committee on science and technology that brings together officials from countries in Europe and the Mediterranean (that is, Arab countries' "neighbors" to the EU – Turkey and Israel) (Rossano *et al.* 2013). These institutions created a rather permanent arena for exchanges of policy experience in the region. The European Commission has funded large "projects" bringing together policy officials, as is the case of the MIRA project, followed by the Medspring project, itself being created before launching a common co-funding program between the EU, European member countries and Mediterranean partners (called ERANET MED, which was preceded by a similar project on agricultural research called ARIMNET), which is foreseen to create a large regional program, called PRIMA. All these initiatives have responded to both policy orientations of the European Commission and intense relations with the national governments of Arab countries that are partners to the EU. None of the large, well-known Arab think-tanks and international policy institutions have triggered discussions on these issues.[34] Finally, we remark that these projects are the only international forums for discussion on policy issues concerning research in Arab countries.[35]

4.5 National systems of innovation

Innovation is distinct from research, and not all innovation is research-based. This is why innovation requires special attention, separate from but related to research. Innovation policies have been developed and sustained quite firmly over the last few years by some governments, for example in Algeria, Egypt, Turkey, Morocco and Tunisia. Other countries have also promoted specific schemes and measures for innovation (Jordan, Lebanon and, to a lesser degree, Syria). Gulf countries have also established specific measures. In recent years a specific emphasis was placed by funding agencies and governments on the development of techno-parks and industrial clusters (Saint Laurent 2005). This policy shift toward innovation (rather than solely research support) was basically done through measures promoting innovation in the public sector and contacts between the public and private sectors in many forms: engineering networks; technology transfer units; fiscal measures; and funding for start-ups and venture capital. As we already mentioned, to varying degrees all the countries of the Arab region were profoundly affected by the example of the EU in its promotion of innovation and the instruments it established to measure it, such as the European Innovation Scoreboard (M'henni and Arvanitis 2012).[36]

The science parks, recently established in several Arab countries, including all of the monarchies of the Gulf, is the most emblematic type of measure toward innovation. The parks are usually part of a broader policy of promoting enterprise and partnerships in innovation, as well as research between the private and public sectors. This helps to explain the relative optimism of business executives interviewed about innovation in the Gulf for the World Bank Survey conveyed also through the Competitiveness Indicators of the World Economic Forum. These executives were particularly enthusiastic about prospects in Qatar and Saudi Arabia, which were ranked 11 and 21, respectively, out of 142 countries. Science parks have also been developed in the Maghreb, mainly in Tunisia and Morocco. For Tunisia, it has been a systematic policy to promote what it calls technopoles. In Morocco, some initial difficulties in establishing successful science parks have recently begun to give way to results. A first appraisal of science parks in Morocco and Tunisia concludes that it is too early to draw conclusive observations (Arvanitis and M'henni 2010). Nevertheless, this is an effort that undoubtedly contributed to the creation of new companies, and in some cases the creation of very successful medium to large companies. Most of these parks function as nurseries and incubators, as well as technopoles. Lebanon has what is probably one of the most successful of such initiatives, called Berytech, which has emerged as a private initiative of the School of Engineering Université Saint-Joseph (see Chapter 4). In 2009, Jordan launched El-Hassan Science Park as part of a major science project in Amman, and Egypt established its own Mubarak Science Park (which has since changed its name) (UNESCO 2010b: 256) These experiments have been extremely slow to come about and will probably need to be revamped in the future.

King Abdulaziz City for Science and Technology (KACST) is also an interesting example, since it is cumulating functions of the Saudi Arabian national science agency and its national laboratories under the scheme of a science park. The science agency function involves science and technology policy-making, data collection, funding of external research and services such as the patent office. KACST is a "science city" with three components: research, innovation and services for the public and private sectors. It has 15 research teams in different disciplines and three programs on industrial property, an incubator and innovation centers, plus a grant system "to encourage excellence and innovation." In 2011, KACST had a budget of almost US$0.5 billion, offering grants to 64 researchers and research teams. It is interesting that only 23 percent of KACST's budget is invested in basic science, while the remainder is distributed among the applied sciences (31 percent in medicine, 27 percent in engineering and 16 percent in agriculture) (KACST 2012: 105). It hosts over 2,500 employees and is in charge of the national science and technology policy, coordination of research and other government agencies, as well as performance of research, support to capacity building and technology transfers and international cooperation. The case of KACST is exceptional since it concentrates all science policy functions and performance of research in the kingdom. Additionally, Saudi Arabia is feeding its own scientific personnel and does not rely so strongly on foreign professors and researchers as the United Arab Emirates and Qatar. Nonetheless, we should remember that the accumulation of all functions in the science promotion is also a sign of a certain difficulty in generating a large and complex innovation system. The interesting aspect here is that the whole research system is concentrated in a single "science city," and what is expected is that the concentration of resources will generate a virtuous performance.

A first appraisal of innovation policies in some Arab countries has concluded that measures to promote innovation cannot be evaluated properly because of the lack of comparative standards (Arvanitis and M'henni 2010). Direct measures to promote innovation through SME-oriented programs, technoparks and incubators are easy to measure; however, even this is not done, in particular because statistics on the productive sectors are not sufficient. What is also becoming apparent after more than ten years of systematic effort in various countries is that policies have usually been short-term and success is expected to be easy and immediate; long-term efforts are not encouraged. Examples like technoparks in Casablanca, Egyptian Smart Village close to Cairo, the Berytech incubator in Beirut or the El-Ghazala technopark in Tunis are thus quite exceptional for having survived beyond the short term. It is interesting to note that Berytech owes its extraordinary longevity and success to the fact that it benefits from autonomous management based on the permanent institutional support of a university; El-Ghazala in Tunisia owes a great part of its longevity to the existence of the School of Telecommunications, even though the companies inside the technopark do not have linkages with the school as strong as might be expected. In both cases, support is not financial but rather consists of the provision of an institutional background. These two examples in what can probably be considered the two most contrary national research and innovation systems, the Lebanese and the Tunisian, show that relations between the private and the public sectors are anything but straightforward. Institutional support goes far beyond financial support and relates to the creation of an ecosystem conducive to technological development. Nonetheless, some assessments tend to doubt the efficiency of the linkage between the universities or engineering schools and departments included in the technoparks in Tunisia (Mezouaghi 2006).

What these policies show, beyond the rather centralized and very much controlled by the state character of the experiences already mentioned in the previous section, is the adoption of a network paradigm by most Arab countries. This paradigm consists of the promotion of a series of common policies that are dedicated to creating linkages mainly between research and enterprises: technology transfer units in universities and engineering schools; funding including venture capital; credit schemes favoring technological development, etc.; engineering networks; promotion of intermediate technical centers; and business associations related to innovation and technological development. Moreover, after a careful revision of policy measures in the Maghreb countries, Jordan and Egypt, experts could underline that these countries have practically experienced all forms of support for economic development oriented toward "innovation" in all its forms.[37] What seemed to lack was not imaginative policy measures, but rather sustainability and permanence of the support policies. The network paradigm certainly has the advantage of flexible arrangements. It is also strongly inspired by innovation policy concepts developed in Europe, and specifically

France. Finally, it has the additional characteristic of challenging the public research sector by asking it to establish linkages to the economy without endangering the institutional and political position of academic institutions.

We have suggested in our assessment of innovation policies that this "French style" of technology policy is very much congruent with the centralized governance of research in France, which can be found also in Maghreb countries, Egypt and Saudi Arabia. We can extend the argument to all the Arab countries: the networking has been very much preferred to other possible policy orientations. In effect, this emphasis on techno-economic networks is not the only possibility for innovation policies. Other possible orientations could have been the development of businesses with a strong public investment component, strong public–private alliances where the main partners could have been the large public corporations, preferential policies toward international investors, favoring medium-sized enterprises as "champions" in their sector, the development of strong public technical centers and the support of national preference policies related to strong industrial sectors. Many of these other options assume a strong industrial policy with choices in term of industrial sectors, something that has become a rarity, and a very strong back-up by the state. The paradox in Arab countries is that the apparently decentralized model offered by the networking paradigm has been so eagerly adopted. These policies aimed at promoting networks are relatively new and have not received a serious evaluation. This paradox of a decentralized mode of action and a rather centralized governance of all new structures can be explained by many factors, among which is the fact that network-oriented support is less demanding in terms of institutional restructuring. Moreover, we believe that what is at stake is the creation of a whole set of new actors that populate the social and economic space between firms and public authorities (Arvanitis and M'henni 2010: 233–269). We have proposed to call this ecosystem populated by units of technology transfer, start-ups, incubators, technology poles and science parks, as well as new companies that emerge around these concepts, a world of innovation (ESTIME 2007). The emergence of this world of innovation could contribute to the strengthening of industrial structures, creating a rather service-oriented sector that revolves around innovation. And, probably, that also explains the success of this way of promoting innovation.

It should be added that, within the framework of the Barcelona Process for European–Mediterranean cooperation, the EU has also suggested more innovation-related actions in the hope of creating a "Euro-Mediterranean Innovation Space" (EMIS) (Pasimeni *et al.* 2007). The idea stems from the abundant linkages between Europe and Mediterranean countries in research (Arvanitis *et al.* 2013a). But it never was embodied adequately into support of projects, as was the case for research relations. So the creation of a common "innovation space" from north, to south and eastern banks of the Mediterranean Sea is still an idea, an unaccomplished promise. Building a common *research* space is quite different from promoting an *innovation* space, the latter being rather more difficult than the former. Moreover, as we already mentioned, the monitoring of research is a difficult task, partially done through the management of projects and programs, whereas monitoring technology and innovation policy in the Arab region is still not performed.

4.6 Producing the knowledge economy

Many international organizations, bilateral donors and NGOs have sought to assist in the transformation of Arab countries' development models from low-cost to knowledge-based production: the EU, the OECD, UNESCO, UNIDO and ALECSO are only a few examples. Finally, the World Bank has actively promoted the policies in favor of a knowledge economy in the region, making assessments that are based on the knowledge assessment methodology (KAM). The KAM calculates a composite indicator called the knowledge economy index. It identifies a series of indicators (or pillars) concerning economic incentives, education, ICT and innovation. Research is only a small element among others in the World Bank framework (Reiffers and Aubert 2002), as also is the case of the Competitiveness Report of the World Economic Forum (Schwab and Sala-i-Martín 2012). It is included under the name of "innovation pillar": Arab countries rank rather low on this innovation pillar, which is based on the number of researchers, patent counts and journal articles.

As we have underlined above, on all these indicators Arab countries show low figures, without doubt. But the knowledge indexes say nothing on the dynamic that explains all these low figures. The more recent CMI/World Bank (2013) report, "Transforming Arab Economies," shows that there is a positive correlation between the country's position on the "innovation index" and their gross domestic product (GDP) per capita, except for the very rich countries (the anomaly here is rather the very high GDP per capita, something common to all resource-rich countries, rather than the low innovation performance). This has also been the result of the previous KAM index calculation (Al Maktoum Foundation and UNDP 2009: 183). In other words, despite the high GDP in oil-producing Arab countries, the ranking on the innovation and scientific research index remains very low in comparison to other Arab countries with lower incomes, or to other countries. Again, Tunisia, Jordan and Morocco perform relatively better, or rather more like the bulk of countries in the world (CMI 2013: 83). Thus, when saying, as the Arab Knowledge Report mentions, and as the CMI (2013) report repeats, that Arab countries do not show a positive correlation between GDP and innovation, it concerns only the oil-rich countries, mainly Gulf countries, and Algeria. The other countries, including the large Egyptian research system, are in a middle position, correlating rather low indicators concerning research and innovation with low GDP per capita.

Figure 1.4 reports the World Bank "innovation index" as it is computed by the KAM. The UAE ranks highest among Arab countries, followed by Qatar and then Jordan. In comparison to 1995, 12 Arab countries show a decrease in their index value for this pillar, and only five Arab countries show an increase. The Arab Knowledge Report (Al Maktoum Foundation and UNDP 2009), from where we take this figure, adds:

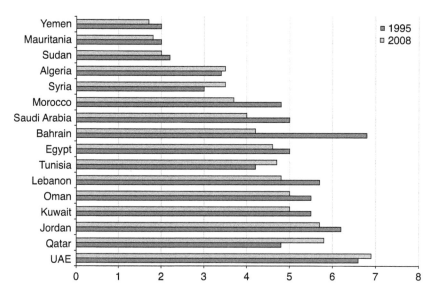

Figure 1.4 Innovation index for 17 Arab countries (World Bank knowledge economy
indicators) (source: UNDP and Al Maktoum Foundation 2009; data from KAM,
World Bank).

Notes
Innovation index was calculated by the World Bank based on
* researchers per 10,000 inhabitants;
* FDI per 100 inhabitants;
* trade (exports + imports) per 100 inhabitants;
* science and engineering students (percentage of total students);
* credit to private sector (percentage of domestic credit);
* domestic credit provided by banking sector (percentage of GDP);
* stocks trade turnover ratio (%);
* market capitalization of listed companies (percentage of GDP).

It should be noted that the innovation system index value of a number of
developing countries rose in 2005 in comparison to 1995. China achieved
the highest increase in this value (1.06), followed by Turkey (0.71) and then
Malaysia (0.63). Globally, the ranking of the Arab region decreased,
whereas Southeast Asia achieved the highest increase due to the improved
levels reached by India and Sri Lanka.

(p. 182)

The argument of the Arab Knowledge Report consists in explaining that the
Arab countries should be more actively engaged in research, and the KAM
indexes serve as a warning. Before explaining what is problematic with this presentation, let us see what happened after the Global Innovation Index was
devised from INSEAD, which has only existed since 2007, while the KAM was
older.

In effect, we could also refer to the rather robust and more complete analysis provided by the Global Innovation Index (GII) (INSEAD *et al.* 2013). If we refer to the 2014 GII, we find even worse results: all Arab countries are under-performing in all indicators and when compared to GDP, with the exception of Jordan and UAE (INSEAD *et al.* 2014: 26).[38] We can cite the comment made by the GII Report (Figure 1.5):

> Three of the six countries of the Gulf Cooperation Council (GCC) come next [in the ranking]: the United Arab Emirates (36th), Saudi Arabia (38th), and Qatar (47th). With per capita incomes ranging from PPP\$29,813.16 (Oman, 75th) to PPP\$98,813.66 (Qatar), most GCC economies achieve rankings below those of their peers in GDP per capita (with the exception of the UAE, which performs on par with those of its peers), a feature common to most resource-rich economies. [...] the regional (MENA and Western Asia) rankings are now more dispersed: Bahrain (62nd) comes behind Turkey (54th), Armenia (65th) and Kuwait (69th) come behind Jordan (64th), and Oman (75th) comes behind Georgia (74th). At the bottom of the regional rankings we find Lebanon (77th), Tunisia (78th), Morocco (84th), Egypt (99th), Azerbaijan (101st), Algeria (133rd), and Yemen (141st). [...] Armenia, Jordan, and Georgia remain in the group of innovation learners, while Saudi Arabia, Lebanon, Azerbaijan, Yemen, Algeria, Bahrain, Oman, Kuwait, and Qatar show below-par performances compared to their income levels.
>
> (GII 2014: 35)

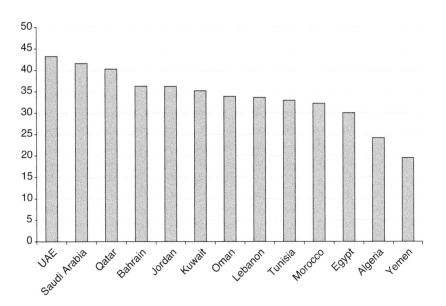

Figure 1.5 Global Innovation Index for Arab countries (source: GII 2014).

Overall, the mix of countries inside Middle East and North Africa (MENA) is so diverse that mean indicators for this "region" are meaningless. This is precisely why we proposed the above exercise in typology, identifying four quite different profiles. The GII takes great care not to be flawed methodologically, but in the end it is just a ranking: the indexes, even when balanced and carefully controlled, as is the case of the GII, cannot reflect the dynamics of the research and innovation system, nor understand the determinants that explain change. Of course, one can doubt whether what these indicators produce is not evidence on the actors inside the research and innovation system; it seems that they produce the knowledge economy itself, that is a new value system. A serious analysis of the innovation system cannot rely on the ranking of countries on a single scale, which is very much an exercise in international relations and relates to the image a government wants to give to its action. Good evidence is provided by the position of Morocco on the GII. Morocco improved its position inside the GII 2014 (ranked 84th) as compared to 2012 (ranked 88th) by creating a task force inside the Ministry of Economics that worked with the GII team in order to show that Morocco's innovation-related activities were better than predicted, and to also appear as an author of an article on human resources inside the 2014 report (INSEAD and Dutta 2012; INSEAD *et al.* 2014). The knowledge economy concerns also the knowledge of the evaluation methods used to valorize knowledge.

4.7 *Toward indicators that help position actors*

If one seriously wanted to monitor efforts to promote innovation, they would need to focus on actual actors of the research system: start-ups, incubators, technopoles or technoparks, industrial clusters, programs of technological upgrading, network activities between research and technical institutions with firms, such as consultancies, technical alliances between technical centers and companies. One would also need to have a general overview of actual policies – not of the "innovation system" as imagined by science and technology policy consultants, but as it actually works. In the first decade of the century, the national systems of innovation (NSIs) have been used as a unifying concept in order to assess research and innovation.[39] Strangely enough, promoters of the NSI approach have quite easily switched to the "knowledge economy" paradigm. The slippage from one to the other is paradoxical since, reading the OECD documents when it was actively promoting the NSI approach (thanks to the seminal work of Bengt-Åke Lundvall), the underlining paradigm is rather a structural argument that relates innovation to links between enterprises and productive and technical providers and clients; it is an approach that relates to industrial economics rather than the economic and financial value of knowledge. The main advantage of the NSI approach was to figure out the real actors of the system, the actual institutions that are part of the system.

On the contrary, the knowledge economy approach, by the scale it chooses to focus on, is deducing abstract behaviors from types of actors. It produces highly contestable indexes that are supposed to translate the competition among countries. The World Economic Forum, which has a clear ideological agenda in promoting free-market, reduced state, no barriers to international trade, deregulation of labor markets and freedom for businesses has titled its indicators a Competitiveness indicator. The high ranking of the small, rich and business-oriented small economies of the Gulf was then no surprise. The fact that we find similar rankings with the other methodologies (KAM or GII) proves the indicators are the same, and thus the results are similar. In fact, the overall paradigm is the same: produce a uni-dimensional measuring instrument that would oblige entering the competition by accepting the terms valorized by this unique measurement instrument.

It is not really the place here to pursue a deeper critique of these methodologies, although we can mention that they appeared once the developmentalist paradigm had been abandoned in the late 1980s. In the case of the Arab economies, they blinded more than opened the eyes of the analysts. None of the social conditions, the cognitive environment, the present political forces have ever been analyzed with the help of any of these indicators. The repeated half-truths on under-performing Arab economies was accompanying the political discourse on the "exceptionality" of the Arab political systems. These general diagnoses concerning research and innovation under the flag of the "knowledge economy" are not helping us to understand the real difficulties. Evidently, the knowledge economy credo didn't open the eyes of economists and policy-makers on what was really happening in the Arab countries – in their own countries!

If we want to go beyond the ranking approach, we should then re-engage in a structural analysis of innovation into economic activities, maybe less ambitious but more grounded than the NSI approach.[40]

5 Investment and funding in research

We have shown that the GERD (gross expenditure on research and development) occupies a middle position as a differentiating indicator in the factorial analysis presented above; it is not closely related to any particular country profile. Of course, larger countries will tend to spend more. Overall, however, funding appears to play an indirect role in defining the profile of a research system; the position of a country in the typology that we have presented above is loosely correlated to the amounts dedicated to research.

Perhaps a cautionary note is in order on the financial input data used in this book. Most rely on estimates, and the field experience of the authors suggests that the data are currently not being cross-checked. Rather, they are declarations made by national authorities, coming from very diverse sources. Most strikingly, national statistical institutions are not the ones providing data on research and innovation. Nor are the ministries that may be in charge of industry, agriculture or other services. In the specific case of telecommunications and information technologies, relevant government ministries have led specific initiatives; this is the case in practically all the Maghreb countries, as well as Egypt and Lebanon.

In nearly all of these countries, the authorities in charge of foreign investment have enjoyed regulatory powers, and as such have tried to produce specific data on the telecommunications sector. Rarely, however, have such initiatives been orchestrated in conjunction with a more general overview of research and innovation activities. Usually, basic statistics such as GERD come from estimates made by the ministry or council in charge of higher education or research. In the Arab world, there is a lack of confidence regarding these data reported by those who themselves will be judged upon it. Moreover since practically 70 percent of the costs of research and development are public expenses, and these are largely channeled through central state budgets, ministries in charge of budgets and finance may not be inclined to release statistics on research expenditures either, since they only report budgets (that is, non-executed financial provisions given through the national budgetary procedures). Finally, some sources used in international statistics, such as COMSTECH data normally used by international organizations, are strikingly different from most other sources. The methodology used for collecting and analyzing the data is not published. Finally, some discrepancies may cast serious doubt on certain figures. For example, some countries report both high GERD and low contribution to education as a whole: this is the case for both the Sudan and Qatar. Great caution should be exercised regarding the use of a single indicator.

UNESCO, through its Montreal-based Institute of Statistics, has undertaken to validate data in the Arab region, an effort which can only be encouraged; the first result of trying to collect rigorous data produced a lot of missing data for many countries, including countries where the collection of the data has been done, but it has not been validated in order to be published in the UNESCO database. The aim here would be not only to provide more transparency regarding public statistical data, but also to improve the confidence of non-public entities (in particular, private companies) in reporting on research and innovation by the Arab states.

5.1 Expenditures for research

Table 1.7 and Figure 1.6 show this absence of relation between the type of research system and the GERD as a percentage of GDP. Morocco and Tunisia are the two only countries spending more than 0.7 percent of their GDP in research and development. In the case of Tunisia, the estimate was modified by the Ministry of Higher Education and Research after the revolution of 2011.

GERD has been low in Arab countries for almost four decades and is lower than the world average at between 0.1 percent and 1.2 percent of GDP. OECD countries devote about 2.2 percent of GDP to research and development. There are signs of change, however. Egypt's GERD has remained stable at about 0.23 percent since 2007; prior to the outbreak of the revolution, the government had planned to raise it to 1.0 percent over five years, and had engaged in reform of the governance of research and innovation based on more competitive funding, more funding for research at public universities and more active government

Table 1.7 Distribution of countries according to GDP per head and GERD

Country	GDP^f 2010	GDP per capita^f (2010)	Public expenditure on education as percentage of GDP (2008)	Public expenditure on education as percentage of total government expenditure (2008)	GERD (as a percentage of GDP) (2007)^a	Type of research system (see Table 1.5)
Tunisia	44.3	4,170.9	6.4	16.5	1.20^e 0.8^e	3
Morocco	90.8	2,882.1	5.7	25.7	0.75	1
Libya^b	80.4	9,511.4	2.7	19.8	0.70^b	2
Qatar	127.3	59,989.8	2.4	8.24	0.33	4
Jordan	26.4	4,199.4	4.9	20.6	0.30	3
Sudan	65.2	1,985.6	0.4	4.1	0.30	2
Egypt^b	218.4	2,450.3	3.8	11.9	0.23^b	1
Lebanon^c	37.1	8,951.1	2.0	8.1	0.20	3
UAE	297.6	45,614.5	0.9	27.2	0.20	4
Oman	57.8^d	15,996.3	4.3	22.6	0.17	2
Algeria	160.7	3,995.8	4.3	20.3	0.16	1
Syria	59.9	2,615.1	4.9	16.7	0.12	2
Kuwait	124.3	27,835.4	6.6	14.8	0.09	3
Saudi Arabia	451.3	14,744.6	5.7	19.3	0.05	1
Bahrain	22.4	19,817.3	2.9	11.7	0.04	4
Iraq	84.1	2,107.9	5.1	6.4	–	2
Mauritania	3.4	975.4	4.4	15.6	–	2
Yemen	25.3	1,060.9	5.2	16	–	2

Source: Based on Arab Knowledge Report, table 5.4, p. 193. GDP is provided by IMF estimates, billion dollars, current prices.

Notes
a World Bank (2012).
b Libya, Egypt: COMSTECH data.
c Lebanon: National Council for Scientific Research (CNRS).
d Oman: statistics for 2014.
e Tunisia: 2007 data and re-evaluated data; GERD has been re-evaluated after 2011.
f IMF estimates: World Economic Outlook database, 2010.

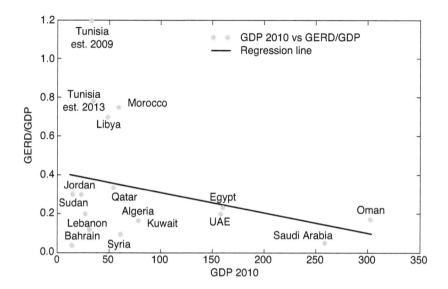

Figure 1.6 Correlation between GDP and GERD to GDP ratio (source: authors' own calculation).

structures. Although the revolution interrupted this reform process, it seems that these orientations for science and technology will be maintained. Something similar has happened in Tunisia. Prior to the revolution, Tunisia's GERD had been climbing steadily since 2000; in 2007 it was the leading Arab state for research and development intensity, at just over 1.2 percent of GDP. Even if this figure was exaggerated and re-evaluated to around 0.8 percent, it shows that Tunisia probably will maintain the advantage it has acquired over almost ten years of institutional modeling, given that, until now, the newly elected Tunisian government has not sought to challenge them (M'henni and Arvanitis 2012). Saudi Arabia, whose per capita GDP is the fifth highest in the region, adopted a national plan for science and technology in 2003 and structured KACST as its main funding institution. However, it was still ranked second-to-last in terms of research and development spending as a percentage of GDP, at 0.05 percent, ahead of Bahrain, at 0.04 percent. It really translates the fact that research is not related only to the abundance of financial resources.

There is no congruence between GERD and either GDP or GDP per capita. Indeed, investment in research is not linked to GDP in a simplistic, linear fashion. Apart from Tunisia (even after the revision of its GERD which brings it closer to 0.8 percent of GDP) and Morocco, two countries that have shown a marked tendency to support research, all Arab countries have had a rather sluggish growth of their public expenses devoted to research. Some rich countries, such as the UAE, do not invest proportionally in the development of science. This, however, relates more to the capacity to spend, which is not related to GDP so much as administrative capabilities and institutions. In fact, the UAE is among the countries with the highest growth in number of publications over the last ten years. This growth is not related to its very high GDP; much depended on the pro-research stance of the government, political system, and ambient values, in particular with regards to religion, the historical connection to Great Britain and international support.

Since authoritarianism has often forced Arab scientists to flee their countries, they end up contributing to the GDP of Western industrial states, rather than the states of the Arab region. However, the private sector and public companies in the productive sector also are partly responsible. Over the next three years (as of 2012), more than half of the companies surveyed for the World Economic Forum survey expected to increase the level of their research and development investment in the Arab region. We have no way to measure that.

Indeed, we have no valid measurement of the private sector involvement in R&D and innovation. It is usually considered that the private sector investment in R&D is very low. On a scale from 1 to 7, the estimated figures would range from 3.9 (Oman) and 3.8 (Tunisia) to a low 2.6 (Bahrain). Caution should be used with this assessment, which one can also find reproduced from the World Bank KAM, but it is in fact a figure imported from an opinion survey of business executives (more than 4,000 respondents in 2004) that is performed for the World Economic Forum.[41] The business leaders' opinion surveys reflect the opinion of individuals that are not necessarily very knowledgeable on the amounts spent in R&D. Hard data probably would provide a different image. For example, with the innovation survey in Lebanon we could make estimates concerning private investment in R&D that are not only higher than expected, but also higher than the GERD estimated until now by the Lebanese National Council for Scientific Research, which is practically entirely in public expenses.[42] Something similar happened with the figures estimated from the innovation survey in Tunisia (20 percent of business expenses in GERD) and Morocco (23 percent).[43] The efforts of the private sector in financing research is still largely unknown for the Arab countries. Our guess would be that at least between one-fifth and one-quarter of GERD is financed by businesses, but in ways and forms that make it invisible in the national statistics.

Also, the WEF result is skewed by the presence of foreign companies in the survey. Among those foreign companies, only around 40 percent plan to increase their R&D investment in the region over the next three years. Public companies that are run as private businesses but have a real monopoly are also systematically under-investing in research. Following a review of Mediterranean countries, a working group on innovation in the MIRA project concluded that very few large companies report research and development activities; among them are Sonade in Tunisia, and Sonatrach and Cevital in Algeria (Khelfaoui 2006). Morocco seemed to be in a slightly better position, but in most cases this related to highly profitable companies exploiting natural resources. Leaving oil and petroleum resources to one side, Morocco's Office Chérifien des Phosphates (OCP), one of the largest phosphate producers in the world, invests 1 percent of its sales in R&D (its sales have been estimated at around US$7 billion per year *c.*2012). A large part of that investment is not related to internal R&D but, as it is called by the upper management of OCP, to "open innovation," which consists of contracting and outsourcing research. This example comes from a company with a comparatively favorable prospect for R&D; moreover, Morocco is sharply increasing R&D investments in very strategic areas, not limited to foreign investment.

Foreign investment is usually sought in order to improve R&D. In fact, when foreign companies invest in R&D, they do little for local technological upgrading. In Tunisia, foreign-owned enterprises have a negligible impact on the economy. The analysis of the innovation survey (Gabsi *et al.* 2008) shows that foreign companies do not invest in R&D, nor do they invest in innovation locally. More generally, and contrary to popular opinion (and to the World Bank assessment, for example in its 2013 report "Transforming Arab Economies"), the same holds true for foreign direct investment in most countries. Internationalization of R&D is rather stable worldwide (at around 23 percent as shown by Larédo and his colleagues (Laurens *et al.* 2014). An exception appears to be China, where more than 400 research centers belonging to foreign companies have opened. But still, none of these appear to translate that investment into local technological innovation, except in the value chains directly related to the companies that own the R&D facilities (Mouton *et al.* 2014; Bironneau 2012). It follows that technological development and innovation in China, as elsewhere, relies heavily on public action by the government rather than foreign investment, even in very applied technologies such as biotech or nanotechnologies (Oulion and Arvanitis 2014). Studies on the R&D strategies of large global companies tend to confirm this main tendency, of a relatively independent development of R&D closely related to strategic decisions at a corporate level and local innovation. The main motives for a multinational to spend in R&D and local innovation outside its main production sites are all of a technological nature, and less market-related. There is no reason why the Arab region would be an exception.

For the most part, R&D centers in the Arab region are relatively small and focus on late-stage development, rather than basic research. Only recently have new initiatives and partnerships been established between the private and public sectors to promote research. Moreover, following some trials and tribulations, Maghreb countries have demonstrated that technology transfer units from universities to the productive sector are relatively inefficient. Most support given to research, development and innovation by national authorities is directed toward SMEs, based on the claim that in the economies of the Arab region, SMEs form not only the bulk of companies (up to 95 percent in most countries), but also provide most employment. This preference for SMEs has been the basis of "upgrading programs" from Mexico to Tunisia, and Chile to Thailand. The EU has been very keen to fund these upgrading schemes in North Africa. The results are always far below expectations and it is usually claimed that the fault lies with the programs and their management. After so many years of upgrading programs, it is time for an alternative explanation. What is needed is a diversification of economic investment: support for large investment projects in highly competitive areas (even by providing direct support to large companies, something all large economies do on a permanent basis); strong support to innovative projects in smaller entities, whatever the sector, but with regularity and in line with company growth; strong support for middle-sized (300 employees) companies with a proven record of technical success and economic strength, but insufficient investment capacity. Such policies would have a far better chance of success than the usual university-managed (and inefficient) technology transfer units or the small loans to tiny companies with no economic prospects.

From fieldwork done in many universities and technological poles or incubators, it appears that successful experiences, both entrepreneurial and innovative, are more numerous than is usually estimated. That was the conclusion reached by innovation surveys conducted in Lebanon, Morocco and Tunisia. For Lebanon, based on a 2010–2011 survey, 60.3 percent of the surveyed firms have to some extent introduced or modified products, processes and services to some degree (Arvanitis 2013).[44] Only the Egyptian survey on innovation found low levels of innovative activity and a more difficult economic environment than Maghreb countries.

A study on Jordan found a decent level of R&D spending in the private sector: 30 percent, compared to 70 percent for the public sector (this figure appears to be the highest in ESCWA countries). There is an incubator (called Oasis) with a proven record of transforming entrepreneurial ventures into viable businesses.[45] The Higher Council for Science and Technology has also pushed an initiative known as "A Professor in Every Factory" (launched in 2003), which sends academics into factories during the summer vacation. More importantly, a recent initiative, funded by a common EU–Jordan fund, is a €4 million scientific research and technological development (SRTD) program, which funds innovation-related activities in the private sector. Most of these programs have targeted SMEs. In Algeria, there are interesting examples from public companies which work in fields as varied as hydrocarbons, iron and steel, electronics, chemistry and food and agriculture. Some have centers for R&D while others have only simple units of research. They have had in most cases a quite difficult conversion to R&D (Khelfaoui 2004: 80). In the Sudan, there is the remarkable example of the Kenana Sugar Company (KSC), which used extensive innovation and created a whole internal techno-economic ecosystem. KSC introduced "green" harvesting in the region, supported by the acquisition of mechanical harvesters which allow the elimination of cane burning prior to harvesting. The waste cane leafage is converted into fodder. The same company also introduced efficient irrigation techniques, new products based on traditional sugar by-products, such as molasses and bagasses to produce animal feed and ethanol, and environment-friendly energy sources. KSC collaborates with different Sudani universities and has received their students. Recently it created a post-doc fellowship to foster this industry–academia link. Examples such as this one can be found everywhere, in particular in large companies that use natural resources, but are still rare. What is more worrisome is that, overall, larger companies are investing relatively little in R&D when one compares their income and their innovation-related expenses. The effort to invest in technology is certainly higher for medium-sized companies. A report on incentives for innovation in Morocco demonstrated this quite clearly: very efficient and up-to-date technological companies are occupying specific niches, investing massively in human resources and maintaining a very extended and strong network of providers and technical experience. All of these companies are small or medium-sized (around 300 personnel). They also tend to incorporate know-how and innovation bred internally rather than through external alliances. This is a finding that is repeated again and again in practically all innovation surveys. Thus, although investment in R&D is in absolute terms caused by large companies, often backed by public investment or public ownership (like OCP, MENAGEM, Domaines agricoles in Morocco, ONAS, CNI Sonede in Tunisia, Sonatrach or Cevital in Algeria, most telecom companies in all of these countries), based on natural resources (oil, gas, agriculture) or in infrastructural technologies (water, construction of roads, telecommunications), the most efficient in using technological investment, although lower scale, are medium-sized companies. Both the economics and the sociology of investment in innovation, research and technology is different for larger and medium-sized companies, something that is not apparent in statistics or composite indexes used to compare the achievement of one or other country. To our knowledge, the formidable resource of the Arab economies should rely on these rather smaller productive units.

In brief, when GERD is used as a measure of national scientific and technological advancement, the results for the Arab region are disappointing overall, despite the significant differences between countries, and despite numerous examples of introducing innovation rather successfully in specific companies. The annual share per Arab citizen of expenditure on scientific research does not exceed US$10, compared to the Malaysian citizen's annual share of US$33. In some small European countries such as Ireland and Finland, these figures are much higher, with annual expenditures on scientific research per capita reaching US$575 and US$1,304, respectively (UNDP 2009: 193). What we hypothesize is that the productive structures and other institutional and organizational matters count as much as political and social determinants in explaining this low investment in technologies and innovation, and the relatively limited, until now, investment in R&D. That also explains why GERD measures mainly public funding in the Arab countries, whereas in industrialized countries its is a more or less balanced distribution between public and private funding.

5.2 The debate on external funding and implications for research

> Demands addressed to research should themselves be examined critically
> (Hannoyer 1996: 401; authors' translation)

Most universities in the Arab world, where research is performed, don't have a serious budget for research. Research in the universities, and even in public research organizations, relies on external funding, both nationally and internationally. Among the foreign sources, as we said above, the EU has become a very frequent and strong partner. We found, astonishingly, the Jordanian universities' budgets are often designated to salaries and wages; the major bulk of funding comes from the EU, the biggest donor, followed by the United States and Japan, and most recently Arab countries from the Gulf. We've been told that some of these funds have political conditionality.[46] In any case, without external funding research in Jordan University or JUST in Irbid, the two largest research universities would be much reduced. The same is true for Lebanon. Universities in Lebanon, with the exception of Lebanese University, the American University of Beirut (AUB) and Université Saint-Joseph (USJ) have practically no budgets dedicated to research. AUB and USJ *c.*2012 announced an internal budget for research around US$1 million. But already in 2012 AUB received more than US$7 million from external sources of funding, and Lebanese University has notable support for research coming from French cooperation and other international funding (Arab funds, the United States, foundations and Iran). The EU has strong participation in all the research projects we have seen in Lebanon, followed mainly by the French cooperation and US funds (the latter mainly in health sciences) (see Chapter 3). What these figures show is that researchers know how to obtain funding when they are engaged in research, and the money from within their own institutions is certainly not sufficient. International funding is tied to a series of international collaborations and, thus, the research system is a worldwide system that concerns both international collaboration and funding.

Shana Cohen (2014) rings alarm bells on the impact of international aid flows and the process of global market integration in Morocco on the role of academia, not only in terms of research topic orientation but also intellectual debate on social and political subjects. She considers that a neoliberal approach to education and research may be held responsible for changes in the structure and assessment of academic work. Other researchers echo Cohen's concern, yet are less alarmist. For instance, for Jacques Gaillard (2014) there is an ongoing and growing debate, particularly in Europe, about whether the increasing reliance on competitive project funding at the expense of core funding may result in giving priority to short-term and low-risk projects to the detriment of longer-term fundamental research and/or high-risk projects as well as non-priority areas. A very similar argument has been proposed in Latin America by P. Kreimer (Kreimer and Zabala 2008), who believes, at least for the case of Argentina, that the integration of researchers in international projects is in reality a form of subordination to the orientations from hegemonic countries. There are also concerns that this trend may impact the capacity of an institution to invest in infrastructure and long-term institutional and capacity building activities.

As we have shown in other contexts, the very concept of a non-hegemonic country expresses this very unequal position in the world research system based on the idea that countries that do not have the capacity to influence the research agenda. Thus we rather prefer to talk of non-hegemonic countries instead of developing countries, for instance, because the actual system of research is not structured only around an opposition between a center and a periphery, but rather a multiplicity of cores, and a variety of peripheries; it doesn't consider exclusively developing economies but all those that progressively build a research capability and enter into research, and, most importantly, the key in understanding what is going on is not the relative positions of the countries in between, or respective to the "centers," but rather their relations to funding organizations present at the international level (Arvanitis 2011a: 636).

5.3 National funding agencies

In fact, the funding context in Arab countries is changing very quickly.[47] A number of new funding agencies have appeared or have been consolidated in recent years. Either as full-fledged public funding bodies, distributing funds by calls for projects (the Académie des Sciences Hassan II in Morocco, the Science and Technology Development Fund (STDF) in Egypt, Scientific Research Support Fund in Jordan, the National Council for Scientific Research (CNRS) Grant Research Program in Lebanon, the Qatar Foundation), or as specific funding programs inserted inside an already existing national institution (see the case of the "Fond national de la recherche scientifique et du développement technologique [FNRSDT]" in Morocco, managed by the CNRST, or the RDI fund in Egypt which is an office of the Ministry for Higher Education and Research).

The funds mobilized through the agencies represent around 1 percent of GERD, with the notable exception of Tunisia, which uses core funding rather than call for projects, although, as we have mentioned the labeling and evaluation system used in Tunisia could be considered as a national competition for research funds. Concerning these new funds that are obtained through competitive calls for projects, the situation in some of the Arab countries we know of is the following:

- The Egyptian STDF represents around 1.8 percent of GERD (considering the sharp increase of public funding for research that took place in 2011, from 0.28 percent of GDP in 2010 to 0.4 percent in 2011); before this massive increase of overall public expenditures, STDF represented around 4.5 percent of GERD.
- In Jordan, SRSF represents nearly one-fifth (18 percent) of GERD as estimated in 2008. The computation as a percentage of GDP is quite difficult to make: SRSF represents JD4 million per year for a GERD of JD22 million as reported in some documents, but that would mean 0.11 percent of GDP, not the 0.34 percent claimed by the government; if this latter figure is correct, then GERD should be close to JD63 million. In any case, the fund is now the main tool for funding research with public money.
- Lebanon mostly funds through competitive calls. Its funding represented an average of US$700,000 per year on average in the period 2007–2011; in 2013 US$1.1 million was allocated to 36 new projects. Roughly, that represents a very small amount that is equal to the annual intra-mural budget for

research in AUB or USJ. In other words, the main public funding instrument is roughly equivalent to the research budget of the two largest universities of the country (and probably also of the national Lebanese University, since it also spends approximately the same amount for research internally).

- Qatar announced a QNRF budget of US$180 million for 2014, which represents less than 1 percent of GDP[48] (far away from the more than 2 percent of GDP announced in research, but nonetheless a gigantic amount when compared to the number of personnel); QNRF is the main funding instrument in Qatar and distributes all funds for research, and the Qatar University received 45 percent of these funds.
- The Moroccan FNSRSDT represents 1.75 percent of GERD. It should be remembered that this fund is a new venture for the Moroccan government, and a very strategic one.
- The Tunisian funding for research projects is largely outside any call for projects. Core funding to labs and research units represents 16 percent of GERD, and it is not channeled through calls, except the so-called "Federative programs," which is about €1 million per year (0.40 percent of GERD). Nonetheless, as we have mentioned already, this money is distributed based on a national-level evaluation where research laboratories and teams need to submit a four-year projection of their activities. In other words, the labeling program of Tunisia can be considered a form of project-based funding. A national agency, the ANPR, has the possibility to fund research and innovation projects, and its €350,000 budget represents 0.15 percent of GERD.

As a comparison, we can remember that the French National Agency for Research (ANR) represents approximately 2 percent of GERD in France, and GERD is 2.24 percent of GDP; the NSF in the United States, with its nearly US$7 billion budget, represents 1.63 percent of the US GERD (GERD is 2.85 percent of GDP).

The figures in Table 1.8 show a profound change in policy orientation in the Arab countries, which is taking place rather rapidly.

Table 1.8 Summary of funding capability mobilized by the national funding agencies (*c.*2012)

Country	Fund	Percentage GERD/actual amount
Egypt	STDF	1.8%/US$14 million
Egypt	RDI	US$6 million
Jordan	SRSF	JD4 million
Lebanon	CNRS-GRP	US$1.1 million
Qatar	QNRF	US$180 million
Morocco	FNRSDT	1.76%/300–500 million Dh; €26–44 million)
Tunisia	Federative projects	€1 million
All Arab countries	Arab Council for the Social Sciences	Total budget of ACSS is less than US$2 million

Source: own research, project MENAFUND.

If we analyze the funding agencies, we can summarize the various functions as follows:

- Define national policy for research.
- Coordinate between different research institutions.
- Manage research centers performing research.
- Manage the status of the research activity inside higher education institutions.
- Manage programs and specific funds.
- Select and manage funding of scholarships to students and researchers.
- Support publishing of scientific journals and publications.
- Promote valorization (technology transfer) of research performed in scientific institutions.
- Evaluate the effects of policies.
- Collect statistics on research.
- Diffuse scientific culture.

As Chris Caswill (2005) insists, funding agencies provide more than funding. They provide resources for research, maximize organizational resources, facilitate "input of ideas" as Caswill calls it, quality control and interconnection between research centers. Cordero and his colleagues (2008) add "knowledge translation" as another function, as they notice an increasing interest in knowledge transfer to users and different stakeholders.[49] Funding agencies use many strategies in order to increase incentives for researchers to engage in knowledge "translation." The UK Department for International Development (DFID) examined the rules for university rankings and modified the research assessment exercise (which rates universities according to what they publish in high-level journals). Canada's International Development and Research Center (IDRC) has small grants available to move research into practice and policy. In Brazil, the State of São Paulo Research Foundation (FAPESP) funds partnerships between private enterprises and public agencies for funding basic research and developing technology based on locally conducted basic science (see Chapter 5). Many more examples could be given.

Sources of funding have become very diverse and researchers may choose the foundation that fits their research agenda. A number of national and international funds for science, technology and innovation have been set up in recent years. Among these funds are the Kuwait Foundation for the Advancement of Sciences (1978), the Qatar Foundation (1995), the Mohammed bin Rashid al-Maktoum Foundation in the United Arab Emirates (2007) and the Middle East Science Fund in Jordan (2009). Among them, only Qatar set the bar high by calling for the allocation of 2.8 percent of the general budget to support scientific research in the mid-2008. The establishment of the EU–Egypt Innovation Fund in 2008 was intended to support projects for applied research on a competitive basis, with special emphasis on innovation (Mouton and Waast 2009). Other foundations are smaller scale, such as the Arab Thought Foundation (funded by Saudi

Arabia and based in Beirut) and the Arab Science and Technology Foundation (ASTF) (UAE). Nonetheless, these Arab foundations do not seem do provide funding conducive to team work that they pledged for the research, but are setting up spectacular events such as prizes for best book or best woman researcher, etc.

5.4 Some hypotheses on the increase of funding in Arab countries

The creation of the funding agencies was closely linked to changes in the institutional landscape that concerned the policy-making structure rather than the performing institutions (universities and public research organizations). Reasons for change are always multiple, depend on the political situation, and can be read as the result of different forces that translate into a (temporary) political "equilibrium," in particular when the policy-making agencies are concerned. We only mention some of these concerning Egypt, Morocco and Tunisia.

In Egypt, these changes happened some years before the popular revolution that brought the end of the Mubarak regime. It was related to a change in the person acting as the minister of higher education and research, who proposed the modification to the policy-making structure. By dismantling the old Academy of Science, which was transformed into an advisory board, and re-integrating policy orientation functions inside the ministry, the new ministry regrouped all policy functions under its authority. It also abandoned the old soviet structure that had modeled the national research center and the Academy. In the process, policy coordination functions became clearly apparent as the most important ones. The change was very closely linked to the EU, which offered strong financial support, around 2007, and became the financial basis of the RDI program. Moreover, the EU appeared as a larger framework in which national research could be both embedded and obtain additional funding. The compatibility between the EU mode of action (funding through specific calls) allowed progressive legitimization of the funding by projects within the Egyptian scientific community.

In Morocco, an overall re-engineering of the policy-making functions was expected for many years – in fact, after the creation of the Académie des Sciences Hassan II (2006) and the non-replacement of the director for research who occupied the function of director of CNRST (2008). In the meantime, the ministry drafted various diagnoses of the state of research and governance of the research system (since 2005), and headed various bilateral projects with the EU, and was subject to a whole re-engineering process. Again, the government used the advice provided by the EU, mainly through bilateral projects (M2ERA and Twinning project). These provided inputs on the possible transformations of the institutional set-up. A plan of action for 2013–2016 was the product of this intense policy-making exercise.

Both Egypt and Morocco had a multipolar research system, under an apparently very hierarchical system, and in both cases it became apparent that reinforcing research passed through a consolidated coordination. The agency model appears thus as an adequate tool for this coordination through funding.

In Tunisia, changes were less the result of the revolution than a process of accommodating competing political forces. The whole political process made apparent strong oppositions that were embodied in specific offices and ministries with strongly diverging views on how to implement policy. The main changes in the overall policy-making structure was, most probably, the creation of the national evaluation committee (CNEARS) that labeled laboratories and research teams in order for them to receive public research funds. The second orientation that played an important role was the creation of the technopoles. Although much less was done than planned, technopoles posed a question of the connection of society to national needs. Also, a notable difference was that, contrary to Egypt and Morocco, Tunisia, under the Ben Ali regime, was very cautious concerning EU funds. International cooperation was closely monitored by each minister and, in some cases, collaborative projects could not be implemented because of a veto issued by the office of the minister. When the regime fell, although the whole policy infrastructure was very loosely modified, changes happened only concerning this opening to the EU. It became suddenly an open battlefield on who by and how the bilateral program with the EU should be monitored, opposing quite openly the Ministry of Industry and the ministry in charge of research. The last years of the Ben Ali regime had been those of a closing down of the system, mainly for reasons of political control. Extreme political tension has nearly paralyzed the research system, which probably survived this deep crisis after the revolution because the labeling structure (the national evaluation committee and the subsequent designation of working research units) that identifies clearly the public performing actors (units and laboratories) has been functional all along. It is thus not entirely strange that Tunisia has been less willing to adopt funding by projects: in fact, its system of approving core budgets for laboratories is a sort of national competition. Moreover, the main difficulty faced by Tunisia was not so much coordination, as in the case of Egypt and Morocco. The agency that could efficiently manage the calls, the ANPR, is still not in charge of the funds, including when this was supposed to be the case. If funding by projects is to be implemented it will probably be the result of pressure not from within the policy-making structure, but from below – that, is from the scientists themselves.

It should also be noted that changes of the institutional framework for policy-making have been affected by the Euro-Mediterranean policy driven for some years by common policy activities, mainly through the Monitoring Committee for Science and Technology and programs funded by the EU[50] (see Section 4.4). The policy objectives of the EU have affected the research institutions (policy-making bodies and performing institutions) on research orientations, and on the management aspects of research projects. It has not been a uniform influence, although the EU has had a one-and-for-all unique "neighboring" policy. There is some debate on the difficult question about the actual influence of the EU and its impact in the Arab countries. We have already mentioned the relatively high support in financial terms channeled through various programs and the participation of Arab researchers into the EU calls for projects (open to all since the 6th

Framework Program). Although the so-called, Barcelona Process triggered by the EU in 1995 has not been a success story in economical and political terms (Moisseron 2005), it appears that scientific cooperation has been rather successful. This is also a paradox since science and technology were not explicitly mentioned in the initial Barcelona Declaration. The influence of the EU on Arab countries has in fact been very different between countries. This effect was quite straightforward in Egypt, with the creation of RDI inside the Ministry of Research, an office that managed the €17 million fund in Egypt. The Scientific and Technological Development Fund (STDF) in Egypt was launched a little time after the RDI program and was certainly influenced by the success of the RDI program, along with bilateral collaborations (e.g., Germany and France). Nonetheless, the example of RDI is quite unique. Research funding agencies in most other countries have been created independently of the EU and under their own terms. The cooperation with the EU, which also increased considerably in most Maghreb countries, has served as a strong incentive for more research and for the structuring of the funding structures. For example, Morocco underwent a long process of reform and finally decided to launch calls under a new national fund, FNRSDT. The launch of this program was driven by previous learning acquired through previous pilot programs (PARS, PROTARS). These previous programs provided very important proportions of laboratory budgets (up to 60 percent in certain cases), and the experience was considered beneficial to those participating in these experiences.

It is thus debatable how much international collaborations and cooperation with the EU influences directly the policy choices or "drive" policy changes. The adoption in Egypt and Jordan of project funding schemes in cooperation with the EU was not entirely related to European cooperation. Something similar happened in Morocco and Tunisia. The 2007 reform of the policy framework in Egypt was embedded in a larger reform of the science policy in the last and short-lived Mubarak government. If these changes were asked for by all the scientific community and took place before 2011, it is also because a larger need for change was felt even inside the policy driven by the authoritarian regimes. The EU relation that we depicted above certainly acted as an incentive, but we cannot affirm that it was the main driver of these changes. Geographic proximity and historical ties account for a lot in the explanation for the rather intense exchanges between the two banks of the Mediterranean Sea.

In brief, the main hypotheses that can explain both the institutional changes as well as the increase in funding in many Arab countries do not seem to us less related to the external influences, or some willingness to modernize the technocratic structure of the state. It is rather the response to real, permanent and politically strong pressure that come from the ground: unemployment, the need for new business opportunities, the changing economic conditions, as well as the increasing scholarly population that seeks, before emigrating, to get a job locally. It is this same pressure that explains the relatively abundant creation of new businesses based on technology and innovation, the extension of research bilateral agreements between rich European countries and non-hegemonic Arab countries. In the social sciences, after the Arab revolutions, but also as a product of the increase in the academic population, the governments needed to respond to the demands for more funding and more working academic space.

6 Conclusion: toward a more diversified research system

The World Bank has indeed designed a Knowledge Economy Index (KEI) and a set of policy recommendations for the future based on the liberalization of the economy: more science and technology, more innovation, more entrepreneurship, more privatization, more flexible markets and less state control. This model has ranked Arab countries in such a way as to champion Gulf states as models of Arab knowledge economies (Figure 1.7). When comparing the KEI and the GII, one finds differences that are mainly due to a stronger emphasis on economic

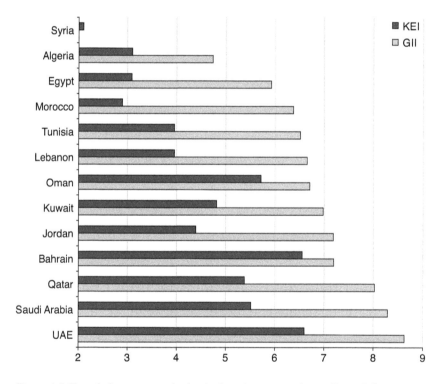

Figure 1.7 Knowledge economy in the Arab region: comparison of knowledge economy index (KEI, World Bank) and Global Innovation Index (GII) 2012 (source: KEI, World Bank, reproduced in "Transforming Arab Economies," p. 28. For GII, same as Figure 1.5).

Notes
Ranking based on the calulated value of the GII and KEI, normalized on a sale from 1 to 10. Minimum KEI is Syria at 1.9 and maximum is UAE at 6.6. For GII, minimum is Algeria at 4.7 and maximum is UAE at 8.6. Syria is not calculated in GII. GII is more consistent with the analysis presented above.

and financial conditions in the Gulf countries. The UAE, Bahrain and Oman lead in the KEI index, whereas the UAE, Saudi Arabia and Qatar lead in the GII. Interestingly, the countries that have a longer research tradition and permanent effort on the part of the government, such as Lebanon and Tunisia, do not fare well in the KEI but rather better in the GII (one should remember that the ranking is worldwide). GII also gives higher grades than KEI to countries that we have proven to be rather larger research systems, with the exception of Algeria, which gets lower marks on both indexes. The detail of the comparison is not really telling us about more than this quite unequal treatment between oil-rich countries and middle-income economies. The normative behind this glorification of Gulf countries looks very much as an overestimation of rich and small countries versus middle-income countries. Is this really what the knowledge economy should boil down to? Does this reflect the diversity we tried to analyze in the above pages?

We advocate for a more diversified model, which would take into account the various types of sciences and the different roles played by the state, depending on the nature of the economy and societal issues at stakes.

The multiplicity of research centers and actors is growing. This is true in all Arab countries; innovation and research policies insist on coordination rather than production and funding, and coordination of various entities, rather than production of knowledge in public mission-oriented research organizations, becomes the new principal orientation of policy. Nothing can tell us today if this is beneficial or not. Managing more complex institutional models is probably more complicated for a state that wants to control everything. Arab countries do share a common feature: their governments are afraid to give up control over the institutions. Moreover, coordinating various research performing structures in different areas and under different organizational modalities will be less easy than the older policies geared toward "capacity building." It supposes, in a given country, the government will agree to take into account a rather wider span of actors than it used to do, participate in defining the agenda outside the sole objectives and priorities of its own agencies and needs, accept being challenged on its own ground and on its sovereign decisions by agencies that are richer, stronger and with different objectives than its own. All of these new policies contradict the usual command-and-control habits of policy-makers in Arab countries.

Innovation policy is probably one among many other areas where these governance issues will be abundant. The diversity of firms, the need for specialized expertise, the necessity to seek funding, the fact that Academia will also claim for better management rules, openness and autonomy, as much as for more funding will put additional pressure on the research and innovation governance. Moreover, most of the research and innovation activities need to be performed in close connection between national and foreign researchers, investors and academics.

We don't believe that imposing a uniform knowledge economy view will unlock creativity and resources. On the contrary, everything out of the last ten to five years, including the revolutions, tells us another story, where multiple actors will fight over rare resources by creating multiple decentralized research units, either in companies, or in private as well as public universities, in technical centers and consultancy companies. It is rather a chance for the future, although it will raise new issues concerning the labelization of research, the certification of quality, the coordination of different entities and the ability to manage a rather large and decentralized research structure.

Notes

1 See UNESCO Institute of Statistics (Montréal): www.uis.unesco.org.
2 See OECD Directorate of Science, Technology and Innovation: www.oecd.org/sti.
3 COMSTECH is a Ministerial Standing Committee on Scientific and Technological Cooperation established by the Third Summit of the Organization of Islamic Countries (OIC): www.comstech.org.
4 There were strong debates triggered by the UNDP report on knowledge in the Arab region (UNDP 2005). The report was followed by a much less polemic version, co-funded by the Al-Maktoum Foundation, known as the Arab Knowledge Report (Al Maktoum Foundation and UNDP 2009).
5 www.globelics.org.
6 FEMISE, UNIMED, THETYS, UNICHAIN, MEDGRID, ANIMA, among many others. The World Bank in association with the European Investment Bank have created the Centre for Mediterranean Integration (CMI) in an effort to gather forces. The CMI hosts a Knowledge Economy for Growth and Employment in MENA program (http://cmimarseille.org). See the book of the MIRA project, which mentions in some detail the institutional framework of research and cooperation in the Euro-Med area (Morini *et al.* 2013).
7 Published as an article.
8 For Southeast Asia, see the special issue of the *Journal of Science, Technology and Society*, March 2006 Vol. 11, No. 1. In particular, the introductory article by Intara-kumnerd and Vang on China; see *China Innovation Inc.* (Bironneau 2012).
9 Again, we maybe appear over pessimistic in this regard, but the relatively scarce research activity in the history of science is a case in point. Although all governments and official meetings talk about the glorious past of Arab science, it is very rare to find good reliable research on these topics. History of science has, unfortunately, been mobilized by nationalistic discourse. See the case of the creation of a national research center for history of science in Syria.
10 The socio-economic literature is abundant on these matters. A recent case of reflection can be found in the study published by Leresche *et al.* (2009), which examines the opinions on science in the European Union based on a very large opinion poll.
11 www.globalinnovationindex.org.
12 www.e-marefa.net.
13 This database contains 1,015 academic and statistical journals issued by various bodies (universities, research centers, public statistical departments, central banks, scientific associations, regional organizations) in the Arab world in three languages: Arabic, English and French. E-Marefa database provides 100,000 articles and statistical reports, 11,000 theses and dissertations (Masters and PhD) and 7,500 book reviews issued in the Arab world. This database involves over 275 universities, research centers, statistical apparatus and regional organizations in the Arab world in 19 countries. These bodies supply their journals and publications to Marefa database on a regular and continuous basis. Other than E-Marefa, there are also two databases: one for all science, called al Manhal (www.almanhal.com) but its coverage is much

less important than E-Marefa. The second concerns only literature on education (produced in the Arab world or about it), called Shamaa (*šabakat al-maʿlūmāt al-ʿarabiyya at-tarbawiyya*, i.e., Arab Educational Information Network). Currently about 20,000 studies are documented in Shamaa, 5,000 with their full text.

14 Good examples are the tools proposed by Loet Leydesdorff or the IFRIS Cortext platform (www.ifris.org). The bibliometric work once based on exploiting online data, went next to desktop research and now returns to online collaborative research. For Chapter 8 we have used the network analysis tools of Cortext.

15 We can mention the work collected in the books of the Alfonso network, coordinated by Roland Waast, to which both authors of this book contributed (El-Kenz and Waast 2013; Gaillard *et al.* 1997a).

16 A good overview of issues on this topic can be found in the European Science Foundation report (ESF 2012). Many research organizations have issued reports in the recent years on this topic. Science Europe, a lobbying organization created by mostly European agencies and public research organizations is elaborating a general recommendation on the issue.

17 Recently, French research institutions such as the Institut de recherche agronomique (INRA) and the Centre de coopération internationale en recherche agronomique pour le développement (CIRAD) have demonstrated the complexity of this exercise when applied research and technologies are involved. Long before that, the International Foundation for Science (IFS), an entity that funds scientists that create their own research laboratories upon returning to their home countries, developed a "dashboard" of indicators that includes publication data and in-house surveying; this methodology, called MESIA, is a good example of a program-oriented impact assessment. Technopolis, a European academic-based consulting firm specialized on science and technology policies, has also developed an impact assessment methodology based on the measurement of relevance, efficacy, efficiency and an array of indicators that could reflect the measurement of impacts of research programs. The EU was particularly prolific on this topic in the 1990s (Callon *et al.* 1997).

18 Science Europe, a lobbying body that groups most European agencies and public research organizations, is developing an analysis of the measurement of the impact of research (www.scienceeurope.org).

19 See our take on the subject in a small opinion article: "Ranking Arab Universities: A Farce" available at: http://tadweenpublishing.com/blogs/news/18584321-ranking-arab-universities-a-farce.

20 Even those are rarely performed. An example of such a scoreboard has been produced by Waast and Rossi (2009) and published only on the MIRA website (www.miraproject.eu). These authors have published an article that shows how to articulate the macro bibliometric indicators and more detailed micro indicators in the case of Arab countries (Waast and Rossi 2010). All documents concerning this issue in the Mediterranean are published on the MIRA website under the topic: "WP2 – Observatory of the EU-MPC Cooperation in S&T Public Library."

21 These changes in the policy framework have been analyzed in the frame of Euro-Med cooperation (Arvanitis *et al.* 2013a). They have been the subject of research in the Arab world headed by the authors of this book (Arvanitis *et al.* 2014).

22 No Varimax rotation was made.

23 Anne-Marie Moulin has written many interesting analyses of these research fields that were linked to health. She has proposed a very stimulating synthesis (Moulin 2015).

24 This center, along with all the 15 international agricultural research centers, are coordinated by the Consultative Group on International Agricultural Research, based in Washington (www.cgiar.org).

25 A survey of Euro-Mediterranean observatories has been undertaken by the Medspring project. Survey analysis by R. Artweh, A. Riss, S. Sanna and R. Arvanitis, updated June 2014 (http://medspring.eu). This is ongoing research with an objective to

produce a complete analysis by the end of 2016, and concerns mainly, but not exclusively, environmental observatories.

26 Figures have changed since this assessment, but more or less the numbers are close. For a complete overview see ESTIME background report on Tunisia (M'henni 2007; www.estime.ird.fr/article240.html).

27 See the special issue on higher education and elites in the *Cahiers de la Recherche sur l'Education et les Savoirs, N° 14 (2015)*, by E. Gérard and Anne-Catherine Wagner.

28 Even if it has been probably publicized as far better than it really is, because of preference for science and technology since long ago, that was conformed under the authoritarian regime of Ben Ali, Tunisia still has a very impressive record for research in academic environments.

29 Rachid Ghrir, "Evaluation de la recherche en Tunisie," Atelier ESTIME, Alger, July 2006. Recently, Dr. Ghrir explained the ins and outs of this policy in a Forum for Research Funders in the Arab Countries, Cairo, December 2015. The first description of the process has been detailed in the ESTIME national background report for Tunisia (M'henni 2007).

30 A study of the major changes in the policy framework in Egypt has been written by Kyriaki Papageorgiou, as part of the Scoping study on "Research Granting Councils and Funds in the Middle East and North Africa (MENA)" directed by S. Hanafi and R. Arvanitis (2012–2014), funded by the International Development Research Center (Canada).

31 Gaillard, J. and Afifi, A. I. (2013). Jumelage institutionnel (MA09/ENP-AP/OT14) "Appui au Système national de la recherche (SNR) au Maroc pour une intégration à l'Espace européen de la recherche (EER)" and report by Arvantis *et al.* (2012) on incentives for research. See also the background reports for ESTIME by Kamal Mellakh (2007) and Jamal Assad (2007).

32 For a review of these documents and the innovation surveys, see Arvanitis and M'henni (2010). In Tunisia, see the third part of the report directed by Hatem M'henni (2007) as well as the report by Abderraouf Hsaini (2007). For Morocco, see above.

33 Projects MIRA and MEDSPRING, and funding programs such as ARIMNET, ERANET MED and PRIMA (in process at the time of writing).

34 The Arab Thought Foundation and the Al-Maktoum Foundation have issued many reports on the state of science and technology, none tackling this issue.

35 Let us remember that both Turkey and Israel, which have buoyant research and innovation, have been less interested in these exchanges since both countries are associated countries to the EU, and thus contribute and participate into the European Framework Programs as full members.

36 The Arab League is still promoting very actively the making of an Arab innovation scoreboard, in partnership with the European Investment Bank.

37 Apart from the already mentioned article by Arvanitis and M'henni (2010), a series of reports inside Euro-Mediterranean projects MIRA and MEDSPRING have focused on these innovation promotion policies. Most unpublished material has been used repeatedly by government officials when designing new policy measures.

38 The team calculates efficient innovation by comparing input/output composite indicators. See details in the GII (INSEAD *et al.* 2014: 3–27).

39 Good examples of this type of analysis in the Arab world has been the work of A. Djeflat – see his latest book (Andersson and Djeflat 2013).

40 This claim, to our knowledge, is rather rare; but see the thesis of Roberto Lopez-Martinez (2006).

41 As cited by the Arab Knowledge Report (Al Maktoum Foundation and UNDP 2009: 193). The report mentions: "The private sector makes a relatively active contribution to funding research in Oman, Tunisia, Qatar, and Saudi Arabia, with an indicator ranging from 3.5 to 3.9 (with 1 being the lowest and 7 the highest)." This figure

(private sector spending on R&D) is an estimate, apparently based on the Executive Opinion Survey performed by the World Economic Forum. See World Economic Forum 2002/2003 Report, page 40. The methodology and survey results are not published. Two years later, the WEF report's executive summary mentions (p. xviii): "Survey data for these countries [United Arab Emirates, Saudi Arabia, Bahrain, Egypt, Gambia, Uganda, Zambia, Nigeria, Mali, Chad, Angola] have high within-country variance. Until the reliability of survey responses improves, with future educational efforts and improved sampling in these countries, their rankings should be interpreted with caution."

42 Data still not published at the time of writing; we have respected the embargo on the report, which will be published later in 2015.

43 In 1996, estimated business expenses in R&D were $US22.6 million. It is a very unreliable data published by ESCWA (1998: 19). R&D expenditures for 1996 (22.6 million) and 1992 (3.7 million).

44 Overall in the sample and for the years 2010 and 2011, 45.2 percent of firms introduced new or improved products, 29.5 percent introduced new or improved services and 43.7 percent introduced new or improved manufacturing processes (Arvanitis 2013). Similar figures appear in all innovation surveys, with the notable exception of Egypt, which indicates much lower figures.

45 SWOT analysis of Jordan Science System, ESCWA (unpublished report).

46 In Jordan, some researchers we interviewed were reluctant to participate in European or American research projects due to Israeli researchers' participation. They stated that they believe that such projects aimed at the integration of Israel in the region.

47 A lot of the information on funding comes from our research with Canada IDRC (Arvanitis *et al.* 2014).

48 We have no estimates for GERD for Qatar and figures do not fit quite well; another source of information mentions that Qatar National University funded research for US$220 million, which looks to be an extraordinary amount (this is close to the budget of a medium-sized institute with fewer than 900 researchers and fewer than 2,000 personnel in France, for example). Moreover QU announces it receives US$266 million from QNRF – an average of 40 million per year.

49 They surveyed research funding organizations in the health sector in six countries in Latin America, Asia and Africa to identify the extent to which they promote "knowledge translation."

50 Most information on these Euro-Mediterranean policy framework changes as well as about the MoCo are publish in a book by Morini *et al.* (2013).

2 Scientific publication

Growth, specialization and internationalization

Usually, scientific production is measured by indicators based on two types of data: the number of publications, mainly in refereed international scientific journals, articles in collective books, proceedings and books; and the citations received by published articles. Studying the use of citations needs a database that includes the references of articles; only two bibliographic multidisciplinary databases offer this: Thomson Reuters' Web of Science (WoS) or Elsevier's Scopus. These two databases were created for bibliometric purposes. Other specialized databases or other large multidisciplinary databases (for example, the French PASCAL) are usually not used in bibliometric analysis – with some exceptions.

These two databases provide a "stable" reference required in order to do comparative analyses. But none of these databases explain, in any explicit way, their choices of journals. In a time when the whole publishing system is changing, this comes as a real difficulty. Moreover, both the WoS and Scopus have some strong biases. It is not very difficult to identify some of these biases that are well known, such as the preference for English, the very poor representation of journals produced outside the United States and the very US-centric set of journals in the social sciences. It is more difficult to measure the effect of these biases and that comes as a real difficulty when doing statistical analyses. The WoS, since it is older, created by the promoters of bibliometrics, is supposedly more stable than Scopus, although it has been shown that both deliver similar results. This holds true for large countries only, and for statistical analyses of fields with a large number of publications (because of the statistical size of the sample of publications). It is probably not true for the analysis of country-specific data, when these countries have small rates of scholarly production; that is, practically all Arabic countries.

Another issue with the databases is their coverage of certain fields. It appears that they underestimate certain domains, while tending to overestimate others: for instance, the biomedical sciences are better covered by the WoS. Books and other forms of publication, more frequent in the social sciences and humanities, are poorly covered by both databases (although they attempt to at least partially cover edited books). Every small journal in the United States is covered in the Social Sciences Citation Index (in WoS), but many widely circulated journals outside the United States are missing; this is true for publications from Europe as well as from other countries and regions. The underlying model of WoS and Scopus is a commercial world centered in the United States, a model that has been challenged even for so-called "hard" sciences.[1]

We have looked at the case of the American University of Beirut (AUB) in order to determine how much of its total scholarly production is reported by international databases. The example makes sense because AUB has a good level of publications in English in major journals. The record of unreported publications, as we will see, can be relatively high.

1 Rapid growth of publication

If we look at the geographical distribution of scientific production by the number of articles over time (1978–2008), we realize that the distribution has changed, mainly because of two long-term tendencies: the absolute number of publications has grown immensely, and we have seen the appearance of a non-English-speaking "periphery" in Brazil, then South Korea and Taiwan, followed by China (Figures 2.1 and 2.2). The basic structure of the geographical distribution of world production has thus moved from a basic center–periphery model to a multipolar world. Of course, the main countries are still largely dominating the world production, but the periphery has exploded. First, the countries composing what Arvanitis and Chatelin (1988) named the "first periphery," mainly English-speaking countries, has been growing but at a relatively slower rate than other countries. Since this statement, emerging economies out of this first periphery, mainly India, China and Brazil, and to some lesser extent smaller producers, have appeared. If we remain at this national-level scale, the periphery becomes multi-centered. If we had examined the data at the level of disciplines, it would have been clear that the periphery is even more complex, since some countries specialize in specific domains.

Still, the total number of scientific articles is low in Arab countries. A recent report indicates that in 2007 the number of Arab scientific publications (approximately 15,000 papers) was equivalent to the scholarly output of Brazil and South Korea in 1985 (Mrad 2011). Moreover, the number of articles published annually per 100 researchers varies from two publications in four Arab countries to around 100 in Kuwait. Obviously, the last figure hides some artifact (or a publication practice, common in some domains, where the lab chief signs all articles produced by his team regardless of whether he has been involved in the actual research work). A very rough estimate could be as follows: if the total number of university teaching staff in the Arab region is calculated at 180,000 (head count) plus an additional 30,000 researchers working full-time in specialized centers, we could then consider there to be around 210,000 Arab researchers. Yet these specialized scientists produce only 5,000 academic papers per year, equal to 24 scientific papers per 1,000 university professors and full-time researchers (UNDP 2009: 201).

This is the result of the underinvestment in research that has already been mentioned above. What is reassuring, however, is the fact that growth over the

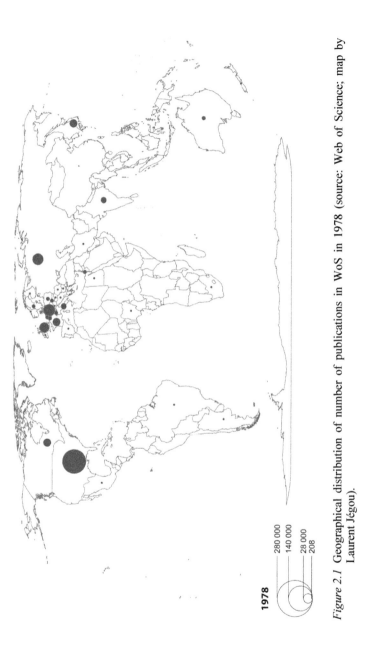

Figure 2.1 Geographical distribution of number of publications in WoS in 1978 (source: Web of Science; map by Laurent Jégou).

Figure 2.2 Geographical distribution of number of publications in WoS in 2008 (source: Web of Science; map by Laurent Jégou).

2008

280 000
140 000
28 000
208

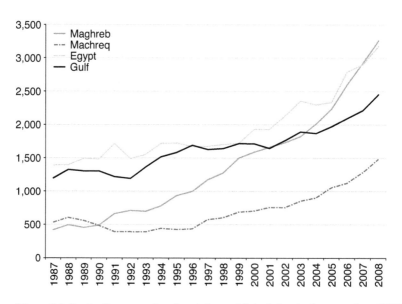

Figure 2.3 Production growth of articles published in Arab countries (1987–2008) (sources: data, Web of Science; computation, P. L. Rossi [IRD]; data published in the Arab Knowledge Report (Al Maktoum Foundation and UNDP 2009: 197).

last 20 years has been impressive. Growth rates are above the world average for publications, and comparable to three emerging countries: Chile, Thailand and South Africa (Table 2.1). As we mentioned in the first chapter, since 2007 many of the Arab countries, in particular those in close relation with the EU, have implemented quite strong reforms of the policy framework. Table 2.1 was produced before these new policies. Nonetheless, the growth rate was taken just before that. This timing detail is important: the Arab region was invisible to computation some 20 years ago, representing a mere 1.5 per 1,000 of world production. It now begins to appear as an emerging knowledge production location.

This growth finds its explanation mainly in the extremely strong growth of the Maghreb countries (Figure 2.4). Tunisia has quadrupled its publications in less than a decade (from 540 in 2000 to 2026 in 2008), achieving a 2.05 per 1,000 share of global publications. Morocco also had a very strong surge in production slightly earlier, between 1998 and 2004. Explanations collected in Morocco in 2004 by one of us, was that Morocco had experienced a surge of production because of Moroccan scientists living in France that had progressively returned to Morocco. If this sounds reasonable it also shows that local conditions were not that favorable to scientific research, or at least not as much as in Tunisia. Algeria has also undergone a recent rapid expansion, but such a rich country with such a strong academic population should have shown much higher levels of production.

Table 2.1 Growth rates and comparisons of some Arab countries

	Morocco	Algeria	Tunisia	Egypt	Jordan	Lebanon	Syria	Chile	Thai	South Africa
Scores SCI 2006[b]	756	728	1,079	2,743	421[a]	481[a]	146[a]	2,972[a]	2,235[a]	3,330
Per 1,000, world shares 2004[c]	1.26	0.73	1.08	3.42	0.69	0.48	0.16	3.04	2.43	4.64

Source: Science Citation Index (SCI) (2006).

Notes
a SCI (2005) (non-expanded).
b Calculation by P.L. Rossi/IRD.
c Calculation by OST (data for ESTIME project, see Arvanitis 2007).

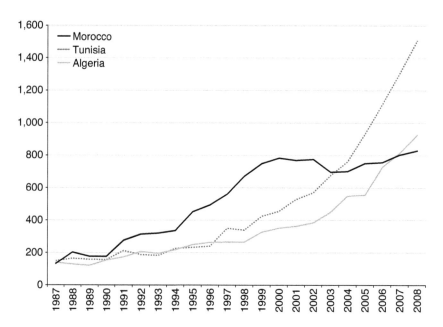

Figure 2.4 Production of Maghreb countries (1987–2008) (sources: data, Web of Science; computation, P. L. Rossi [IRD]).

Jordan and Lebanon, in the Machreq, have also known strong production. Jordan has woken-up and shows a continuous and rapid growth that surpasses Lebanon (Figure 2.5). Finally, one should note the spectacular growth of the United Arab Emirates and Saudi Arabia (Figure 2.6). Egypt experienced sluggish growth during the early 2000s, but experienced a surge in production over the later years (after 2007) which compares rather well when looking at its close contender, Saudi Arabia (Figure 2.7). The main reason probably lies in the new effort to promote research, since 2007, including a policy of investment in science. Funding has increased, alongside opportunities to collaborate with foreign scientists. Moreover, as the Tunisian example shows, the recognition of the research activities inside the public budgets and inside the universities, with clearly identifiable budgets and teams, with an agenda that is defined for a four-year period (in the particular case of Tunisia), played a fundamental role, as we will demonstrate in these pages. The cases of Egypt, Jordan and Tunisia show that a strong institutional change in the policy toward research funding seems to have triggered a real shift in production. More money distributed through competitive projects, international collaborative projects and recognition of research activities seems to be a key feature in all these countries. The reason why this particular mix of funding instruments is functioning will be the object of the concluding remarks of this part of the book.

In terms of book production, 20 Arab countries produce 6,000 books per year, compared to 102,000 in North America (Lord 2008). There are as many

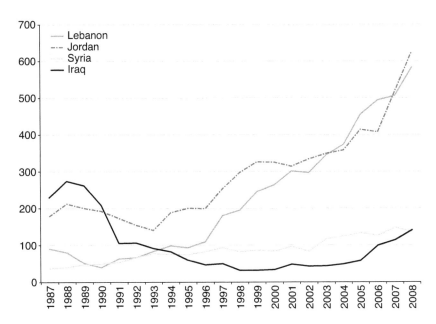

Figure 2.5 Production of Machreq countries (1987–2008) (sources: data, Web of Science; computation, P. L. Rossi [IRD]).

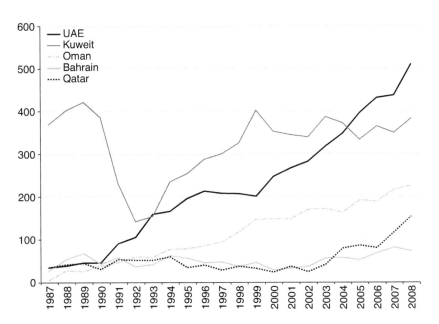

Figure 2.6 Production of Gulf small countries (1987–2008) (sources: data, Web of Science; computation, P. L. Rossi [IRD]).

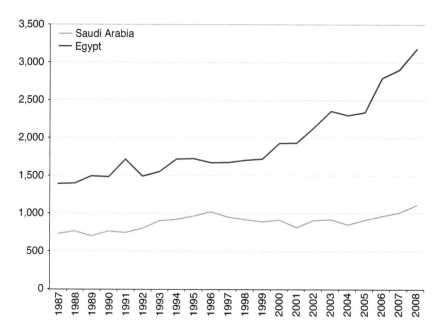

Figure 2.7 Production of Egypt and Saudi Arabia (1987–2008) (sources: data, Web of Science; computation, P. L. Rossi [IRD]).

translations published annually in Greece as in all Arab countries (Mermier 2005). This relatively low rate of production in the Arab region has been the topic of many discussions, in particular in the social sciences, where we have no good information sources for publications for the whole Arab region. There is, however, one notable exception – the Maghreb countries. In Casablanca, the Abdulaziz Foundation keeps relatively exhaustive records of production in the humanities and social sciences for all Maghreb countries. It also keeps track of publications in the humanities and social sciences produced elsewhere which focus on the Maghreb region. This very exceptional source of information has been used, to our knowledge, only once for bibliometric purposes (Waast *et al.* 2010). The ESTIME project mobilized the librarians of this Foundation and we now have good figures which were used by the Social Science World Report of UNESCO (Figure 2.8).

Moreover, the Abdulaziz Foundation database shows the highly differentiated forms of production in fields such as history, economics, sociology and anthropology (Al-Khatib 2014) (Figure 2.9). It indicates the dominance of the humanities (literature studies and history, mainly, and in general identity, culture and political life) and the surprising decline of publications on economics, although the subject matter of enterprises is among the most important ones. This is even more surprising given that business management is among the most rapidly growing areas of study in practically all Arab countries.

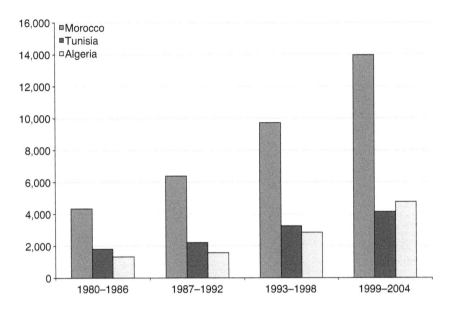

Figure 2.8 Production in the social sciences (1980–2004) (sources: Abdulaziz Foundation, Casablanca; treatments, P. L. Rossi and C. Richard-Waast).

Finally, rare are the repositories of Arab books that can allow us to provide some assessment of book production in the Arab world. We should, however, highlight the importance of newly established Arab e-book publisher al-Nile and Furat, based in Beirut. Other recent efforts are to gather e-copy of Arab Masters' and PhD dissertations, such as the portal of the Egyptian Universities Libraries Consortium. In addition to the Egyptian theses, the Consortium provides access to books and periodicals published by the Egyptian universities.[2]

2 A marked specialization pattern

When looking at the distribution by areas of science, we find a very particular mix of disciplines prevails in the Arab countries (Figure 2.10). Clinical sciences and medicine are very frequent and most strikingly they are followed by very applied disciplines from engineering sciences, to physical sciences and computer sciences. Agriculture, biological sciences and environmental sciences, which have grown a lot, still represent a more modest part of the production. The 2009 edition of the Arab Knowledge Report showed some even more striking figures (p. 198) – which we don't reproduce here because of a total absence of explanation of the sources of the database that is used. Nonetheless, let us mention they were considering that energy sciences (engineering mostly) accounted for 47 percent of the production, followed by the environmental and agricultural sciences (24 percent), and basic sciences with only 15 percent. It should be

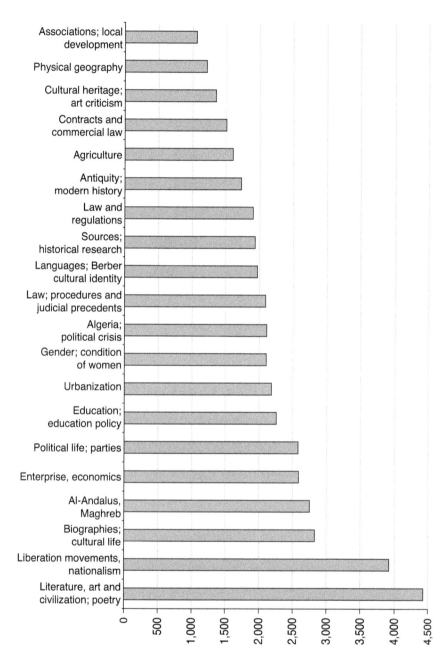

Figure 2.9 Domains of production in the social sciences in the Maghreb countries (1985–2004) (sources: Abdulaziz Foundation, Casablanca; computation, P. L. Rossi and C. Richard-Waast).

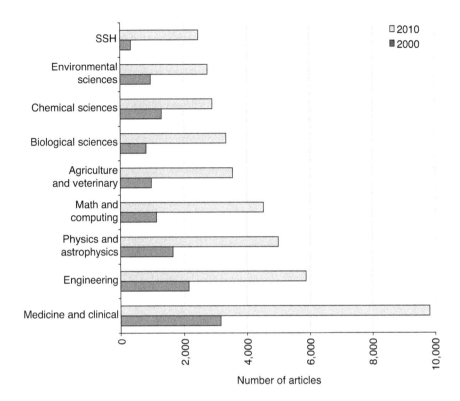

Figure 2.10 Scientific articles according to domains (sources: SciMago webpage, based on Scopus database; treatments, R. Arvanitis).

remembered that these publication data by discipline or research domain can be very different for different databases.

We know, from field interviews, that engineering in all senses is the dominant discipline in most Arab countries, with the notable exceptions of Tunisia and Lebanon. Egypt, Morocco and Algeria are all strong in chemistry, primarily organic chemistry, chemical engineering and physio-chemical characterizations of specific materials. Clinical medicine is a research strength for Jordan, Kuwait, Lebanon, Oman and Saudi Arabia, Tunisia and the United Arab Emirates. Syria's strength lies in plant and animal science, largely due to the presence of ICARDA, an international institute belonging to the Consultative Group for International Agricultural Research Centers, which is based in Aleppo. Qatar also makes its mark in engineering (Naim and Rahman 2009).

To understand the scientific publication development, we will refer to the concept of specialization patterns, i.e., percentage of publications in each specialty out of the total publications worldwide. The specialization index is equal to 1 when activity of the country in a given domain is similar to the world production, above 1 if there is a specialization in the specific domain, and below 1 if there is less specialization. Figure 2.11 shows the specialization patterns for eight countries from 2000 to 2010, based on Scopus data.

We can see the contrast between the ultra-specialized Algeria in engineering sciences, to Morocco with its more "basic sciences" orientation (and a surge in biology and genetics). Egypt, Saudi Arabia and to a lesser extent Jordan have a very marked engineering and chemistry profile, with the added "new") emphasis on environmental sciences. Lebanon with its clinical sciences and computer sciences, and Tunisia with the life sciences (which explains the rare mix of chemico-physical sciences with agricultural and environmental) and computer sciences.

Tunisia has become closer in its production profile to Lebanon, which is quite different from other countries. The case of Lebanon is very special: It has a

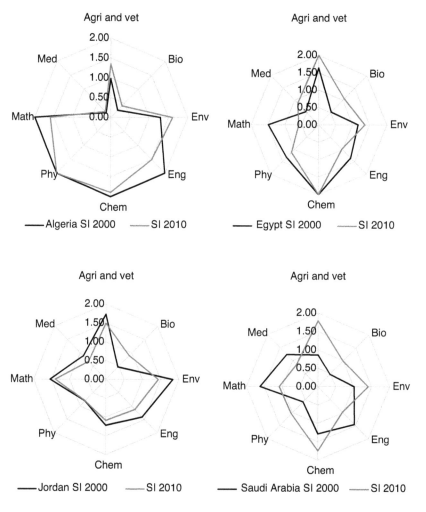

Figure 2.11 Specialization patterns in selected Arab countries (sources: SciMago webpage, based on Scopus database; our computation and presentation).

strong medical research core of two large hospitals, namely the AUB Medical Center and Hotel Dieu de France, both attached to large private universities (AUB and USJ) (see Chapter 4). There is also a growing number of publications from the Lebanese University and Balamand University, which both have well-regarded university hospitals. Nonetheless, most of Lebanon's production in this area is affiliated with AUB and its Medical Center, which has historical prestige in the region. Moreover, AUB has made a strong effort to promote the scientific production of its personnel, which has translated into impressive overall production figures.

Jordan is moving in a similar direction: although coming from a typically engineering-dominated landscape of research, it is now evolving toward producing more research which will be based on a recognized medical capability. Nevertheless, the dominant figure in Jordan remains engineering-related areas of specialization.

Finally, UAE, a new scientific country, is making the most of environmental sciences, engineering and computer sciences.

Tunisia and Egypt have seen the most important changes in the ten intervening years: Tunisia has greatly increased its production in the agricultural sciences and diminished its specialization in mathematics. Egypt, primarily because the size of the production involved is more important, has considerably diminished its over-specialization in chemistry. This is a good sign, because in this particular case most publications on chemistry were routine analyses of specific chemico-physical characteristics of materials. Now, the country produces a more even spread of publications in various domains. It is also striking to note the similarity in the specialization profiles of Egypt and Saudi Arabia (low in medical sciences and biology, high in engineering). Finally, it is interesting to compare two countries that are very similar in size but have quite different profiles. Jordan has a stronger emphasis on engineering, environmental sciences and, surprisingly, social sciences. As a word of caution, it should be mentioned that figures for social science disciplines are still relatively low (and probably more sensitive to changes in the specialization indicators). By contrast, Lebanon has stronger specializations in biological sciences, agricultural sciences and clinical medicine. Interestingly, there is a slowdown in medical specializations in Lebanon to the benefit of the biological sciences, a more basic set of sciences. This is probably a sign of a growing emphasis on research.

Compared to the data published by the ESTIME project, for 1993 and 2004, based on data from the WoS (OST computations), one can observe strong variations. These are partly due to the differences in the databases Scopus in our computations here, and WoS, for OST, as well as of different groupings of scientific specialties into large "domains." We try here to avoid the monopolistic reference to either one or the other database. Also, we have not included the social sciences which are too small a selection of journals to really make sense, as we will show later in this chapter. The actual data – including social sciences and humanities (SSH) – is published in the appendices of this book. What has changed remains important.

For example, Morocco had no real specialization except mathematics and computer sciences. This has now changed markedly. Tunisia was more clearly specialized in medical sciences than it is now, when environmental sciences and biology have been dominating (and as far as we know, biotechnology). Lebanon has been more stable in its specialization pattern, with a marked preference to life sciences and computing (which is also translated in active start-ups in the productive sector in informatics and computer applications). What appears also as a general feature is the fact that the specialization patterns which were rather stable over time are changing rapidly. Two main directions appear in these evolutions: the progressive appearance of environmental sciences (also very applied) and the marked preference for computer sciences in many of these countries. For an overview of the whole Arab countries (see appendices) we computed the same specialization patterns for all Arab countries for 2000 and 2010 (Figure 2.12).

The overall pattern of specialization and growth for the Arab region, because of the importance of some countries in size (Egypt, Saudi Arabia, Algeria) is also very much geared toward the chemical sciences and agricultural sciences. As we see, the environment appears as a new domain of specialty, which we believe is influenced by increased funding for environmental sciences, primarily from Europe but also internationally. Figure 2.13 shows the relative shares of the scientific large domains and their evolution over time. We see the growth of agriculture, environmental sciences and biology. We also see the slowing down of the "mathematical" overspecialization. Finally, although clinical sciences are important for the region, they represent a very small share of the world production.

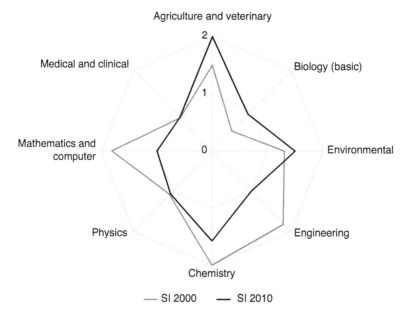

Figure 2.12 Specialization index of whole Arab region (2000–2010) (sources: SciMago webpage, based on Scopus database; our computation).

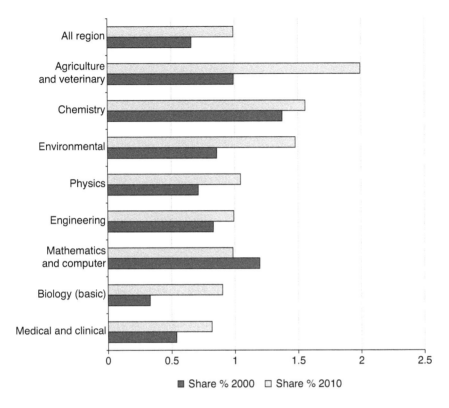

Figure 2.13 Relative shares by discipline of whole of Arab region 2000–2010 (percentage of discipline) (sources: SciMago webpage, based on Scopus database;
our computation).

3 Low citations, low impact?

What is most striking is that figures of citations received by the publications in
Arab countries are still low in comparison to those published in other regions of
the world. Whereas the average number of citations for a single paper from the
United States is 3.82 (one of the highest averages worldwide), and the average
for a South Korean paper is 1.51, the average number of citations from the Arab
region ranges from 0.99 for Lebanon to 0.60 for Egypt. The figure can be as low
as 0.01 in other Arab countries. These very low figures of received citations do
not reflect differences in language, since all the data pertains to English material
published and reported by the Thomson and Scopus databases.

Citations measure influence, much more than impact. They are closely related
to the distribution of prestige and reputation in the scientific community. Even
though they do not necessarily measure quality (as was claimed by the inventor
of the citation measurement, E. Garfield), they do reflect the way in which the

scientific community uses its publications. It should be noted that more than half of the world's science production is not cited at all. Since measures based on citations depend on time, many indicators have been proposed to take into account this factor. The H-index is one of the most popular measures, designed by Hirsch precisely in order to record this effect of age in relation to citations and publications. The logic behind the H-index is that the longer a career, the more likely citations become. One way to take this cumulative effect into account without giving it a decisive advantage is to detect the number of citations received in relation to the number of publications. The H-index, for present purposes, is the number of articles within a given country (H) that have received at least H citations. An H-index of "30" would mean that this country has 30 publications that all received at least 30 citations. To arrive at this result, the country in question would need to have far more than 30 publications. The index measures a certain level of permanence.

The issue here is that the H-index can vary widely, with some articles receiving a very high margin of citations. This is usually the case when an institution inherits the work of a large number of researchers that have been very productive in their former institutions, or associate researchers from other countries with very high citation scores. The H-index has several drawbacks, but it is especially problematic when used to measure publications on a collective rather than individual scale – including measurements taken at the national level. The variety of publication and citation practices across fields is not correctly represented by this indicator, resulting in a situation where fields known to be highly productive, both in terms of papers and of citations, impose a global norm.

Nevertheless, this figure is rather low for Arab countries. For example, Scimago,[3] which reports statistics calculated on Scopus data, reports H-indexes for the whole period 1996–2013 (Table 2.2). By way of comparison, the United States (an outlier in all these statistics) has an H-index of 1,518, followed by the United Kingdom with 943. Further down are Germany (814), France (742), Canada (725), Japan (694) and Italy (645). The Central European countries have H-indexes between 200 and 350. China, as the second largest producer of papers in that period, has a relatively low index of 436, meaning the number of papers that received a high flow of citations is low. It should be noted that the H-index is indeed sensitive to the scale of production (the more articles are produced, the greater the probability of high flows of citations), longevity and regularity.

Table 2.2 confirms this analysis and shows not only the low figures of Arab countries but also two countries with "irregular" behavior with respect to this citation indicator. The fourth country is Lebanon, which has a much higher H-index (109) than expected. This is due to high production in the biomedical fields and reflects a real engagement in internationally recognized research. The UAE also demonstrates a higher-than-expected H-index (100). For many reasons, the UAE has engaged in what seems to be progress toward internationally recognized research. These high figures could also be the result of growing numbers of expatriates in the UAE.

Table 2.2 Scientific production and the H-index (1996–2013)

World rank	Country	Documents	Citable documents	Citations	Self-citations	Citations per document	H-index
42	Egypt	104,784	102,181	659,779	132,942	8.42	148
45	Saudi Arabia	74,210	71,129	403,827	63,995	8.09	144
55	Morocco	31,277	29,822	195,079	36,093	7.88	109
68	Lebanon	15,840	14,744	123,586	12,411	10.72	109
63	United Arab Emirates	22,874	21,785	131,259	14,245	8.42	100
52	Tunisia	44,798	42,808	218,166	48,839	7.39	97
64	Jordan	22,753	22,273	136,316	18,084	8.04	92
69	Kuwait	15,446	14,933	113,984	14,771	8.52	92
56	Algeria	31,153	30,665	137,505	26,895	7.1	89
78	Oman	9,663	9,076	56,077	6,914	7.96	74
101	Syria	4,591	4,420	36,200	4,631	10.91	64
89	Qatar	7,692	7,326	34,654	4,056	6.63	60
100	Sudan	4,700	4,547	31,807	4,301	10.22	58
110	Palestine	3,343	3,193	18,626	2,580	8.43	48
90	Iraq	7,603	7,233	20,555	2,644	5.37	46
109	Bahrain	3,753	3,490	16,340	1,735	5.59	43
122	Yemen	2,074	2,018	11,792	1,390	9.04	42
111	Libya	3,217	3,116	11,939	759	5.66	41
169	Mauritania	400	383	3,382	205	10.15	28
170	Eritrea	399	387	3,754	308	9.99	28
206	Somalia	77	70	420	20	8.6	13

Source: Scimago based on Scopus data.

In any case these numbers, like any others in bibliometrics, should be used very cautiously and not all their stakes are scientific, but sometime commercial and ideological. Below we will develop some thoughts about the problematic impact factor and the invisible knowledge before concluding this section with the questions posed by this new market of information created by the ranking of universities.

3.1 The problematic impact factor

The most famous bibliometric indicator is the impact factor, which measures the mean number of citations received by a journal compared to the total number of articles published by the journal. It is very different from one field to another, and most importantly, it is not very robust (which means it varies significantly when changing the number of cited articles), as well as various other statistical difficulties. There has also been a fierce controversy regarding the use of the impact factor, which is in part due to its availability since it is regularly published by the Thomson WoS (in its science citation index reports), and has existed since Eugene Garfield introduced it in the 1960s (before WoS was acquired by Thomson Reuters it was a private venture of Garfield's, called the Institute for Scientific Information). Still, it appears clear that the main difficulty is that the impact factor is based exclusively on the citations received by a single journal; therefore it can be easily manipulated by an unscrupulous journal editor, as has been brilliantly shown by R. Monastersky (2005).

Before discussing theses indexes for the Arab world, we should mention that critics against such quantitative measurements of scientific production and reputation have gained momentum. Critics (Molinié and Bodenhausen 2010; Ernst 2010; Piron 2010) either discredit totally such measurements or request to combine it with qualitative assessments. Noble Prize winner Richard Ernst (2010: 90) is among the strong opponents to any form of such measurement:

   i Let us formulate a creed of scientists and researchers of all kind: never ever use, quote, or even consult science citation indices! Let us appeal to the pride and honesty of researchers to derive their judgments exclusively by careful studies of the literature and other scientific evidence. It is better to refuse to comply with requests than to base your judgment on numeric bibliometric indicators! Let us incorporate this creed into our teaching, discrediting "number games" as incompatible with our goals of objectivity, credibility, fairness, and social responsibility, as researchers.

  ii Let us establish, on the Internet, a generally accessible Webpage to list agencies, journals, and individuals who regularly use and misuse bibliometric measures in their judgments. Let us encourage researchers to add their critical commentaries to this database to identify notorious violators of the above creed. We may call this database "Bibliometric Discredibility Pillory" or BDP. It could be that an enthusiastic bibliometrics fan might even be inclined to apply the standard bibliometric evaluation tools to this database to establish a "Bibliometric Discredibility Index" or BDI to identify the worst offenders of academic credibility.

iii Let us discredit specifically rating agencies and their managers that have established and regularly publish science citation indices and university ranking lists; agencies that enrich themselves on the account of science quality, and cause more harm than good. Let us urge funding agencies to never ever support projects that intend to further extend bibliometrics based on merely counting citations.

In effect, bibliometric indicators when applied to individuals are absurd. Worse, they have become quasi-routine since the invention of the H-index, which was conceived by a physicist who wanted the citation figures to reflect the life-long effort of a scientist.[4] The success of the H-index should be seriously taken into account: it means that the demand from institutions to use simple metrics is also adopted by individuals, even despite their own willingness. When a young researcher is hired, his publications will be measured. When a junior staff professor goes into seeking external funding for his projects, the selection committees will merely look at the numbers. When associate professors enter the "tenure track" they will be evaluated by their colleagues (not only their peers) and measures will become the ultimate razor blade. What this tells us is the fact that scientific competition for financial resources has become the main driving force of science. And the metrics created are also based on the data corpus (the bibliographic databases): the competition of Thomson Reuter (commercializing the WoS) and Elsevier (commercializing Scopus) to gain this market is a clear sign that this battle is not any longer "scientific" but clearly commercial.

3.2 The question of undercoverage

Citation measurements have encouraged a certain concentration of production into journals that are registered in the WoS database, which was once thought to represent "mainstream science." This poses a real difficulty to countries lacking a significant history of scientific publication, since the game seems strictly limited to a very small number of players (Gaillard 2010a).

It should be remembered that the lack of local journals in Scopus and WoS databases is partly responsible for the low figures. The inclusion of journals, however, is usually based upon two conditions of regularity and good readership. A researcher recently conducted a census of publications in the two databases that are produced in countries bordering the Mediterranean (Table 2.3) and found a decent amount of local journals in countries where the research system is consolidated. A large country like Turkey now counts 143 journals in Scopus and 73 in WoS (or 70 in 2015). It should be underlined that many of these journals publish in English (360 titles in 2015 in the WoS – that is 40 percent of the journals reported as published in the Mediterranean region) or are publishing at least an English summary. Many journals have also chosen to publish in English and their local language. The WoS reports 200 such multilingual journals in the same set of Mediterranean

Table 2.3 Local journals published in Mediterranean countries in Scopus and WoS databases

	Scopus	Web of Science, 2010 SCI + SSCI + A&HCI	Web of Science, 2015 SCI + SSCI + A&HCI	Journal in Wos as percentage of number of titles 2015
EU countries				
France	773	251	264	1.95
Italy	572	168	186	1.37
Spain	356	163	160	1.18
Greece	39	18	20	0.15
Slovenia	29	25	24	0.18
Croatia	104	62	53	0.39
Cyprus	2	0	0	0.00
Malta	1	0	1	0.01
Non-EU countries				
Bosnia-Herzegovina	2	4	1	0.01
Montenegro	0	0	0	–
Albania	0	0	0	–
Eastern Mediterranean				
Turkey	143	73	70	0.52
Israel	70	25	17	0.13
Lebanon	4	0	0	–
Syria	0	0	0	–
South Mediterranean				
Egypt	14	3	4	0.03
Tunisia	2	0	0	–
Algeria	1	0	0	–
Morocco	1	0	0	–
Libya	0	0	0	–
Total	2,084	792	893	5.90

Source: analysis provided by Bülent Karasözen (unpublished data, 2010). Last column is author's own calculation based on Thomson Reuters website; list of journals (SCI, 2015; AHCI and SSCI, 2014).

Notes

SCI = Science Citation Index Expanded; SSCI = Social Sciences Citation Index; AHCI = Arts & Humanities Citation Index. Total number of titles in Web of Science (2015) = 13,563 titles, out of which 4,461 were published in the USA (32.9%) and 6,478 in other "core" countries (Canada, Japan, UK, Germany, France, other Western Europe, Italy, Spain, etc.) (47.8%).

countries. Nonetheless, as we can see from Table 2.3, Maghreb countries, Egypt and Lebanon have very few or no journals. It is not that there are no such journals (we can name without much thought *Insanyat* (Algeria), *Idafat* (Lebanon), *Journal of Lebanese Science* (Lebanon), *Cahiers du CREAD* (Algeria), *Critique économique* (Morocco), all of which have a decent and regular circulation, not to mention the 396 journals specialized on the Maghreb region indexed by the Foundation Abdulaziz in Casablanca[5]). Quality alone cannot be held responsible for this situation. Generally speaking, a large share of the publications from natural sciences as well as from the social sciences and humanities is not indexed in these databases.

This undercoverage in not new for countries of the periphery, but it is persistent, and as Arvanitis and Chatelin (1988) show, the periphery countries get discouraged by this situation, although they have produced more than 50 percent of the world production in areas that are directly relevant to them. Ismael Rafols, one of the authors of the Leiden Manifesto, reminds us that conventional bibliometric analysis is systematically biased against non-English languages, developing countries, applied sciences (in particular engineering), and interdisciplinary research.[6] He also shows, as had Arvanitis and Chatelin 27 years ago, that when using a specific database (for example CAB Abstracts, which is focused on agriculture and global health), production reported is much larger for low-income countries. India, for instance, has four times more publications in CAB than in WoS. The consequences can be very direct for this under-representation and it is not only an interest in data that should guide us. It has consequences, for instance, on the kind of research that is done for rice, genetically modified crops, plant nutrition and the like. It also has consequences because the knowledge produced locally is not correctly assessed in international comparisons.

The pressure for publishing in some very few "internationally recognized" journals discourages production in local journals (Hanafi 2010). Arab science periodicals included in international databases (other than Scopus or WoS) number no more than 500, about one-third of which are published by Egyptian universities and research centers; the other two-thirds are divided between Morocco, Jordan and Iraq. Arab science journals suffer from fundamental problems such as irregular publishing, lack of objective peer review and the unedited publication of the proceedings of conferences and seminars. Additionally, some of these periodicals are not regarded as credible for academic promotion purposes, leading many researchers and academics to prefer publication in international, peer-reviewed journals (UNDP 2009: 200).

4 Invisible knowledge

There is a tendency among all Arab public and private universities to adopt the American promotion system, which boils down to identifying research only when it is published in a "refereed international scientific journal," preferably one with high "impact factor." Authors are generally encouraged to make the decision about where to publish based on this impact factor; this has consequences for both the publications and the prestige of regional universities.

In order to understand how a university department's publications are distributed, we studied the amount and type of production of publications accounted for by the international databases, as well as those not covered by them. We took the example of the AUB, a university that is typical in the sense that it has an explicit policy of encouraging its professors to publish in high-impact journals.

In spite of this policy, we were positively surprised to find that AUB professors produce many books over time (Table 2.4). From 2001 to 2014 they published 208 books, which are mostly invisible in WoS or Scopus. Most of these books (71 percent) are published by professors within the Faculty of Arts and Sciences (Table 2.5). Contrary to what some argue, namely that full professors become relaxed over time and don't produce much, Table 2.6 shows that more than half of these books were published by professors. Knowledge production for the social sciences is as cumulative over time as any other scientific discipline. And if our hypothesis that scientific production is very much related to the promotion system holds true, this strong production of books should be related to the regular growth of the total production of the AUB, a topic we tackle in Chapter 4. In terms of language, only ten of over 147 books in SSH are published in Arabic (7 percent). This certain lack of interest to communicate their message locally is a puzzle we examine in Chapter 9.

We wanted to examine the total production of knowledge by AUB's professors in many forms (articles, books, manuals) from 2006 to 2008. It should be noted that contrary to our expectations, it was not easy to collect the information at the level of the departments. There is no regularity nor even completeness in

Table 2.4 Average number of books per year (AUB)

Period	Average number of books per year	Total
2001–2005	8	40
2006–2010	16	79
2011–May 2014	22	89

Source: AUB data, provided by Librarian AUB.

Table 2.5 Distribution of professors by faculty

Faculty	Number of books (2001–2014)	Percentage
Faculty of Arts and Sciences	147	71
Faculty of Engineering and Architecture	24	12
Faculty of Agricultural and Food Sciences	15	7
Faculty of Medicine	12	6
Olayan School of Business	5	2
Faculty of Health Sciences	5	2

Source: AUB data, provided by Librarian AUB.

Note
Faculty of Arts and Sciences contains both natural and social sciences. Most social sciences are located in that faculty.

Table 2.6 Distribution of number of books by rank of professors

Rank	No.
Lecturer/instructor	14
Assistant professor	18
Associate professor	61
Professor	112
Professor emeritus	2
Total	207

Source: AUB data, provided by Librarian AUB.

the documents we received. The only faculty that realized a bibliometric survey was the Faculty of Medicine, an activity that was not always appreciated by professors at the AUB Medical Center. After discovering the very unequal status of the information available, we focused on the Faculty of Arts and Sciences of AUB, which includes a varied number of disciplines in basic sciences (natural and social sciences). We have only selected here the "publishing" faculty members: 50 in the natural sciences (physics, chemistry, astronomy, geology, mathematics, computer sciences, mainly) and 80 in the social and human sciences (literature, civilization, history, language, sociology and anthropology, economics, education and political sciences).

Table 2.7 gives the data for the period covered by three annual reports that we found complete. We analyze here only the following: articles (whatever the status of the journal), books, edited books, chapters and published proceedings. We exclude thus many other productions such as videos, leaflets, various dissemination articles and some newspaper articles (which we will examine later in Chapter 9).

To begin with, we found that annual reports *under-reported* the production of their faculty members, either due simply to faults in the reporting or sometimes because dates of publications are not the same – authors tend to report on the date they deliver a paper to a publisher, the publisher (journal or publisher of books) delivers in the following year (or sometimes even years!). In our case we found 62 such references that were reported in the databases but not in the annual reports. These concern mainly the natural sciences (15 percent of their references) who do not seem to bother so much with the annual reports, since most of their production is in journal articles.

After pooling the annual reports and the database references, we found that the databases reported 32 percent of the production of the faculty, even after adding those unreported references. Now, it seems, we also under-estimate this figure, because we base our calculations on the actual finding of the references in the databases. Curiously, many of these references are published in peer-reviewed journals, but the specific reference seems absent from an online interrogation of both Scopus and WoS. In the publication lists, reported by professors in the annual reports of the Faculty of Arts and Sciences, we noted the mentions of 46 indexed journals and 84 not indexed by WoS or Scopus. In the

Table 2.7 Example of the Faculty of Arts and Sciences of AUB (basic sciences): publications 2006–2008 reported by annual reports and databases

	Number produced	Percentage of total	Number in SSH	SSH, percentage of total	Number in natural sciences	Natural sciences, percentage of total
Reported in annual reports (a)	630	91	311	98	317	85
References found in databases Scopus and WoS not reported in annual reports (b)	62	9	6	1.9	56	15
Invisible knowledge (production not reported by the databases)	475	69	272	86	202	54
Total publications (a + b)	692	100	317	100	373	100

smaller Faculty of Agriculture and Food Science, publications appear in 11 journals that are indexed and six that are not indexed. Nevertheless, we still have a high number of non-reported productions which we call "invisible knowledge."

In other words, 68 percent of the production is not reported in the two main multidisciplinary databases that are usually used to report the bibliometric activity of an institution. As expected, the proportion of "invisible" knowledge in the humanities and social sciences was found to be higher than in the natural sciences. But still, the proportions are very high (86 percent for the social sciences and 54 percent for the natural sciences). Given that we are in an English-speaking university that obtains in these years external funding from European and American funds, both public and private, for more than $US14 million, and that produces a substantial number of publications (from 3.9 articles or other products for the SSH to 6.3 articles or other productions in the natural sciences), we can cast serious doubts on the validity of those university rankings based on either Scopus or Web of Science.

Thus, the issue is not confined to the social sciences and humanities, but exists in all sciences to varying degrees. The debates about the international databases are usually making the assumption that core countries will have a better coverage than peripheral countries. A study by Siversten (2014) shows very similar results on the coverage of the publications in Norway. He analyzes the coverage of 70,500 scholarly publications from the higher education sector in Norway for 2005–2012 and finds that while Scopus and WoS cover most of the publications in natural sciences and health sciences (respectively, 83 percent and 80 percent of all publications), this coverage decreases significantly for engineering, social sciences and humanities (respectively, 67 percent, 39 percent and 30 percent). Similarly, a study many years ago on the production of science departments in Mexico in the chemical sciences showed very similar results, in which the faculty of chemistry of UNAM (the largest university in the world) reported less than 19 percent of their production in the databases (Russell *et al.* 1995: 488).

In brief, what is "invisible" to the international databases may be visible outside the academic community. It may also relate to local uses and local communities where researchers live. Perhaps this tendency (conscious and unconscious) to separate the university from community plays an important role in marginalizing the university. The pressure exercised by the university upon their professors to publish in the high-impact journals is part of an ideology that supports the ranking of universities, as we will see in the following section.

5 Ranking universities

One of the most perverse consequences of privatization is the rise of instrumental rationality, the global ranking of universities in terms of "excellence," which serves to guide investment decisions of corporations looking to outsource research or direct wealthy parents to reliable credentialing for their children.

(Burawoy 2014)

In November 2014, *US News*, extending its previous experience, published the Best Arab Region Universities. According to this ranking, the "best" five Arab universities are: King Saud University (Riyad, Saudi Arabia [SA]), King Abdulaziz University (Jeddah – SA), King Abdullah University of Science & Technology (Thuwal, SA), Cairo University, and the AUB. Beyond this overall ranking, the newspaper offers rankings in each scientific field, an approximation of academic disciplines. While the whole concept of ranking is problematic, the ranking concerning the SSH is fundamentally flawed since most of SSH production is in Arabic and the Arabic-language journals are not indexed by Scopus. This section will assess this ranking, as well as other rankings of universities.

Ranking universities is related to the idea of the knowledge economy. Although the most famous ranking has been the well-known rankings produced by Jiaotong University in Shanghai, it was not the first one. Doctoral schools in the United States were ranked by the National Research Council in 1982, and the newspaper *US News and World Report* produced their first ranking of undergraduate university programs in 1983. *Business Week* (1988) and the *Financial Times* (1989) produced a ranking of MBAs in the United States and United Kingdom. Nonetheless, the Shanghai ranking in 2003 produced a shock because of its worldwide scope, focused purely on research and the rare mix of indicators that included publications and Nobel Prizes. The origin of this ranking is interesting in itself: It was supposed to provide a list of good (or eligible) universities for Chinese students receiving scholarships for studies abroad. In other words, it was supposed to provide guidance to the government on the way to upgrade the academic quality of its doctoral students going abroad, who were also expected to return with a prestigious diploma. In some countries, alternative rankings have been proposed; in Germany (CHE ranking in 2002 and post-grad ranking in 2007), France (Ecole des Mines ranking in 2007) and the UK (*Times Higher Education* in 2004). The EU has been quite attentive to the generalization of the ranking of universities and tried to promote alternative ways of thinking that would replace the notion of ranking by the notion of "strategic positioning" proposed by indicator specialists in Europe (Lepori *et al.* 2008; European Commission 2010).

The huge success of these rankings can be explained by many factors (Debailly 2010): the globalization of research and higher education as a collection of competitive markets; market for universities, students, professors and publications; the close connection that private universities establish between the salaries and "prestige" as measured apparently by rankings; the development of evaluation procedures based on indicators instead of the peer assessments, and which promote individual success – "excellence"; the further deregulation and privatization of higher education in countries where research and higher education are part of the world image of hegemony (see the case of the UK, for example, or the resistance of the French university and engineering schools system to rankings). The predominance of metrics that relate evaluation to simple performance indicators has also been at the very heart of New Public Management, and more generally of managerial approaches to research and higher education policy (Debailly and Pin 2012). Evidently, those promoting ideologically privatization and less state involvement in the economy will favor these rankings and metrics of excellence. More recently, the debates have left the criticism of rankings that seems relatively inefficient to the promotion of impact measurement. A whole new field for research evaluation is thus emerging. In the meantime, *US News* continues to produce its rankings regularly, a nice commercial venture since readers of magazines and newspapers find it reassuring to locate their school in those rankings. Very little is known about how much of this effort actually influences decisions to choose a school, but it certainly has a nice impact on sales of the newspapers. While other rankings take into account teaching and research (such as *Times Higher Education*),[7] *US News* focuses only on one research output: the indexed publication in Scopus.

The Arab countries, mainly in the Gulf, have actively promoted commercially based universities, either public or private, close to this worldwide market of competences, where money buys prestige, and petroleum funds excellence. Rankings fit well in this search for excellence and market competition. Some universities have been denounced in newspapers and scientific journals as hiring shadow professors who spend almost no time there but agree, for a high price, to list all of their publications with that university, or publish some of their papers with their affiliation listed to the university. The actual scale of this phenomenon is still not known, but probably affects only marginally the actual level of scientific research. Nonetheless, it does affect the image of the universities and the countries in the rankings produced by the Competitiveness reports and World Bank assessments of knowledge-based economy. In November 2014, *US News*, extending its previous experience, published the Best Arab Region Universities.[8] This ranking, contrary to its US equivalent, is based solely on raw numbers of articles, citations and other indicators provided by Scopus, another commercial venture headed by Elsevier. This means they are not scaled against the number of academic staff an institution employs. Contrary to WoS, Scopus seemed to welcome additional journals, some of which are questionable, as we will see later on. In fact, both databases seem to cover in very similar ways the scientific production in aggregate figures for statistically large datasets. When zooming down to specific countries that produce small numbers of publications, or even particular institutions, the number of methodological shortcomings makes things even more difficult. Still today, there is no accepted standard in bibliometric evaluations and rankings are not at all favored by specialists in the field.

Thus, university rankings should be taken for what they are: commercial activities that describe a private sector knowledge market and try to provide tools for it. The *US News* ranking of Arab universities has all the flaws of rankings and additionally is based on a very thin database. If we look to the 448 "Arab" journals included in the Scopus list, we find that 67 percent of them belong to two problematic publishers, Hindawi (based in Cairo) and Bentham (based in Sharja, UAE) (Table 2.8). Both are mentioned as a "questionable publisher" by the Beall listing, which lists "Potential, possible, or probable

Table 2.8 Distribution of journals based in the Arab world by publishers

Journals publisher	No.	Percentage
Hindawi Publishing Corporation	146	33
Bentham Science Publishers	151	34
Universities Press	151	34
Total	448	100

predatory scholarly open-access publishers."[9] "Predatory journals" are those that unprofessionally exploit the author-pays model, something that became a business itself with the appearance of open-access publishing (it is also named "Gold Open Access" as opposed to entirely free open access journals, called "Green Open Access"). Typically, these publishers spam professional email lists, broadly soliciting article submissions for the clear purpose of gaining additional income. Operating essentially as vanity presses, these publishers typically have a low article acceptance threshold, with a false-front or non-existent peer-review process. Unlike professional publishing operations, whether subscription-based or ethically sound open access, these predatory publishers add little value to scholarship, pay little attention to digital preservation and operate using fly-by-night, unsustainable business models. What is even more troubling is that many rather good scientists in Arab countries, because of the pressure to publish, get fooled by the name of a journal – or pretend to – such as "European Journal of Scientific Research."

As we mentioned in the introduction, according to this ranking the "best" five Arab universities are: King Saud University, King Abdulaziz University, King Abdullah University of Science & Technology, Cairo University, and the AUB. Beyond this overall ranking, the newspaper offers rankings in each scientific field, an approximation to academic disciplines.[10] Concerning the SSH, the ranking is fundamentally flawed since most SSH production is in Arabic and the Arabic-language journals are not indexed by Scopus. Only two journals in the list are produced in Arabic (one from Kuwait and another from Jordan)[11] among the seven journals based in the Arabic world. In the Arab world you have around 300 academic journals that are in Arabic that are ignored.

Rankings are not indicative of research, nor are they used for evaluation of research, even in very competitive environments. Rankings are not used for funding decisions and probably have never had any real impact on choosing a career since other features such as location, cost, proximity and previous knowledge of an academic institution play a more important role than any ranking. They only serve a symbolic, political and highly ideological function in that they legitimize the idea of benchmarking among different universities. If some effect is to be found it is in triggering fierce controversies among academics and academic managers on the respective merits of their own institutions, discussions that never go beyond the frontiers of the small world that is concerned by the figures. Bahram Bekhradnia, president of Britain's Higher Education Policy

Institute, described ranking as following: "they're worse than useless. They're positively dangerous. I've heard presidents say this all over the world: I'll do anything to increase my ranking, and nothing to harm it" (*The Economist* 2015). Prospective pupils and families that read these rankings will probably be happy or disconcerted by their choices (future or present) but will give little credit to figures that relate very loosely to the actual academic status and practice.

As Bourdieu once wrote, "standardization benefits the dominant." These rankings want to consolidate the idea of a single standard, a fits-all measure, independently of content, orientation, location or resources. Instead of thinking about universities as a social institution that fits a certain environment, in terms of *ecology* (biodiversity adapted to its environment), it is thought of in terms of *hierarchy* (how to attain the title of *"the best"* when competing against the US\$41-billion-endowment Harvard University). Limited to this elite formation function, the university becomes a caricature of itself. Effects in the country or the territory, activities beyond publishing, research, community services, participation in public debates, influence of policy decisions, contribution to local political life, dissemination of both knowledge and arts, social organization, become invisible in these one-dimensional rankings. Even the actual contribution of individuals highly devoted and loyal to their own home institution becomes a footnote in the career of academic faculty members. Rather more worrying is the fact the promotion reports, that are produced for promotion inside universities and decide the professional death or life of candidates, are contaminated by the benchmarking and managerial view of "excellence" that obscures all other dimension that are not part of the ranking in terms of publications. Ranking is thus part of an academic *celebrity model* that operates at a global level, in a selective way, as globalization itself.

While we are not enthusiastic toward any ranking, if a ranking is a must-have, then we can think of alternative ways of conducting ranking or promotion criteria for individual professors. Some principles to be taken into account:

- All indicators should be scaled against the number of academic staff a university employs.
- Bibliometrics may inform, but not replace peer review.
- Creation of national/language portal (such as The Flemish Academic Bibliographic Database for SSH). The newly established E-Marefa and al-Manhal are a starting point for the Arab world, but they still insufficient and it is better to have national or official pan-Arab organizations create such portals.
- Benchmark the whole life-cycle of research (i.e., including knowledge transfer and public or policy-oriented research activities). We admit that not all research should have an immediate relevance to local society. Thus research should be classified by temporality (research that needs time to have output [because of lengthy fieldwork or because of political sensitivity of its content] versus research that yields quick results) and by public/policy relevance and knowledge transfer/innovation (looking at how much research

income an institution earns from industry). If the trend will be kept to quantify that, indicators of public/policy activities for the relevant research should be developed, including when these activities will become relevant to public and policy debates.

6 International scientific collaborations

As a result of the growing complexity of science, the ease of face-to-face contact, the internet, and government incentives, science and technology activities are being conducted in an increasingly international manner. In all fields of research, international collaboration is crucial to research projects. Mostly viewed as a positive aspect of research, international collaborations are becoming an integral part of research. This is so much so that we can easily distinguish a global strategy in research from an internationalization strategy. The latter is mainly based on the idea that a local focus is first needed and then it is possible to deploy an internationalization strategy that would enhance the scientific capacities of individual researchers and institutions through participation in international research networks. The former is becoming common in large research networks and assumes competences to be located anywhere in the world, and that for each new research topic one would need to have a coordination of hundreds of teams spread over the surface of the globe. This is largely the case of global objects like biodiversity, climate change, the human genome and a multiplicity of other subjects that simply could not be researched if it were not for the existence of such international research networks. In both cases, either in internationalization or in globalization of research activities, the underlying assumption is that one can nurture a research capacity, branch it internationally and use foreign partnerships to consolidate local research. The daily experience of researchers in developing countries is that international cooperation helps researchers to join ideas and move forward at a faster pace. It also entirely changes the local perception of what research is about. As a Jordanian interviewee stated:

> the European projects [to which I participated] have helped change the negative perspective Jordanians have towards the concept of heritage. Whereas architectural heritage, for example, used to seem shameful and many felt the need to destroy their old homes and build new modern ones, many Jordanians now respect traditional architecture and architectural and civilizational heritage.

In a recent book concerning international collaborations between Latin America and Europe, Gaillard and Arvanitis (2013) insist on the fact that not all international scientific partnerships occur under the umbrella of cooperation programs. According to several authors (e.g., Wagner 2008), the decision to work together is essentially a personal one based on mutual interests and complementary skills, and international collaboration functions as a global self-organizing system through collective action at the level of researchers themselves (Leydesdorff and Wagner 2008). These views of scientific collaboration stressing the individual researcher alone need to be qualified. The researcher is presented as the hero of international collaboration, taking decisions where individual interests would be the main driver; this explanation is based on the idea that the individual recognizes potentially interesting collaborators and is able to evaluate the expected outcomes of the planned collaboration. This could probably be the case for experienced and relatively senior researchers who enjoy world repute. It does not reflect the case of younger researchers who usually do not have access to all potential choices for initiating successful and fruitful collaboration. Moreover, for an individual to be able to objectively "choose" his collaborators, he/she needs to be embedded in his/her local environment, institutionally, politically and economically.

The existence of a local scientific community as well as the institutionalization of scientific activity play a very important role, since it is through participation in local training and local scientific teams that the young individual scientist can become increasingly involved in international collaboration. That explains also why international collaboration is so much linked to training at the doctoral and post-doc level. Personal decisions are important, but choices are also influenced by other factors that go far beyond what we are usually ready to accept when assuming that international scientific collaborations are beneficial. A possible way to examine what constrains and influences decisions to collaborate would be to scale the issue at different levels:

- the national policy environment (and instruments existing at the researchers' institution) that directly affects the decision to collaborate on the basis of the instruments available for the scientific collaborations but also, indirectly, on the basis of the national political and economic context;
- the international level, involving wider networks of collaborations through which scientists can find opportunities for international collaborations. This level should include global issues as well as actors that are very active at an international level;
- finally, the individual level, choice of discipline, career pattern and personal contacts.

In their article "Where is science going?" Diana Hicks and Sylvan Katz note that "International collaboration is often singled out for special mention. It has been a concern of recent European Union science policies and of bibliometric analysis." They find that "the increased cost of certain instruments, the increased scope of many problems, the global reach of research-intensive multinational companies, and increased travel and communication are combining to make the scientific community even more transnational" (Hicks and Katz 1996: 394). These drivers for international collaboration have been confirmed by a recent review of topics on the theme, prepared as a background document for the European Commission (Boekholt *et al.* 2009). They were also strongly confirmed by a study one of us coordinated in the Mediterranean countries, based on a survey questionnaire, called the "MIRA Survey on International Collaborations," addressed to 4,000 researchers from the northern and southern banks of the Mediterranean (Gaillard *et al.* 2013). Most results of the survey have been published in the collective book of the MIRA project (Morini *et al.* 2013), a cooperative policy-oriented project that joined the policy dialogue between the EU and Mediterranean countries (Arab countries and Israel and Turkey, which are Associated Countries to the EU Framework Programs).

6.1 International co-authorship

The indicator most often used to capture the scale or intensity of international collaboration in science and technology is co-publications of authors from two or more different countries. Co-publication analysis can tell us something about the relative importance of international collaboration that leads to tangible outputs (publications) and the nature of the cooperation in terms of countries and disciplines.[12] What the story of these indicators tell us is the spectacular growth of international cooperation, as measured by co-authorships, at the international level. As has been reported by Gaillard and Arvanitis (2013), 30 percent of the world's scientific and technical articles had authors from two or more countries in 2006, compared with slightly more than 10 percent in 1988. One-quarter (26.6 percent) of all articles with American authors had one or more non-American co-authors in 2006; the percentage is similar for the Asia-8 group of countries,[13] and slightly lower for China and Japan (NSF and OST 2008). Between 2001 and 2006, international co-publications increased in all countries except China, Turkey and Brazil. The higher rate for the 15 key members of the EU (EU-15), at 36 percent in 2006, partly reflects the EU's emphasis on collaboration among member countries as well as the relatively small science base of some EU members. The high level of collaboration among all other countries (46 percent in 2006) may reflect science establishments that are small (for example, in developing countries) or in the process of being rebuilt (as is the case in Eastern Europe).

It is acknowledged that developing economies have high and increasing co-authorship figures; the smaller the country, the higher this proportion of co-authorship (Gaillard 2010a). Co-authorships tend to be proportionally lower for larger countries with a growing scientific community. Thus in China, Brazil and Turkey, the number of co-authorships has fallen as a percentage of total production, a result of rapidly growing scientific production and the diversification of scientific communities.

In the Arab countries, the growth of co-authored articles has been higher than that of the overall production (Figure 2.14). Since 2005–2007 we also witness an acceleration of the pace of co-authorship and it has, apparently, a direct impact on the growth of the production by local researchers as well. In this case, we are talking of Arab countries that have increased their scientific cooperation with the EU.

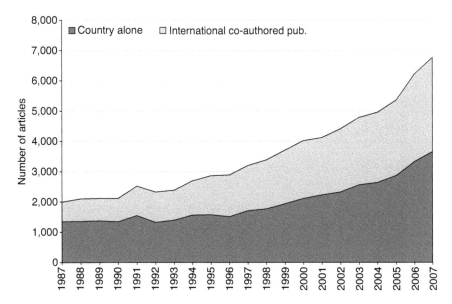

Figure 2.14 Growth of production and international co-authorship of selected Arab countries (1987–2008) (source: SCI 2008; calculation, P. L. Rossi [IRD]).

Note
Countries include Jordan, Lebanon, Egypt, Algeria, Tunisia and Morocco.

Table 2.9 presents data on overall scientific production in 2000 and 2010, based on Scopus data, alongside the corresponding shares of co-publications. Increasingly, Arab scholarship is done in cooperation with scholars abroad, shown by the difference between 2000 and 2010. Co-authorship is indeed extremely high for small producers (including the UAE, Syria, Qatar, Libya, Yemen, the Sudan and Mauritania), while larger producers fall in the mid-range. Egypt has an exceptionally low figure of co-publications. However, the share of co-authorships is expected to grow in Egypt, as in other countries. The standard situation for most Arab countries appears to be a rate of co-authorship accounting for approximately half of all publications.

Nonetheless, co-authorship patterns are very different from one country to the other (Figure 2.15). Egypt (with 35 percent of co-publications) in 2007 has still a low proportion of co-publications. Smaller countries like Jordan (49 percent) and Lebanon (52 percent) have higher levels of co-publications with researchers from foreign countries. Maghreb countries have higher proportions, mainly with France. Tunisia, the fastest-growing science-producing country in the region, has the lowest level of co-publications (47 percent) of Maghreb countries; on the contrary, Morocco and Algeria, with a proportion of 60 percent of co-authored articles, can be considered as open to cooperation. Even growing in numbers, co-publications tend to diminish relatively (but not in absolute terms).

Table 2.9 Publications and co-authorship in Arab countries (2000 and 2010)

Country	Documents 2000	Documents 2010	Percentage international collaboration (2000)	Percentage international collaboration (2010)	World share (%) (2000)	World share (%) (2010)
Egypt	2,858	8,459	28.1	40.2	0.24	0.4
Saudi Arabia	1,835	5,739	26.1	56.2	0.15	0.26
Tunisia	755	4,415	39.7	43.9	0.06	0.2
Algeria	495	2,862	51.5	52.5	0.04	0.13
Morocco	1,184	2,277	51.4	47.6	0.1	0.1
Jordan	627	2,062	30.46	41.46	0.05	0.09
UAE	425	2,059	47.5	58.2	0.04	0.09
Lebanon	448	1,259	38.4	54.6	0.04	0.06
Kuwait	568	1,050	27.9	45.7	0.05	0.05
Oman	255	779	42.4	60.7	0.02	0.04
Iraq	91	724	16.0	30	0.01	0.03
Qatar	58	693	34.5	69.6	0	0.03
Libya	72	468	34.7	51.9	0.01	0.02
Sudan	99	466	55.6	59.2	0.01	0.02
Syria	139	402	52.5	62	0.01	0.02
Palestine	40	281	50.0	50.9	0	0.01
Bahrain	89	266	15.73	42.48	0.01	0.01
Yemen	41	198	68.3	70.2	0	0.01
Mauritania	14	20	78.6	100	0	0

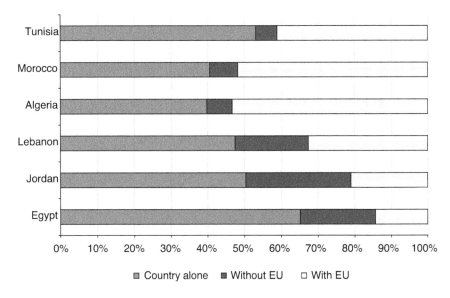

Figure 2.15 Publications and co-publications of selected Arab countries, with or without EU partners (2007) (source: SCI Extended – Thomson Reuters; computation. P. L. Rossi [IRD]).

In fact, the overall pattern of French-speaking Maghreb countries is similar: co-publications with France have grown but proportionally less rapidly than the overall production and new partners are appearing from outside Europe (mainly the United States and Canada) and from inside Europe (Spain, Italy and Germany).

6.2 The dynamic of research collaborations

As we have shown above, the specialization pattern of publications of these countries, largely oriented toward chemistry, physics and engineering, is different from European countries. They also favor mathematics, mainly in Maghreb and Lebanon. By contrast, they also under-publish in life sciences (biology, bio-medicine). Tunisia and Lebanon are exceptions, since they have a relatively strong medical and biomedical basis. This orientation in favor of basic biological and bio-medical research is also the general tendency of many European countries. Moreover, European countries seem to deploy more research activities in "basic" science, whereas Arab countries seem to prefer quite clearly technology-oriented and applied research, as confirmed by the MIRA Survey on International Collaborations (Figure 2.16). Thus the expectations of Arab country researchers are more "applied," technology-oriented than for Europeans. The same survey shows also that access to equipment and use of equipment is a stronger motivation than it is for Europeans.

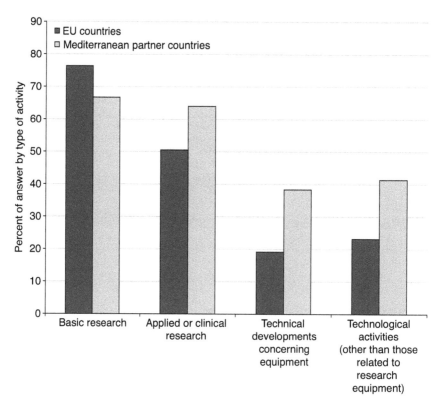

Figure 2.16 Type of research in research collaborations, percentage responses to the question: "*Could you indicate the relative importance of each type of research in your collaborations?*" as "important" and "major contribution to this type of research" (MIRA survey) (source: MIRA Survey, unpublished report).

These specializations patterns are very important because countries tend to reinforce their specialization over time rather than diversify, since research (and technological development) are activities that are "path dependent," that is, they depend on the former choices, thus feeding on previous work and accumulated competences. So the dynamic implemented by the collaborations may not have been so much that of a continuous quest and permanent search for better opportunities, but rather that of an initial choice that triggers a long period of exchanges between researchers and, of course, securing the necessary resources for that.

When asked about the drivers to collaborate internationally, the responses show a quite homogeneous set of answers; almost all of the proposed reasons were considered as "important" or "major" for more than half of the respondents to the MIRA Survey (Figure 2.17). The prime reasons to collaborate internationally are directly linked to advanced scientific interests: "Access to new and

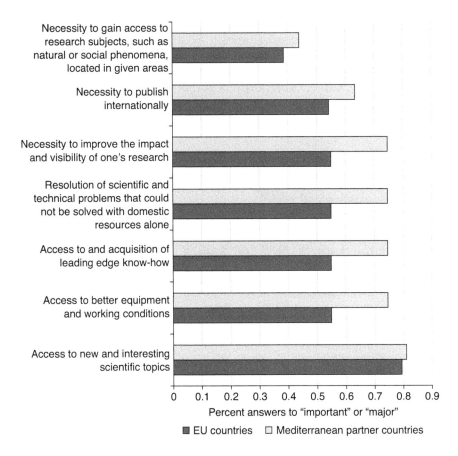

Figure 2.17 Major drivers for international collaborations (source: MIRA Survey).

interesting scientific topics" for 80.2 percent of the entire group (79.4 percent in Europe and 81 percent in the Mediterranean partner countries [MPCs]), followed by the "Necessity to improve the impact and visibility of one's research" for 67 percent of the group (61.5 percent in Europe, 72.5 percent in the MPCs). Not surprisingly, "Access to better equipment and working conditions" is a more important reason for the MPCs, with 74.5 percent than for Europe (54.9 percent). The proposed motivation, which gathers less interest in the surveyed population, is: "Necessity to gain access to research subjects, such as natural or social phenomena, located in given areas." Nevertheless, the interest remains quite important and 44 percent of researchers in the MPCs and 38.6 percent of their European counterparts declare that it as either "important" or "major" for them.

More than half of the surveyed population in the MIRA Survey (55 percent of the entire group) did apply to international calls for tenders involving international scientific collaboration. Scientists working in Europe participated more than their partners from MPCs (61 percent and 49.4 percent, respectively). A number of reasons were suggested to characterize motivations to participate in an international call for proposals (Figure 2.18). Almost all the motivations were considered as "important" or "essential" by the majority of the respondents in the two regions, apart from "Reach new technologies/competences not available in my country" which, not surprisingly, is the last one given by people working in Europe (44.8 percent) but ranked second for people working in the MPCs (67 percent). In both regions, the most important criterion was money: "access to international funding" (Europe 83.8 percent, MPCs 85.3 percent). Globally, the

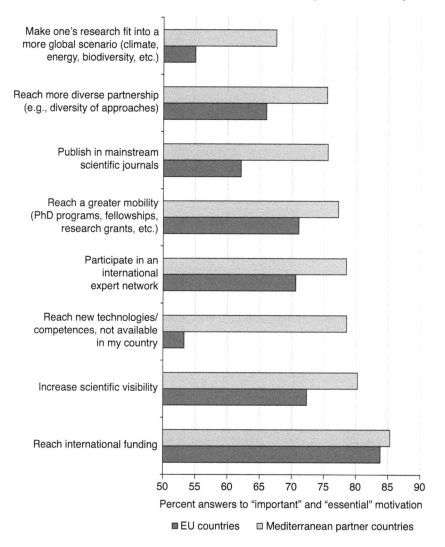

Figure 2.18 Motivations to engage into international collaborative projects (source: MIRA Survey).

proposed motivations are more explicitly acknowledged in MPCs (between 52 percent and 79.7 percent of positive opinions expressed for all proposed motivations); nevertheless, motivations linked to visibility, mobility and networking rank very highly in both regions.

The MIRA Survey was an exceptional opportunity to measure some of the factors affecting international collaborations. It is important to underline that the asymmetry of collaborations, which was recognized as a source of tension and a major issue in the 1970s and 1980s, has developed into a more equal partnership. This is not specific to the Arab countries or the Mediterranean, but to all international collaborations, as has been shown by Gaillard and Arvanitis (2014) in their survey of international collaborations between Europe and Latin America. Moreover, those who engage in these collaborations are older than the overall population of scientists in both the MPCs and Europe. This would tend to confirm that researchers in their mid-career stages (40 years and above) are more likely to collaborate internationally than those who are in their early or late career stage.

Interestingly, there are none who disagree that international collaboration is a win–win process that benefits all partners. The expectations related to participation in international calls for proposals involving scientific collaboration are very high, and the declared derived outcomes are very significant in both regions. International collaboration addresses and involves very dedicated and goal-oriented individual scientists in all countries, scientists who seek to increase and improve their scientific capacities and develop greater international recognition.

The 4,340 scientists who answered the survey belong to quite homogeneous categories in the two regions, including the 1,828 scientists from Arab countries. There are no marked differences in age and gender between respondents from the MPCs and EU countries: in the two regions, the surveyed group is older than the overall scientific population and women represent close to one-quarter of the respondents. The respondents work mainly in universities, in the public sector and research is their main activity, i.e., they spend more time on research than on teaching and other activities such as administration and consulting.

The survey confirms the great mobility of scientists even prior to international collaboration, although with differences depending on the country and region. At the time of the survey, between 7.6 percent and 11.5 percent of the surveyed population could be considered as being part of the science and technology diaspora (meaning they are living in a country other than their country of nationality). Compared with the figures on high-skilled migrants reported today, this percentage is very high. Science is an international activity.

Scientific collaboration between the two regions is often the result of this mobility. Over 69 percent of the scientists have collaborated or published scientific papers with colleagues met during long stays abroad, and 50 percent did so with colleagues who were trained or had visited their own institution. Nevertheless, these results state clearly the strong connecting role of scientific conferences. More than half of the respondents have collaborated or co-published with scientists from other countries that they met only at scientific conferences (58 percent of scientists in Europe and 44.7 percent in the MPCs).

The prime reasons to collaborate internationally are directly linked to advanced scientific interests: "Access to new and interesting scientific topics" for 80.2 percent of the entire group (79.4 percent in Europe and 81 percent in the MPCs), followed by the "Necessity to improve the impact and visibility of one's research" for 67 percent of the group (61.5 percent in Europe, 72.5 percent in the MPCs). While quite homogeneous between the two groups, the expectations are higher in the MPCs and more tangible effects are expected as "Access to better equipment and working conditions" motivates 74.5 percent of the MPC scientists against 54.9 percent of their European colleagues. On the other side, the lack of collaborative programs is perceived as the major constraint in the two regions to collaborate internationally (more than 80 percent in the two regions).

The outcomes of collaborations are also many, not different in the two regions and directly linked to the professional improvement in knowledge and recognition of the respondents. They are, from the most important and by decreasing order: "increase in the total amount of their publications" (EU 66.4 percent, MPCs 62.8 percent), "increased international scientific recognition" (EU 64.6 percent, MPCs 62.6 percent), "participation in new scientific projects" (EU 64.2 percent, MPCs 61.9 percent) and "greater recognition in their scientific fields" (EU 60.7 percent, MPCs 61.6 percent). Nevertheless, more tangible outcomes are more highly prized among the MPC scientists, like "learning new techniques" (EU 47.4 percent, MPCs 65.1 percent) and "access to equipments not available in their country" (EU 28 percent, MPCs 49.9 percent).

While a majority (55 percent) of scientists in the overall survey population responded to calls for proposals involving international scientific collaboration, the extent of this participation differed clearly between the two regions: 61 percent for scientists working in EU countries, 49.4 percent for those working in the MPCs. However, analyzing the scientists' participation in calls for proposals gives a very balanced picture of the two country groupings. The responses indicate that for approximately two-thirds of the scientists (EU 64.2 percent, MPCs 66.1 percent) the project was initiated by their laboratory or institution alone or together with one or more partner laboratories. A large proportion of the respondents (EU 38.7 percent, MPCs 41.9 percent) reported that they were project coordinators. The large majority of the scientists in both regions were directly involved in budget allocation (EU 64.7 percent, MPCs 51.7 percent) and task assignment (EU 91.7 percent, MPCs 66.1 percent).

On "involvement in the projects," the results show a very high level of satisfaction in both regions; 83.8 percent of MPCs scientists and 85 percent of scientists working in Europe felt they were able to get involved as extensively as they wanted. The responses given in the two regions about the level of individual contribution in the projects almost follow the same pattern, but scientists working in the MPCs were more likely to rate their contribution as "essential" (EU 40.2 percent, MPCs 48.5 percent). Nevertheless, a large majority of the respondents (EU 85 percent, MPCs 85.8 percent) rated their contribution to the project either as "important for the progress of the project" or "essential for the conduct of the project."

6.3 Scientific partners of Arab countries

The hierarchy of countries with which partnerships are pursued is very sensitive to policy. It has also changed rapidly in the last decade. France has been a privileged partner for Morocco, Algeria and, to a lesser extent, Tunisia. In general, France is the main scientific funder for international projects in the Mediterranean region, through bilateral programs. The appearance of Saudi Arabia, Italy and Spain as frequent co-authors is remarkable. It relates to a proactive policy of international cooperation on the part of the authorities of these countries as much as to the growth of research activity. Spain, for example, has seen a massive growth in its international collaborations, in particular (and understandably) with Latin America. It has also seen more cooperation with Morocco and other Maghreb countries. Italy has had a very sharp increase in its participation in international programs with neighboring countries in areas of its competence (cultural heritage, archaeology, agricultural sciences, food sciences). The more "traditional" players (France and the United States) have seen their relative share diminish, but nevertheless saw growth in the context of increasing collaborations and co-authored publications (Table 2.10). However, co-authorship with the EU has grown in all countries (even those usually "preferring" the United States), and this is directly due to the effort by the EU to open its programs systematically to non-EU partners (Arvanitis 2012).

The case of Lebanon is interesting because not only do we see more international co-authorship (Figure 2.19), where co-publication increased from 22 percent in 1987 to 55 percent in 2006, but also a progressive re-orientation toward more collaborations with European partners.

But not only do the bibliometric studies agree in finding a sharp increase in scientific collaboration. Other sources of information confirm this increase. Figure 2.20 shows the participation of major research funding available in Europe for international cooperation, namely the European Framework Program. The figure shows the participation in the Seventh Framework Program, one year before it ended, with a sample of 151 projects; when the program was terminated, a total of 168 projects had been funded for a total amount of €430 million.[14] Arab Mediterranean countries comprise 304 institutions and EU countries comprise 1,328 institutions. Other participants include Associated Countries (Israel and Turkey) with 65 participations, and other countries with 303 participations.

6.3 Inter-Arab cooperation

Our investigation of research practices at AUB, the Lebanese University (LU) and USJ (in Chapter 4) shows limited Arab inter-regional cooperation (Hanafi *et al.* 2013). This concurs with the work of Antoine Zahlan, who points out that there have been some 1,000 research papers published on aquifers by scientists, though few scientists collaborate to enable them to bring their expertise to serve the entire region (Zahlan 2012: 193). The extraordinary National Priorities Research Program (NPRP) (hosted by the Qatar Foundation (QF) in 2006) has

Table 2.10 Partner countries of three Arab producers

Rank	Tunisia		Egypt		Lebanon	
	Country	Percentage	Country	Percentage	Country	Percentage
1	France	77.0	United States	27.9	France	37.0
2	United States	5.7	Germany	14.9	United States	32.3
3	Germany	4.1	Saudi Arabia	12.4	United Kingdom	10.1
4	Italy	3.7	Japan	10.3	Canada	6.9
5	Belgium	3.6	United Kingdom	8.6	Bahrain	4.5
6	Canada	3.6	Canada	5.3	Italy	3.8
7	United Kingdom	3.1	Italy	4.1	Saudi Arabia	3.2
8	Morocco	2.2	Belgium	3.1	Germany	–
9	Spain	2.1	France	2.9	Australia	–
10	Algeria	1.5	Spain	2.2	Egypt	–

Sources: Web of Science; data treated by OST, France (for ESTIME project). Published in UNDP and Al Maktoum Foundation, 2009, p. 199.

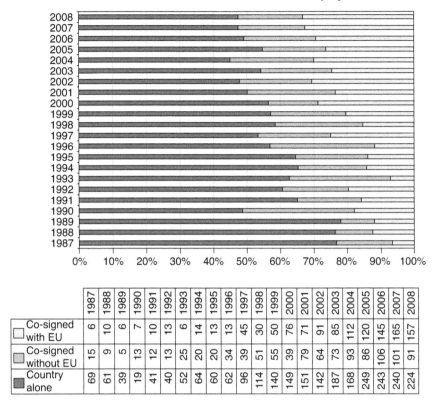

	1987	1988	1989	1990	1991	1992	1993	1994	1995	1996	1997	1998	1999	2000	2001	2002	2003	2004	2005	2006	2007	2008
Co-signed with EU	6	10	6	7	10	13	6	14	13	13	45	30	50	76	71	91	85	112	120	145	165	157
Co-signed without EU	15	9	5	13	12	13	25	20	20	34	39	51	55	39	79	64	73	93	86	106	101	91
Country alone	69	61	39	19	41	40	52	64	60	62	96	114	140	149	151	142	187	168	249	243	240	224

Figure 2.19 Publications and co-authorship: Lebanon 1987–2008.

many collaborations, but few are with the Arab world (15 percent of total awarded collaborative institutions and 13 percent of the total awarded proposals). One of the hypotheses could be the poor advice of some of the experts in terms of education[15] and research: after all, why would a famous American corporation, such as RAND, encourage QA to carry-out an inter-Arab collaboration? RAND is indeed a "non-profit" global policy think-tank first formed to offer research and analysis to the US armed forces by Douglas Aircraft Company. It is currently financed by the US government, private endowment, corporations including the healthcare industry and universities.[16] As QF recently ended its contact with RAND, we hope Qatar would rethink its inter-Arab collaboration.

In the Gulf area, we notice a recent increase in co-publications within the Gulf region (Table 2.12). As we see, the UAE and Saudi Arabia have the most co-publications, although these figures vary (23 and 19 publications, respectively) (Hitti 2011). Still, figures are low.

Collaboration is weak even within the same country. Our survey in Lebanon among AUB faculty found that interviewees at AUB collaborate both with other

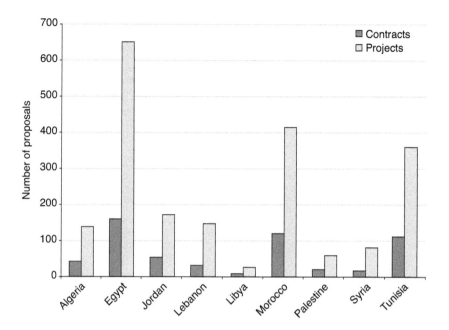

Figure 2.20 Arab participation (partner countries to EU) in the EU's Seventh Framework Program (2007–2011) (source: Cordis database; data up-to-date on 15 November 2011).

Note
151 projects evaluated at that time in the Cordis database with Mediterranean countries participation. "Projects" means submitted projects. "Contracts" means mainlisted projects in order to negotiate a final contract. Actual contracts may have been lower. The data do not cover the whole period of the Seventh Framework Program, only 2007–2011.

faculty members at AUB and with other researchers abroad, notably through contacts formed during PhD and post-doctoral years. However, very few had ever collaborated with researchers in Lebanon not affiliated with AUB. A professor in the Faculty of Medicine mentioned that "scientists in the Arab region do not communicate with one another – they tend to remain in the same field, whereas scientists abroad communicate and evolve in their research" (Hanafi *et al.* 2013). This is a quite common, but partly faulty, perception. In fact, the survey done on international collaboration by the MIRA project tends to show that the behavior of Arab scientists is not very different from that of their European, Turkish or Israeli counterparts. The main difference between Arab researchers and Europeans is instead a lack of time to do research (Gaillard *et al.* forthcoming) and it may be the difficulty of obtaining a visa to northern countries that impedes many researchers from being trained in Western laboratories, as one professor from Yarmouk University reported.

Table 2.11 Geographical distribution of NPRP (2007–2011)

Region	Collaborative institutions submitted		Collaborative institutions awarded		Proposals submitted	Proposals awarded	
	Number		*Number*	*Percentage*	*Number*	*Number*	*Percentage*
Arab	271		27	15	171	35	13
Canada	97		15	8	103	26	9
America	558		66	37	525	137	50
UK	181		30	17	111	22	8
EU	447		17	9	130	15	5
Asia and Australia	393		24	13	207	41	15
Total	1,947		179	100	1,247	276	100

Source: Al-Taie (2013).

Table 2.12 Co-publication between the Gulf countries (2005)

Country	Bahrain	Kuwait	Oman	Qatar	Saudi Arabia	UAE	GCC	Total
Bahrain	0	0	1	0	4	3	2	10
Kuwait	0	0	3	0	4	5	3	15
Oman	1	3	0	1	3	4	1	13
Qatar	0	0	1	0	1	4	2	8
Saudi Arabia	4	4	3	1	0	5	2	19
UAE	3	5	4	4	5	0	2	23
GCC	2	3	1	2	2	2	0	12
Total	10	15	13	8	19	23	12	88

Source: Scopus cited by Zahlan (2012: 162).

7 Conclusion

There are many reasons for the relatively low production of knowledge on science in the Arab countries, but we can mention the four most important. First, in spite of the fact that most researchers in the Arab region belong to higher education institutions, *research is often not on the agenda of these universities*. Many professors would probably engage in more research if their institution relied on an explicit statement favoring research, which is rarely the case.

Second, *the university promotion system* used by these institutions profoundly affects the productivity of faculty members. In the best cases, the recruitment and promotion systems mention the necessity to present a certain number of publications; in many cases, the system is not so clear and no such rule is made explicit. One issue worthy of notice is the type of documentation required as evidence of production. Another issue is the balance between publications and other types of activities.

Third, *local journals published in Arabic are rare*. Local periodicals of good scientific stature should be encouraged, not as academic department information papers but as relevant disciplinary ventures. This would promote the image of science in society; it would help young researchers to publish their work; and it would provide a venue for the diffusion of local scientific activity. While "five stars" professors are capable of publishing books, young researchers need journals to publish their articles. Certain common pitfalls are to be avoided, such as irregular publication schedules, a lack of objective peer review and irrelevant topics to the local society.

Fourth, *the lack of a systematic analysis of research program impact*. A notable effort is being made to create observatories and indicators in science and technology in the region, but no sufficient effort was made to tackle the issue of the impact of research and the role of publications (MIRA 2011).

Notes

1 A landmark in this discussion has been the Paris UNESCO-ORSTOM Conference in 1990, proceedings published by Arvanitis and Gaillard (1992), freely available at the Horizon database: http://horizon.documentation.ird.fr/exl-doc/pleins_textes/pleins_textes_6/colloques2/36935.pdf.
2 See http://srv5.eulc.edu.eg/eulc_v5/libraries/start.aspx?ScopeID=1.&.
3 The Scimago Journal and Country Rank is a portal that includes the journals and country scientific indicators developed from the information contained in the Scopus database.
4 The H-index, named after the Argentinian physicist Jorge Hirsch, was proposed in 2005. An H-index is the highest number (H) of articles that are cited at least H times. The index works very differently from one scientific field to another.
5 http://act.fondation.org.ma/fondation1_fr/perio_lat.asp.
6 Ismael Rafols, personal communication, based on ongoing research (under-reporting research relevant to local needs in the Global South; database biases in the representation of knowledge in rice). To be presented in an international conference on the transformation of research systems, January 2016 (Paris).
7 This ranking is based on 13 performance indicators, grouped into five areas. Teaching: the learning environment (worth 30 percent of the overall ranking score). Research: volume, income and reputation (worth 30 percent). Citations: research influence (worth 30 percent). Industry income: innovation (worth 2.5 percent). International outlook: staff, students and research (worth 7.5 percent). See www.timeshighereducation.co.uk/world-university-rankings/2014–15/world-ranking/methodology.
8 www.usnews.com/education/arab-region-universities.
9 http://scholarlyoa.com/publishers.
10 Disciplines in academia do not necessarily follow the classification by fields used in databases. Moreover, indicators are very sensitive to changes in the numbers of articles that have been indexed by the database. Finally, the production of a specific university can be strongly underestimated due to incorrect affiliations and wrong or different forms of writing a specific affiliation. Databases like Scopus and WoS have tried to correctly follow-up the affiliations of authors but there are still large parts of the production that can be missed.
11 A few other journals publish in both English and Arabic, such as the *Arab Gulf Journal for Scientific Research.*
12 See, for instance, Glänzel (2001); Adams *et al.* (2007); Schmoch and Schubert (2008); Mattsson *et al.* (2008).
13 Asia-8 is composed of South Korea, India, Indonesia, Malaysia, Philippines, Singapore, Taiwan and Thailand.
14 The data on the participation of Arab countries in the preceding EU Sixth Framework Program have been published in the Arab Knowledge Report (Al Maktoum Foundation and UNDP 2009: 193).
15 The most flagrant poor advice was to push a sudden shift into English language in the Qatari school curricula. According to Ramzi Nasser (2014), students coming out of schools performed at the lower quartile in the standardized tests at the SAT and TOEFL internationally in 1999. In 2011 Qatar was ranked low in the average math scores of fourth-grade students.
16 "Research and development" has long since expanded to working with other governments, private foundations, international organizations and commercial organizations on a host of non-defense issues. RAND Europe is located in Cambridge, United Kingdom, and Brussels, Belgium. The RAND-Qatar Policy Institute is in Doha, Qatar (since 2003). The RAND-Qatar Policy Institute has been instrumental in setting up the Qatar National Research Fund for defining the QEERI research portfolio. For further information the reader is encouraged to go to www.rand.org/qatar.html.

3 Universities, researchers and diaspora

The institution, as keeper of past research and promoting new activities in line with today's needs, is protecting research as a profession but research, as a mode of living, is protecting the institution against itself and its permanent temptation to be out of this world.

(Hannoyer 1996: 394; authors' translation)

Knowledge production cannot be understood without investigating both the locus of research (institutions) and the researchers themselves. As far as Arab countries are concerned, research is very much concentrated in universities. Few countries have research centers, usually mission-oriented (agriculture), and very little research is done by private enterprises. Thus, research depends strongly on the university context, and the Arab countries in this respect are a laboratory of new globalized developments concerning higher education, where numerous new universities appear, mainly private, and where the pressures of international-ization, privatization and globalization are very strong (Romani 2012).

1 Universities as teaching and research institutions

Higher education varies strongly in the Arab world from country to country. Algeria, Egypt and Morocco are on the path to mass higher education; hence they possess a larger reservoir of teachers doing research. Some countries lacking a proper university system are also on the ascendant, including Libya, Syria and Iraq (which in fact had a famous educational system before war ravaged the country). The rest have developed a national system with universal access, but limited capacity.

Since the emblematic *Beit al Hikma* (House of Wisdom) in twelfth-century Baghdad – which remains a permanent historical remembrance as important for Arabs as is the Athens Lykeion for the Western world – higher education has historically played a central role in forming elites endowed with a cultural capital. By completing studies as law makers, doctors or engineers, students who already belonged to the economic and political elite were acquiring high prestige (and a social function) in a typical reproductive manner. Following independences, and in close relation to the political national projects, we witness a very profound transformation of the universities, in the Arab world as elsewhere, where different types of universities compete on an international market of competences. Universities were strongly related to the training of the state personnel, in a typical developmental scheme, in a dominant position where some schools and universities were asked to provide all the necessary highly trained personnel needed for developing the country. For some 30 years, this need has been modified, mainly through a marketization of knowledge (both in teaching and research) and the diversification of the resources that fund the activities of the universities. As a consequence, a diversification of the training of the universities is ongoing, not entirely due to its own internal needs and dynamic, but with the help of very active policies that have "accompanied" the institutional changes. Additionally, in many Arab countries, the language of interaction has been different from one university to the other, and other languages than Arabic have been used, such as English and French, for teaching and also as working languages. Language issues are indeed very sensitive and political (Suleiman 2003; Hitti 2011).

1.1 The different types of universities

One can find three – or maybe four, as we will see – types of universities in the Arab region. The first type is the public university, which absorbs the overwhelming majority of students. Being often a national university, it generally uses Arabic-language curricula. Political censorship and repression has limited critical approaches, especially in public institutions (UNDP 2003). Maghreb countries (with the exception of Libya) and Egypt have been examples of these public universities. The massification of education in Egypt, Syria and Maghreb countries, where a free education allows a large proportion of the population access to it, albeit very important in the post-independence era, has led to an increase in the quantity of students but at the expense of the quality of the training offered. In addition, universities have been plagued with various difficulties: lack of proper faculty salary, poor libraries and teaching resources, out-dated curricula,[1] enormous logjams of students, lack of financial resources for research and poor knowledge of foreign languages. All these factors affect the level of education in these universities. In many national universities in the Arab region, the vast majority of faculty members are hampered by heavy teaching loads and institutional administrative work (Hanafi 2011). A faculty member at Yarmouk University (Jordan) pointed this out: "I have done a lot of teaching, capacity building and obtaining projects for the university." The university professors do not suffer the pressure of publication everywhere in the same way. In the Arab east, Lebanon and Jordan mainly, the pressure is very strong. On the contrary, in Maghreb countries, there was, until recently, no relation between publication and promotion. According to the Moroccan sociologist Mohamed Cherkaoui (2008), only 45 percent of social science professors in Moroccan national universities have published at least once (academic journal, book, report, newspapers).

Faculties of Medicine have usually escaped the common diseases of the public universities, in particular in Egypt. They remain prestigious, recruit the sons of the elite, work as public services in close relation with important hospitals, and allow for a certain mix of public professional activity with private practice (Moulin 2015). They also shelter research activities that translate into abundant clinical papers, but research is usually the place for biologists rather than medical doctors, less prestigious an activity than medical practice, which might also (partly) explain why bio-medical research has a strong female research potential in all Arab countries. In any case, national public universities remain the backbone of higher education and are the main locus of research.

The second type of university is the selective private university. The older ones were founded by missionaries, and related to a religious educational project. One can find these universities mainly in Lebanon and the Arab east, as private non-profit universities which attract the elite and upper middle class. We can mention some of the more prestigious: the English-speaking American University of Beirut (AUB), its immediate competitor, the French-speaking Université Saint Joseph (USJ), and the American University in Cairo, or the Lebanese-American University. Lebanon hosts also some smaller community-driven universities (the pontifical Notre Dame University, the Holy Spirit of Kaslik University, and so on) (see Chapter 4). Most of these Christian universities were only marginally teaching religious matters or theology, contrary to the old and prestigious Islamic universities such as Al-Azar in Cairo (but in fact installed as a university only in 1961), Zitouna University (integrated in 1961 as a Faculty of Theology in the University of Tunis), Al-Quaraouiyine University in Morocco or the more recent Islamic University in Medina (also founded in 1961, known for its Wahhabi orientation).

The creation of private universities has not always been the result of marketization, as shown in the case of Lebanon, where there was no public university until the foundation of the Lebanese University in 1951. The older Christian private universities are very selective, rather expensive, teach exclusively in English or French and have a distinct linkage to specific social classes and communities. They fit quite well the description of a university described by Bourdieu (1984: 214), which entails a fundamentally conservative institution that reproduces and reinforces social class distinctions.

Less consistent with this view are the new private universities. One such example is the Lebanese International University (founded in 2000) which really is very emblematic of this switch from mass education to market education (Kabbanji 2012: 6). "Lebanon is the country of the 32 banks and 41 universities" was the comment of an interviewee, which gives the exact measure of the exceptionality of the Lebanese case. Nonetheless, the buoyant private sector is certainly meeting some social and economic needs, in this case directly linked to the knowledge economy. It challenges directly the older selective not-for-profit universities by creating a market that is disconnected from the old social hierarchies.

Until recently, except for Lebanon, only the Gulf countries had known these market-oriented universities.[2] Usually prestigious, linked to the United States, funded by oil (see the emblematic case of King Abdullah University of Science and Technology [KAUST] launched by a personal contribution of the king and a contribution of ARAMCO, creating a trust fund), these universities are hiring renowned foreign professors, very generously remunerated, in exchange for high article production and the establishment of strong foreign linkages. More recently, the branding of a foreign university locally is becoming a new strategy. It still remains to know whether this merchandising will finally produce a local dynamic, although it seems the extreme internationalization is the main orientation of these rather unique university institutions.[3] In other countries than the oil-rich Gulf economies, privatization has become a strong tendency. Jordan opened its first private for-profit university in 1990, followed by Egypt and Syria. In Morocco, for a long time there existed only one private university, but two new private establishments were founded in 2006 (Université Internationale de Rabat) and 2008 (École de Gouvernance et d'Économie de Rabat). The emergence of private universities has accelerated the two-tier education system that has different speeds and segregates social classes (Akkari 2009).

The creation of different types of elite-training institutions, more or less linked to the local economy and society, has many impacts on society that go beyond that of research or access to the labor market (Bristol-Rhys 2008), and sometimes with paradoxical effects. For instance, Tremblay (2011) highlights the fact that women's access to the expensive private universities in the Gulf has not translated into their access to the labor market. The university becomes a major site of struggles over the production of cultural norms, as well as of social inequalities (Bourdieu 1984; Ringer 1991; Sabour 1988). Hanafi (2011) has already shown the compartmentalization of scholarly activities in the Arab universities and the demise of the university as a public sphere. Among the aspects that concern this new context, research plays a particular role in defining "selectiveness" of universities, but also in producing the conditions for distinctions based not only on previous social status, but new social inequalities based on knowledge.

1.2 Research in the universities

Research has mainly, until now, been rooted in the public universities and the older selective universities. The existence of good universities is an essential aspect for research to exist, but hardly the only one. A research "system" needs not only talented persons and good training, but also a variety of other institutions (mission-oriented research centers, technology transfer mechanisms, training facilities, specific infrastructure, recurrent funding, stable social and political conditions, collectively approved management rules and many others) that help ground research inside the university and give the ability to address national demands, propose novel solutions to societal challenges, or simply identify viable, unnoticed, promising niches for new knowledge creation (Mouton and Waast 2009).

Tables 3.1 and 3.2 summarize some of the indicators concerning available resources inside the university system and the research potential. Preparing

Table 3.1 Distribution of countries according to GDP per capita and number of researchers per million inhabitants

Country	Expenditures in higher education				Number of universities (2006)	Students				
	Million US$ (2008)	Percentage of GDP (2008)	Percentage of government budget (2007)	Per student (2007)		Number of students (2007)	MSc students (2006) in science and technology	MA students (2006) in social sciences and humanities	PhD students (2006) in science and technology	PhD students (2006) in social sciences and humanities
Egypt	1,300	0.8		$757	31	1,776,699	50,287	28,445	14,609	9,202
Iraq										
Syria	454	1.04	3.57	$814		558,131				
Libya					13					
Algeria	636	0.8			26		15,308	9,873	7,689	4,917
Mauritania					1					
Morocco	777	0.92	3.8	$2,748	15	282,724	6,117	6,500	6,702	4,147
Tunisia	681.80	2.04	6.45	$1,948	?	350,000	6,854	11,730		
Bahrain					16		83	468	1	0
Kuwait					9					
Oman					4		263	302	1	0
Qatar					7					
Saudi Arabia	6,100	1.30	1.90	$8,186	17	670,341	3,403	5,733	338	1,862
UAE					33	30,200				
Sudan					21					
Yemen							496	1,494		
Jordan				$763	26	200,000	779	799	30	
Lebanon	118	0.5		$1,635	41	147,600				6

Table 3.2 Researchers

Country	Researchers		Researchers per one million inhabitants (2007)	Estimates on full-time equivalents (FTEs) (2008)	FTEs per million population (2007)	Number of scientists and engineers in refereed journals (2010)
	Number of researchers (2005)					
Egypt	33,481		420	13,941	617	7,669
Iraq						499
Syria						75
Libya	390		61			24
Algeria	5,764		170	5,944	170	2,283
Mauritania				411		19
Morocco	17,516		166	4,699	647	1,877
Tunisia	25,445		492	5,625	1,588	4,041
Bahrain	1,000		1,759.33			222
Kuwait	158		152	634	166	894
Oman	1,200		613.08	548	19.71	698
Qatar	10.5		42	789	464.12	567
Saudi Arabia	716.07		41			5,176
UAE	3,500		3,314.5	875	116.66	1,717
Sudan	12,615		290			
Yemen				486		
Jordan	42,151		280	2,223	1,952	
Lebanon	13,316		200	565	178	

researchers begins with investing in higher education. This is shown with state education budgets ranging from 0.8 percent of GDP for Egypt and Algeria to 1.2 percent of GDP in Tunisia. However, actual investment is larger, as budget allocations do not include private and not-for-profit universities.

Higher education institutions produce a huge number of students: approximately 1.8 million in Egypt, including 102,000 graduate students; and 750,000 in Saudi Arabia, including 11,000 graduate students. The number of students in the Arab region has increased considerably, from 5.4 million in 2000 to 7.3 million in 2008. In 2000, there were 1,907 students for every 100,000 inhabitants. By 2008, this number had increased to 2,185 (UNESCO 2010a: 68). These figures explain part of the complicated equation in the Arab countries. Figure 3.1 shows the development of the academics in Arab universities, which has been steadily increasing since 1965. Note, however, that figures in Egypt and the Gulf began to increase only in 1995. In 2008 Arab countries spent $16.26 billion on higher education for 6.62 million students (Mrad 2011). Even if the formerly very steep increase in the curve should begin to flatten, it remains the case that the growth of the learned world is increasing greatly in the Arab populations. This learned portion of the population battles now to find its role inside the economy. If only one explanation should have been brought to explain the acceptance of the "knowledge economy" as a project for the Arab world, maybe it lies there: the huge number of persons that have university degrees and seek a job in their country.

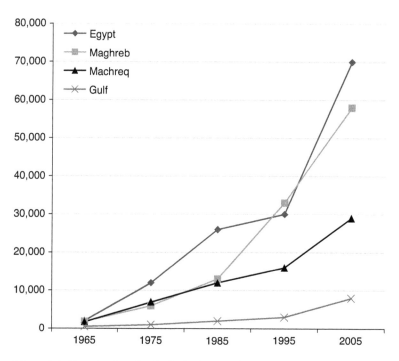

Figure 3.1 Growth of academics in Arab countries (1965–2005) (source: Waast 2010).

It is very difficult to draw a direct correlation between the number of graduates and the number of researchers, as many students and academics do not go into research. And effectively, the share of "publishing" academics, visible in the international arena, moreover through publications in refereed journals indexed by the Web of Science (WoS) or Scopus is certainly much smaller than the actual numbers of graduates. The reason is not only related to language but to the fact that many Arab universities are not research universities, even if their bylaws state otherwise. From 33,481 researchers in Egypt, statistics suggest that 13,941 are on full-time equivalent (FTE), but indeed only half of them will publish in refereed journals. The FTE in Egypt (at least for those years before the new policy framework) was certainly exaggerated, as we know it is rare for the actual research activity of teaching staff in public and most private universities to exceed 5–10 percent of their total academic duties, whereas it forms 35–50 percent of academic duties in European and American universities (UNDP 2009: 190).

Thus, researchers are located mainly in universities and public research centers.[4] In a country like Egypt, which has some strong public research centers, higher education hosts 65 percent of R&D (IDSC 2007; UNESCO 2010b: 257). In countries where the public funding is not oriented toward public research centers but rather the universities, the proportion of university faculty members dedicated to research can grow very high. Finally, private for-profit universities seem unable to invest as strongly as public universities or selective private universities into research.

Finally, a word is necessary on gender distribution. A recent study that relies primarily on government data from ten Arab countries (Salih 2008) shows that women accounted for 40 percent of researchers in Egypt and Kuwait, 30 percent in Algeria and Qatar and 20 percent in Morocco and Jordan. Their numbers fell to between 14 and 4 percent in Oman, Yemen and Mauritania.[5] In the MIRA Survey, women represent around one-third of the sample. Interestingly, more women are located in the biological sciences than engineering, and they can be predominant in high-level international institutions dedicated exclusively to research.

2 The ingredients of a scientific community

Scientific communities are structured to support competition as well as cooperation within its members. They usually have different functions: the formation of research teams and vibrant scientific associations, publishing and circulating ideas and research results, debating scientific subjects, peer reviewing and recruiting of their future peers. In brief, the concept of scientific communities relies on the idea that an interested collection of individuals, beyond their particular institutional affiliation, will join in an effort to investigate a particular object: a soil, the climate, a material, a disease, a process, a theorem, a social activity. As research grows, the nature of these objects changes and the frontiers between the objects and the methods to study them change also.

Contrary to an academic discipline that needs to identify cohorts of students under the same name (e.g., history, biology, mathematics, geography, sociology, physics), research is more interested in the shifting frontiers between disciplinary borders. Scientific communities are thus moving also and depend upon the vigor of the research activity itself, the resources available, the personnel that can be mobilized. The landscape of research is thus much more mobile and complex than institutional distinctions in academia. In the non-hegemonic countries and the developing countries, it has been argued, a long time ago, that they lack effective "scientific communities" (Gaillard *et al.* 1997b). Nonetheless, this statement signals two interconnected processes: a process of institutionalization of science (the creation of institutions, structures, funding and evaluation mechanisms) and the creation of fora for the discussion. These two processes seem to be usually connected, although, as is mentioned by Hocine (Khelfaoui 2004) in the case of Algeria, this is not necessarily the case. One can have an "institutionalization without professionalization," in the sense that the scientific profession is not vibrant, whereas the universities and the research centers, as well as other institutions, exist – at least nominally.

2.1 Two pillars: scientific associations and solid research teams

The creation of scientific community needs two pillars: scientific "associations" (we use the word in a large sense, not in the sense of an NGO), and research "teams" (collectives of recognized researchers, working together). Or, to put it differently, a scientific community is composed of peers and colleagues. The peers are recognized by other peers – it's the definition of a peer. A chemist working on catalysis will be immediately recognized as a "catalyst" by a French, Algerian or American catalyst. They write in the same journals, they publish on the same subjects and they participate in the same conferences. Historically, scientific associations have played a fundamental role in overcoming the institutional limitations and at the same time opening research avenues. This was the origin of the famous British Association for the Advancement of Science and its little sister in the Americas, the AAAS. They are important not only because of a need to discuss and exchange, but also because they permit validation of a topic, a method, a procedure, a research result. Publication itself comes well after this previous circulation of ideas and preliminary results. That is where the actual results get a social value.

In the Arab world, scientific associations are few and rather low in activity, with some notable exceptions. In the social sciences, the Lebanese and Tunisian associations for sociology, the Lebanese, Egyptian and Sudanese ones for psychology seem rather active. Less so the association in basic sciences, like soil sciences or the environment, mainly because the large worldwide associations are dominant and provide the usual fora for research. In the applied science, medical doctors and engineers are particularly well organized, but this relates rather to the professional aspects, the defense of the working conditions, like the professional unions, the self-organizing bodies like the Orders of Medics or

Lawyers. They also take charge in the scientific lectures, training and continuous education of their members. In Jordan, our survey shows that the state does not encourage the establishment of scientific associations unless members are co-opted (e.g., Jordanian Sociological Association). At the regional level, there are again many associations, but often inactive. The Arab sociological association has only two activities: summer schools for graduate students and a journal. The Arab Society for Economic Research has (supposedly annual) conferences (13 since 1989) and a journal issued four times per year. One should highlight the effort conducted by the Center for Arab Unity Studies (CAUS), the Arab Center for Research and Policy Studies (ACRPS) and recently by the Arab Council for Social Science (ACSS) for their role triggering regional encounters. CAUS has helped four Arab scientific association by co-publishing their journals.[6] There are also two pan-Arab/pan-Islamic organizations – the Arab League Educational, Cultural and Scientific Organization (ALECSO), and the Islamic Education, Science and Culture Organization (ISESCO) – both of which played a minor role in organizing the Arab scientific community.

The second pillar is the consolidation of research teams. The role of universities and the state could be decisive in this respect. The best example in the last years in the Arab world has been Tunisia, as we already mentioned in Chapter 1. This country had been experiencing sluggish growth in its scientific production until the end of the 1990s. After that, it decided to reform its research funding system. Intriguingly, Tunisia has a very centralized research system, which served its purpose. In effect, contrary to a general tendency around the world, Tunisia preferred to emphasize core funding rather than competitive project funding. It based the funding mechanism on a national evaluation system that permits the identification of research units that will receive funding directly by the Ministry of Research, rather than project calls. The evaluation is done by an independent body: the National Evaluation Committee of Scientific Research Activities (CNEARS), established in 1996, which is responsible for the evaluation of activities of scientific research programs, projects and results. It also evaluates the public research organizations and research programs of private companies that benefit from public support. After 2008, the CNEARS identified around 330 units and 250 laboratories. These entities, mainly inside the universities and public research organizations, sign a contract with the ministry that allows them to guarantee their basic funding and covers salaries for permanent staff and other running costs (65 percent) and the rest for the investment budget (35 percent). This has stabilized the research structures inside universities and research centers on a four-year basis, with an interim evaluation after two years. Additionally, the same units can access non-targeted project-based funding representing around 16 percent of gross expenditure in research and development (GERD). This competitive project funding mechanism, called PRF, encourages labs to create research consortia. This system explains why the need for an agency on a project basis was less felt in Tunisia. Let us also remember that this system has been particularly effective since Tunisia has increased its production four-fold since the early year 2000s.

It should be mentioned also for the record that Tunisia was the home, in the late 1980s, of the only genuine experiment of an independent funding agency generated by the scientific community itself: the National Foundation for Scientific Research in Tunisia (1989–1992). This particular political creation, a short-lived experiment, was the product of a particular political situation when Tunisia had abandoned its programming of research period and when scientist and academics, led by a respected and highly esteemed professor of physics, Professor Ali El-Hili, proposed to the government the creation of this agency (Siino 2004: 273–281). The agency was dismissed not because of its inefficiency; on the contrary, all Tunisian scientists that experienced this period insist that it was a very efficient and agile institution. It disappeared because of a strong political disagreement internal to the Tunisian administration which was resolved by the creation of a Secrétariat d'Etat à la Recherche Scientifique inside the Ministry of Higher Education. El-Hili himself stated that the death of his foundation was the victory of the administrative routine against political innovation (Siino 2004: 281). In any case, this was the only genuine independent agency that ever existed in the Arab world.

In the last years, in all Arab countries there was the creation of a new policy framework, very much influenced by relations with the European Union (EU). It consists of creating funding agencies that distribute funds based on project competition. The immediate success of these funds in Egypt or Morocco, and the eager willingness of researchers to participate in the competition, is very telling of the need for "clean" procedures that permit identification of the research activity. As we have shown in a recent report (Arvanitis *et al.* 2014), the funding agencies have had a massive response to the calls for projects that they have launched in the late years in an effort to promote research. Funding has increased, alongside opportunities to collaborate with foreign scientists. Moreover, as the Tunisian example shows, the recognition of the research activities inside the public budgets and inside the universities, with clearly identifiable budgets and teams, with an agenda that is defined for a specific period (four years in the particular case of Tunisia), played a fundamental role. The cases of Egypt, Jordan and Tunisia show that a strong institutional change in the policy toward research funding seems to have triggered a real shift in production. More money distributed through competitive projects, international collaborative projects and recognition of research activities seem to be key features in all these countries. The reason why this particular mix of funding instruments is functioning will be the object of the concluding remarks of this part of the book. For the time being, we should insist on the fact that all these procedures are helping research teams to get adequate funding and recognition for their research activities.

State support is essential in this process, as is generally the case for all research-related activities. We can suggest two examples of insufficient state support that hindered research. Each Arab country counts on a strong institution for statistics and population studies that produce census data as well as labor, revenues and household surveys. Many researchers we interviewed complained that detailed statistics were not available for researchers: either they were expensive or simply inaccessible, considered as a state secret.[7] Authoritarian Arab states (Yahya 2014)[8] have used statistics as a bio-political tool in the Foucauldian sense of control and surveillance of their population, but certainly not as a research instrument.

A second example comes from Qatar, which for a few years has offered important funding for research that aims at serving the local and international research community. Qatar announced a QNRF budget of US$180 million for 2014, which represents less than 1 percent of GDP[9] (far away from the more than 2 percent of GDP announced in research, but nonetheless a gigantic amount when compared to the number of personnel); QNRF is the main funding instrument in Qatar and distributes all funds for research, and Qatar University received 45 percent of these funds. But when we browse the WoS, it hardly feels like "local" research teams are at play. Many of the authors were temporarily affiliated to one of the Qatari research institutions and ended up outside of this country. The normative imposes that 65 percent of funding and 50 percent of the research effort should be spent in Qatar, but even with this provision it does not really seem possible to consolidate Qatari research teams. It is rather that the Qatari model consists of associating very closely the local research community with international co-authors. Moreover, as we mentioned above, "Qatari" here does not refer only to Qatari nationals but also to residents of Qatar, more often than not Arabs spending most of their professional life in Qatar.

The weak institutionalization of the scientific community makes the scientific field (*champ* in the sense of Bourdieu) easy to influence by exogenous social and political forces. The lack of autonomy of the scientific field relates to both the weak institutionalization and to a weak self-organization. The lack of autonomy is problematic because it gives a rather strong leverage position to bureaucrats, administrators, provosts, chancellors, deans, university presidents and other academic authorities based, as Bourdieu (1984) mentions, on the "bureaucratic principles of temporal powers over the scientific field."[10] Without the recognition of a specific research activity, without a certain autonomy and freedom of speech, research will never prosper, and not only because of the authoritarian regimes. As a young professor from the University of Jordan said:

> Professors do research, only motivated by the need for promotion and personal interest.... When the university decides to fund research, some of our faculty hides the information. The old guard, those who have good relationships with the university bureaucrats, are the ones who capture most of the grants.[11]

2.2 Weak institutionalization

Scientific communities play an active role in regulating the debates over scientific results. In recent years, the debates on hot issues have become public, and what was once discussed internally has become the subject of public controversies.

This is the case of genomic research, reproductive technologies, genetically modified organisms (GMOs) used in agriculture as seed, climate change, risk management, vaccine campaigns, AIDS cures, and many other such subjects. For such debates, research should be discussed for its cognitive and epistemological content, as well as the sociological conditions that influence it. But it is rather rare to have such debates in the Arab world. What gets in the way is a certain suspected bias related to the sources of funding of research centers or the personality of a researcher. Why this happens seems to us also the result of this weak institutionalization. Particular researchers cannot count on the support of their peers in this kind of debate, in part because locally there are too few peers that could serve as regulators of the debates.

An associate professor in humanities at AUB explained

> there is no scientific community in my field, regionally scholars are isolated. There are a lot of people who work on linguistics in Jordan, they do a lot of conferences (in English), but I don't go there because my university does not value such connection.

An assistant professor, also in humanities, mentions that "there is no scientific community," but while he does not "exchange work with people in the department and others at AUB or other universities, I don't feel isolated or alone, but neither am I part of a scientific community." An assistant professor in basic sciences informed us that "research in Lebanon is more difficult than in the States or in Germany, because isolation is the main problem." What appears from these comments, and more generally in the survey done inside the AUB, was that professors are rather good at connecting with foreign networks, at finding external funding, and at locating the right publishing outlets internationally. Simultaneously they don't feel the need for more local insertion. Of course, this is a generalization, but it is based on the majority of the interviews at AUB. In the Lebanese University, some professors said they were fighting against what they call an "elite-oriented" structure, seeking "to be inserted into the local intellectual life," to "participate in the reconstruction of the country" and other similar declarations that show a clear rejection of the tendency of the AUB "to be oriented towards the US and less engaged locally." It seems that the weak institutionalization plays the role of increasing this opposition between the local and the foreign, the participation in the relevant national development issues or the international agenda. As decisions to enter into a research topic, a debate, a research activity seem to be taken individually, rather than guided by some collective body, the researcher is immediately confronted with a basic dilemma: either he gets inserted and recognized internationally or he remains locally subject to economic and other pressures that will weaken his research.

What has appeared clearly from this work in Lebanon, which we will review in more detail in the next chapter, is the extreme fragmentation of the scientific field. It takes the form of compartmentalization of the scientific community, not only in the social sciences, as we have heard, but also in "hard" sciences.

In Lebanon, the very few people who work in nano-technology are dispersed, one in each research university without collaboration between them. In the social sciences, the division we have just pointed to, between the "elite" scientists that publish abroad and the locally based ones, produce also a compartmentalized elite.[12]

Before advancing, it might be useful to mention the argument we have heard so often. Lebanon is a small country, thus it is difficult to have a "critical mass" in any scientific domain. This lack of "critical mass" is also raised elsewhere (e.g., Mouton and Waast 2009). The concentration of knowledge production is a well-documented phenomenon: a small number of establishments and scientists produce the bulk of results in most sciences. A more refined analysis (per establishment and per field and topic) may, however, give a better result: in countries such as Morocco and Jordan (even in leading establishments), there are no more than a bunch of successful research niches; and within each of these, no more than ten very active researchers and 20 more episodic contributors (Kleiche and Waast 2008). As a result, the quality of national research remains fragile and there may be problems regarding the reproduction, updating and renewal of research methods, and research topics.

Usually, the notion of "critical mass" is used to explain that after a certain quantity of personnel and resources are accumulated, some successful process is triggered that favors research. The idea was clearly stated by De Solla Price (1963) when he was explaining the creation of a scientific community leading to "big science," in particular in fields established following World War II, such as nuclear and high-energy physics. However, no one has yet proven what is the "right" critical mass for triggering the construction of a scientific community. The concept has in fact no empirical basis, and the statistical calculation offered by De Solla Price was limited to a period of exceptional growth within the research community. Of course, numbers count, and having 60 researchers in an area is certainly better than having only one or two, although research can be the result of collaboration and these could very well be maintained by "low-level" activity. But there is no minimal figure: what certainly happens is the need to have a way to demonstrate collectively the validity of the knowledge produced. In the absence of a research community, of strong institutions, and enough activity for discussions, whatever the size, there will be no "critical mass."

2.3 Research as an autonomous activity

We can offer no solution to the difficulties posed by this weak – or non-existent – scientific community. As Roland Waast (2006) has stated, research gets strong when there is an unspoken "pact" between scientists and society. This pact is the following: researchers get sufficient autonomy, even political autonomy, and means to work, but they, in turn, will guarantee the quality of their production, that they will be as "objective" as possible, as useful as possible, producing both useful and valid knowledge of which the country can be proud. In Maghreb countries, this political recognition of research as an element of a national political project has been effective only in Tunisia. Morocco, after the authoritarian rule of Hassan II, began a political process that consolidated, in part, research – for example, with the creation of the Academy of Science, ironically called "Hassan II Academy of Science and Technology." Algeria, precisely because of the civil war, has been profoundly divided on the role of knowledge and culture in the political construction of the nation. In Lebanon, because of the existence of old and strong universities, a certain independence of the CNRS from other public administrations (following the UNESCO precepts of the 1960s that consisted of recommending researchers to manage scientific councils), research has been developed and is strongly connected internationally, but rarely has it been in a position to have sufficient strength locally and freedom from the sectarian system that rules the country. A paradox seems to unfold these days in Egypt, where the changes occur from inside the state, from the Ministry of Research, for reasons that are still unclear although we can mention the very strong connection built by science administrators and the scientists themselves with European partners.

What seems to be decisive is not so much the number of researchers but rather the connections of the research activity with non-research activities, be they economic, social or otherwise. Maybe it is useful to remember this elegant representation of the multiple functions research can satisfy called the "Rose of Winds" of research (Figure 3.2). Research produces knowledge that is certified

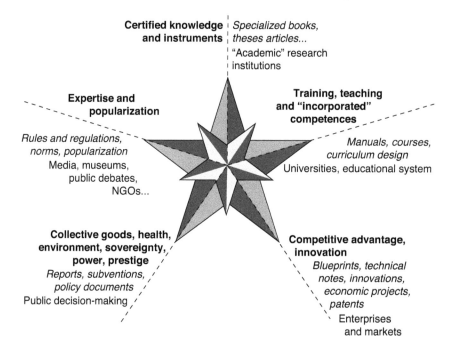

Figure 3.2 The "Rose of Winds" of research (source: Callon *et al.* 1997/Art by Lila Paleologou www.pelpal.gr).

to be valid (by the publication system, the reviewing by peers, and all procedures where knowledge is evaluated by other scientists), and its production is visible (and measurable!) in scientific journals and other publications; but, it also produces "incorporated" knowledge, that is knowledge that belongs to very specific persons that have received adequate training and are the only ones to adequately manage this knowledge; it produces knowledge that permits circulation of ideas, objects and material outside the scientific community (which explains why the phrase "popularization of science" was in use); it can produce a certain knowledge that is more complex than the relatively easy-to-manage expertise, a knowledge that is shared with non-scientists, for example when building a science base for public policies, that accompanies public agencies or private actors in implementing a specific policy for public goods and other difficult-to-manage issues; finally, specific actors can integrate knowledge produced by research (patenting, common developments, etc), either by buying knowledge or incorporating researchers themselves, as is the case with R&D collaborations between private companies and public research laboratories. In a more critical stance, Burawoy (2005) has also insisted on the connection between research and society (see Chapter 5), which relies on different uses of the knowledge produced by research.

3 Scientific diasporas: brain-drain and brain-gain

Currently, brain-drain is a major concern in the Arab region. Figures released by the Organisation for Economic Co-operation and Development (OECD) show that around one million highly qualified persons of Arab origin reside in the OECD countries. This number corresponds to 10 percent of the highly qualified population in the Arab region, and 20 percent of the corresponding population for the Maghreb countries (Wahishi 2010: 7).[13] In Table 3.3 we can see the number of Arab expatriates and the percentage of highly skilled expatriates by country of birth.

Mouton and Waast give us more details from the United States as the National Science Foundation in 2000 revealed that there are thousands of Arab scientists and engineers living in the United States: 12,500 Egyptians, 11,500 Lebanese, 5,000 Syrians, 4,000 Jordanians and 2,500 Palestinians (Mouton and Waast 2009). Scientists from Morocco and Tunisia tend to head for Europe (Siino 2004; Waast *et al.* 2010; UNESCO 2010a: 271). As can be seen in Table 3.3, the total number of researchers in Lebanon is only slightly larger than the number of Lebanese researchers employed in R&D in the United States. This shows the importance of the phenomenon of brain-drain.

The Arab region is considered one of the most active in exporting highly qualified human capital equipped with university degrees. Indeed, human capital is among the region's major exports, possibly equal to oil and gas in value. What little data are available support this claim: 45 percent of Arab students who study abroad do not return to their home countries; 34 percent of skilled doctors in Britain are Arabs; and the Arab region has contributed 31 percent of the skilled migration from developing states to the West, including 50 percent of doctors,

Table 3.3 Total number of Arab expatriates and percentage of highly skilled expatriates by country of birth

Country	Total number of expatriates	Of which highly skilled (percentage)
Algeria	1,301,076	16.4
Bahrain	7,424	40.6
Egypt	274,833	51.2
Iraq	294,967	28.2
Jordan	575,992	48.9
Kuwait	37,591	44.1
Lebanon	332,270	32.9
Libya	27,481	43.4
Mauritania	14,813	18.5
Morocco	1,364,754	14.8
Palestine	14,798	43.8
Oman	2,753	36.9
Qatar	3,384	43.3
Saudi Arabia	34,646	35.4
Sudan	42,086	40.5
Syria	126,372	34.1
Tunisia	371,274	17.7
UAE	14,589	23.9
Yemen	32,428	19.3

Source: Dumont and Lemaître 1985, table A26, using various sources and OECD calculations.

23 percent of engineers and 15 percent of scientists (Zahlan 2012; UNDP 2009: 208). Over 200,000 PhD holders (80 percent of all Arab doctorate holders), unable to connect with the local economy, emigrate (Mrad 2011). An IRD expert report on "scientific diasporas" reported on this topic in 2003, including an exceptional study by Jean Johnson, from which we extracted some indicators, alongside data from the ESTIME project (Table 3.4). There is a need to better understand the reasons for the scientific diaspora in relation to general emigration from the Arab region.

Table 3.4 Brain-drain from the Middle East: number of scientists and engineers established in the United States, 2000

	Egypt	Lebanon	Jordan	Syria	Palestine	Kuwait	Maghreb
Established in the United States	12,500	11,500	4,000	5,000	2,000	2,400	Few
Employed in R&D	4,400	4,900	2,000	1,800	700	1,200	Few
Researchers in the country*	75,000	6,000	6,500	N/A	N/A	2,400	40,000
Researchers in the country (FTE)*	15,000	600	750	400	N/A	500	8,000

Sources: Barré *et al.* (2003). * ESTIME www.estime.ird.fr.

The situation is very different in the Maghreb and the rest of the Arab region. According to the National Science Foundation, very few scientists from the Maghreb are established in the United States; rather, scientists from the Maghreb head to Europe (mainly France; Figure 3.3) and, more recently, Canada. A bibliometric study in the social sciences has recently proven that 60 percent of the most productive social scientists from Algeria are now living and employed abroad (50 percent of the 200 most productive, authoring more than one-third of Algeria's scientific production over the last 25 years). The proportion of Moroccan authors living abroad is much lower, representing 15 percent of the most productive (Waast and Rossi 2009). According to the Algerian trade unions, the number of Algerian scientists established abroad had increased from 2,400 in 1984 to 27,500 in 1994; in 1995, 90 percent of scholarship holders had never returned from abroad. To this should be added the well-known exodus of "highly qualified persons" (including a number of leading researchers and academics) during the civil war of the 1990s (Khelfaoui 2004). However, Hocine Labde-laoui argues that because of many "push" factors in France and an improvement of the situation in Algeria, many Algerian faculty and researchers have been convinced to return to their country (Lablaoui 2010).

There is a range of opinions on brain-drain. In many countries, the official point of view is that these emigrants are despicable traitors, who prefer their own material well-being to the interests of their homeland. Added to that is the claim

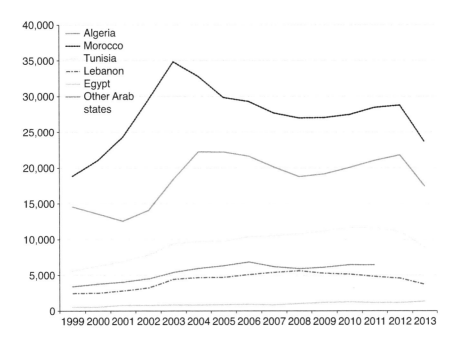

Figure 3.3 Number of Moroccans, Algerians and Tunisians in French universities (source: French Ministry of Higher Education; UNESCO).

that there is a deliberate "pirating of brains" by the wealthiest countries, at the expense of the poor countries which bore the costs of their education (Mouton and Waast 2009).

Researchers are not the only ones fleeing these countries, and there is no reason for them to remain hostages of governments that do not care (or know how) to use their talents. Moreover, this argument seems to indicate the idea that highly skilled individuals, because of their training, are somehow the property of the state. The view draws back to the concept of state-driven development, which was predominant in the post-World War II era (Gaillard *et al.* 1997b; Amsden 2001). Some recent studies have convincingly proven that most researchers' attitudes depend on national science policies, and on the movements of international industry. The North African case has been well-documented: if the profession is decently treated (status, income), scientific life can go on, and brain-drain is much lower. In these cases, students return home upon the completion of degrees abroad. They may give up lucrative careers in the emigration countries, preferring (managerial) positions in their home environment (Gérard and Kleiche 2002).

Another feature is noteworthy: since the decision of some multinational firms to invest in Morocco in 2010 (in high-tech production, and even in development research), the country has had to hastily develop a training plan to double the number of graduate engineers; it has been only partially able to meet this objective. Part of Morocco's appeal to these firms is the quality of its "elite" engineering schools (modeled on the example of French "Grandes Ecoles"); the same holds true of Tunisia. The lowered cost of managerial salaries in these Maghreb countries combined with the quality of the engineering training make these countries attractive to subsidiaries of multinational firms.

Another opinion is that there is no real brain-drain, but rather a natural flow of scientists to the best places in which to exercise their talents. The "marketplace of knowledge" will determine their settlement to the best effect, each place in the world will have what it "deserves," and the task of governments is to offer the best conditions to retain the best researchers. This view is becoming predominant and is attached to the multi-polar world system that has been emerging since the late 1980s, with the state's loss of control over their own training-to-employment system. However, some countries had very restrictive systems of scholarships for their most talented young students, which permitted them to be trained abroad in exchange for a promise of employment, usually in the public sector, upon their return. Such has been the case for example in Syria, and returnees that "escaped" their return obligation had to pay fines or, worse, had to confront menacing security services. Thus international mobility is not given, even for the highly skilled. Dumont and Lemaître argue that the largest developing countries seem not to be significantly affected by brain-drain, and indeed may benefit from the indirect effects of mobility; meanwhile, some of the smallest countries, especially in the Caribbean and Africa, face the emigration of large portions of their elite (Dumont and Lemaître 2005).

To overcome brain-drain, the working conditions for researchers should be improved (through provision of an environment conducive to research and the increase of their salaries). In Africa many studies show how brain drain has been, if not reversed, at least slowed down by simply providing better conditions. As Meyer *et al.* argue, there are two possible policies for developing countries to tap their expatriate professional communities, either through a policy of repatriation (a return option), or a policy of remote mobilization and connection to scientific, technological and cultural programs at home (a diaspora option) (Meyer *et al.* 1997). Here, we will develop three options: top-down initiatives for higher education, temporary recruitment of expatriate experts and networking with the diaspora.

3.1 Top-down initiatives in higher education

Three regional initiatives exemplify recent top-down initiatives in higher education: Qatar's Education City,[14] the Masdar Institute in Abu Dhabi and the KAUST in Saudi Arabia. The two first initiatives have adopted "branding" strategies, while the third relies more on local expertise. They are all, to different degrees, likely to reduce the level of brain-drain in Arab countries, which have been hit by an exodus of talent, but it is too early to know the outcome as so far there are mixed results.

Some Gulf countries are now offering excellent facilities to international enterprises and universities in order to attract and territorialize them. For instance, the University of King Abdel Aziz attracted 20 scientists from the UK in 2012 by providing each one US$1 million for their research. So far, however, it has not found niches of excellence. This top-down initiative can originate with the state or private institutions. In the latter, one can highlight the effort of the AUB and other universities in Lebanon in attempting to reverse the brain-drain of medical doctors. Based on a 2009 survey conducted among Lebanese doctors practicing in the United States,[15] 6 percent of the 286 participants were willing to relocate to Lebanon, and one-third were willing to relocate to the Arab Gulf. Slightly more than half were willing to relocate to Lebanon as a base for clinical missions to the Gulf. These findings suggest that there is a possibility to make Lebanon a regional "academic hub" by recruiting Lebanese medical graduates practicing abroad (Akl *et al.* 2012). It is also worth mentioning that Berytech was initially conceived as a way to repatriate young professionals that were fleeing the country (see Chapter 4).

3.2 Brain-gain: temporary recruitment of expatriate experts

While connectivity between the diaspora and the homeland is an important factor in fostering physical return, a temporary physical return may be the only possible option for many skilled expatriates, a category whose participation is vital to the construction of the Arab region, especially following the popular uprisings of recent years. In this case, it is possible for Arab governments or the international community to harness this group and facilitate the transmission of their expertise for the benefit of their homelands. These efforts were made in many

Arab countries, but notably in Palestinian territories, Lebanon, Tunisia and Morocco. Here, we will present the Palestinian case to see what lessons can be learned for the Arab region.

These two policies have both been employed in Palestine: in the first through a UNDP program that encourages repatriation, called TOKTEN (Transfer of Knowledge Through Expatriate Nationals) (Hanafi 2008); and in the second through an internet-based network called PALESTA (Palestinian Scientists and Technologists Abroad).

The TOKTEN concept is an interesting mechanism for tapping expatriate human resources and mobilizing them to undertake short-term consultancies in their countries of origin. The UNDP, which implemented TOKTEN in order to utilize the expertise of expatriates, demonstrated that emigrants who had achieved professional success aboard were enthusiastic about providing short-term technical assistance to their country of origin. Indeed, many of these individuals returned and settled permanently in their home countries. This program has been applied over the past 22 years in 30 different countries, resulting in the application of thousands of technical assistance missions by expatriate professionals to their countries of origin (UNDP 2000). One of the main catalysts for the creation of the TOKTEN program was the growing necessity of counteracting brain-drain from developing countries to the first world. Over the course of the 1990s, the program created databases of expatriate experts and gave assignments to more than 400 of them per annum to volunteer projects[16] to their countries of origin for periods ranging from one to six months. TOKTEN volunteers have served in government, the private sector, academic institutions and NGOs.

One of the most successful TOKTEN programs has been in Palestine, with over 170 Palestinian experts contributing their time and expertise. Palestinian TOKTEN consultants have helped reform the treatment of kidney disease in Palestine and have guided the development of macro-economic frameworks and planning. TOKTEN skills have also been brought to bear in the realm of computer and information technology, on city planning, on university curriculum development and academic networking, on the upgrading of film and television capacities and on cultural preservation, including the Bethlehem 2000 project. TOKTEN has generated some genuine success stories in Palestine, such as the construction and opening of the international airport in Gaza. In this case, nine TOKTEN consultants had stayed on and constituted the backbone of the airport's operations (UNDP 2000: 1–2).

The TOKTEN experience also provided returnee experts with a first-hand taste of life in their homeland and encouraged them to settle (within the limits of Israeli immigration control) for the long term. In fact, 34 TOKTEN experts, about one-fifth of the total, continued living in Palestine following the end of their TOKTEN assignment. The TOKTEN returnees have come mainly from Jordan and the United States, two countries with Palestinian communities that have kept close ties with family networks in the West Bank and Gaza. TOKTEN participation should be considered quite high for Palestine, which currently experiences the Israeli politics of spacio-cide and rendering the social and economic life of the Palestinians there very difficult. In Lebanon, where expatriates do not experience similar problems in acquiring residency, only six out of 36, or one-sixth, resettled in Lebanon following the end of their TOKTEN mission (Ghattas 1999).

Finally, the TOKTEN program raises questions concerning the nation state framework's capacity to deal with brain-drain. In an increasingly globalized skill and labor market, developing countries are rarely able to compete with developed countries that offer far higher wages. In such cases, TOKTEN facilitates a degree of compensation for countries of origin. In the Palestinian context, such a mechanism can be of vital significance, given the current political and economic situation, which does not encourage (and in fact bars) the homecoming of refugees and members of the diaspora, and where the outflow of skilled individuals is likely to continue.

TOKTEN should be used carefully. Both in the Palestinian territories and Tunisia, despite its "positive" efforts to reverse the brain-drain, it brought expatriates home for visits but some interviewees complained that it has unintentionally contributed to downgrading the local university scientists (for the Tunisian case, see Siino 2004: 374–376)

3.3 Network with the diaspora: the PALESTA case

While the return of skilled and professional individuals has been marginal under TOKTEN's low-capacity programs, the ambitious PALESTA network project sought to directly connect a larger group of professionals in the diaspora to the center. PALESTA, an internet-based network, has as its objective the harnessing of the scientific and technological knowledge of Palestinian expatriate professionals for the benefit of development efforts in Palestine. There are two similar pioneering networks that deal with South Africa and Colombia: SANSA (South African Network of Skills Abroad) and Red Caldas (the Network of Colombian Technologists and Scientists Abroad) (Meyer *et al.* 1997; Gaillard 2007).

PALESTA's network, a hybrid constructed by the Palestinian Ministry of Planning and International Cooperation's Science and Technology Planning Unit with UNDP support, was launched in 1997. The network includes a database of expatriate Palestinian scientists and professionals and discussion lists for secure discussion among participants as they contribute their technical knowledge and experience in addressing issues of importance to the development of the Palestinian economy. The network functions as a kind of professional gateway, providing current job listings and information on developments in many public, private and non-governmental organizations in Palestine, as well as workshops and public events.

Despite PALESTA's ambitious objectives, however, our analysis of this network demonstrates mixed results.[17] From one side, PALESTA's electronic discussion list has had a positive effect by providing space for a new experience of community and a rewarding in-gathering that has been diverse and egalitarian. The network has, in a limited way, created a tangible social space that has generated a kind of collective self-conscious for a worldwide professional expatriate community. Communication through PALESTA or a similar network allows mutual identification for actors and allows inferences to be made concerning their associations (Meyer *et al.* 1997: 7). From the other side, the virtual community has its limits. A critical examination reveals a tendency, as Wilson suggests, toward "thinning the complexities of human engagement to the level of a one-dimensional transaction and a detaching of the user from the political and social responsibilities of the real space environment" (Wilson 1997: 158). Although PALESTA members numbered more than 1,000, data suggest that only 20 percent had participated regularly in email exchanges. This technology, however, is not a panacea for the lack of physical connectivity of the Palestinian diaspora. PALESTA's weak overall effect reflected an over-reliance on a technological approach where connectivity is based mainly on electronic exchange, with very few concrete projects launched via the network. Similarly, Gaillard and Gaillard have pointed out that:

> the diaspora model will never be a low cost, self-sufficient answer to Africa's scientific needs. Its effectiveness depends crucially on the internal dynamics of the home-based scientific communities. After all, a network of expatriates is at best an extension of a national scientific community, not a substitute. Efforts should therefore, first and foremost, focus on strengthening national scientific capacity particularly training and recruiting the next generation of scientists. If this is not done, the diaspora will only be a smart cloak hiding shabby clothes.
>
> (Gaillard and Gaillard 2003)

4 Conclusion

We would like to summarize some of the options the Arab world should prioritize, highlighting some major issues and their policy implications.

4.1 Fixing the cycle between research, universities and society

The major issue revealed in our research is that the cycle between research, universities and society has been broken. The results of this disconnect have varied depending on the domain of economic, political or social life under consideration. As we mentioned when discussing the various functions of research, there is an insufficient appraisal of activities that are not directly linked to the production of scientific articles and books.

One of the most important aspects of the broken cycle has been the working conditions of researchers within their institutions. Most researchers in Arab countries belong to universities, and their primary responsibilities include teaching. Generally, these universities do not support their research activities. There will be no real progress if universities do not actively promote research in their own teams, within their own departments and faculties. Action here will necessarily be related to creating internal funding research opportunities, both for individuals and teams. External funding administrative support for the development of research activities will also be necessary. In many universities in Morocco, we have been told that the use of external funding by the actual research teams is close to impossible. This is true for all kind of research.

In the absence of substantial support from institutions, research will always be a marginal activity. However, research has also been too narrowly related to the individual promotion of professors. In this case, "research" has acquired a distorted meaning, since its only significance is its reception by colleagues and the university administration, and only for a specific person. On the contrary, research should be promoted as a collective endeavor, with shared activities and common working plans.

4.2 Making innovation a clearly stated objective of public policy

Arab countries have small patenting rates. This is usually used as a reason to conclude that more patenting should be encouraged. Policies have been designed that are supposed to promote the development of research into patents; however, this is only a small part of the more general issue of connecting research to the economy and society. Business incubators, technoparks or high-tech industrial clusters are not necessarily a panacea, or at least will probably be less of a solution than was initially thought. However, this is not to say that these efforts should be abandoned. On the contrary, these are usually meaningful initiatives and, as far as they serve to connect business practitioners, companies and real markets, they should be promoted and supported. Technoparks are also part of an Arab regional economy, and they cannot function without developing strong links with actual economic and social entities that surround them; thus, they should be included in regional development planning and economic programs that support local businesses.

It is often claimed that industry expresses little demand for the local university and research community of locally based technical centers. This is only partially true. All innovation surveys conducted so far show that there is innovation going on in ways that are difficult to measure. Lebanon, Morocco and Tunisia repeatedly conducted innovation surveys and it cannot be said that industry does not need R&D or innovation. More than half of the enterprises surveyed (even 60 percent in the case of Lebanon) had developed innovative projects, but most had been carried out without university participation (as an institution, though many of its researchers did) (see Chapter 4). Of course, this innovative activity depends upon the size and the sector of the companies. It should be noted that innovation is much more important in the headquarters of the multinationals than in their local branches (even in sectors such as pharmaceuticals, chemistry and electronics). Success stories indicated that innovation can be found in larger "medium-sized" companies, defined as having around 300 employees, based on long technical expertise fed by continuous improvement in actual markets and interactions with clients and providers.

The same holds true for universities. There is abundant anecdotal material in various universities showing strong linkages between teams and companies, based on long-term relationships and expertise. As an example, the Faculty of Science of USJ in Lebanon has a very long history of contact with the wine industry, the cement industry and the agro-food industry. They have built very strong relationships in these sectors that are funding research inside the lab as well as providing contact with industrialists. In Egypt, there have been numerous groups of companies in the information and communication technology (ICT) sector that have developed their technological learning based on university expertise. Innovation surveys indicate that these efforts require further development. They have argued that there is no shortage of innovation, only a lack of support. Less than 10 percent of companies are aware of the support schemes offered by the government in any of the countries where similar surveys have been done (Egypt, Morocco and Tunisia). It may be that they will develop in the future, as is hoped, for example, with the plan "*Maroc Innovation*," launched in Morocco in 2012.

The situation today is paradoxical. On the one hand, there is growth in innovation activities, in all kind of companies and even firms that were not interested in this activity several years ago. On the other hand, innovation surveys indicate a low level of interest on the part of the companies in public support for innovation. Companies surveyed mention many reasons for this lack of interest, but two key factors emerge: a lack of information on the support schemes, and little involvement in them. Another aspect is mentioned often: companies show a low level of confidence when the state is involved. One way to re-establish this confidence would be to channel public support through market-based entities that companies can then act on through the market and have a close working relation with the public entities that provide said support. It should also be noted that if the state shows more support for establishing an appropriate legal framework and makes use of resources to promote the participation of the private sector in research, companies will respond better to state initiatives. The state should then show that its interest is not the "business as usual" approach and that technological development will benefit from exceptional support measures. A preference should be given to collaborative work between technical entities (labs, centers, research teams) and companies. Preference should also be given to companies that wish to develop internal R&D activities. Entrepreneurship is often said to be lacking in the Arab region, which is used to explain the low level of innovation. We believe this not to be the case; rather, it appears that entrepreneurship is the region's most abundant resource. What appears to be more difficult is securing regular market support and continuing expansion. As the initial investment costs in R&D are probably less focused on research than on development, support schemes should provide for more than "one shot deal" support. Single support schemes will always be short-term. Such an effort would require more concerted action between the public entities involved in promoting economic activities.

4.3 Making research a political topic

During the Arab Summit in March 2010, the heads of state in attendance adopted a resolution mandating the General Secretariat of the League of Arab States to develop a science and technology strategy for the entire Arab region, in coordination with specialized Arab and international bodies. This strategy was to be submitted to the 2011 Arab Summit for adoption, and was expected to address the important issue of facilitating the mobility of scientists within the region and to enhance collaborative research with the sizeable community of expatriate Arab scientists. Both the strategy and the subsequent Arab Science and Technology Plan of Action (ASTPA) will be drawn up by a panel of experts from the region, with the institutional support of the Arab League Educational, Cultural and Scientific Organization (ALECSO), the Union of Arab Scientific Research Councils and UNESCO, among others. ASTPA will design both national and pan-Arab initiatives in 14 priority areas, including water, food, agriculture and energy. It is also expected to recommend the launch of an online Arab science and technology observatory to monitor the science and technology scene in Arab states and highlight any shortcomings in implementation. One of the keys to implementing measures at the country level will be identifying the challenges Arab countries face at the domestic level and establishing research as a stand-alone topic for political discourse. Political support for research and innovation at the highest level is required, coupled with affirmative government action, an upgrade of existing science, technology and innovation infrastructure and an increase in GERD.

At the same time, lessons learned from the experiences of several countries in Latin America suggest the importance of connectivity at the level of institutions and of individual researchers. Thus, both top-down and bottom-up approaches are required.

4.4 Research arrangements: diversification and scientific priorities

Can one talk of a science "system" in many of these countries, as they do not exhibit typical systemic characteristics (Mouton and Waast 2009)? It is perhaps a more apt metaphor to describe the situation of the research in most of the Arab countries by science or research arrangements, rather than science systems. The research landscape in each Arab country is fragmented and small in scale, and institutions are not typically aligned through input, process and output flows, and there is no systemic behavior in response to external changes and demands. Rather, the image is of an "assemblage" of fragile, somewhat disconnected and constantly under-resourced institutions. Here we would like to raise two issues for the future: the centralized vs. diversified model and the issue of research autonomy.

Within research units, there is a variety of research activities that can be developed. As research activity grows, all countries experience a certain level of diversification. What can normally be found in a good research system is usually a wide range of specialists. But when the overall number of scientists is small, there may be a situation where you find one or two specialists in each area. They usually feel quite alone and few among them would have the capacity to sustain a large team of specialists over time. Small research systems must then confront this situation, and often experience difficulty in forcing the creation of larger teams.

This issue is a complex one and there are many ways of dealing with it. The institutional complexity of research arrangements always poses a dilemma. As a way to offer a sound proposal for discussion, one should examine the type of funding that would be drafted according to priorities. "Priorities" is not a very good term since it harkens back to the 1970s, when national planning was fashionable. Moreover, recent exercises in priority-setting in Arab countries have tended to produce a catalogue, which is possibly relevant but not feasible with local resources. A very good example is the Science and Technology and Innovation Program (STIP) designed by CNRS in Lebanon, but no funding was available at the time it was drafted (see Chapter 4). We find the same thing in Jordan.

An alternative way of tackling the funding issue would be to draft a catalogue not on the basis of declared priorities (whatever forecasting exercise be used), but by combining these declared priorities with actors funding them. It is not our purpose here to detail this exercise, but it would be interesting to have a real forecasting exercise that combines the possibility of actual actors in the field. A possible differentiation would be as follows:

- A few strategic funding programs with strong linkages to the productive sector. The pursuit of some programs which imply energetic support from the state in areas considered "strategic" and applied research, where the public authorities promote active collaborations or "clusters" with dynamic firms. We have already mentioned this aspect above. It is necessary here to add that funding would then be given priority when the alliances and collaborations are made. The areas for funding are well known: water, desertification, renewable sources of energy and agro-food, etc. The main evaluation criteria would be the program's relevance to the local economy and the level of linkages to the productive sector.

- Promotion of some research areas with clear socio-economic objectives that are specific to the country, where users and social actors are present, and where economic interest is not the first objective – for example, health. It is good to remember that in some countries university incubators in areas not considered "strategic" have been very commercially successful. As the Lebanese CNRS has stated, "if you consider health-related research a cost, consider disease!" What is needed is some support to these areas, which are not immediately profitable, but where interaction with final users is of paramount importance. Consider, for example, the construction industry, which has developed its new building materials based on intense exchanges between the companies that build, those producing the material and designers and architects. These areas related to real users could also recollect and use local knowledge, for example in agriculture, medicine, pharmaceuticals and fisheries. "Traditional knowledge" is better introduced into research and new developments when it is linked to communities that use this traditional knowledge. The main criteria here would be relevance to social needs and the creation of strong teams.

• Areas of basic sciences. These are areas where collaboration with foreign colleagues will be actively sought out, where the objective is neither socio-economic, nor driven by innovation. The rationale for such programs is that a country, as small as it may be, needs to have an eye open to developments made elsewhere. If Caroline Wagner (2008) is right, the smaller the country the more beneficial this link to foreign research. Doctoral students are a good investment if interesting employment schemes are devised for them following the completion of their studies. We should add to Wagner's proposal that this strategy should not only be related to domains with an existing local productive base (such as hospitals), but also to the "domains of the future." Excellence and novelty should be the main evaluation criteria.

All these strategies require funding, which could be distributed through many different schemes: scholarships to students working with companies, funding of collaborative projects, direct subvention to research projects, etc. Two aspects of the experience of many countries bear repeating:

Identify research: Research needs to be clearly identified and not only included into larger objectives like industrialization, provision of food or health-care and other socio-economic objectives. Public budgets should clearly identify research as a goal. If not, a powerful alliance of some social groups and economic interests will always eclipse it.

Stabilize teams: Funding should go to teams, not individuals. Building teams takes time. Very short-term research assignments can kill teams, which have to adapt quickly and respond to the offer, and function as consultancies instead of consolidating their human resources and equipment. This is why funding should not come only in the form of project funding under competitive schemes, but should also offer a stabilizing mechanism, a system that permits the maintenance of quality research and at the same time grow its own resources. The experience of the Tunisian "labelization" system (label as research teams specific entities and link a specific funding to a specific roadmap presented by this research team over a four-year period) is perhaps the best example, since it generated a stable increase in research activities over a very short time in Tunisian universities.

4.5 Consolidating teams

There is a real need for "stabilizing" mechanisms and promoting "unifying" research arrangements. In effect, naming "clusters of activities" is not a sufficient strategy to induce the creation of strong teams around specific objectives. A mechanism is also required to guarantee regular funding in the medium term, and not exclusively from outside sources. This mechanism needs to be driven by both universities and central state institutions which can guarantee the validity of the "team projects."

Research in a social and economic environment that shows little interest in research is possible. The AUB is a good example; Lebanon does not boast an environment particularly conducive to research, but nor has it been hostile to scientific innovation. Still, no real incentives for research exist, with the National Council for Scientific Research historically supporting pre-existing research areas rather than promoting new ones. Usually, these areas of research have arrived in Lebanon through Lebanese professors returning from France or the United states and developing research activities alongside their former European or American colleagues. International cooperation is thus the main tool of consolidating a competence: it does not permit, however, the development of its own basis of research themes of greater local relevance. Biomedical research at AUB grew in this manner and in a symbiotic relationship with the medical practice at the university hospital. Thus, the professionalization of medicine entailed conducting research. This is not the exception but the rule, as can be shown in other universities and university hospitals in Lebanon. One of the researchers we interviewed at USJ, who has an impressive record of publications, described himself as a doctor, not a researcher, and he mostly promotes a research team, not an individual practice. He developed an area of expertise that is unique in the world and specifically relevant to Lebanon, where medical diagnosis and lab research co-exist.

We can try to generalize from this example by saying that lack of professionalization in specific activities is part of the riddle of research. The more professionals there are the more research will be required. When professionals become more demanding, research gains in importance and value. This is how contacts have been built between companies and universities in many countries; but this contact does not happen through funding alone.

In the late 1970s, when the research system in Brazil was beginning to grow, a Brazilian sociologist conducted a series of interviews with researchers in many fields under the title "Islands of Competence" (Oliveira 1984). This is a most accurate description of the situation in some Arab countries: a series of islands of competence, niches of peculiar expertise which have been built or are being built. These islands are relatively independent of one another, even in similar domains. They objectively sought the best expertise and avoided local competition. They also played on national pride as a means of securing funding. Local networking will be avoided. This experience was common to most Latin American countries during the 1980s and 1990s. New institutions were created, geared toward building bridges between productive entities and universities. However, these countries, like Tunisia some ten years later, created "national systems of research" that served mainly as promotion systems, identifying and consolidating the research activity of individuals. These evaluation structures of research funded an additional incentive for good publication patterns. Universities adopted similar schemes. Brazil, in contrast to Mexico and Chile, adopted incentive schemes that were collective rather than individual.

Today, this gives Brazil a decisive advantage in research. These evaluating/ labeling schemes, with their different forms, have been strong instruments for the promotion of research. They benefit research for many reasons, including the fact that they allow for the clear identification of specific activities related to research. They may also lead to better living conditions for researchers.

4.6 Doctoral programs and post-doctorate fellowship

In universities, a large part of the research activity should be included within the general framework of the Masters and PhD programs. These need to be designed in such a way as to lead to research, in particular for PhD programs. There will be no research-efficient faculty if they cannot relate the teaching activity of PhD seminars to research orientations. Moreover, the use of cooperative or shared doctoral programs with foreign universities could be a lever for more research in the university environment. France has designed "sandwich doctorates" with double diplomas from French and foreign institutions, and these have been received quite enthusiastically by both French universities and their partners abroad. They also have the advantage of promoting long-term relations between teams in both countries.

Another important aspect related to the institutional capability to support research is the existence of post-doctorate fellowship and grants, which are rare in the Arab region. For instance, according to our survey of research practices, very few Lebanese members of the AUB's faculty have benefited from post-doctoral fellowships; those who have, completed their fellowships outside the Arab region. Meanwhile, at the largest university in Lebanon, the Lebanese University, no post-doctoral system exists, a situation common to many other universities. Many Arab universities give grants for research only to full professors, who are normally over the age of 50. One professor of biology in her early sixties at Cairo University declared in a fieldwork interview that "now that I am a full professor, I can begin research!" There is a great deal of room to increase support to young faculty by promoting fellowships. None of these measures can be of any success if both funders and employers (in this case the university administration) are not involved in a common strategy.

4.7 Local, regional and international collaboration

All the studies and interviews we have had access to show that there are very few synergies between different scientific institutions at either the national or regional level: joint projects between Arab scientific research institutions working in similar fields remain extremely rare, even within the same country.

It is clear that scientific networks at the level of sub-disciplines could be promoted and that resources from Gulf countries would be useful in that effort. Many reasons make us doubt the feasibility of programs at this level, drawing upon the experience of the EU. The Framework Programs, established in 1984, had the purpose of supporting European research projects that combined different teams from different countries. This worked surprisingly well and quickly.

It should be said that, at that time, funding for research in European countries was usually done by regular budgetary provisions to research institutions, whereas the EU was proposing funding projects through competitive calls.[18] Nonetheless, the EU "framework funding" came in handy and worked well, among other reasons because the European Commission's research activities were parallel to those of the construction of European institutions in other areas (economy, agricultural funding and so on). Moreover, the Framework Programs obliged the national research system to be internationalized at least within the boundaries of Europe. In the case of inter-Arab cooperation, there is little cooperation and research is isolated in this endeavor. A recent ESCWA report (2014), *Arab Integration: A 21st Century Development Imperative*, established a sad observation on the lack of inter-Arab cooperation in research as well as in other domains. Additionally, a recent evaluation of the EU Seventh Framework Program cooperation shows that EU funding to non-EU partners (possible since the Fifth Framework Program in practically all areas and since the sixth in all programs of the EU) is quite low. International cooperation with non-EU partners is basically done through funding directly with European partners. More than €400 million has been distributed to projects involving Mediterranean partner countries; the partners in Mediterranean countries in these projects received approximately 10 percent of this total funding.

Bilateral programs may prove more efficient, and it should be remembered that European countries have not abandoned their bilateral funding of research and higher education in neighboring regions. France, Italy, Spain, Germany and to a lesser extent the United Kingdom have been active in funding research through bilateral programs in the Arab region. Even the best ideas for realizing the full potential of the region, through the use of funding from the Gulf or any other source, does not make sense if not accompanied by a policy with stated objectives.

Having said that, despite the fact that inter-Arab cooperation is quite low, more funding is available and we believe that only time will tell if the increasing money from institutions such as the Qatar Foundation will fill the gap. The once-stated objective of "national self-reliance," whether referring to individual states or to the pan-Arab ideal, is probably best forgotten. Rather, we believe that the driving force behind the development of research in the region will not be funding so much as the professionalization of funding mechanisms. For example, the Qatar Foundation's support for medical research has been appreciated by the research teams involved because of the seriousness and professionalism of the evaluation mechanism. As one researcher said, "they had done their homework, and they select very good teams." Funding research is a profession, and there is a clear need for transparency and professional regulations for the use of money from competitive funds. It is also clear that no research will ever grow satisfactorily if the internal mechanisms currently in use by most institutions for spending external funds are not modified. Today, the problem is less a lack of funds than a lack of management capacity to spend them. It would be our recommendation to promote systems of management for research and innovation, and make them a topic of high priority for training in the near future.

A closely related issue is the fact that networking as an objective of funded projects is very efficient. Again, the experience of the EU Framework Programs shows the strong capacity for more research and better-oriented programs as a result of networking. Projects that are by themselves small networks always tend to expand in order to interest larger networks. The professional networking is thus particularly efficient and grounded in the actual practice of research. There is no reason why this kind of networking wouldn't work in specific professional areas. Again, this seems possible only at the level of disciplines or specific subjects.

This kind of "linking" strategy, which is based on exploiting the networks of research, would make sense if it permits relatively strong research teams to participate. In that case, strong poles of the network that bring together many researchers working on the same topic would be able to profit from the flow of resources. Participation in international collaborative networks without a parallel consolidation strategy would be like entering a river; it will end by dissolving in the sea. However, networks/links are not a sufficient strategy; they need to be complemented by the consolidation of teams as discussed above. This consolidation seems impossible without state support and intervention. The motivation and form of state participation can vary a great deal: it can range from the routine management of public institutions conducting research on a centralized model (Tunisia) to the fostering of a multiplicity of universities with no common regulatory framework (Lebanon). This is different from the way the World Bank has promoted the "knowledge economy." As we mentioned in Chapter 1, the World Bank has indeed designed a Knowledge Economy Index (KEI) and a set of policy recommendations for the future based on the liberalization of the economy and less state control. We advocate for a more diversified model, which would take into account the various types of sciences and the different roles played by the state, depending on the issue being addressed.

4.8 Academic journals

Writing is part of the research process. Publishing in journals becomes part of the basic infrastructure to encourage research. It is in all the sciences that the Arab world needs more journals to publish scientific results (Hanafi 2011; Hanafi and Arvanitis 2013a). The objective should be to create a dynamic of exchange between members of the scientific community locally and to mobilize allies from peers, the public and decision-makers. It should be noted that the main dynamic behind the publication of journals is the existence of a lively scientific community. Large publishing companies (Elsevier, Kluwer) have taken strong commercial positions, making the scientific community an instrument of commercial objectives. With the advent of Open Science, strong protests have emerged from working scientists who have used the force of "social digital networks" to mobilize the community, giving way to a renewal of peer partnerships. The Arab world could profit intellectually from this movement.

4.9 Diaspora options

As demonstrated earlier in this chapter, there are many lessons to be learned from the two Palestinian experiences highlighted, namely the TOKTEN program and the PALESTA network. Zewail City of Science and Technology also aims to link the Egyptian scientists abroad to this city. It is extremely important for governments and international organizations to encourage networking with the diaspora and the temporary recruitment of scientific expatriates to work or volunteer in their countries of origin. Every Arab country stands to benefit from similar initiatives, which cost little to run but have the potential to harness development in the Arab region.

Notes

1 For an example, see Badawi (2009) on the sad reality of the curricula in sociology in Egypt.
2 The recent growth of private universities in Jordan could also be given as an example.
3 See the ongoing work of Sébastien Mosbah-Natanson and Pauline Huet on the United Arab Emirates, or the work of Claire Beaudevin.
4 These centers are generally specialized in specific spheres of public interest (agriculture, nuclear and space technologies, health) with a continuum from basic to applied research. They are often favored by governments, which give priority to their funding because they contribute to areas of national strategic importance and are commissioned to generate more practical outcomes (IFI 2011).
5 Thirty percent of 125,000 university faculty members in Arab countries are women. Some researchers have put this figure at over 170,000 for the end of the 2000 decade (Waast *et al.* 2010), but this could be due to the inclusion of individuals who teach at more than one university, meaning they would be counted more than once (UNESCO 2010a: 71).
6 These journals are *Idafat, Arab Journal of Sociology, Journal of Economic Research, Journal of Political Studies* and *Arab Journal and Translation.*
7 We found a very striking case in Egypt, where a researcher who is an officer in one of the state-run statistical centers refused to deliver data on poverty unless she could be co-author of the publication.
8 Or, of course, by colonial powers such as Israeli authority (Yahya 2014).
9 We have no estimates for GERD for Qatar and figures do not fit well; another source of information mentions that Qatar National University funded research for US$220 million, which appears to be an extraordinary amount (this is close to the budget of a medium-sized institute with fewer than 900 researchers and fewer than 2000 personnel in France, for example). Moreover, Qatar University announced it has received US$266 million from QNRF – an average of US$40 million per year.
10 For Fernanda Beigel (2011), the distinction between both temporal and scientific capitals is not simple at all, as they can both be intertwined, particularly given the evolution of the international publishing system. The distinction is itself conceptually debatable, as it is based on a metaphor taken from the opposition between "religiosity" and "temporality," which reveals a trust in the "purity" of a specific autonomist project.
11 Some researchers are even skeptical whether we can use the concept of professional (not to mention scientific) field. For the Palestinian case, see Inkster (1991) and Romani (2008).
12 Hotayt (1996: 35) notices that Lebanese PhD and Masters students don't refer to the work published in other universities in Lebanon. In the same way, scholars cite very rarely publications of their local peers (Hachem 1996).

13 It appears that immigrants are "more qualified" than the native-born population. In the OECD area as a whole, the share of people with tertiary education is higher for the foreign-born (23.6 per cent) than for the native-born (19.1 per cent) (Dumont and Lemaître 2005). It should be remembered that immigrant populations have played a fundamental role in the economic and technological growth of many industrialized countries, in Europe, North America, etc. (Rosenberg 1982; Inkster 1991).

14 A branding strategy consists of inviting a famous foreign university or institution to create a local branch and use its name in the country. The Qatar Foundation has funded the Qatar Education City, which includes branches of eight elite international universities, delivering "world-class programs chosen to ensure Qatar is equipped with essential skills and specialties." The schools are: Texas A&M University at Qatar, Weill Cornell Medical College in Qatar, Georgetown University School of Foreign Service, Virginia Commonwealth University in Qatar, Carnegie Mellon University, Northwestern University in Qatar, Ecole des Hautes Etudes Commerciales (HEC Paris) and University College London Qatar. The city is also home to educational institutions for children and teenagers, and research institutions such as the RAND-Qatar Policy Institute, the Qatar Science & Technology Park and the QNRF. The Qatar Education City is also the home of the Qatar Music Academy and Qatar Symphony Orchestra.

15 Of a sample of 500 physicians contacted by researchers, 286 participated in the survey.

16 In Palestine, TOKTEN consultants receive US$2,000 if junior and US$3,000 if senior, in addition to paid travel and miscellaneous expenditures.

17 This assessment is based on the findings of an evaluation study conducted by Sari Hanafi (2008).

18 The exception was the UK research council, which were funding a lot of their research through competitive calls inside the UK.

4 Practicing research in Lebanon

Institutions and internationalization

Studies conducted over the past decade have identified the contours of the research system in Lebanon. This chapter is an overview of the institutional organization of research in Lebanon and the main challenges this small country, with rather strong academic institutions, has to face. Indeed, the four million inhabitants of Lebanon[1] share some features that make it quite different from the neighboring Arab countries: high levels of education and a large student population;[2] a significant scientific production; the recognized quality of its physicians and its hospitals; a high rate of emigration; and an economy that is primarily driven toward services. It is also a parliamentary democracy but at the same time a society divided into communities officially recognized by the political system and partly by its Constitution, inherited from the French protectorate. It is also a country deeply marked by a long and bloody civil war (1975–1990) (Abou-Rjeily and Labaki 1993).[3] This sectarian system is reflected in the recruitment of public officers, particularly in the case of the Lebanese University, the largest university in the country, which includes half of the student population. In addition, Lebanon has a large portion of refugees: first, 250,000 Palestinian refugees since 1948 (a population that is very marginalized by the absence of their basic rights in Lebanon, such as the right to work or to own property, among others) and the recent waves of Syrian refugees since the onset of the Syrian uprising. These refugees constituted, in April 2014, one-quarter of the Lebanese population. It is thus a rich country, weakened by an unstable political situation that creates an unfavorable environment for research and innovation.

Until 2006, very few papers described research in Lebanon.[4] The journal of the Lebanese Association of Women researchers, *Bahithat*, gathered in one issue (no. 3, 1996–1997) a collection of articles, essentially essays that are not always based on data, on the state of research in the Arab world, mainly in Lebanon. This is probably the first systematic collection on this topic.[5] In 2006, a research team was set up to investigate different aspects of the research organization as part of project ESTIME (2005–2007).[6] A report by Jacques Gaillard (2007) presents an overview of the institutional system. This project was also the opportunity for some major fieldwork on research practices in the natural sciences, the social sciences, the innovation system and research funding available locally.[7] This was the only comprehensive work on the research system and since then, despite several attempts, research in Lebanon has not been the object of such a general assessment.

Since then, one can find some analysis of the situation of research in Lebanon mainly in reports on the entire Arab world (UNDP 2004; 2005; 2009; Al Maktoum Foundation and UNDP 2009; Arab Thought Foundation 2009; chapters dedicated to the Arab states in the UNESCO *World Science Report*). All these general reports on the Arab world follow the tracks of the three first UNDP reports on Human Development in the Arab world. The latter had been insisting on the importance of education, research, the role of women and freedom of speech and opinions, as engines of progress. The 2009 *Arab Knowledge Report* Al-Maktoum Foundation and UNDP 2009) has insisted on the importance of a knowledge society and dedicated a whole chapter to scientific research. All these reports give Lebanon the image of a middle-rank economy among the Arab economies. We find this surprising, given the number of rather mature and renowned academic institutions, as well as the high level of qualifications of its population. As we mentioned in the introduction of this book, Antoine Zahlan (2012), who lives and works in Lebanon, has published a comprehensive study, mainly based on bibliometric data and insights from his own experience as an engineer. He maintains that research is not developed in the Arab region mainly because of the absence of a political project based on national sovereignty. Lebanon is not exactly Zahlan's target, but his argument about sovereignty rings true with particular strength in a country that is strangled by foreign forces.

When looking at Lebanon's case we must thus remember that its situation is particular on more than one dimension, especially in what concerns intellectual life, scientific research and academic presence. It has also demonstrated a solid tradition of scientific collaboration which makes it more interesting. In all these aspects, Lebanon ranks rather favorably compared to its neighbors. However, if these above-mentioned international organizations (World Bank, UNDP, etc.) persist in giving this country a rather unfavorable view, it is mainly because of the unfavorable conditions for business and political instability. For example, in the first innovation survey ever conducted in the country (Arvanitis 2014), over 78 percent of companies surveyed declared that the political and security situation in Lebanon is a factor that impedes innovation (as well as research and development in firms). Lebanon also offers one of the very few innovative business incubators (Berytech) that is functional and successful in the Arab region. These features make Lebanon a distinct case and of particular interest. And, as we will review in this chapter, Lebanon rates rather favorably in terms of quality of research; despite the abominable political environment, it is still a place that offers quality research. This, by itself, is a paradox.

1 A rather satisfactory scientific production

A first attempt to evaluate the research in Lebanon is the analysis of its production of items in large databases. Figure 4.1 shows the scientific production for the period since 1975, the onset of the civil war, until the year following the

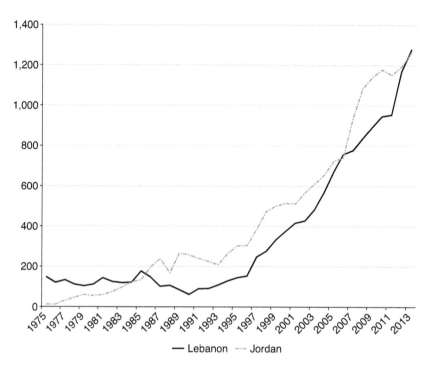

Figure 4.1 Production of articles in Lebanon and Jordan (1975–2013) (source: Web of Science; online interrogation in April 2014 includes the SCI, SSCI and Proceedings).

signing of the Taif Agreement (1990) – considered to be the formal end of the war. The production curve starts rising (1991–1997), and then increases rapidly until 2006, the year of the Israeli bombing of Lebanon, and restarts more slowly thereafter. After 2010, the curve jumps impressively. Currently, the average production of articles listed in the Web of Science (WoS) is around 1,600 items per year;[8] there are 1,300 articles per year in Scopus. The influence of the short "war" (in fact, the bombing of Lebanon by Israel) in July 2006 was particularly bad, and many people, at the time, fled the country. Increasingly this political unrest is affecting everyday life, a "detail" never to be forgotten. Since 2011, the country has greatly accelerated its production to reach the same level as Jordan. Yet the latter country, which has made considerable efforts to improve its research system (Larzillière 2010), has probably twice as many researchers as Lebanon.[9] This means Lebanon is above not only its neighboring Jordan, but well above the average Arab country. This is due mainly to two unrelated fields of research: the clinical medicine fields (a very productive field worldwide, as Gaillard (2010) reminds us), which represents more than 40 percent of the Lebanese production, in particular oncology, hematology, surgery, endocrinology and clinical general medicine; and engineering-related areas, mainly algorithmic electronic engineering, computer sciences, telecommunications and mathematical research related to these areas. Chemistry is a very important discipline (solid state, catalysis, organic chemistry, but also analytical chemistry of medicinal substances). In that, the rare mix of disciplines makes the profile of Lebanon close to that of Tunisia, and rather different from the engineering-dominated profile of Egypt or Algeria. It is also interesting to note that practically all co-authored articles of Lebanon with Saudi Arabia are located in the medical fields.

Concerning the production of social sciences and humanities (SSH), methodological difficulties led us to attempt to estimate the number of articles in Arabic for the period 2006–2013 using a new academic database that started recently to include many Arab academic journals (E-Marefa). We get the figure of 164 items, giving an average of 20.5 articles per year.[10] In the WoS over the period 2000–2011 we counted 558 English-language articles and we note a sharp increase since 2009; we find 59 items per year on average over the comparable period of the two samples (2006–2011). The Scopus database records 130 items in SSH for the year 2010. The growing production in these SSH fields is an extremely recent trend. It parallels the strong growth we noted since 2011 for the entire Lebanese production. However, this figure, certainly fewer than 150 articles per year, seems overall relatively low. Previously, we had expressed the idea of an opposition between those who publish locally and perish globally and those who publish globally and perish locally (Hanafi 2011); in reality, it would seem that the local production is quite low and that the large majority of SSH researchers *perish both locally and globally*.

2 The main pillars of research in Lebanon

To understand the growth of research in Lebanon since the civil war (despite the slowdown of 2006–2011), one should identify growing centers of research activity: universities (representing around 95 percent of the production, including hospitals), the National Council for Scientific Research (CNRS) with its program of support for research, national research centers and private research centers. Figure 4.2 shows the importance of leading universities and research centers in the country. As outlined, this distribution is not consistent with the actual distribution of researchers by institutions. UL has the largest number of professors. AUB and USJ are of similar size, as is the case of LAU and Balamand. The CNRS has a very small (and productive) number of researchers.

As we already mentioned, the profile of scientific publications in Lebanon (indexed in the WoS) is quite different from that of neighboring countries. Indeed, the Arab countries have a strong specialization in engineering and materials science, while Lebanon (Tunisia as well) is highly oriented toward the medical sciences.

In addition, we note that the Lebanese share of global production (Figure 4.3), according to Scimago data based on Scopus,[11] increased by 30 percent in the ten years between 2000 and 2010, representing 0.347 per 1,000, an honorable proportion for a country of four million inhabitants and probably around 1,200

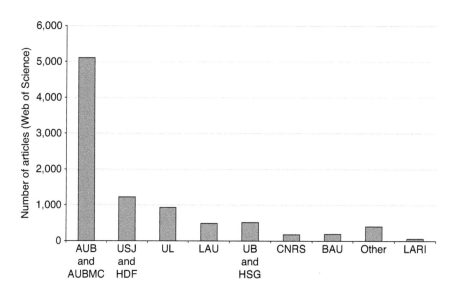

Figure 4.2 Scientific production of the main Lebanese institutions (2000–2011) (source: Web of Science, treated by C. Tayoun/R. Arvanitis, July 2012).

Notes
AUB and AUBMC: American University of Beirut and its Medical Center (ex. AUH); USJ and HDF: Université Saint-Joseph of Beirut and Hotel Dieu de France hospital; LAU: Lebanese American University; UL: Lebanese University (public and largest university); UB and HSG: Balamand University and Saint Georges Hospital; CNRS: National Council for Scientific Research (four research centers); BAU: Beirut Arab University; LARI: Institute of Agricultural Research.

full-time equivalent (FTE) researchers. This figure is a sharp progression compared to 1999 (0.08 per 1,000) and 2004 (0.13 per 1,000);[12] some domains have increased dramatically, from two to three times higher than world production in areas such as mathematics and computer science especially (+329 percent), social sciences (+333 percent) and engineering (+259 percent), biology (+245 percent) and agricultural sciences (+221 percent).[13] These increases are also reflected in research projects funded by the CNRS, as we will indicate below.

2.1 Universities

There are 47 licensed universities (only 41 are active on the ground); all but the Lebanese University are private, and 12 of them have faculties of science or engineering. However, as shown in Table 4.1, the scientific production is concentrated in a few universities: the American University of Beirut (AUB), which has a high-level university hospital; the University Saint-Joseph of Beirut (USJ), which has the largest hospital in the city of Beirut (University Hospital Hôtel Dieu de France);[14] the Lebanese University; the Lebanese American University (LAU), a rather recent and expensive private university; Balamand University,

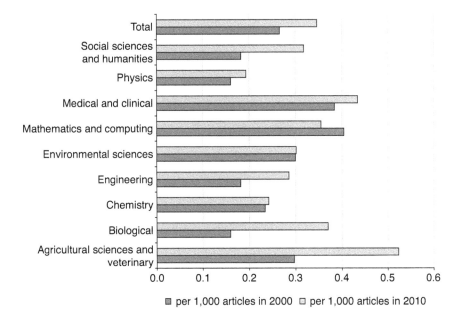

Figure 4.3 Share of world production of Lebanon (comparison 2000 and 2010) (source: indicators from Scimago, based on SCOPUS; analysis in October 2012).

an orthodox university whose main campus is located near Tripoli and to which is attached the Hospital Saint-Georges; and finally the Beirut Arab University (BAU), an Arab-speaking private university founded as a chapter of the University of Alexandria in Egypt that acquired full autonomy in recent years, teaching in Arabic and English (Gaillard 2010b).

Several other universities have established directions for research, including the Holy Spirit University of Kaslik and the Notre Dame University (NDU) (both are Catholic universities adopting an American model of liberal arts education), but their contribution to research is still modest and based on a few faculty members. Over a period of 11 years (2000–2011),[15] production represents less than 5 percent of publications in the country, while the top five research universities are, in the same period, 94.6 percent of the production. This shows a certain stabilization of the research concentration over time.

The importance of research in universities is unrelated to the number of students. Indeed, the LU is the largest (73,698 students in 2011/2012), followed by the BAU (11,392 students), USJ (9,362 students), the AUB (7,826 students), the NDU (6,827 students), the Holy Spirit of Kaslik University (6,645 students) and the LAU (6,320 students).[16]

Table 4.1 Main institutions performing research in Lebanon

Universities or research centers	Annual publications 2009–2011[a]	Personnel R&D FTE[b]	R&D spending[b]	Total professors[c]	Students[c]	Year of foundation
American University of Beirut (AUB) + Center Medical AUB	265	100	17.8	813	7,000	1866
Lebanese University (LU)	122	150	11.4	4,400	73,000	1953
Université St Joseph (USJ) + Hotel Dieu	65	90	8.0	1,830	9,400	1875
Lebanese American University (LAU)	65	10	All together: 0	180	6,300	1924
Univ. Balamand (BU) + Hop. St. Georges	38	20		940	2,800	1988
Beirut Arab University (BAU)	17	10		670	11,000	1960
34 other universities	55	>50		4,900	39,000	Three or four per year since 1996
CNRS: four research centers	21	50	5.5			
LARI (agricultural research)	All	55	5.2			
IRI (industrial center)		10	0.3			
Five other research centers		30				

Notes
a Publications in WoS, compiled by Claude Tayoun.
b Estimation published in Gaillard (2007).
c From Ministry of Education and Higher Education.

2.1.1 The American University of Beirut and Université Saint-Joseph

The two major private research universities in Lebanon are among the oldest universities in the region. The current AUB was founded in 1866 as the Syrian Evangelical College, followed by the creation of the USJ in 1875, founded by the Jesuits. Competition between the two universities is real, even if it is denied by their respective authorities; in this race, AUB outpaces USJ very strongly, especially because of its connection to the Arab economic and business elites. It has become, after the civil war, the main elite university in the country, as evidenced by the choice of the university by those who come from the best schools, including the French-language schools – Grand Lycée, Jesuits schools and Collège Protestant. USJ played a key historical role in the formation and production of political elites and public servants until the civil war (Kabbanji 2012); today, the Faculty of Political Science and Law is still very important. By contrast, AUB is the main producer of scientific articles and books, with 63.7 percent of production over the period 2000–2011; USJ has attained a modest 15.5 percent of the scientific publications in Lebanon.[17] The English language and the fact that AUB academics are often trained in the United States largely facilitate the publication of journal articles in English. Nonetheless, the multidisciplinary and multi-lingual AUB journal *al-Abhâth* was an outlet for Arab debates before the civil war, especially in history (Raymond 2013).

This inequality is impressive considering that the two universities have a similar size; it has been the subject of a thorough evaluation requested by the new rector of the USJ in 2012 and it is a source of concern among the faculty of the university. In a remarkable (and unpublished) self-study, based on 92 interviews conducted in-house, including the conclusion of debates in many meetings and a substantive work on the contents of the research, USJ has revealed its strengths and weaknesses concerning scientific research.[18] The report proposes structural changes to improve the situation of research and encourage tenured professors to publish in a more systematic way. This most surprising and frank self-criticism, which is a very rare exercise, reveals the acute perception of the fragility of the current situation. However, USJ has a promising Faculty of Science that is research-oriented, yet has only 24 tenured professors (what the university calls "encadrés"). In addition, this faculty has very close links with a large number of industrial companies (especially in chemistry, cement and food and wine industries) that fund its research activities.[19] The same university founded the Berytech incubator that is now one of the most dynamic around the Mediterranean.[20] AUB was, paradoxically, less successful in its contacts with industry despite the existence of a center for the promotion of entrepreneurship,[21] and two small incubators (launched in 2015). Despite the fact that its clientèle remains the economic elite, its research orientation is rather based on a conception of research not really linked to business but rather to publications.

Research in universities is mostly related to the need for promotion rather than the relevance of the topics to the country. We know that this assertion constitutes a controversial claim and there are many counter examples.[22] However, after conducting a thorough survey of academics at three universities (AUB, USJ and LU), this finding seems obvious: the output of the research is publications in English-language journals indexed with a high "impact factor." Professors at Lebanese universities have accepted this norm and we think many practical reasons explain this fact.

Teaching is very demanding and research time is limited. Only a small fraction of the academic population is really dedicated to research. In the MIRA Survey (discussed in Chapter 3), among the 117 Lebanese researchers of the survey, who are mainly dedicated full-time and experienced researchers, only 13.5 percent declare spending more than half of their time on research.[23] Around 50 percent spend up to one-third of their time on research. But as Figure 4.4 shows, most of the time is dedicated to teaching. Let us remember that the sample is slightly skewed toward professors with more experience, although the Lebanese sample is definitely younger than the overall sample (EU or other Mediterranean countries): 37.1 percent are under 40 years old. In any case, as shown in Figure 4.5, research is far from being the sole activity of the Lebanese academics. The data presented here hide a very skewed distribution, where a very few people dedicate a lot of time to research and most spend rather a standard one-third/two-thirds to research/teaching. This is not unexpected since we find here a typical opposition between profiles of the careers of academics one finds in large universities in Europe: those who invest almost exclusively in

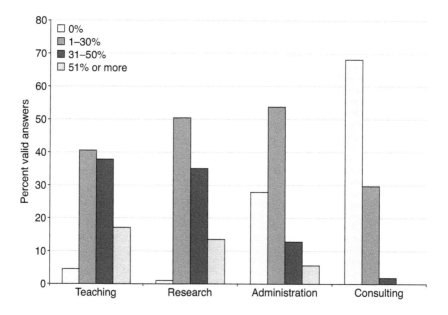

Figure 4.4 Time dedicated to academic activities (source: MIRA Survey).

Notes
Survey results to this question corresponds to 110 answers in Lebanon, 1,941 for EU researchers and 2,094 for Mediterranean countries (including Lebanon).

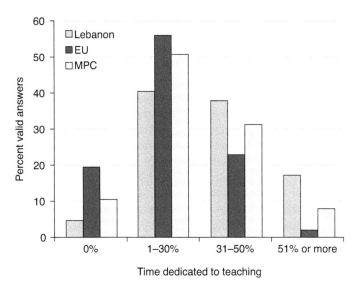

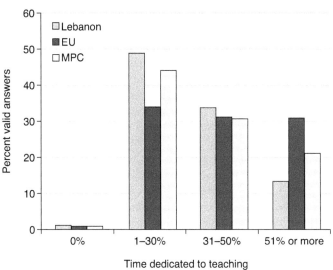

Figure 4.5 Teaching and research activities. Comparison between Lebanese, EU and Mediterranean countries' professors/researchers (source: MIRA Survey).

Note
Survey results as in Figure 4.4. EU: European Union researchers. MPC: Mediterranean partner countries to the EU.

research and those who build careers around teaching, research and service activities have unequal rewards (Louvel and Valette 2014). Research is easier to account for than "academic services" or even teaching, since one can rely on simple bibliometrics. It appears that the university has a preference for this method of rewarding advancement rather than the more complex careers built on service given to the university, since international rankings favor this easy counting. It does not make it easier to be in Lebanon, where the pressure is higher since the university imposes the research activity and tries to play the game. This whole issue is complex and it is highly political inside the university structure; it should be handled less simplistically than by solely rewarding research activity. Responsibility for this is not only on the administration of the university, nor is it the sole result of the increasing commodification of higher education. A perfectly functional market for academic knowledge could also favor quality criteria that are not reduced to a ranking based on publications (see Chapter 2). The very heart of the "knowledge economy" should be a priority for all universities. The university and the country certainly lose due to this rather simplistic approach, and it seems to us that denouncing the commodification of higher education – although it is necessary – should not be an excuse to evade the debate.

Professors are increasingly aware of the uncomfortable situation the promotion system entails, but promotion cannot "wait" (there is a risk of ending their contracts), and many academics opt for irrelevant, small research that results in quick publication. Working with the aim of rapid publication is not an easy task either. Many interviewees affirm that foreign "international" journals are often reluctant to mention local specificities, even the name of the country (Lebanon has very bad press in the United States, and many Americans still believe the country is a ruined desert), or to refer to the political and social life of the country. We have had examples of authors explaining to us how a paper finally was accepted when the title eliminated the word "Middle East." Apart from specialized publications, this still seems not to be at all a marginal attitude coming from editors of science journals. Additionally, we have found (see Chapter 7) that language has an important effect on the scientific production, particularly in the social sciences; the marginalization of the Arabic language, even in the social sciences and humanities is quite important. Maghreb French-speaking countries, for reasons that have not been fully explained, seem more often to publish in Arabic (Arvanitis *et al.* 2010). In brief, the publication system functions as a lock-in device that imprisons researchers in a hierarchy of knowledge which is essential for their promotion, over which they have little control, as pointed out by Wiebke Keim (2010) for the social sciences in non-hegemonic countries.

When comparing AUB and USJ it is apparent that publications do not have the same role in the promotion system. AUB has imposed for many years that academics should publish a certain number of articles in recognized journals or books (in the case of SSH), a mandatory requirement when seeking promotion. Despite the directive specified by the provost not to stick to counting publications and to make qualitative assessments, academics themselves tend to count the number of articles by applying the rule of "one paper per year" and, after seven years a professor who has not published a minimum of seven articles will either be demoted or forced to leave the university. This aggressive standard probably explains much of the incentive for publication. USJ does not really take into account research in the promotion and career of academics, despite strong recommendations expressed by various bodies of the university, and this is an aspect that was highlighted by the internal working group on research, which conducted the assessment of research activities we mentioned above. Today, USJ is certainly under-producing, and this is not solely due to lack of incentives. The net result is that USJ does not hold its position in the context of increasing competition between universities in the Arab region.

Other differences between the two universities are important to mention. AUB follows a secular American system whose courses are taught exclusively in English (this was not always the case); it is widely multi-confessional and the recruitment base consists not only of children of the elite but also of the middle-class (and sometimes popular classes, thanks to a scholarship system). USJ teaches rather more in French, and even if it advocates multi-confessionalism and tolerance, it is still very marked as a university with a religious orientation: its rector is also a Jesuit priest. The civil war has profoundly influenced these institutions and a collateral effect of the war has been a weakening of the USJ, which no longer holds a quasi-monopoly on the training of the political and judicial elite (in the cabinet in 2014 only two ministers are from USJ). In addition, USJ felt more strongly the pressure exerted by the commodification of the higher education sector, denounced by Kabbanji (2012). Less expensive than its English competitors (AUB and LAU), USJ agreed to open its doors to the middle-classes. They used historically to enroll in smaller, private universities as well as the LU. Everything suggests that the middle-class is also the most weakened by the political situation of permanent crisis in Lebanon since the assassination of Rafik Hariri in 2005 (Traboulsi 2014).[24]

Recall that the AUB and USJ are certainly private universities by status, but they are primarily non-profit institutions. As private entities, research is more easily accepted and there is no particular difficulty in defending the idea that research can serve private interests, and therefore funding can also be private. From this point of view, the two institutions have, without any doubt, created strong instrumental platforms with high-level equipment. Sometime there is a terrible overlap: we have seen, for example, three sets of MNR equipment for research located in a small area of less than $10 \, \text{km}^2$.[25] The lack of sharing of major equipment is the result of the fragmentation of the academic space.

In terms of research funding, the two universities are experiencing a significant difference. The part of the budget of the university dedicated to research is roughly the same in both universities (around US$1 million) outside the Faculty of Medicine at AUB, which has additional own funding of about US$250,000 annually that comes from deductions of the honorarium's clinical consultation. This serves both to finance research projects and call for projects internally. However, AUB seems more effective at managing external funding, which in total is around US$7 million annually (AUB registered 306 projects from external financing between 2007 and 2011) (Hanafi *et al.* 2013). USJ has no mechanism to count external financing, but given the diversity of identified projects (TEMPUS, FP7 projects, CEDRE, French ANR projects, AUF, USAID, etc.), we expect an important level of external funding also for the USJ, but much less than that of AUB.

2.1.2 The public Lebanese University

Well after the creation of the private universities, the LU was created in 1951, as a public university and a counterweight to private universities (its policy was to occupy the academic fields that were not taught in the other universities). It was also thought of as a place of integration and inter-confessionalism. The LU was a place of all political debates (Favier 2004) and student struggles: political struggles and war often found fertile ground among the strongly mobilized student population in 1958 and in 1975. Despite the proliferation of small, private universities, the LU provides affordable tuition that attract almost half of the student population coming not only from the popular class, but also the middle class. At the time of its creation, the project of a national university was strongly framed by its relative position among existing universities, and its founders sought to do their best to "create fields that are not covered by other universities"; thus the first rector of the university, Fouad Ephrem Boustany, had long opposed the creation of a medical school in order to not compete with AUB and USJ (Favier 2004: 71–72). The real date of university creation could be said to be 1959, when three faculties and an Institute of Social Sciences were created. The civil war marked a profound rupture because the university was divided into different campuses/branches. This branching into different geographical areas ended up in a sectarian division of the university. Adnan El-Amine (1998) shows that each campus, except the central one in Beirut, became a representative of one of the sectarian groups:

> the risk of university branches [...] falling under pressure of local and factional interests is very real, particularly as appointments of Directors and teachers in these branches became bargaining chips in the market of nepotism and personal rather than academic interests.
>
> (Bashshur 2006: 11)

The academic field in the LU became thus not only a field of scientific forces, usual in the academic setting where faculties and departments fight for scarce resources, but also a battlefield – a structured arena within which professors and administrators, because they have different positions and proclivities, struggle to (re)define the very structure and boundaries of the field. To escape this sectarian division, other Lebanese universities that were forced to branch have adopted a strategy of (re)unification by concentrating disciplines in one campus only, such as the case of the LAU (Kriener 2014).

However, schools and faculties are partially grouped, and in recent years the Graduate School of Science and Technology has created a broad platform with the bulk of science students located in Beirut (al-Hadath campus). This effort is supported by the National Council for Scientific Research, which funds many research grants for students and projects submitted to the program of research. In addition, the Graduate School is supported by scholarships for Masters and PhD students to study mainly in France with French or Franco-Lebanese funding (AUF, Embassy of France, CEDRE program). The creation of this multidisciplinary graduate school appears as a revolution in the organization of the LU and "it could be achieved through the implementation of the LMD system that created a fertile ground for reform." (Z. Saad, interview on 20 July 2011). The project could be completed because "it was the will of our president to give a great importance to research." Our interviewee insists on the pivotal role played by the students, "the centerpiece of this system. By creating labs and platforms, they come here to work all day, they are integrated into research teams. Student involvement and support (grants and good working conditions) are consolidating the research teams."

The major issue at stake is not just financial, even if visibility allows better access to finance; it is to transform research in the LU that until recently, including in the experimental sciences, was conceived as an individual activity (Gaillard 2007). Despite the short life of a central research committee between 2001 and 2006, which distributed funds to more than 500 projects, its impact in consolidating research teams was very significant. However, many researchers who actually are not permanent employees of the university and the "old guard" of professors seemed less interested in research (Kabbanji 2010). The project of the Graduate School (*Ecole Doctorale*) was also one of the recommendations of an internal report evaluating research (never published) (Gaillard 2007). These recommendations were: the creation of units associated to the CNRS, a program that was finally established by the CNRS; the development of a database of academics and students (still non-existent); support for research projects in some relevant areas, relying on a set of common equipment (the platform is finally a reality as we have mentioned); and a mechanism for funding research projects which today still does not exist. The Graduate School in social sciences is in a phase of restructuring, and has not yet borne fruit, especially due to greater dispersion of its campuses in different geographical areas.

2.1.3 Other universities

To complete our quick overview of the major universities, we can report that the LAU has also made an effort to strengthen its presence in research. It is a university whose precursor was a Presbyterian girls' college founded in 1924. The university got its status of higher education institution in 1996 and now has seven faculties. The university numbered more than 8,000 students in 2013. After 2004, one of the objectives included in its accreditation process by an American organization was to integrate research in education. However, apart from specific areas, research remains a marginal activity at LAU.

The BAU, formerly a chapter of Alexandria University, was created as a counterweight to the Christian universities. It has long attracted a majority of Palestinian and Arab students. Its growth has slowed, but it remains a major university in the institutional landscape structure and gradually is consolidating its research activities. The big news in the academic landscape is the emergence of small private universities. One of them, the Lebanese International University (LIU), has shown very rapid growth – within seven years it has approached the size of the BAU in terms of number of students (Kabbanji 2012). This university has started to appear among the institutions that are answering calls for research projects of the CNRS in the bio-medical field.

The renewed interest in research is part of the reconstruction process after the civil war (1975–1990). Research is seen as necessary for the country's elite universities. It is partly a by-product of the growth of universities, trying to consolidate their international level by promoting research. However, universities play little role in the research orientation as they don't have any specific strategy. Their research is the byproduct of the research activities of individual professors that are willing to pursue research and to publish. Finally, it should be noted that an important driver for research is the bio-medical and clinical research that takes place in the Faculties of Medical Sciences as well as in hospitals across the country.

Academic research in Lebanon seems to match quite well this important finding of Roland Waast (2006): research can only be the result of a pact created and agreed by society (its elites, its constituent bodies, its political organs, its higher education institutions) with researchers, which gives research the necessary conditions for the exercise of a living, diverse, open, free research that will be properly financially supported. This pact can have many motivations, political or economic, cultural or religious, even antagonistic ones. But it has to be built upon reaching a usually tacit agreement (therefore the name of a "pact") that allows research to exist. The example of Tunisia, even beyond the authoritarian period, or of South Africa and Israel, are part of these examples that correspond to those situations in which society and knowledge go hand in hand, where the strategic importance of the research is provided by national institutions in order to affirm national sovereignty, to speak like Antoine Zahlan. This question goes well beyond Lebanon and concerns very directly many countries that have a fragmented research landscape. The CNRS, the only policy-making institution for research in the country, has tried to address this question for 50 years.

2.2 The public research centers

Public research centers play an important role, even if they are very reduced in the number of personnel. Public research centers are mainly involved in applied research, and four of them belong to the CNRS; the Center for Agricultural Research (LARI) belongs to the Ministry of Agriculture. These research centers conduct research missions in order to maintain a database of relevant information on national resources (food security and agriculture, natural resource management, environmental protection, observation of flora and fauna, mapping, monitoring of nuclear radiation, etc.) and to support legislation and national policies. CNRS and LARI have around 25 researchers. The budget for these public centers comes mainly from the state, especially with regard to salaries. In addition, there are some other centers whose main mission is neither teaching nor research, such as the Industrial Research Institute (IRI) (for scientific testing and analysis)[26] and the Central Administration of Statistics (CAS) (state agency for economic and demographic statistics).[27] It is important to note in this context that in 2012 salaries of CNRS researchers were reassessed and pension plans revalued, as was the case for the public university. These changes should attract academics in search of research careers.

Note that some of these public research centers, although modest in size, have long historical trajectories. This is the case of one of the four CNRS research centers that was founded in 1975 in geophysics. It followed the Ksara Observatory (1920–1975), which was run by Jesuits, and was for many years the only observatory in the eastern Mediterranean. The agricultural research center dates back to the creation of an agricultural station in Tal Amara in the Bekaa Valley after Lebanon gained independence (1946) as a training center, supported by French technical assistance. The Center for Remote Sensing, Center for Marine Sciences (in Batroun) and the Lebanese Atomic Energy Commission (founded in 1996 with the support of the IAEA) were all established as centers of the CNRS.

The civil war interrupted the activity of these centers. For example, the marine research center was moved from Batroun to Jounieh (closer to Beirut) during the war and returned to its original location after the war. By their small size, these centers remain fragile as evidenced by the misadventure of the fifth CNRS center specializing in renewable energies. A Saudi agency had financed the establishment of the center and then hired its nine researchers to work in Saudi Arabia. That was the end of this research center. Recently, the CNRS has ruled against significant funding of this type as this may endanger the existence of the centers.

The four CNRS centers are highly involved in activities supported by international funding through international cooperation with the IAEA, the EU, Italian and French bilateral cooperation, as well as many international institutions: CIHEAM, FAO, UNDP, ICARDA, ACSAD and the World Bank. Without this funding, projects would be significantly smaller.

LARI is in a similar situation. It's the only public institution dedicated to agricultural research; however, it is not the only institution conducting agricultural research: Faculties of Agriculture at AUB and LU, as well as CNRS centers, are also working on issues such as soil, fertilization, etc. LARI researchers dedicate about 60 percent of their time to research. Moreover, until 2006 LARI was exclusively financed by public funds. It is only recently that it began to look for external funding and international collaborations (Gaillard 2007: 28ff.).

2.3 *The private research centers*

Lastly, we should mention a multitude of privately managed research centers that aim at providing research and consultancies for public, private, national and international clients. Most of these private centers are concentrated in the social sciences and their origins, motivations and funding are very diverse, but in general they tend to provide studies that have a policy objective (on education, migration, public management, economic affairs, international relations, etc.). The second type of private centre is the R&D unit of industrial enterprises, on which, until the 2012 innovation survey of CNRS, we had absolutely no previous information.

The private centers, one should say "small" private research centers, are usually research NGOs that raise funds and respond to external commands. They are probably less important numerically than is usually perceived: for instance, the IFPO survey of researchers in the social sciences and research centers counted 71 researchers out of which only nine belonged to these private centers (Zakhia 2007). In the MIRA Survey, discussed below, only ten people were identified as from a private center, out of 117 researchers. However, most common is the situation where researchers and academics are hired by a private center for a specific project and publish as part of the center's activity. In this way they escape the institutional structure of the university, get paid more, and curiously enough, publish their work only as part of the NGO. Thus, among the 45 social scientists interviewed by J. Kabbanji and his team, 22 reported having received funding for research from a Lebanese research center (Kabbanji 2010). Hanafi (2007; 2010) examines the mushrooming of centers that have sprung up in Palestine, Lebanon, Egypt (and to a lesser extent, Jordan). It can be explained by the multiplicity of funding sources available, mainly from European and American donors, as well as United Nations agencies, who all seem to prefer to fund these NGOs rather than the universities. The fear of the funders seems to be that the universities will "swallow" the funds without delivering results. Most probably what happens here is that the relation is a personal one, not an institutional demand. This has translated into the emergence of the "intellectual entrepreneurs" (Romani 2001), "expert-sociologists" (Kabbanji 2005) or "consultants" (El-Kenz 2005a; 2005b) who have become part of the networks of the donor agencies, who know how to manage the cognitive and cultural codes of the donor agencies in their research field. These researchers produce mainly empirical work, with little theoretical basis. But the main characteristic of these centers is that they are located outside the universities and at the same time use the academic personnel. The Issam Fares Institute at AUB identifies in a survey it made on the subject of "policy-oriented research centers," 240 "policy research institutes" in the Arab countries, with the largest number in Lebanon, Palestine and Morocco: 40 percent of these centers were independent organizations (IFI 2011). The study concluded on the "lack of research capacity in most of these centers, the interference of funders and governments in their orientations, and the lack of transparency in the making of public policy."

The recent creation of the Arab Council for the Social Sciences (ACSS), with the support of foreign funds dedicated to research for development, attempts to support the strengthening of social sciences research. It aims at supporting researchers based in academic and research institutions. This is a very exceptional initiative and only time will tell if the scientific community in the Arab world will respond to the ACSS call. That would probably be the best response to the challenge mentioned in the Issam Fares Institute (IFI) in its 2011 report and the endemic weakness of the social sciences: their distance from the institutional harbor that should be the universities. The re-integration of the activities deployed by these centers into the universities would probably help overcome the fragmentation of the social sciences community, and, by way of consequence, enrich the public debates about the challenges facing Arab societies.

Finally, it is important to note that in the industrial sector, R&D centers are integrated into companies. The innovation survey that concerned the activities of companies in 2010 and 2011 in Lebanon helped to quantify the existence of centers of industrial R&D in the country: 23 percent of companies have R&D units and 38.7 percent carry out R&D without having a formal R&D unit in their company. For small and medium enterprises, these R&D centers/units are usually small (between 1.7 and 2.8 employees on average), while this average reaches 18 people for the seven larger companies of this survey. From this representative survey of the industrial sector of the country, Rigas Arvanitis (2014) estimated around US$120 million spending on research activities in 2011. This is the first time Lebanon could dispose of such an estimation that reveals real opportunities for applied research that have been neglected by the universities, except for a few initiatives. At the national level, in addition to the above-mentioned Berytech incubator, we should mention the Lebanese Industrial Research Achievements Program (LIRA) that was initiated by the Lebanese Industrial Research Association. It aims at facilitating contacts between the private sectors and universities. Every two years LIRA funds, on the basis of a public technology forum, research applied to industry.

However, the same innovation survey conducted in the industrial sector and ICT companies noted the almost total absence of links between the private sector and academic researchers or research centers in the development of industrial products and processes. As for universities, the establishment of a system of promotion based on the number of publications discourages academics from developing relationships with companies that are necessarily time-consuming and not recognized by the promotion system. In addition, universities are badly equipped to support the drafting and filing of patents, which is usually expensive. In brief, there is, strictly speaking, no technology transfer units dealing with technology transfer in Lebanese universities. All contacts that we have mentioned so far, such as the ones in the Faculty of Science of USJ, are direct and personal contacts developed with industrial enterprises.

3 A national research policy with an international orientation

3.1 The CNRS and its research support programs

The CNRS combines three functions: a funding agency for research, a council (*majliss*) of science and technology to coordinate research activities at a national level and to establish national policy research, and research performance in research units (four research centers).

In its function as funding agency, the CNRS has distributed research grants through calls for proposals submitted by universities and national research centers since 1962. The funding program lasted 13 years and was interrupted in 1975 by the civil war. The new support program was subsequently formalized in 1998. Continuing this consolidation, in 2005–2006, the CNRS developed a national policy for science and technology whose implementation was interrupted by the assassination of Prime Minister Rafik Hariri in February 2005. This event marked a watershed: after this period the financial situation of CNRS became much more difficult.

CNRS finances research projects in different fields by providing small grants. Its objective is to encourage the maintenance of research activities primarily at universities. Therefore, it was – and remains – quite open to various fields; however, its calls for proposals have not been very competitive because of limited funding (average of US$2,500 per project annually). In 2000 a reorganization of the call for proposals was undertaken whereby the selection committees that evaluate and shortlist projects were consolidated and it is now the board that makes the decision to award grants. This Grant Research Program (GRP) was accompanied by associated research units (ARUs) that provide funding for projects taking place between several institutions. As of 2004 the program has been open to SSH, requiring a modification in CNRS regulations.

The program certainly has a structuring effect on research in the country. First, obtaining a grant from CNRS is more about quality than a financial windfall, as the monetary support is small. In addition, it is the only national program funding research. AUB, for example, often provides extra funding for the projects that were initially selected by the CNRS. Finally, the project application must also come from the institutions and not individual researchers, requiring that the institutional affiliation be kept informed, maintain approval and manage the request in a transparent way.

In the seven years following the reorganization of the program (2000–2006), 614 projects were approved for a total budget of US$3.2 million. The selection rate at that time had a relatively high acceptance rate of around 48.5 percent. In the next period (2007–2011), the CNRS funded a total budget of US$3.782 million in 14 academic and research institutions (Table 4.2). There has therefore been a decrease in funding from the CNRS in real monetary terms because inflation was on average 1.3 percent in 2000–2006 and 5.7 percent (10 percent in 2008 following the global financial crisis) in 2007–2011. Finally, the average

Table 4.2 Distribution of financial support from CNRS by scientific areas (2007–2011)

Discipline	No. projects	Amount (thousand US$)	Percentage of total funding
Basic science, engineering and IT	130	1,333	35.57
Medical sciences, public health and biology	92	1,200	31.75
Environmental and natural resources	50	561	14.70
Agriculture and food technology	30	400	10.45
Social sciences and humanities	44	287	4.53
Total	346	3,782	100.00

Source: data extracted from *Five Years Report, 2007–2011*, National Council for Scientific Research (CNRS), pp. 12–14.

number of projects funded per year fell from 87 projects per year on average to 69 projects. The year 2012 was particularly difficult for the CNRS as it "lost" nearly one-third of its budget; however it was reinstated the following year. Again, as we detailed in the previous section, in times of political instability research is not a political priority for the government (which came after a provisional government as it took almost a year and a half to form after the political crisis of 2011). In 2014, US$450,000 was allocated to fund 60 new projects (selected from 151 proposals). The success rate of projects has been significantly lowered compared to the beginning of the decade, with 40 percent of projects[28] approved against almost 50 percent in 2000.

Figure 4.6 shows the distribution over the last three years. A few institutions have received grants: the AUB won almost half of these grants (44.6 percent in 2007–2011), followed by the LU (27.6 percent) and CNRS research centers (8 percent). It is remarkable that USJ gets fewer projects (3.6 percent) than Balamand University (4.6 percent) and thus is at the same level of participation as the LAU (3.2 percent). USJ researchers clearly prefer bilateral international financing and other funding sources. Researchers from CNRS research centers also seem to have an advantage, especially when considering their relatively small number. Finally, note that the distribution by institutions is substantially the same since 2000, despite the greater institutionalization and structuring of research that has occurred over the past decade.

In contrast, distribution by field has changed significantly (Figure 4.7). The once dominant medical sciences are now less important than the basic sciences and engineering (a decrease of 20 percent that benefits mainly basic sciences and engineering, which show an increase of 30 percent). This change reflects a rebalancing of university research that comes from an improved research capability in disciplines other than medicine. The number and quality of projects has not diminished, according to the observations of grant managers, but the competition becomes stronger and the quality has rather improved. In short, what reflects this change is a consolidation of academic research. Only weak financial means would hinder the CNRS expansion.

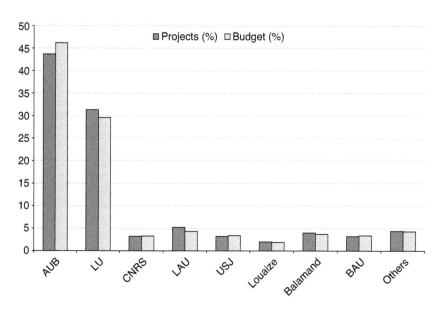

Figure 4.6 Percentage of total approved projects and percentage of total GRP budget, 2010–2013 (source: CNRS).

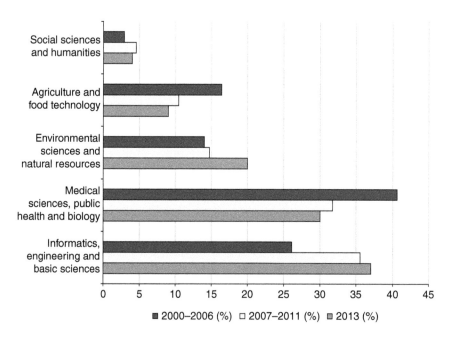

Figure 4.7 Distribution of grants by disciplines: comparison of the periods 2000–2006, 2007–2011 and 2013 (source: CNRS).

CNRS also awards scholarships to students to complete their PhD abroad or in Lebanon. Since its launch in 1962 (until 2012), the CNRS has distributed 999 scholarships for study abroad. During the period 1999–2012, of the 277 scholarships, 244 were for PhDs in France, 14 in England and five each in the United States, Canada and Belgium. Scholarships are also awarded to students enrolled abroad who carry out their work in Lebanon. Finally, since 2001, the CNRS awards scholarships ("Awards for Excellence" program) to students with the best baccalaureate-level achievement.

3.2 Drafting a national policy document

The CNRS is responsible, through its mandate, for national research policy. To do so, it established a national plan for scientific research. In 2001, the CNRS mobilized a UNESCO expert to develop an exercise in defining national priorities and sector recommendations. The resulting STIP document (Science, Technology, and Innovation Policy – CNRS 2006) emerged after consultation workshops with 30 experts, most of them researchers and academics. The Action Plan was approved in 2002 by the CNRS and the government, but its implementation, planned to begin in 2005, was interrupted by the assassination of Prime Minister Hariri. However, some of the proposed activities have succeeded. On the one hand, the CNRS has earned its reputation as a coordinating body for research, one of the major objectives of the plan. Although ordinary people are not aware of the council, the small research community does know of it and refer to it in different ways. On the other hand, many of the opportunities identified by the work of experts in the STIP (industry, ICT, agriculture, environment, medicine and public health) have actually triggered several activities supported by the CNRS: creation of associated research units; participation in the selection committee of the Franco-Lebanese CEDRE program; support of the development of international projects; parliamentary activities when they relate to natural resources; realization of an innovation survey in collaboration with the World Bank and the Office of the Prime Minister; seismic hazard mapping in collaboration with the French Research Institute for Development and USJ; the launching of an observatory of science and technology (LORDI) in cooperation with a French research institute (IRD); activities aimed at structuring the national science community with the support of the Lebanese Association for the Advancement of Science (LAAS); publication of the *Lebanese Science Journal*, a refereed journal; and support for thematic scientific meetings.

Nevertheless, it can be said that beyond the STIP document, there is no *explicit research policy of the CNRS*.[29] But an implicit policy exists and is embodied in its support for teams and scholarships to researchers, which is mainly a capacity building policy, with a preference for some research topics all related to the environment and natural resources. This orientation has recently been further strengthened by the creation in 2013 of a Lebanese Observatory on the Environment (O-LIFE) as a platform for the coordination of research in the country. The Italian Cooperation has also donated more than €5 million with the launch of an oceanographic vessel and the establishment of a wide CANA project on marine and coastal resources in relation to the Center of Marine Research. The CNRS has also been heavily involved in the Euro-Mediterranean projects proposed by the EU.[30] Thus, it would be unfair to limit the role of the CNRS only to capacity building and project funding: all CNRS international activities are now the heart of its objectives.

4 The fragmented Lebanese science community

We have tried in the above pages to describe the Lebanese research system. Among its ingredients we found the universities, the research units inside the universities, a small number of mission-oriented public research centers, numerous small private policy-oriented NGOs, and an unexpectedly high number of industrial R&D units; a rather strong human base but mainly focused on teaching and clinical practice rather than research per se; some public funding and high foreign sources of funding; and since few years ago relatively decent salaries to the academic sector, even in the public sector. We observed the total absence of technology transfer units but a solid technological incubator. If it were not for the political instability, Lebanon appears to be a rather strong "research system." Nonetheless, what we observe also is the extreme fragmentation of the Lebanese scientific community, not only on disciplinary grounds, but also institutionally. This fragmentation goes hand in hand with a strong internationalization of research.

We use two separate surveys to highlight these aspects. The first is a survey of 65 academics-researchers of the AUB (Hanafi *et al.* 2013).[31] The second source consists of the responses of Lebanese researchers in the MIRA Survey of collaboration between European researchers and researchers from southern Mediterranean countries in 2011–2012 (Gaillard *et al.* 2013).[32]

The MIRA Survey identified 117 researchers based in Lebanon who worked in cooperation with European colleagues (86 men and 31 women made up 73.5 percent and 26.5 percent of the sample, similar to the average distribution in the survey). The low proportion of women was also the same for European respondents. But in Lebanon, most women were in the younger age range. The Lebanese responses correspond to 5.2 percent of the responses of Mediterranean countries. Of the total, 85.5 percent are professors and 8.5 percent are full-time researchers; 42 percent of interviewees are managers of institutions (6 faculty directors, 26 heads of departments and 17 heads of laboratories). Many of these academics spend most of their time in teaching, as we showed above; research is generally not their main activity. Indeed, only 13.5 percent spend half of their time or more conducting research against 33 percent for teaching activities. They are, therefore, first and foremost teachers. Consultancy, as it is declared, holds, contrary to our expectations, very little time and this is also confirmed by the interviews. By contrast, those who are related to private research centers and NGOs conduct short-term research according to focused requests, mainly (but not exclusively) in the social sciences. Rarely are these results published (Hanafi

2011). Moreover, the main clients are international organizations in Lebanon: UN agencies, as well as European and North American foundations and donors, as we mentioned above (see Section 1.3). It is a very powerful driver toward fragmenting the social sciences and neither the CNRS nor the foreign research institutions that collaborate with academics in Lebanon have been able to draft a policy that has the objective of overcoming the institutional dispersion.[33]

The majority of the survey is located in the research fields that are dominant in the country, such as engineering and medicine and clinical sciences (Figure 4.8). They are followed by the environmental sciences (earth sciences, astronomy, oceanography, ecology, agriculture, biology of fauna and flora, basic biology, etc.) and mathematics and computer sciences. Note that the medical sciences are the majority in the country's production, and the survey sample is under-representing this field. The survey sample is drawn from WoS authors, especially those who are co-authors with a European colleague. We have not tried to corrected the anti-SSH bias of the WoS, nor have we tried to "force" one or another discipline. With the important exception concerning the fact that medical and clinical sciences are under-represented, the distribution by disciplines is fairly consistent with the publications (Figure 4.9). Finally, the importance of environmental sciences is consistent with the active role taken by CNRS research centers in these areas (see above, the distribution by areas of the research projects obtained from the CNRS).

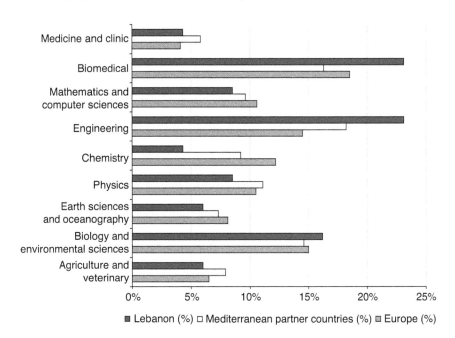

Figure 4.8 Distribution of MIRA respondents by disciplines; comparison Lebanon, Mediterranean and European countries (source: MIRA Survey; computation by the authors).

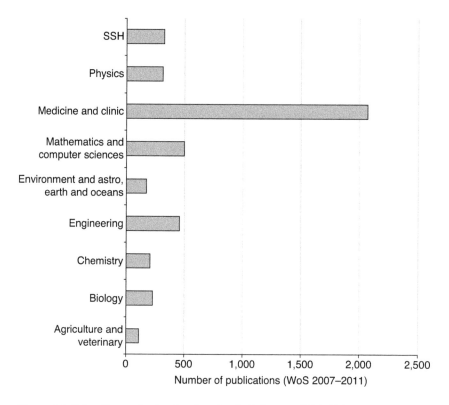

Figure 4.9 Scientific production by domains in Lebanon, 2009–2011 (source: Web of Science, treated by C. Tayoun/R. Arvanitis, July 2012).

5 The context of international collaborations

We have shown (Section 6.2 of Chapter 2) the importance of international collaborations. Particularly for the case of Lebanon, we have seen that the increased collaborations took place with European partners rather than the usual North American partners, particularly when looking at the English-speaking universities. Chapter 2 explains how the international collaborations in Arab countries are closely linked to international mobility for studies and stays abroad. In the case of Lebanon this is a feature that is strongly accentuated.

5.1 International openness since the training years

Many respondents to the survey pursued their studies abroad (86 percent) (Table 4.3). This figure is particularly high. The average for the Mediterranean countries surveyed is 40 percent; it is 15 percent for Europeans. One-third of the Lebanese sample has a post-doc and 22 people (68.7 percent among those with a post-doc) indicate having done this post-doc abroad. This result is consistent

Table 4.3 Studies and post-doc abroad

	Number	Percentage
You did your whole studies abroad	102	85.7
You did a post-doc	32	26.9
You did part or all this post-doc abroad	22	18.5

Source: Survey MIRA.

with the average among the researchers from Mediterranean countries (69 percent of researchers in these countries have a post-doc abroad), but obviously much higher than the rate for the European researchers (29 percent); it only reflects the existence of a multiplicity of research centers in European countries compared with the Mediterranean countries.

In addition, the Lebanese stay on average much longer abroad. It should also be noted that 29.4 percent of respondents have a second nationality (14 French, six Canadians, four Americans and ten from other countries). More than half of the Lebanese population has indeed dual nationality (Kasparian 2003); the country has for long been a country of emigration and it still is.

There is another significant difference between Lebanese researchers and those in other Arab countries, which is the very strong connection to France. In the public LU, where classes are given in Arabic, many professors speak and publish mainly in French, especially in the social sciences. The Graduate School of the Faculty of Science of the LU recently reorganized and has built its capacity building project on many collaborations and partnerships with French universities. This is also the case of USJ and many predominantly Christian universities (Holy Spirit of Kaslik University, NDU, Balamand). Anecdotal evidence at AUB, which teaches in English, confirms also a strong connection to France. Contacts of English-speaking universities with North American funding agencies seem also to be easier. In this manner, multilinguism helps this "internationalization by the language" that is rooted in Lebanon's history; it might have a relation also to the relevance of research with the local society and economy.

5.2 Frameworks of international cooperation

We stressed the rather low public or university budgets dedicated to research. International cooperation helps to fill this gap. Table 4.4 shows the framework in which collaborations take place according to the researchers interviewed for the MIRA Survey. Note that the share of researchers engaged in international collaborations in Lebanon is much higher than in the case of other Mediterranean countries and, remarkably, within international projects. The other specificity of Lebanon is its very strong connection to the Gulf countries. An unpublished survey on Lebanese professionals[34] working abroad has shown the importance of their activities in the Gulf region.

Table 4.4 If these collaborations still continue today, please give the framework in which they take place (percentage of number of responses)

	Lebanon	Percentage	Mediterranean countries	Percentage
Without official framework	57	72.2	1,104	58.5
Bilateral cooperation	55	71.4	920	48.8
International project	25	53.2	461	24.4
EU project	22	50.0	402	21.3
Foreign public project	16	42.1	234	12.4
Foreign private project	3	12.0	51	2.7
Arab-funded project	12	35.3	90	4.8
Total responses	117		1,887	

Source: Survey MIRA.

Thus, according to the Lebanese researchers surveyed in MIRA, international collaborations are essential: they allow them to have access to new and interesting scientific topics (85.5 percent), to improve the impact and visibility of one's research (82.4 percent), to resolve scientific and technical problems that could not be solved with domestic resources alone (80.8 percent), to publish internationally (76.9 percent), access to better equipment and working conditions (76.8 percent) and to acquire leading-edge know-how (76.7 percent). By contrast, in the survey, collaborations are less related to the need to gain access to research subjects (such as natural or social phenomena, located in given areas) (46.1 percent).

For these possible objectives to engage in international collaborations, Lebanese respondents reported their motivations: access to international funding is very important (90.5 percent of responses), followed by the possibility of achieving greater mobility (84.5 percent), reaching more diverse partnerships (including diversity of approaches) (82.7 percent), participating in international expert networks (88.5 percent), making one's research fit into a more global scenario (79.8 percent) or increasing the scientific visibility (85.4 percent). The ability to publish internationally appears to be the most frequently cited motivation (91.3 percent) and we do wonder whether this motivation is not induced by the university promotion system.

The AUB survey that we conducted concurs to a large degree with the MIRA Survey results but provides further qualitative data. At AUB, interviewees collaborate both with other faculty members at AUB, as well as with other researchers abroad, notably through contacts formed during PhD and post-doctoral years abroad. Interviewees were asked if they were connected to a network either locally, regionally or internationally (Table 4.5). More than 60 percent were "connected" locally or internationally, much fewer regionally (only one-third).[35] As we can see, the international connections are more frequent and relate to the foreign education of the AUB professors. This is also fully supported by the numerous extra-mural grants that AUB obtained. In the field of engineering, one professor with extensive experience in international projects said:

Table 4.5 Connections of AUB professors to local, regional or international networks (%)

	Locally	*Regionally*	*Internationally*
Not connected	35	45	20
Connected	50	31	53
Very well connected	15	7	7
N/A		17	20

Source: our survey at AUB.

collaboration is more competitive in the United States; you often feel like you're doing an original thing in Lebanon, because many fields have yet to be researched due to a lag. In America, there are many referral centers. In Lebanon however, there is only one referral center, which means everyone knows who you are.

On the contrary, not many are connected at the "regional" (that is, in neighboring countries) level, either because they do not have the money (here, "time and money") to go to a neighboring country, or because they simply do not feel interested by what happens there (which we have been told often and in various forms). One assistant professor put it in a cynical way "Using the money for travels. You don't use the university grant for a presentation in a close country. You use it to go to the US or Europe. I go to a country where I expect to see new things!" Others noted that "researchers from Arab countries do not communicate among themselves; they remain in their field long while foreign researchers progress much faster in their research" (associate professor of medicine).

In spite of declarations by our interviewees, rare are the cases of local collaboration, often induced by material issues, such as the ARU on urban pollution which is an AUB–USJ collaboration. Eight of these associations among universities, supported by the CNRS, exist. This policy is very recent; it is obliging universities to pool resources around a project across a two-year period, pooling also resources from CNRS and the two universities. It is a way to create a viable research capacity (instrumentation, common training) between different groups, usually one or two professors from the associated universities. Researchers appreciate this policy and the CNRS has already eight of these ARUs.

Internally, it was often found that professors collaborate with their students (as research assistants or simply because they are gearing their students' work toward their own research):

A big part of my work consists in taking students to a PhD level with the hope that they will come back to Lebanon and contribute to ongoing projects, so they would come back to something they already know and build on existing projects.

(Professor in basic sciences)

This type of collaboration with students is common, although as Katz and Martin (1997: 5) show, the word "collaboration" is understood between peers (i.e., scientists of similar standing).[36] For Lebanon, the collaboration of students is not at all institutionalized: it remains a personal decision of the professor, and the student does not necessarily get involved further in the research projects. This close connection of students and professors is weakened when there is no doctoral schools (as is the case of the AUB, which delivers very few PhDs), contrary to the LU or USJ (or even any of the other universities that deliver doctoral degrees). The absence of the doctoral degree (or PhD) at the AUB is probably also increasing this dominant trait of a research activity that is not directly linked to local objectives but mainly to international publications. Students graduated from AUB are directly oriented toward an American university, since they obtain a US degree.[37]

Coming back to the MIRA Survey, we could mention that difficulties establishing collaborative programs should not be underestimated. Among the Lebanese responses, 79.7 percent believe that the lack of cooperation frameworks is the main reason they do not engage in international projects; 45 percent report inter-institutional difficulty; and 40 percent report that the establishment of collaborations is time consuming, time being the rarest resource in the Lebanese research system (especially in LU and USJ).

Collaborations are related with the thesis director (usually at the beginning of a career), some colleague met in the lab or in the institution one has worked at (and this correlates strongly with stays abroad, which in the case of the Lebanese are longer and more frequent than other Arab countries in the Mediterranean basin), colleagues met while they were visiting (as is the case of the authors of this book) and scientists met in conferences. It is important to underline that diasporic scientists are not so frequently mentioned (17 percent of ongoing collaborations, slightly higher than the 13 percent in Arab countries). Finally, people that have never been met before are mentioned by 10 percent of the Lebanese (against 13 percent in other Arab countries and 18 percent in the EU). The relations are definitely individual in the case of the Lebanese and, more often than not, face to face. This might be interpreted as a sign of the rather dispersed nature of collaborations (as well as hiding a large array of situations difficult to summarize in a series of answers to a questionnaire).

Unlike the natural sciences, in the social sciences, international funding is not really related to the formation of research teams. In our interviews, there were many who mentioned sources of funding from the UN agencies or foundations (Ford, Heinrich Böll, Friedrich-Ebert, etc.). Too specific or too tied to a particular person, these funds also raise a fundamental question about the type of objects and methodologies that may be relevant in Western countries without meeting the national reality. Similarly, Candice Raymond (2013), studying the research of historians in Lebanon, notices that collaborations occur between Lebanese and Western researchers.

We already mentioned the Arab Council for the Social Sciences created recently, which tries to foster local research and also inter-institutional – as opposed to individual – cooperation. Other centers like the Center for Arab Unity Studies (CAUS) and the Arab Center for Studies and Policy (Doha Institute)

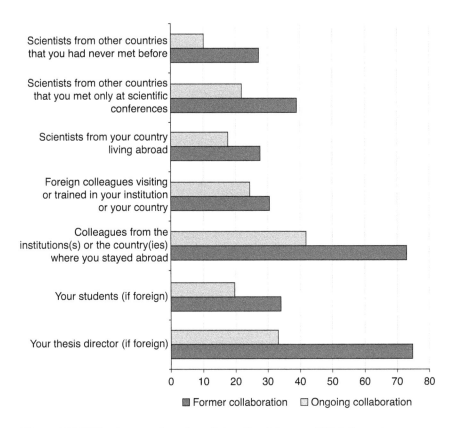

Figure 4.10 With whom are done the collaborations? (source: MIRA Survey).

create platforms for inter-Arab cooperation. We have also seen a series of networks of universities in the Mediterranean region (Thetys, driven by the University of Marseille, or UNIMED by the University of Rome) that also prepare to respond to EU calls. But overall, it seems that the international teams in the social sciences are still rare and collaborations are driven by individuals.

Some international projects don't fund research but merely workshops. One typical example are projects funded by the French *Agence Nationale de la Recherche* (ANR) – this agency has not taken into account, in its ruling, the participation of non-European partners. Lebanese researchers involved in six such projects[38] were frustrated that the research expenses by third-parties were not covered, even for research assistants.[39] The participant observation we have shows very diminished results from three or four meetings every six to nine months where people say almost the same thing. Many "local" researchers end up without having their contribution published: they contribute only to two among 20 publications resulting from these ANR projects. This does not necessarily mean a simple hegemony of the French research team, but rather some difficulty from the side of the Arab researchers in avoiding disagreements or even preferring this low-cost solution. Additionally, these projects do not fund translations.

Finally, the absence of international collaboration is often voluntary, sometimes for personal or ideological reasons. We were amazed to find some faculty who speak perfect English and French unwilling to communicate with their peers abroad. They state clearly that they are not interested. These cases who adopt this kind of extreme "counter-hegemonic" position are not very common.[40]

In summary, in the natural sciences, collaborations are developed inside strong institutional frameworks. For historical reasons, many relationships are established with France, as we have shown. This trend is now reflected in stronger collaborations in the framework of European projects. Increasingly, these collaborations go through PhD co-supervisions – a new practice favored by French universities that has become fairly common with Lebanese PhD students. Articles co-authored with Europeans have risen sharply. Few collaborations have developed with other researchers in the Arab countries and the Middle East, although it appears that the Gulf countries are becoming a new location of interest for collaborations (many Lebanese are working in Gulf universities).

Finally we should admit that there is a tension between the internationalization of research and its local relevance. One researcher from USJ put it clearly that when Lebanese researchers do not have links to the local private sector, they end up looking for international collaboration. This was repeated by a professor of engineering at AUB, confirming that the "University should not be an ivory tower. We don't go to the private sector. Let it come to us if they need us. We have our reputation." As Figure 4.11 suggests, we may schematically consider AUB as the most institutionalized, USJ (specifically in applied research) as the most locally relevant and LU as the missed opportunity to be locally or globally relevant.

5.3 Jordan vs. Lebanon

It is very interesting to contrast the relatively internationalized Lebanese case with the less internationalized Jordanian case.

Lebanese academics have more often graduated from abroad than have their Jordanian counterparts. In Jordan, two-thirds of the sample graduated with a BA from Jordan, followed by Arab countries (Egypt, Lebanon, Iraq, Kuwait and Saudi Arabia) and a very few from other countries. The percentage of those that graduated from Jordan drops to less than half (46 percent) for the Masters degree and 8 percent for the PhD. The main destination of the Masters and PhD is the United States. The Jordanian government has privileged this country for its scholarship program. Compared to Lebanon, Jordanian academics have graduated from many non-Western countries, including Arab countries, most of them in SSH. The reason behind that is often financial. Rare Jordanian academics have a fellowship after their PhD. However, many have a job during their career outside of Jordan. The main destination is the Gulf countries, where salaries are much higher than in Jordanian universities.

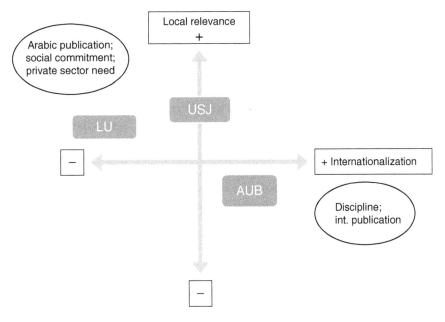

Figure 4.11 Lebanese universities between relevancy and internationalization (theoretical representation).

This difference will have implications for networking with other academics. A majority of interviewed academics in Jordan declared being well-connected or just connected at local, regional and international levels (respectively 69, 65 and 71 percent) (see Table 4.6). What differentiates Jordan from Lebanon is a relatively more integrated research community locally and regionally which is the reason many graduated from Arab countries and worked in some of them (mainly in the Gulf).

Linguistic abilities of Jordanian academics are lower than those of their Lebanese counterparts. These abilities play a large role in the level of engagement of

Table 4.6 Different levels of networking for Jordanian professors

	Locally		Regionally		Internationally	
	Number	*Percentage*	*Number*	*Percentage*	*Number*	*Percentage*
Not connected at all	12	17	11	16	11	16
Weakly connected	9	13	13	19	9	13
Connected	38	55	36	51	28	40
Very well connected	10	14	10	14	22	31
Total	69	100	70	100	70	100

Source: survey among 73 academics in Jordan performed by Abeldhakim Al Husban.

researchers with global research projects or global scientific research networks. While most of the researchers at the department of science and engineering don't suffer from any linguistic inabilities since many of them are graduates from Western universities, many of those who specialize in the humanities, education and religious studies do have difficulties with foreign languages and, often, only speak Arabic. Therefore, their participation in global conferences is very limited, so much so that some have never participated in a conference outside of Jordan. However, it is interesting to note that a large majority of the Jordanian inter-viewees declared having membership of a regional or international scientific association or society (Table 4.7).

In terms of domains of research, those who are connected to regional or inter-national research projects are largely skewed in favor of the natural sciences, engineering and applied sciences; rare are the professors in education, literature, art or religious studies, as most of the latter are graduated from non-Western countries.

6 Conclusion

Crossing our ethnographic and prosopographic information with bibliometric and institutional analysis, we contributed to a more objective view of the research dynamics in Lebanon. Research is like the country's image: deeply fragmented, certainly largely due to the fragmentation of universities, but also, paradoxically, to its openness to the international community. If international collaborations are a necessary ingredient to develop research, and even vital for a small country like Lebanon (as pointed out by Caroline Wagner [2006]), the fact remains that they may result in some thematic dispersion. Insofar as the CNRS has failed to implement its planned research policy, it is difficult to speak of a national research strategy. Nonetheless, the institution has shown a policy resolutely turned toward the international, only constrained by the lack of locally available choices. Universities, even the most productive ones such as the AUB, do not have any real research policy, except to help professors to make the necessary contacts and build lasting relationships with foreign partners. Unlike other universities, however, AUB has strengthened the management of external funds based on an efficient specialized service that is not limited to managing funds, but performs "fund raising," searching for external funding sources.

Table 4.7 Affiliation of Jordanians to a regional or international association

	No	*Percentage*
Regional (Arab world)	17	23
International	12	16
Both	36	49
No membership	8	11
Total	73	100

For faculty members, the research activities are sometimes difficult to fit into their schedule and only the pressure of their career forces them to undertake research. So, for many of them, and since they are in contact with foreign researchers, research remains a fairly individual activity. The lack of structured teams is still a reality for most areas and higher education institutions. Recent efforts such as the Faculty of Science of USJ or the Graduate School of Science and Technology of LU, mentioned in this chapter, indicate a willingness to go beyond this situation. The limits of this structuring exercise remain in the difficulty to produce research that is relevantly connected to social actors beyond academia. This second challenge is more difficult to meet.

CNRS nevertheless remains, as much by its funding program as its ability to mobilize resources abroad, the only organization capable of coordinating research. In addition, academics engaged in research are willing to work with the CNRS in the framework of actions clearly defined. Its chronic lack of staff, however, induces always a certain dispersion that is difficult to escape. Moreover, in the particular case of the social sciences, the effort to create a structured program should rely on an internal capability to construct such a policy. Moreover, it will always be difficult to compete with a multitude of financial offers made by international donors. The collaboration with a regional initiative such as the Arab Academy of Social Sciences would probably be necessary. In the context of a weak state and under budget constraints, only the work of individuals and private companies seems to create engines for effective initiatives in research as well as innovation.

We have insisted in the earlier chapters, as well as in the case of the Lebanese research system, on the two main challenges: the need to overcome the fragmentation by grouping initiatives, institutions and laboratories, gathering people in common projects, in brief providing ground for a vibrant scientific community; and the need to produce research that is linked to the needs of the country, relevant for the development of its economy and its social sector, and not exclusively producing articles in the highly recognized journals. We began by referring to the work of Antoine Zahlan, who has had the enormous merit of insisting on the need for relevance, in Lebanon as in all Arab countries, and give research a proper space that it deserves. Nevertheless, the relevance of research cannot be limited to issues of training and management; it is also a political decision and, as such, requires a reflection on how to mobilize actors beyond the university and the research centers.

Notes

1 For political reasons, there has been no census in Lebanon since 1932, with the pretext not to change the religious community balance.
2 Nahas (2009: 15) mentions a ratio of the number of students per 100,000 inhabitants of 0.4143, one of the highest in the Arab world.
3 The civil war in Lebanon has been among the worst civil wars of the century: one-third of the population was displaced, 150,000 persons were killed, 180,000 wounded, 13,000 kidnapped, 17,000 disappeared and 13,000 handicapped (Abou-Rjeily and Labaki 1993).

4 The CNRS has been the only institution describing its activities with an annual report, until the civil war.

5 To our knowledge, one of the few references to teamwork research in Lebanon is the analysis of Claude Dubar (2006), which describes, in terms of its practical realization, the survey on social classes in Lebanon, published in 1976, an "unlikely collective research" (p. 39) as he called it.

6 As mentioned in preceding chapters, the ESTIME project covered all the countries around the Mediterranean – see final report by Rigas Arvanitis (2007).

7 On the natural sciences, see Kabbanji (2010) and Bechara and Kabbanji (2006). Social sciences: Kabbanji and Moussaoui (2007), Zakhia (2007) and, later published as a book, Kabbanji (2010). A brief report on the innovation system (Kabbanji 2007) and a report on research funding available locally (Hanafi 2007).

8 1,464 items in SCI Expanded + SSCI of WoS for 2014.

9 These unreliable figures published by UNESCO on this subject (or, even worse, those of COMSTECH) again refer to definitions that vary from one country to another. For instance, following the recommendations of the Frascati Manual, Lebanon does not count PhD students as researchers, as does Jordan. See the data contained in the report of the ESCWA (Hanafi and Arvanitis 2013a: 51).

10 The estimate is based on the new database located in Jordan, E-Marefa (www.e--marefa.net) (71 articles) plus the two leading journals in the region, *Idafat: The Arab Journal of Sociology* (21 articles) and the journal *al-Mustaqbal al-Arabi* of the Center of Arab Unity Studies (72 articles) in the period 2006–2013. This center also publishes an English version with a selection of articles previously published in Arabic in the *Journal of Arab Contemporary Arab Affairs*.

11 Country rankings: www.scimagojr.com/countryrank.php.

12 Calculated by the OST for the ESTIME project (Gaillard 2007). The estimation was performed using data from the WoS, which has a journal database smaller than that of Scopus. See Methodological note published on the website: www.estime.irf.fr.

13 Authors' calculations on the basis of articles indexed from the WoS from 2000 to 2011.

14 The first two Lebanese Faculties of Medicine were founded in 1867 (for AUB as an integral part of the university) and the other in 1883 (established at USJ eight years after the founding of the university).

15 We use data here from the database of publications stem from WoS; authors' affiliations were cleaned and corrected by Claude Tayoun, whom we thank. The file contains 8,007 references to authors with affiliations in Lebanon, which corresponds to 18,836 addresses of affiliations (Lebanese and foreign co-authors). This reference file can be used to examine the different aspects of the publication of authors in Lebanon.

16 Statistics are from the Center for Research and Educational Development (CRDP) *Statistical Report, 2010–2011*, affiliated to the Ministry of Education and Higher Education. Cited by R. Dimassi (research in progress).

17 We calculate the data from our database of publications stem from the WoS for the period 2000–2011. We know these data have stirred the personnel of USJ dedicated to research and that the university now has a policy to overcome this weakness.

18 We must remember that USJ had requested an evaluation report from the *Agence d'évaluation de la recherche française* (AERES) in 2009; unfortunately this was superficial and merely reproduced known information and clichés.

19 Many faculty belong to industrialist families; they are a real industrial bourgeoisie, owners of small, medium and some large businesses.

20 Berytech was created in 2001 by USJ. It is the leading technopole/incubator in Lebanon and the region. It seeks to provide a favorable environment for the creation and development of start-up businesses, hence retaining graduates and highly skilled Lebanese who might otherwise emigrate for the sake of their careers. Berytech started

with one pole in Mar Roukos and added a second pole on Damascus Road in 2007. It created its first US$6 million venture capital seed fund for Lebanese technology start-ups in 2008. Several entrepreneurial activities were introduced: incubation awards; entrepreneurship contests; summer schools and regional academies for entrepreneurs; "From idea to start-up" courses for engineers; micro-enterprise acceleration programs; university road shows; local and international exhibitions and workshops; entre-preneur forums; start-up weekends; mentoring programs; and networking events, among other activities. To date, Berytech has housed more than 170 entities, assisted more than 2,000 entrepreneurs in several outreach programs, disbursed more than US$350,000 in grants to start-ups, and invested more than US$5 million in Lebanese technology companies. It was among the first of such institutions in the region to receive accreditation from the EU as a Business Innovation Center, opening access to international networks for its companies and affiliates. In 2012, and with the support of the EU, Berytech launched the Beirut Creative Cluster, grouping more than 30 leading companies in the multimedia industry, and was the European Bronze Label for Cluster Management Excellence. See www.berytech.org.

21 The Center of Entrepreneurship and Innovation was created on 10 July 2008 by the signing of an agreement between "Olayan Business School" of AUB and the Founda-tion of Mohammed Bin Rashid Al Maktoum (Dubai). The latter donated approxi-mately US$5 million for its creation. The center conducts research on regional entrepreneurship and provides economic analysis by sector and country.

22 At AUB, you have some excellent examples in health. In 2014 there was a research study that would improve the lives of epilepsy sufferers conducted by Zaher Dawy's team in collaboration with NeuroPro, a Swiss medical research company. They are working with specially patented algorithms that will be used to develop computer software for a device that can predict an upcoming seizure in patients (see www.aub. edu.lb/news/2014/Pages/fea-epileptic.aspx). In engineering, one can note the extra-ordinary work done in the team of Mona Fawwaz concerning the reconstruction of villages in the south of Lebanon after the 2006 bombings, in addition to al-dahiyya (southern neighborhood of Beirut).

23 The MIRA Survey happens to be the only survey at our disposal on the research practices.

24 Thirty-two percent of students in the university declared their desire to go abroad to continue their studies but also to seek employment (Kasparian 2006), although many fewer will end up capable of doing it.

25 MNR is magnetic nuclear resonance spectroscopy. There is one MNR for physics/chemistry analysis on the AUB campus and a medical one in AUBMC. It is a very expensive piece of equipment that needs to be kept active 24 hours per day, 365 days per year, otherwise it does not work. This equipment costs millions depending on the energy produced (US$3–6 million) in addition to the 10 percent of its cost for mainte-nance (as an average; a machine that costs US$3 million needs US$300,000 per year for maintenance), or, to put it differently, one-fifth of the AUB or USJ internal research budget.

26 See www.iri.org.lb/brief.html.

27 www.cas.gov.lb.

28 This rate is close to what is commonly practiced by most OECD countries or in inter-national institutions.

29 As called by Amilcar Herrera (1971) to distinguish it from the implicit policy, imple-mented by "default" as we would say today.

30 Apart from the research project ESTIME, the CNRS has been very active in MIRA (policy dialogue platform), and since late 2013: MEDSPRING (follower of MIRA), ERANET MED (co-funding that has produced a US$5 million fund in 2013) and PRIMA, a regional program in the making. The details of these activities can be found in the book from the end of the MIRA project (Morini *et al.* 2013).

31 We drew a representative sample of 321 professors from AUB with a doctorate (PhD) selected randomly among two professors from each department of the university. Details of the sampling and its characteristics can be found in our article published in 2013 (Hanafi *et al.* 2013). Our survey is focused on researchers of LU and USJ, but the analysis is still in progress.

32 The MIRA (www.miraproject.eu) Survey was answered by 4,340 researchers from 38 countries (27 in Europe and 11 Mediterranean country partners of the EU) that have co-authored articles or have collaborated in joint projects (Gaillard *et al.* 2013). Researchers in the social sciences accounted for a small part of the sample since the sample was basically conceived through the WoS database.

33 To our knowledge, only one such initiative has been drafted at present, called ODYSCE, which is an initiative of the researchers supported by the CNRS (an ARU) that joins AUB, USJ, LU and LAU, as well as the French IRD. The French institute IFPO is trying to embark on a similar objective, but oriented toward the French-speaking students exclusively.

34 Rita Yazigi, personal communication, 2013.

35 Here regional networks refer to the Arab region. However, one should note that some AUB historians have particularly developed connections with Turkish colleagues. Abdul-Rahim Abu-Husayn participated to many conference in Turkey (Raymond 2013) and Nadia Sheikh translated her book into Turkish.

36 In this connection, Hagstrom (author of a famous survey on science and its reward system in 1966) made a curious observation about the relationship between teachers and students, namely that in some teachers' minds, students do not count as collaborators. During his interviews, he asked scientists of co-authored papers if the work was carried out in "collaboration" with others. A number of scientists replied "no" although most or all of their papers had been jointly written with students (Katz and Martin 1997: 5).

37 The AUB operates under a charter granted by the Education Department of the State of New York in 1863, which registers the university's degree programs. AUB degrees are also recognized by the Lebanese government through the equivalence committees of the Ministry of Education and Higher Education: www.aub.edu.lb/accreditation/Pages/index.aspx.

38 "Projets: Hauran III, Tanmia," "Mobilités, Frontières et Conflits dans les Espaces Israélo-Palestiniens," "Du Golfe arabo-persique à l'Europe: entre violences et," Projet CITADAIN, and finally "Les Palestiniens entre Etat et diaspora."

39 This is a particularity of the ANR projects only, since the ruling for ANR projects concerned initially only French teams. Usually, EU projects have the possibility of direct funding toward all types of eligible costs.

40 Research in international social science is increasingly published in English, with extensive reference to American and European publications (Gingras and Mosbah-Natanson 2010). Yet Wiebke Keim noted that some people resist, that

> the only way to develop a real and practical "non hegemonic potential" would suppose to refuse the participation in this common arena and to refuse naming this arena the central arena of the discipline. And it happens, more often practically than in theoretical terms, when a scientific community becomes large enough it can move towards alternative for a—local or regional, sometimes non-academic; then the North-American sociology loses its importance and the foundation of the divide between center and periphery dissolves.
>
> (Keim, 2010: 590)

Part II

The tumultuous development of social science in the Arab region

5 Development and place of production of the social sciences
Different forms of compartmentalization

The essential task of Arab sociology is to carry out critical work within two threads: (a) to deconstruct concepts that have emerged from the sociological knowledge and discourse of those who spoke on behalf of the Arab region, marked by a predominantly Western and ethnocentric ideology; and (b) to simultaneously critique the sociological knowledge and discourse on various Arab societies produced by Arabs themselves.

(Khatabi 1975: 13 [authors' translation])

Orientalism has been denounced, but its critics reproduce very often what they reject. Ethnocentrism in general is the most well distributed thing on earth, and it needs to be uncovered. In the name of difference, very often a "logic of apartheid" is promoted. Unity and diversity, power and knowledge, play a common game that criticism should prevent.

(Hannoyer 1996: 405 [authors' translation])

1 Introduction

The quotes that open this chapter suggest a problematic relationship between the heritage of the Western social sciences and local Arab societies. We join Alain Roussillon (2002), who argues that the introduction of the social sciences in the Arab region coincided with the colonial invasion in the Arab region. Examples may be easily found: Orientalist texts such as the five volumes of the nineteenth-century *Description de l'Egypte*, produced by academics travelling with Napoleon's invading army, are illustrative. There is some confusion over whether it is causal relationship or simply a correlation.

In the late colonial period and after the independence of the Arab states, two major trends of social science emerged: one that denounces the colonial sciences and decolonizes them, and reflects on the social, economic and cultural dependency produced after the independence. Reference to Ibn Khaldoun was a compulsory passage to think of the "specificity" and sometime the "uniqueness" of the Arab world (Kerrou 1991). Influenced by Fanz Fanon and *Tiers-Mondistes*, many social scientists in that time (Anouar Abdelmalek, Taib Tizini, Abdulkarim Khatabi, etc.) were busy with the paradigm of identity, and sometimes so exhausted by this that they did not produce research that might show us how a rupture can be established with the "colonial research." The second trend, the "developmentalists," was so absorbed by the development of the national project and adopted often the paradigm of modernization that has often neglected the study of social actors performing behind development projects. Abdelwahab Bouhdiba (1970 : 8–9) wrote once "*toute sociologie est une sociologie du développement.*" Generally speaking there are two problematic processes in the Arab world: institutionalization of the social science as academic disciplines and the professionalization of the social scientists (sociologists, anthropologists, geographers, etc.).

Only since the 1970s have fragmented social science groups emerged in the Arab region. Politically, these groups have been in agreement with French and to a much lesser extent American social science. They were involved in the service of a political process, namely the engineering of a new society. The fundamental issue for social scientists after independence, and this is true for all post-colonial societies, is how to serve the state, the nation or the modern project pursued by the nation. This project, whether communist, socialist, nationalist or even pro-American, was concerned with the country's need for a modern administration and economic sector. This absorbed the social sciences into resolving technical problems, rather than being critical of them. It is interesting to know that when Fuad Chehab became president of Lebanon in 1958, he ordered a social, economic and urban plan for Beirut. He was told that no one in Lebanon can do it and he needed to bring in French experts. After that, he ordered the establishment of the Institute of Social Science in 1959. The graduates of this institute, for a long time, have been hired as civil servants in different ministries to deal with social and economic problems of Lebanon. This resembles the cameralism that flourished in Germany from the middle of the sixteenth to the end of the eighteenth century. The central issue was how the welfare of the state might be secured, and their whole social theory radiated from this central task (Albion 2001).

So far these two sets of paradigms (identity/decolonization/Ibn Khaldounian and developmentalism/modernization) are still operating in the Arab sociology, but one should add the new one – that of the paradigm of cultural representations: a paradigm that puts more emphasis on social actors' representations than social structures that influence why these presentations take place. There is nothing wrong with these paradigms. However, the only concern we may have is the balance between the different social research productions that are based on these paradigms.

Curiously, there are few serious works on the state of the art on social science in the Arab world that allow us to speak here of the trajectory of this field. Some authors attempt to provide a critical assessment of the social sciences (or one of their disciplines) produced by or about the Arab world. Some were more interested to show their failure (Binder 1976); others are more nuanced (Kerrou 1991) and discipline-centered (Shami and Naguib 2013; Timothy 2002; Kabbanji 2014). All, except Kerrou, have done their assessment based mainly on English-language production. The contribution of Shami and Naguib is particularly interesting as they show the predominance of the research on national identity and the fact that this happened at the expense of investigating ethnic minorities and how minorities were often studied in their relationship to the majority, and not to understand their particularism.

Other assessments are more inclusive and take into account the local production of knowledge, such as the state of the art in Arab anthropology of Baqader and Rashiq (2012). While Abu-Baker Baqader sees the weakness of the anthropological production in the Arab East in the fact that it did not operate a "rupture with the Western paradigm," Hassan Rashiq is more optimistic about the development of North African anthropology. For him, this discipline emerged within the field of sociology in the 1960s and focused on the political field but became quickly autonomous and mature. One can mention also the very interesting study of Hasan Rachik and Rahma Bourqia (2011) on the genesis and development of Moroccan sociology.

As an intellectual movement, Arab social science has been heterogeneous and only a historicized and contextualized analysis can account for its continual reconstruction to meet the changing dynamics of the Arab world.

In this chapter and following ones, we will not do another examination of the state of the art in social science, but we will try to locate the size and the place of production of social science in the Arab world through concrete case studies. By that, we aim at avoiding denouncing failure or celebrating success, or to process with a hindsight bias: our objective is indeed to pursue the retrospective in search of the prospective. Dealing with knowledge production, it is not only what is considered as mainly academic production (articles in refereed journals and specialized books), but in a broad sense, and for this we will use Michael Burawoy's famous typology of sociology (professional, critical, policy and public). In fact, we will develop it to be better projected toward the Arab world and extend it to all the social sciences. We will then tackle them through case studies to illustrate the connection this production has with society and policy-makers.

2 Locus of Arab social research

Nowadays, all Arab countries, with the exception of most of the Gulf monarchies, invest in social research with the help of international aid. Research is done either by universities or research centers, but Arab countries that create a hospitable environment for research are rare. Political repression, censorship and lack of research-based policy hinder the development of such environments.

Scholars from Maghreb involved in the ESTIME project clearly indicated that the phenomenon of research centers, taking the form of NGOs, is not very widespread. However, the case in the Arab Mashrek is quite different. Research centers, whether private or as NGOs, are flourishing, launching several surveys in applied social research for two particular reasons: the first is the peace processes of both Lebanon (after the Taif Agreement of 1989) and Palestine (following signing of the Oslo Accords in 1993), and the second concerning economic liberalization in Jordan and Egypt. The keyword for the donors was "empowerment" of civil society. These centers produce either research or pure consultancy, i.e., perfunctory research with the output often consisting of an unpublished report (IFPO 2007).[1]

The survey carried out in the mid-2000s by Sari Hanafi concerning research centers in the Arab Mashrek shows that research activities have mainly been conducted by two different types of organizations: first, by specialized research organizations such as research centers that have emerged either within or outside university settings (like the Lebanese Center for Policy Studies); and second, by NGOs specialized in development, advocacy and cooperative efforts (Hanafi 2010). For instance, in the Palestinian Territory research production is very marginalized when it comes to university-affiliated institutions (only four centers constituting 10 percent of research output),[2] while the majority of organizations conducting research are NGOs. Some 41 percent of the organizations producing research are specialized bodies, while the rest are NGOs dealing with advocacy and development (Hanafi 2009).

However, there are two exceptional cases in the region: on the one hand, Lebanon and Syria; on the other hand, Egypt. In Lebanon, the university is still the bastion of research: according to the ESTIME survey, 85 percent (60 out of 71) of the researchers included were affiliated with Lebanese universities (IFPO 2007). Syria has a similar profile, but for different reasons: the government still controls what is produced in the social sciences and humanities (SSH). These are strongly apologetic, restricted in their research approaches, controlled by single-party authorities and used for ideological propaganda and political manipulation. Egypt constitutes a unique case in which the importance of public research centered on the social sciences is a phenomenon that dates back to the 1950s. Egypt hosts the National Center for Sociological and Criminological Research (NCSCR) based in Cairo, as well as the semi-public Al-Ahram Center for Strategic Studies. Other centers are university affiliated, like the American Research Center in Egypt (ARCE), which is also based in Cairo.

In Jordan we find a diverse array of research organizations, but more importantly the large majority of these organizations are located outside the premises of universities.

Maghreb countries show the highest output of SSH research, whereas Egypt and the countries of the Arab Mashrek are characterized by relative stagnation in these fields (El-Kenz 2005). Taking the total number of projects supported in all fields in Lebanon, for example, we find that support for projects in SSH research did not exceed 9 percent at the American University of Beirut (AUB), and 5 percent at the National Council for Scientific Research. The situation is comparable for most Arab countries. The reason for this may not lie in a lack of financial or human resources or in the absence of research priorities tied to the daily concerns of members of society, but rather in the weak academic incentives for researchers and university professors, especially in the fields of human and social sciences.

Although universities continue to play a primary role in social science research in the Maghreb, Syria, Libya and Lebanon, more than 80 percent of social science research is produced through research centers or consultative agencies outside of universities, especially in Palestine, Jordan, Egypt, Morocco and to some degree in the countries of the Gulf (Al Maktoum Foundation and UNDP 2009: 202).

According to the 2013 Global Go To Think Tank Index Report (TTCSP 2014), there are many think-tanks and research centers in the Arab region. Most of them have emerged in the last few years (Table 5.1).

Some of these centers are populated by local researchers. The most important centers are Al-Ahram Center for Political and Strategic Studies (ACPSS) (Egypt), the Center for the Arab Unity Studies (Lebanon) and the Arab Center for Research and Policy Studies (ACRPS) (Qatar), Economic Research Forum (Egypt), Tunisian Institute for Strategic Studies (ITES), Amadeus Center (Morocco), Centre des Etudes et Recherches en Sciences Sociales (CERSS) (Morocco), Al Jazeera Centre for Studies (Qatar), Arab Thought Forum (Jordan) and Center for Strategic Studies (Jordan). These centers are half research center and half think-tank. All have an independent entity for the study of SSH, with particular emphasis on the applied social sciences. However, some other centers are branches of international and transnational centers/agencies, like Institut Français du Proche-Orient (IFPO) (Lebanon), Brookings Doha Center (Qatar) and Carnegie Middle East Center (Lebanon). The first category of centers has triggered regional collaboration much more than international, while the second category has done the opposite. The ACSS is aware of this reality and expresses interest in fostering capacity building for local researchers but keeping collaboration and cooperation with both regional and international social science communities. It is interesting to note that most of these centers are outside the premises of the universities and more and more independent of the government. This trend is constant since the beginning of the 1990s. For instance, in 1989, only 7 percent of research centers were independent (Shahid 1989).

In spite of this amazing development in the Arab world, propelled by its ongoing transformation, there are two forces that seek to delegitimize the social sciences: the authoritarian political elite and some ideological groups such as certain religious authorities. Both have taken advantage of the social sciences' problematic origins (their emergence during the colonial era) and their foreign funding.

Table 5.1 Research centers/think-tanks in selected Arabic countries (2013)

Country	No.
Egypt	55
Jordan	40
Tunisia	39
Morocco	30
Lebanon	27
Qatar	10

Source: based on TTCSP (2014).

It is rare in the Arab region to hear of a "white paper" written by social scientists at the request of the public authority and debated in the public sphere. Sociologists work either as elements in the matrix of modernization projects, though not as an independent body, or as servile agents restricted to justifying the government's decisions. Even when the Tunisian dictator Zein Al-Dine Ben Ali used science in his discourse in the 1990s as an ideological weapon in his ruthless struggle against the Tunisian Islamist "obscurantists" (Siino 2004: 362), he did not refer to the social sciences but the harder sciences. Scientific meetings are treated like any other public meetings and are held under police surveillance. In Syria two workshops were canceled suddenly by intelligence services one day before being held: one in education and the other in secularism.[3]

Principled social scientists have been sent to prison, exiled or assassinated. An intelligence officer once told Sari Hanafi: "All of your group [of dissident social scientists] fill less than one bus and can easily be taken to prison!" Generally speaking, Arab authoritarian states have always underestimated the salience of such "bus people," whether defined as dissident intellectuals or more generally the enlightened middle class, in stirring protests. The 2011 revolutions in Tunisia, Libya, Yemen and Egypt served to confirm this view. Sometimes a state is only interested in furbishing its image. The Moroccan sociologist Mohamed Cherkaoui (2008) brings us a very insightful example of such practices. When the Moroccan Ministry of the Interior wanted to promote voting participation in the elections of September 7, 2008, they addressed a communication agency rather than true social science professionals. For him, if the state had initially sought sociologists and political scientists, it would have had a serious study in electoral sociology: one that could determine not only the voting trends but also reasons behind historical abstention. Hasan Rachik and Rahma Bourqia (2011) are more optimistic and consider that the rupture between state and social science is more ideological than effective, but they observe mainly the use of social science only in the form of a problem solving knowledge.

Religious authorities have often felt threatened by social scientists as the two groups competed over the discourse on society. Hanafi's study on family planning in Syria revealed tense television debates involving a religious leader and an activist: the late Sheikh Mohamed Said Ramadan al-Bouti (who argued that Islam is against any form of family planning) against an anti-clericalist activist from the General Union of Syrian Women, a state-sponsored organization. While family planning falls squarely within the domain of sociology and demography, no social scientist was ever consulted for these public debates. Another example can be evoked from Qatar. It is not anecdotal to mention that the Qatari authorities protected themselves from conservative political and religious commissars by asking the Qatari branches of the foreign universities to teach the same curriculum as their program at the university headquarters. However, who would protect professors within these distant universities? In a recent interview, the President of Carnegie Mellon University Qatar, in order to "protect himself," stated that the Qatari authorities were responsible for the university's curriculum. So everyone tries to preempt the debate in a context already problematic as the freedom of expression is very limited. The development of a "sphere for science" could become an extra-territorial space of exception, in the sense that local laws do not necessarily apply to it, bestowing the freedom to criticize the surrounding society, but running the risk of being disconnected from societal needs.

While the social sciences worldwide, along with philosophy, were one of the major tools for reforming religion, this is not the case in the Arab world. In Saudi Arabia, for instance, there are two interesting recently established research centers that are interested in connecting the Sharia (religious studies) to modernity: Namaa Center for Research and Studies and Taseel Center for Studies and Research. Namaa declares in its mission statement the need for moderate Islamic discourse to be integrated with intellectual discourse and its tools for the sake of "conscious development" and of connection to "knowledge and experience [sic] of the contemporary world."[4] A close scrutiny of the activities of the center (studies, lectures, book reviews) shows indeed this connection and integration has been made through philosophical and logical tools, but not through social science. Scholars participating in this endeavor are coming either from religious studies, philosophy, history or are considered simply as intellectuals. The titles of the three studies mentioned in the website are very revealing: "Freedom or Sharia?," "Problems of values between culture and science," and "Averroes' school of thought and its connection to the European renaissance." Already invoking positively Averroes' school of thought is something very new in a country dominated by Salafism and Wahabism. Here, one should highlight the amazing role of the three Maghrebin philosophers Mohamed Abdel Al-Jaberi, Mohamed Arkon and Abdullal Al-Arawi. The two former are some of the most prominent examples of contemporary Arab thought interpreting the classical Arab heritage (*turath*). Of course, there are some exceptions: a sort of light use of social science. One of the Saudi authors that the center of Namaa promotes is Abdullal Sufiani. In 2014 Sufiani held a PhD in education from the Islamic University of Madineh (SA), with an endeavor to do back and forth between education as a science and fiqh, as one can see from the title of his PhD thesis, "Regulations of educational critiques through fatwas of Shaykh al-Islam Ibn Taymiyyah and their application in the field of educational research." In a lecture on "The hidden factors influencing the faqihs" (these are jurisprudents or the religious lawyers of Islam) by Abdullal Sufiani, the lecturer challenges the sacrality of faqihs, using psychology and sociology and referring to Freud and Ibn Khaldoun.[5]

The Taaseel Center[6] has almost the same mission statement, yet the trend of reforming mainstream Islamic dominant schools is less clear. Their interest in rethinking contemporary thought are as important as the Namaa Center, but always through a critical assessment of Western philosopher thinkers, such as Francis Fukuyama (al-Lahibi 2013).[7]

This delegitimization is reinforced by the way social scientists conduct their analysis. Producers of social knowledge in both the West and the Arab region create what is sometimes called the "mythology of uniqueness" of the Arabs.

The Arab region was thought of as a place of cultural specificity and exceptionalism; Muslim immigrants to the West were similarly viewed as an incompatible ontological category predicated on culture (Yılmaz 2012). Many still persist in seeing Arab societies as either a collection of religious devotees or segmented tribal groups. This exceptionalism has distracted from the real debate on societies, politics and culture in the Arab region (Kabbanji 2011), especially in terms of the analysis of social class. Samir Kassir called this the "Arab Malaise" (Kassir 2004), resulting in a situation where, instead of studies of Muslims or Arabs, there are studies of Islam and Arabic.

3 Projection of Burawoy's typology in the Arab world

A little knowledge that acts is worth infinitely more than much knowledge that is idle.

(Gibran Khalil Gibran)

As we previous mentioned, the university system and the system of social knowledge production greatly influence elite formation in the Arab world. Many factors will play a role, but one of them that we will focus on here is compartmentalization of scholarly activities. Universities have often produced compartmentalized elites inside each nation state and they don't communicate with each another: they are either elite that publish globally and perish locally or elite that publish locally and perish globally.

To understand the problem of visibility of the Arab social production, we use the seminal four-dimensional typology elaborated by Michael Burawoy for sociology, applying it more broadly to all of the social sciences. Burawoy distinguishes between four types of sociology: two (*professional* and *critical* sociology) are relevant to academic audiences, and the others (*public* and *policy* sociology) pertain to a wider audience. Professional sociology consists of "multiple intersecting research programs, each with their assumptions, exemplars, defining questions, conceptual apparatuses and evolving theories" (Burawoy 2005: 10). Critical sociology examines the foundations – both the explicit and the implicit, both normative and descriptive – of the research programs of professional sociology. Public sociology "brings sociology into a conversation with publics, understood as people who are themselves involved in conversation. It entails, therefore, a double conversation" (Burawoy 2005: 8) and reciprocal relationships, in which meaningful dialogue fosters mutual education that not only strengthens such publics but also enriches sociological work itself and helps it in setting the research agendas. Community participation in the design of research proposals as well as lectures and workshops with different stakeholders for dissemination of the results of research are forms through which social scientists can interact with the public and determine the relevance of future topics of study, both for the needs of society and the public. Public social science thus has four levels: first, privileging the method of sociological intervention[8] and action research; second, speaking and writing for the public exclusively about the researcher's discipline; third, speaking and writing about the discipline and how it relates to the social, cultural and political world around it; finally, speaking, writing and taking a stand for something far larger than the discipline from which the researcher originated (Lightman 2008). Here, we should admit the public researcher's normative stance without necessarily uncritically espousing a cause (Marezouki 2004; Wieviorka 2000).

Finally, policy sociology's purpose is to provide solutions to problems that are presented to the society, or to legitimate solutions that have already been reached. Some clients (international organizations, ministries, etc.) often request specific studies for their intervention, with a narrow contract (Burawoy 2005: 9).[9]

Beyond social science, many scholars (El-Jardali *et al.* 2012; Brandt and Pope 1997; CIHR 2004) use the concept of knowledge translation that covers both public and policy activities. The Canadian Institutes for Health Research (CIHR) defines it as

> the exchange, synthesis, and ethically-sound application of knowledge—within a complex set of interactions among researchers and users—to accelerate the capture of the benefits of research [...] through improved health, more effective services and products, and a strengthened health care system.
>
> (CIHR 2004)

It was promoted thus for public health and medicine research, but covers now all disciplines.

Lavis *et al.* (2006) provide a framework to assess what should be transferred, to whom, by whom, how and with what effect, using four strategies: push efforts

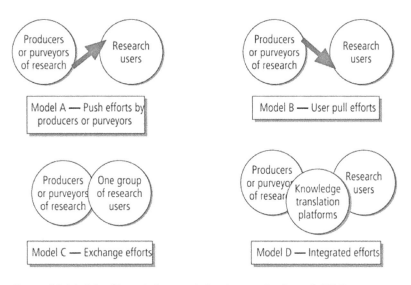

Figure 5.1 Models of knowledge translation (source: Lavis *et al.* 2006).

by researchers or purveyors; user pull efforts; exchange efforts; and integrated efforts.

While all four types of social science are equally represented and being debated in Europe (e.g., Pierre Bourdieu, Alain Touraine and Michel Wieviorka) and partially in North America (e.g., Michael Burawoy, Herbert Gans and David Riesman), this is not the case in the Arab East. The lack of dialogue/debate regarding this issue in the Arab East can be noted from the ratio between published articles, newspaper articles and unpublished reports in 203 CVs of social scientists in the Arab East (see Chapter 9). Research shows that scholars often specialize in one type of social science and there is no debate between these individuals. In the Arab East, the profile of the intellectual is well known: typically, he or she is a theorist who talks about tradition, modernity, authoritarianism, democracy, identity, Arab unity, globalization and so on, but avoids stepping into society to conduct empirical research. Even social scientists are often guilty of pontificating like philosophers, raising questions rather than offering concrete answers. It is even rarer to hear professional social researchers speak in the public sphere. This is due not only to the absence of their products in the mass media or newspapers, but also to the danger of being visible in the authoritarian states.

Projecting Michael Burawoy's typology of the research activities (professional, critical, public and policy) into a model that fits better the Arab world, I will point out four moments:

First, the global/universalistic moment: this Aristotelian moment of the *reason* insisting that social science is like any science and hence needs techniques of conducting research. This requires rather a nomothetic approach to produce data that allow comparability with other contexts. This comparability is the equivalent of the lab experiment in hard science.

Second is the local moment where the notion of consciousness, to speak like Hawari Al-Adi (2014), is very important. The subjectivity of actors and influence of culture become compelling, requiring a more idiographic approach that seeks to fully understand the causes of what happened in a single instance, taking into account the local culture. The first and second moments are the professional and critical moments in Burawoy's typology. However, there is a trend of polarization. For instance, browsing two social science journals in the Arab Gulf, we found that social science is lacking consciousness. Sociology becomes studying micro problems using science techniques but without addressing the authoritarian nature of monarchies there in addition to other power structures. The absence of this moment is also clear where Arab researchers have deserted their traditions, contrary to their European counterparts (Ju'eit 2001).

The third moment is the semi-normative moment, which is similar to the public and policy social science in Burawoy's typology. It involves the application of the two previous moments to engage in a dialogue with the community and with decision-makers. This moment needs to use local/global moments (or professional/critical moments) to solve problems of the society through awareness campaigns, advocacy, lobbying, but also strategies and scenarios. We call it a semi-normative moment because it is mainly driven by scientific results, but with choices that stem often from political, ideological and moral underpinnings.

Our preliminary results of the content analysis of the contribution of Arab social scientists in the public debate showed that social researchers do not often contribute to the public debate: we find more in North Africa than in the Arab East, more in the countries where there is freedom of expression than despotic countries. If there is some use of public sociology there are also some abuses. Two issues can be highlighted. First, the way many social researchers are blurring the necessary boundaries between professional/critical research (a sort of Weberian idea-type of a value-free science) with the normative moment. For instance, writing in a way that one does not know the boundaries between empirical findings and ideology and between the scholar's vocation and the politician's trade. This trend is recurrent in the Arab social science and was reported even in the early 1990s and before (see Kerrou 1991). Second, there is sometimes the figure of prolocutor, in the sense that the *Oxford English Dictionary* puts it – "the use of ambiguous language so as to mislead" – i.e., to use "persuasion to capture free-floating disposable loyalties with success dependent upon their rhetorical capacity to present, create, and appeal to new situations" (Stanton 2009: 223). This is often driven by a mix of fear of the state and of religious authorities.

Finally, there is a normative moment related to the moral, the religious and the Universal Declaration of Human Rights. To reach this moment one needs to engage with all moral entrepreneurs in the society, including religious leaders. Thus far the data gathered from analyzing the op-eds in Lebanese newspapers reveals a very limited dialogue and interaction between these groups (see Chapter 9). For instance, many Lebanese scholars hide themselves behind the position of the majority of Lebanese who reject giving the Palestinians in Lebanon basic human rights (right to work and to own property). They often end their articles by stating that such demands cannot be realized as the majority of Lebanese would refuse it. In taking this position these authors have chosen not to adopt a normative stance that can remind people of morality and the Universal Declaration of Human Rights on this issue.

4 Fragmented research activities

In terms of researchers' profiles, critical social scientists are generally over 50 years old. The trend is often that senior scholars do not do fieldwork. Policy and public social scientists are often male. The high competitiveness and aggressiveness of the consultancy market could explain this male bias.

Some professional and critical social scientists that I interviewed expressed a condescending attitude toward public and policy social research. A recent study surveyed 238 researchers from 12 counties in the Arab region, showing little use of health systems and policy research evidence in health policy-making (El-Jardali *et al.* 2012; cited in IFI-CAPRI 2014).[10] Many other studies deplore the lack of policy impact for many of the research centers (al-Khazendar 2012;

Shehadeh and Saleh Tayyara 1999; Afandi 2012) in the case of Jordan, Yemen and the Arab world in general. One of the reasons for lack of interest is the feeling that policy-makers are not interested in listening to the scientific community. One professor from Jordan reported: "Policy-making is the prerogative of the minister, particularly one whose appointment is subject to tribal, regional, geopolitical, or international considerations upon which the regime accounts for when composing its government."

For a long time, professional researchers have taken a positivist approach and set aside their ethical responsibilities by avoiding both expressing their views (pro or con) in public forums and lobbying public officials. Some scholars (Harb 1996; Balqziz 1999) tend to discourage academics being involved in politics and consider that this cannot be accompanied by any critical discourse. This attitude is more frequent with academics from elite universities. The rupture appears not only by the fact that professional academics don't care about policy, but also the other way round. A glance at the profiles of the consultants conducting policy research for state and international organizations reveals that around three-quarters have never published in academic journals or books, there are no traces of fieldwork and most of the output recycles the work of others. These consultants seem to be lacking consistent reflexivity.

There is unequal competition between policy researchers and other types of social scientists, resulting from the intervention of the donor agencies, who often favor the former, coined "expert social scientists," at the expense of the latter. This reflects what Lee *et al.* (2005) called the tumultuous marriage between social science and social policy, in which the rules of conjugality are never fully established or agreed upon by both parties. For instance, UN agencies sometimes produce policy knowledge which is self-legitimized and disconnected from professional research. The 2009 *Arab Human Development Report*'s text references (UNDP 2009) (other than statistical references) reveal only 30 academic references of 242 (12 percent) and almost half (47 percent) of those references are UN documents (see Table 5.2).

Examination of CVs shows that public social scientists in the Arab East are also often disconnected from professional social scientists. They become experts on any topic they are requested to research by media or public institutions.

Table 5.2 Source of references in the 2009 Arab Human Development Report (UNDP)

	Percentage	*No.*
UN documents	47	113
International organizations	17	40
Internet documents	12	30
Academic publication	12	30
Official documents	9	21
Newspapers	3	8
Total	100	242

Although anecdotal, I have watched TV programs on some Arab channels (al-Jazeera, Future TV, Syrian TV, Palestinian TV and al-Arabiyya) during the last year, to look for the presence of Arab public social scientists. We have noticed a small number of them being interviewed on different topics which are sometimes related to their fields of expertise, but in many cases the topics are not related at all. Reviewing some of these media-savvy scholars' CVs shows that they have not been producing much professional or critical research. Rachid Daif has noted how simplistic the academic discourse in the Lebanese media is (Kabbanji 2010: 78). However Chapter 9 in this book will show more complexity concerning the academic contribution to the op-eds. Similarly, it is rare to find books written by social scientists that are read beyond the academic realm, where they could become the vehicle of a public discussion about the nature of Arab or local society – the nature of its values, and the gap between its promise and its reality, tendencies and malaise.

We can summarize this in Figure 5.2, which shows the following:

• Inflation of policy research in the Arab East at the expense of professional and critical research, by the effect of foreign funding that privileges research that yields directly to recommendations to "resolve" a social problem. This is not the case in the Arab Maghreb.
• Weak public research in all of the Arab world, but particularly in the Arab East.
• There is no connection between the four types of research in the Arab East, while there is a more "healthy" situation in the Francophone Arab countries, where we note balance and overlap between the four types of research; also, the magnitude of the professional research in this latter area is a good indicator of a healthier situation there.

Having said that, we are not suggesting that each scholar should do all four types of social research. However, when there is a trend of compartmentalization

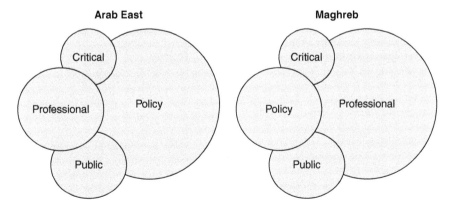

Figure 5.2 Typology of research activities in the Arab world (source: authors).

at the societal level, this risks producing mediocrity in each type of social science and, in particular, risks rendering professional and critical research more elitist and irrelevant (Alatas 2001), disconnected from society's needs. Structures such as universities, donor agencies and media are pushing toward this specialization.

Notes

1 IFPO and ESTIME established a database in 2005 for research centers and researchers. Among the 54 centers, there are 27 which produce reports (gray literature): "In general, NGOs edit either guides, or are very close to the field, and provide trainings, reports, surveys, whereas universities provide mainly proceedings of meetings" (IFPO 2007).

2 Three are connected to Birzeit University (the Public Health Institution, the Law Center and the Birzeit Center for Development Studies) and one is connected to Al-Quds University (the Jerusalem Studies Center). Currently, the number of these centers has tremendously increased in the Palestinian universities.

3 The first was organized by Munir Bashshur in 2003 and the second by Sadeq Jalal al-Azem in 2008.

4 See http://nama-center.com/Default.aspx.

5 See www.nama-center.com/WatchVideo.aspx?id=fEyX248JatY; see also his book (Sufiani 2014).

6 http://taseel.com.

7 See http://taseel.com/display/pub/default.aspx?id=6251&ct=4&ax=3; the reader can see that all references are in Arabic.

8 This method was developed by Alain Touraine (1981).

9 Burawoy typology was discussed by many scholars. Some of them were unhappy about it. See, for example, McLaughlin and Turcotte (2007). Sometimes the importance of the policy stance the professional researcher can offer to policy-makers is downplayed. Some authors have the contradictory position of being committed to the society without thinking about the policy moment, as in the case of Pierre Bourdieu. Often showing contempt for media and political power, he once wrote: "If, as Bachelard says, 'every chemist must fight the alchemist within,' every sociologist must fight the social prophet within that his public asks him to incarnate" (Bourdieu *et al.* 1973: 42).

10 Findings show that only 16 percent of the participants interacted with policy-makers and stakeholders in priority settings, and 19.8 percent involved policy-makers in the process of developing their research. For research dissemination, it was found that researchers are more likely to transfer their research findings to other researchers (67.2 percent) rather than to policy-makers (40.5 percent).

6 Writing sociology in the Arab world

The case of *Idafat*

1 Introduction

Idafat: The Arab Journal of Sociology (hereafter *Idafat*), is a new, refereed, academic journal published by the Arab Association of Sociology, in cooperation with the Center for Arab Unity Studies (CAUS). The journal's main objective is to disseminate research in sociology and anthropology produced in the Arab world and to open debates about social and political problems from disciplinary, national and Arab perspectives. It also aims to introduce international pieces of research, in addition to new trends in sociology and anthropology, to Arab readers. It is published both as hardcopy and online.[1] *Idafat* intends to fill the gap within an academic field of Arab sociology in which there are very few journals that have regular periodicity and longevity (e.g., Kuwait University's *Journal of Social Science and Journal of Social Affairs*, *Umran*, a newly established journal of social science published by the Arab Center for Research and Policy Studies, Doha). Some universities have "national" journals, i.e., social science journals that publish mainly on the local society (e.g., three Arab–French bilingual journals: *Insaniyyat* [Algeria]; *Prologues*; *Études maghrébines* [Morocco]). Other journals are multidisciplinary (*Journal of Damascus University*) and publish often the research conducted by the academics within their university.

Submissions to *Idafat* or book reviews are sent to reviewers, and then presented to the *Idafat* editorial board for consideration. Most authors receive a decision on their article one to three months after submission. The delay is often due to the refusal of scholars to review or the non-respect of reviewers of the proposed deadlines. This reflects the weakness of the professionalization of the scientific community locally and at the regional level (Hanafi and Arvanitis 2013a; Kabbanji 2010). Unlike books, journals are a collective enterprise, one that requires collaboration and collective commitment (Martin 2012a: 838). Thus, studying journals provides an excellent opportunity to observe the situation of the scientific community. Gérard and Kleiche-Dray (2009) provide an exceptional study of how the Arabic–French social science journals in Morocco play a significant role in restructuring the disciplinary field by providing some disciplinary focalization around specific research objects and making visible a core of contributors. Social sciences have been historically highly atomized and it is rare to find a research team around a scientific object or discipline (Gérard and Kleiche 2002).

Idafat was first launched in 2000 as a non-periodic journal (a sort of annual book), published five issues and then stopped for three years before restarting again as a regular journal in the spring of 2008 (with four issues per year). Readers of *Idafat* are not only sociologists but also a wider public, as evidenced by many indicators: some articles are included in syllabi; some articles were browsed by readers 2,500 times in the last two years; and the journal is sold in both bookshops and newspaper kiosks. There are also a few cases in which articles received feedback and counter-arguments.

This chapter analyzes the 18 issues published from 2008 to 2012 by examining some variables such as submission data, author nationality, article keywords and the use of references. The objective is to unfold the way Arab sociologists produce knowledge in sociology. A special focus will be placed on the language of citations and references. This chapter argues that some institutional settings, in addition to the economy of knowledge production, make the balanced use of references in Arabic and foreign languages difficult.

2 Who are the authors of *Idafat*?

As Table 6.1 shows, of the 584 items received by the journal – which include, in addition to numbers of articles, book reviews, review articles and workshop reports, and the issues' editorials – 248 are articles that were selected as the subject of this study. Some 42.5 percent of submitted manuscripts were published in general, but what is relevant is the rate for authors coming from the Arab world (39 percent), as others are often invited to submit papers. It is a rate higher than the 15.5 percent of papers accepted in *Current Sociology*, a journal of the International Sociological Association (Martin 2012b).

As can be noted in Table 6.1, the acceptance rate ranged between one-third and one-half for the foremost countries, according to the nationality of the first author (and not one's place of institutional affiliation). In fact, one cannot rush to the conclusion that this reflects the quality of published manuscripts, as there are three rules of thumb which determine the editorial board's decision to accept or reject manuscripts: first, and the most important criterion, is the manuscript's quality in terms of topic, methodology and theorization; second, the distribution of manuscripts according to countries and subject; and finally, affirmative action as a policy adopted by *Idafat* in favor of young researchers who wish to publish their first study. We distinguish between Arab nationalities and others for analytical reasons. Most articles published by foreign authors are requested from them. *Idafat* translated those articles into Arabic as a policy that sought to introduce new methodologies, approaches and theories in sociology to Arab readers.

To study the distribution of manuscripts according to the nationality of the first author, it was decided to analyze only the articles. They are 57 percent of

Table 6.1 Distribution of submitted pieces by nationality of the first author

Country of nationality	No.	Percentage	Submitted papers	Accepted papers (%)
Morocco	42	16.9	108	38.9
Palestine	39	15.7	96	40.6
Lebanon	32	12.9	98	32.7
Tunisia	30	12.1	61	49.2
Algeria	20	8.1	56	35.7
Egypt	16	6.5	46	34.8
Iraq	14	5.6	39	35.9
Bahrain	3	1.2	7	42.9
Jordan	3	1.2	8	37.5
Saudi Arabia	3	1.2	5	60.0
Kuwait	2	0.8	4	50.0
Libya	2	0.8	4	50.0
Oman	2	0.8	2	100.0
Syria	2	0.8	5	40.0
Mauritania	1	0.4	3	33.3
Qatar	1	0.4	1	100.0
Sudan	1	0.4	4	25.0
United Arab Emirates	1	0.4	1	100.0
Subtotal for the Arab world	**214**	**86.2**	**548**	**39.1**
France	14	5.6	14	100.0
United States	5	2	5	100.0
Germany	3	1.2	5	60.0
Switzerland	2	0.8	2	100.0
Singapore	1	0.4	1	100.0
Pakistan	1	0.4	1	100.0
Netherlands	1	0.4	1	100.0
Austria	1	0.4	1	100.0
Canada	1	0.4	1	100.0
Denmark	1	0.4	1	100.0
Europe	1	0.4	1	100.0
Iran	1	0.4	1	100.0
Jamaica	1	0.4	1	100.0
Japan	1	0.4	1	100.0
Subtotal for other countries	**34**	**13.6**	**36**	**94.4**
Total	**248**	**100**	**584**	**42.5**

the total items (142 articles) (see Table 6.2). Another restriction is adopted by analyzing only manuscripts whose first authors are Arabs (120 articles). These come from across the Arab world, except Yemen, Djibouti and Comoros.

As can be seen in Table 6.3, the three Maghreb countries of Tunisia, Morocco and Algeria have had more contributors to *Idafat* than the others. They published 22, 18 and 17 articles, respectively, constituting 18, 17 and 15 percent of the total number of published articles. This might be attributed to two factors: the quality of local university education in the social sciences compared with

Table 6.2 Types of published pieces

	No.	Percentage
Articles	142	57.3
Book reviews	87	35.1
Conference reports	9	3.6
Editorials	9	3.6
Other	1	0.4
Total	248	100.0

national universities in the Arab East, and a more balanced use of Arab and foreign references, as will be elaborated below. It is not contended that French sociological schools in which the Maghreb scholarship is imbued fit better with the problems of these countries, and perhaps with the Arab world, than the other Western schools. This goes beyond the scope of this study as this hypothesis needs further in-depth research. In this regard it is interesting to compare our results with a similar study that concerns *al-mustaqbal al-Arabi* (Arab Future), also published by the CAUS. Contrary to *Idafat*, the number of contributors from the Arab Maghreb is much lower than that from the Arab East, and institutionally they have a profile more of public intellectuals than academics (Mofleh 2015), a profile of profane scholars, to refer to Raymond (2013), that grow up intellectually outside the premises of the universities and sometime become dissident to mainstream ways of writing.

Lebanese sociologists (who are also under the French influence) ranked fourth (17 articles, representing 14 percent), followed by Palestinian sociologists, whether from Palestine or the diaspora (13 articles, representing 11 percent). (Table 6.3).

In terms of co-authorships, this is rare and rather specific to social science in the region; and when there is co-authorship, it is local and demonstrates the lack of transnational collaboration, which is contrary to the international trend. Some 94 percent of the articles (133 articles) are written by a sole author (Table 6.4).

Concerning the nature of published research, only 29 percent of the articles (37 articles) are based on field research, while a similar number is based on readings (30 percent), and the rest (40 percent) are discussion articles (essays).

Some 84 percent of the articles in *Idafat* are written in Arabic, compared to 16 percent that have been translated from French or English publications written either by foreigners or by Arab diasporic sociologists. The translation process has enabled broader exposure of the Arab reader to classic literature in sociology.

Table 6.3 Distribution of published articles by nationality of the first author

Nationality	No.	Percentage
Tunisia	22	18.3
Morocco	20	16.7
Algeria	18	15
Lebanon	17	14.2
Palestine	13	10.8
Iraq	10	8.3
Egypt	8	6.7
Jordan	3	2.5
Bahrain	2	1.7
Libya	2	1.7
Kuwait	1	0.8
Mauritania	1	0.8
Qatar	1	0.8
Saudi Arabia	1	0.8
Sudan	1	0.8
Total	120	100
Other nationalities	22	
Total	142	

Source: *Idafat*; authors' calculations.

Table 6.4 Co-authoring in *Idafat*

Number of authors	No.	Percentage
1	133	94.3
2	5	3.5
3	2	1.5
4	1	0.7
Total	141	100.0

Source: *Idafat*; authors' calculations.

3 Topics covered

Political sociology and the sociology of migration (24 times each) are two major themes.[2] This is not surprising, given that the Arab world has lived under severe political crises since the independence of these countries, and many of them are poverty-ridden. This has prompted many Arabs to migrate. These countries have also attracted Arab and Asian labor migration. The other topics covered are social theory (20 articles) and historical sociology (18 articles), which also includes theoretical studies about Arab or foreign authors that have contributed to the establishment of Arab and Western sociology. The sociology of religion (13 articles) is also covered because of the importance of the question of religion in Arab culture and Islam in the region. This makes sense, as one cannot imagine a study of the social and political phenomena in the region without taking into account religion as a variable, especially in societies that have not yet completed the process of separation between religion and the state. This topic becomes particularly salient after the Arab uprisings.

Critical studies of the nature of knowledge production in a specific country, or across the Arab world, have occupied the minds of some authors of *Idafat* (nine articles). There are another eight articles on the theme of "youth," six in the genre of gender studies, five on the Arab revolutions, another five relating to culture and four on colonialism (Table 6.5). Concerning gender, it should be admitted that it is still under-represented in the Arab world and it is not mainstreamed in articles dealing with social phenomena. Also rare are studies that deal with social divisions in the Arab world, and particularly the social class division, where each received only one paper.

Table 6.5 Topics covered in *Idafat*

Topic	No.	Topic	No.
Political	24	Sociology of science	2
Migration	24	Trade and worker unions	2
Theory	20	Aesthesis	1
Historical	18	Tribes	1
Religion	13	Corruption	1
Knowledge	9	Cosmopolitism	1
Youth	9	Criminology	1
Gender	6	Demography	1
Arab revolutions	5	Egypt	1
Culture	5	Elderly people	1
Colonialism	4	Family	1
Ethnicity	4	Fashion	1
Islamism	4	Health	1
Sexuality	4	Identity	1
Social movements	4	Ideology	1
Children	3	Iraq	1
Civil society	3	Linguistics	1
Economic	3	Memory	1
Forced migration	3	Palestine	1
Literature	3	Palestinians	1
Semiotics	3	Profession	1
Tunisia	3	Racism	1
Algeria	2	Rural	1
Citizenship	2	Social classes	1
Democracy	2	Social division	1
Education	2	Social psychology	1
Lebanon	2	Urban	1
Morocco	2	Violence	1
Media	2		
Methods	2	Total	220

Source: *Idafat*; authors' calculations.

Table 6.6 Language of references used in the *Idafat* articles

	References in Arabic	References in English	References in French	References in other language
Mean	7.39	6.99	4.87	0.289

Source: *Idafat*; authors' calculations.

This chapter now turns to a very compelling issue, which is the references used by researchers in their articles. Here, the focus will be only on the language of references, leaving aside the network analysis of authors who cite each other throughout *Idafat*. This is still under examination and it allows one to draw conclusions about whether *Idafat* sparks dialogue and debate among sociologists and intellectual communities.

Table 6.6 shows there is, in general, a modest place for the Arabic language versus English and French, as the average use of references in Arabic is 7.4 per article against 7.0 in English, 4.9 for French, and 0.3 for other languages, i.e., those in Arabic represent around one-third of the references.

This was the case despite the relentless efforts made by the *Idafat* editorial board to request authors who had not performed a literature review of the Arabic scholarship to do so. The board and reviewers thus often suggest additional references in Arabic.

It may be useful to examine the distribution of the average use of the references in issues, according to the nationality of the first author, and in an attempt to understand the relationship between university and languages used in the literature.

One may note evidence from Tables 6.6 and 6.7 that authors in the Arab East generally refer more to Arabic references (except Lebanon) compared with Maghreb authors.

4 Conclusion

Our results concur to a large extent with a study conducted by Ahmed Musa Badawi (2010). Comparing Arabic, international and Bengali sociological journals, this study yielded that Arab authors read less literature than their Bangladeshi and international colleagues. They referred to the same reference significantly fewer times than the Bangladeshi and international authors, which Badawi interprets as a sign of uncritical and superficial reception of the research literature.

How can this trend be explained? One should go back to the question of how the Arab sociological community conducts its research, the paucity of library databases which limit their access to academic references and the problem of proficiency in the foreign language. The next chapter examines this question through an online survey of the use of references by researchers who are doing their Masters or PhD degrees.

Table 6.7 Average number of references in the *Idafat* articles, by the first author's nationality (only Arabs) and the percentage of the Arab references

Nationality	References in Arabic	References in English	References in French	References in other language	Total articles	Percentage of the Arab references
Algeria	8.6	2.9	7.4	0.56	18	45.2
Bahrain		14.5	5.0		2	0
Egypt	8.5	7.0	1.1	0.125	8	50.7
Iraq	13.9	1.7	0.1	0.1	10	88
Jordan	17.3				3	100
Kuwait	16.0		11.0		1	59.3
Lebanon	5.1	9.7	2.6		17	29.1
Libya	3.5	4.5			2	45.2
Mauritania	22.0	2.0	12.0		1	61.1
Morocco	8.3	2.7	7.1	0.2	20	45.5
Palestine	13.1	1.3	1.1		13	53.5
Qatar	8.0				1	100
Saudi Arabia	24.0	3.0			1	88.9
Sudan	31.0				1	100
Tunisia	3.1	3.1	7.1		22	23.4
Total	8.43	4.92	4.43	0.58	120	Average: 47.3

Source: *Idafat*; authors' calculations. In gray, average number of references is above the average number of references of the journal (120 articles).

Notes

1 See www.caus.org.lb/Home/electronic_magazine_list3.php?CatID=4. *Idafat* has benefited from funding from the Arab Cultural Fund (London).
2 Each article can cover more than one topic.

7 Social research and language

Is there a marginalization of the Arab language?

I'm not fond of the biological metaphors that talk about the life and death of languages, yet everything around us shows us that a language that does not develop becomes closer to death.

(Calvet 1987; authors' translation)

One day, God wanted to be hired as researcher at INSERM [French public health research institute]. He presented a work he was very proud of: "the creation of the world" and estimated it was an experience whose impact factor, duration of the citation and international visibility were sufficient to justify the job position. One year later he received an advice of the commission : 1) his experiment had not included a control group; 2) the experience was not reproducible; 3) and, above all, the original publications were not in English.

(Chikhani Nacouz 1996: 174; authors' translation)

1 Introduction

Publication is the main communication tool of scientific activity; it entails the diffusion of knowledge, training and peer assessment of scholars. Publications have also been widely studied from a strategic evaluative perspective to identify and measure the productivity of laboratories, disciplines and countries (Arvanitis and Gaillard 1992; Waast 1996; Glänzel 1996). They are currently used from a management and evaluative perspective in order to measure individual productivity and, as such, have become a management tool of funding agencies and policy institutions (Campbell *et al.* 2010). Additionally, the extensive commercial activity surrounding publishing scientific journals and producing large bibliographic databases further enhances non-scientific uses of scientific productions. The publication system in the social sciences, as in all sciences, is thus a global power structure (Alatas 2003; Keim 2008; 2011) which is very unequally distributed worldwide (Gingras and Mosbah-Natanson 2010) and linguistically (Ammon 2010).

By reconsidering publications in social sciences in Arabic, this study attempts to bring the publication practice to the forefront not merely as a diffusion instrument of research results, but as an activity shaping the very core of research practice, which determines the research topic choices, the type of analysis and its writing (Pontille 2003; 2004). We would like to place these issues in the global context of the production in the social sciences in the Arab world (Arvanitis *et al.* 2010; Hanafi 2011). Thus the objective of this chapter is to question the relationship between social research and language by arguing that many factors, including the political economy of publication, globalization and commodification of higher education have marginalized the peripheral languages such as Arabic. This marginalization, we argue, is not necessarily inevitable but indicates a "dependency by choice."

Our reflections are based on a variety of data and fieldwork we have performed, as well as personal, although different, experience of both authors on the structure of scientific research in Lebanon, and organizations performing research in the Arab world (Hanafi and Arvanitis 2013a; 2013b; Hanafi 2011; Arvanitis 2007; Arvanitis and M'henni 2010). We used a specific survey by questionnaire that serves the purpose of organizing the issues at stake. The questionnaire survey concerned the use of references in the PhD and Masters thesis and was answered by 165 persons who hold a Masters or PhD degree from a university in the Arab world, regardless of discipline. This sample cannot be considered in any way representative of the Arab social sciences community, but it points to structural aspects concerning the use of Arabic vs. foreign language sources in doing actual research.

We have used a variety of additional material (bibliometric analysis, interviews with academics in Lebanon and Jordan) in drawing out the hypothesis of this work, mainly from ongoing research that aims at understanding the research practices in all sciences in Arab countries, focusing on the universities, organization and promotion of research, as well as international scientific collaborations.

The evaluation of research production, linked to the university promotion systems, becomes very acute and pivotal. The "high-impact journals," being in English, force to a certain extent the marginalization of the Arabic language. The additional particularity of the Arab world is that many of the new universities (mostly private) teach in English, a foreign language. Old foreign-language universities, with a distinctive tradition in research, are to be found mainly in Lebanon and the Maghreb. Moreover, these are elite universities and the foreign language is part of the identity of that elite. The "scientific" elite is very much linked to these well-known foreign-teaching universities, like the American University of Beirut (AUB) or the Université Saint-Joseph (USJ) in Lebanon. In the Maghreb countries, French has long dominated the social sciences, well after the implementation of the "Arabization" laws that imposed Arabic as the main teaching language. It also appeared that the new universities in the Maghreb responded to demographic pressure, favoring Arabic as the main language, whereas the older universities and higher education schools (like, for example, the schools of Mines and the Institut Agronomique Hassan-II, in Rabat, or Ecole Polytechnique in Algiers) which have stronger research activities continued to use French both as a teaching and scientific production language. This explains the coexistence of linguistically segmented social sciences, and still a strong preeminence of French in the social sciences. We argue that the language of instruction plays a crucial role.

2 From the internationalization to the globalization of the social sciences and universities

Scientific research has gone beyond the internationalization process that began after World War II (Leresche *et al.* 2009): it is now global activity, international by definition, and this fundamental change is profoundly affecting the social sciences. Academic disciplines, areas of technological investments, domains of interests and objects of research were formerly seen through a national lens. Today, disciplines are defined at a global level, they nurture projects funded by international agencies (where even national agencies fund foreign projects), their scope is required to be immediately understandable across the globe, and accessible to all languages and cultures. An indication of this change lies in the expansion of worldwide research projects and more frequent international collaboration (Wagner 2006; 2008; Frenken *et al.* 2010).

Internationalization as a matter of collaboration was seen as an intergovernmental and international activity, a diplomatic activity. Social sciences were less directly involved in the internationalization process since the interest of the states was to promote so-called Big Science, precisely the kind of activities that needed large international networks. This brought about a pattern of communication and publication that was characterized by the domination of the large, developed countries and disciplines such as physics, chemistry and bio-medical research. English was the language of communication, and some journals, mainly American and English academic journals, became "central" tools in the communication strategy (Meadows 1974). The very notion of a scientific community is based on the structure of the publications; the notion of "gatekeepers" and "invisible college" (Crane 1972) emerged from the examination of the work of peers acting as patrons or editors. Not all other languages became secondary in terms of frequency in the academic publications, but any other language than English was considered "provincialism" by the standards of the communication gurus of the day, who knew that the journals formed a very unequal system. Interestingly, this situation was exploited both politically and commercially (Garfield 1996), leading to a worldwide reproduction of this inequality with the excuse of enhancing circulation and efficiency in science (see the arguments of this debate in Arvanitis and Gaillard 1992).

The language issue is of particular importance for the social sciences (Ortiz 2008), although it affects all scientific research. In the earlier stages following World War II, the social sciences were less affected, publishing more often "locally" (in their own country) in the form of books, whereas other disciplines communicated mainly through academic journal articles. After this internationalization phase, scientific research entered a globalization process, where funding opportunities became available internationally on a larger scale than before. At the same time, profound changes affected the demography of scientific disciplines in the 1980s, both on the American continent as well as in Europe (Pontille 2004); as a result, scientists needed to be visible at a global level. Globalization raises issues immediately across the globe, and researchers feel the need to communicate with a variety of colleagues in faraway countries. This global view of research, contrary to the former trend of internationalization, has been directly affecting the social sciences, more than social scientists are willing to accept, and globalization became both an object of research and a way of working (Sassen 2007). We can tentatively link this change to the fact that funding and resources, even in our own institutions, have become intensely dependent upon publication. The credibility cycle that Latour and Woolgar (1979) deciphered long ago (in the biological sciences) is in full swing today (in the social sciences), and influences social sciences most profoundly, with the increase of project funding that is delivered worldwide. This worldwide research system is not, strictly speaking, "internationalized"; rather, it becomes an activity that is *ex ante* globalized. Questions and research issues have to be understandable in every part of the world. Large funding programs and networks that expand throughout the globe: the wider the networks the more probable it is to find researchers from non-hegemonic countries. To be heard, this web of projects is speaking a unified language – English – that leaves little room for "local" languages.

An assessment of the social sciences carried out in South Africa in 1995 (cited by Keim 2008) mentioned that 90 percent of the articles contained in the "Social Science Citation Index" originate from 10 percent of the world's countries. Gingras and Mosbah-Natanson (2010) show that, in the same database, in the 1998–2007 period, 94 percent of the social sciences were published in English as reported by the Web of Science (WoS). Ammon (2010), looking at a more balanced database (the International Bibliography for the Social Sciences), found that English represented 76 percent in 2005. The growth of other languages does not include Arabic. Worse, Arabic is not even among the ten most frequent worldwide languages in the social sciences, which include, among others, Chinese, Dutch, Japanese and Polish in the Ulrich database. Chinese and Polish are absent from WoS in social sciences.

The language domination of English might be the result of the location of research, since most articles originate in North America and Europe. Gingras and Mosbah-Natanson (2010: 151) note that in the social science index of the WoS

> North America is the largest producer of articles in the social sciences, with more than half of the total number of articles, and is the only region publishing an average of more than 10,000 articles per year. With other countries' growing contributions, the North American share of the total is bound to diminish over time: from 61 per cent of the total of social science articles over the period 1988–1997, this percentage drops to 52.2 per cent over the next ten-year period (1998–2007). Europe is the second most important actor in social sciences and its share grew substantially, from 29.1 per cent during 1988–1997 to 38 per cent during 1998–2007.

More disturbing is the fact that citations of articles written in Africa, Latin America and Oceania to other articles in the same region were halved in the same ten-year period. In the period 1993–1995, 22 percent of the references in African papers were to African social science journals. Ten years later, this proportion had fallen to only 11.7 percent. The decline is even stronger in Asia. The two major social science producers, Europe and North America, have experienced a small decline in the references to articles coming from the same region, "indicating better recognition of foreign contributions" (p. 153).

These proportions of language distribution depend a lot on the sources of data/databases used. Nonetheless, English still remains a strongly dominant language in all files reviewed. For example, a very detailed analysis done by Keim (2010) shows that in *Sociological Abstracts* (1995–1998), 45 percent of the production (26,136 references) comes from the United States, 13 percent from the UK, followed by Germany (4.6 percent), Australia (3.9 percent), France (3.6 percent) and the Netherlands (2.9 percent). All other countries have less than 1 percent, and 95 countries (out of 166 "peripheral" countries) have no reference at all. The African continent represents 1.3 percent – less than Spain – while Asia has 3 percent and Latin America 4.1 percent. The Arab world is practically absent from this database. Ten years later (2005–2008), the United States represents 43.5 percent (23,475 references), and the UK 14 percent (7,573 references). Africa represents 2.5 percent, Asia 5.5 percent and Latin America 3.6 percent. There are more data from Ammon (2010) showing that English is the dominant language: since 1965, when Sociological Abstracts began, from 81.7 percent (1965–1970) to 85.5 percent (1995–1998) of documents were in English; this information comes from probably the most balanced database in social sciences, along with International Bibliography of the Social Sciences (IBSS).

3 Language of instruction and language of research

Although language is a highly symbolic marker of identity, multilingual scholars have multilayered identities which open the door to more expansive research agendas and a commitment not only to local and regional contexts, but also to international ones. The language of instruction cannot be chosen exclusively on the basis of political-cultural factors, which are related to identity formation on gaining political independence. There is also a political-economic component which involves recognizing problems related to the dearth of resources that limits the production of required textbooks, as well as problems determined by the marketing strategies of international publishers from core universities (Sultana 1999: 31).

Different languages, therefore, call for different markets, which is what makes the English language extremely important as a tool for instruction. In the Arab states, however, Arabic has been substituted in recently established private universities. There is no plausible reason for the existence of a curriculum that is completely void of sources written in Arabic. A study of 30 syllabi of social science courses taught in USJ, the Lebanese American University (LAU) and the

AUB shows that it is extremely rare (only two references) to find Arabic references, even as secondary reading.

Following Renato Ortiz (2008), we can identify two different critical questions under the language issue: the first one relates to how language provides for a "universal" knowledge. Ortiz correctly points out that universality is a philosophical concept, not a sociological reality. However, globalization has affected the circulation of ideas and concepts in more intense ways than we are ready to accept. Arab countries, for a variety of reasons, have been completely subjected to this pressure. The second question relates to the capacity to think in one's own words. Social sciences are particularly sensitive to the language in which the production circulates and the Arabic language is used very differently. Among Arab scholars, who have received in large proportions instruction in English/ French, the issue is even more crucial: is the reality of their own societies understandable in a "foreign" language? Can we split the use of language between two scientific "functions"? One would relate to the dissemination of ideas and publication, the other would relate to thinking about the societal issues in the "native" language. Is it possible to split this analytic capability that implies reading/ writing in one language and speaking in another? Ortiz (2008), for example, rightfully reminds us that he has no more legitimacy, as a Brazilian sociologist, than a foreigner writing in English about Brazil. But he also clearly implies that language does force you to think differently.

In the Arab world a strange configuration is taking place: social sciences are taught in Arabic, in public (usually large) universities, while some exclusive universities use English or – more rarely – French. The phenomenon also concerns some newly created universities in the Gulf countries, where well-known American or European universities have established branches.

Language of instruction is the product of both policy and history. In general, governments have not been consistent in their policy concerning language in the Arab countries, with some exceptions like Syria that required Arabic as a teaching language in all higher education institutions. History explains the persistence of French in Maghreb universities. The language of university teaching in Algeria has been, officially, Arabic since 1971 but was expanded to practically all disciplines in the social sciences only after 1984. In practice this has been a progressive move depending on the books available rather than policy (Guedjali 2011). French is usually still frequently used in science, technology and medicine. The same is true for Tunisia and Morocco. In Jordan, the Ministry of Higher Education and Scientific Research (2003) acknowledged the need to encourage the Arabization of science, and encouraged scientific research in Arabic, but did not mention the language of instruction. The same happened recently in Saudi Arabia.

In the Gulf, language policy changes constantly. In an interview conducted with the Chairman of Graduate Studies in the Education Department of Qatar University, he claimed that the quick shift from Arabic to English has had negative effects on Masters-level students. First, many female trainees who want to improve their methods of teaching are not allowed entry onto the program because of their weak proficiency in English. As such, the number of enrolled students in the program, which was 35 in 2006, decreased to six students in 2010 after the program's language of instruction changed. At another level, the teachers noticed that the students enrolled in the program do not assimilate or absorb the content of their subject. The teachers made their claims based on observations that the students understood the theories being presented but could not use them in their research projects.

Throughout one of the consultation projects for evaluating sociology programs that were directed in one of the universities in the Gulf (2008–2009), several problems in the curriculum were found. One of these was that the books being used were old and monotonous. It was suggested that a specialized committee be formed in each major field to review their curriculum and substitute their texts with current Arabic literature and translate foreign sources into Arabic where the gap needs to be filled. It was also suggested that the university assesses the enrolled students' proficiency in English as well as how well they can read and process sources in English when needed, and translate some of the texts into Arabic. The university could offer a course or two that teach foreign texts in their original language. Unfortunately, none of these suggestions has been adopted and some of the departments in social sciences have been transformed into English. Some of the Gulf states are experiencing a loss of Arab identity and so they are deliberately focusing on the local folkloric culture, pushed by a mentality of minority; or they are driven by a fascination with globalization. In the latter case, they opt for an isomorphism to foreign institutions and the usage of English.

When two competing languages are used in the same country, language has been used as a selection tool in the higher education system. This is the case in Lebanon and was the case in Algeria. Today, lower classes in Algeria are usually integrating into the social sciences, which are more "Arabicized" than medicine, engineering or natural and exact sciences. Interview data in economics, sociology and law (Benguerna 2011) show the diverse effects of the Arabization policy. In practice, in many universities lecturers and students are switching between Arabic and English (or French), an "innovative accommodation" as it has been called by Zughoul (2000). In North Africa language switching is not only frequent, but almost instinctive (Sultana 1999: 32). In Maghreb, language also affects the labor market, since companies prefer to hire young graduates speaking both French and Arabic rather than exclusively Arabic. It is also a sign of social recognition and identity.

In research, the relation between language and research topics is little known. To our knowledge, there exists only one such study, published in the *World Social Science Report* (Waast *et al.* 2010). It shows that the social science production in Maghreb countries emphasizes different research topics according to the language of publication. Topics from history, literary theory or political sciences are more frequently published in Arabic, while other disciplines such as psychology, economics or sociology are more commonly published in French/ English/Spanish.

The language issue does not only relate to topic choice, but also to the access to knowledge and exposure to other researchers both locally and globally, in the dissemination and discussion of research ideas. What some scholars have been denouncing for many years in the Arab world is that research production in Arabic has been slowly degrading. Ahmad Musa Badawi (2009) notes that the references used in the PhD thesis in sociology in Egyptian universities are old ones, using old theoretical paradigms, mostly lacking a critical stance and creativity; moreover, he considers that the topics are not always relevant to Egyptian society. Jad Melki (2009) notes that in most Lebanese universities literature reviews and essays in media studies are confused with research. Kabbanji (2010) notes that research for a large majority of authors writing in the social sciences relates to individual essays, books and sometimes articles, mostly based on deskwork and probably related to promotion. Hanafi (2011) has been denouncing the fact that many research pieces are local, empirical and remain in the form of reports that are rarely diffused because they are addressed to institutional funders and not for academic purposes. At the same time, Arab scholars of great reputation are numerous in Europe and the United States, and in certain cases the number of nationals of an Arab country among scientists abroad can be larger than the number of researchers in their home country.

In research, the use of English is a generalized practice, even in the Arab world. Table 7.1 shows the use of English, French and Arabic in a large survey carried out in the framework of a European project called MIRA (www.miraproject.eu), answered by 4,340 researchers from 38 countries (27 in Europe and 11 Mediterranean country partners of the EU), that have co-authored articles or have collaborated in joint projects (Gaillard *et al.* 2013). Researchers in the social sciences accounted for a small part of the sample since it was basically conceived through the WoS database.

It is apparent that social scientists in Arab countries use Arabic in higher proportions than in basic sciences (physics, chemistry, biology, etc.) and medical

Table 7.1 Arab researchers' publishing language (MIRA Survey)

	English	*French*	*Arabic*	*Total respondents*
Basic sciences	641	345	49	646
Percentage of respondents in basic sciences	*99.2*	*53.4*	*7.6*	*100.0*
Applied sciences	145	77	15	150
Percentage of respondents in applied sciences	*96.7*	*51.3*	*10.0*	*100.0*
Medical sciences	335	194	52	339
Percentage of respondents in medical sciences	*98.8*	*57.2*	*15.3*	*100.0*
Social science and humanities	26	18	12	30
Percentage of respondents in SSH	*86.7*	*60.0*	*40.0*	*100.0*
Total	1,147	634	128	1,165
Percentage of respondents in all fields	*98.5*	*54.4*	*11.0*	*100.0*

Source: MIRA Survey; calculations by the authors.

sciences (bio-medicine and clinical sciences). It is interesting to note that social sciences and humanities (SSH) and applied sciences in other countries more frequently use languages different to English (the answers are not exclusive). Let us observe that the 1,184 Arab scientists that answered this survey are probably older than the general population of researchers, have co-published with a foreign (European) partner, and are engaged internationally. An additional comment concerns language: it appears that all researchers having co-published with foreign colleagues publish in extremely high proportions in English, whatever the country of origin, nationality, country of residence, age or professional status. Their mother tongue, whether European or not, is used in moderate proportions and more frequently than not as a secondary language to report scientific results. Science communicates in written form in English, even though it can be practiced in the local language.

4 A survey on language use in Arabic research

The survey we performed was placed online between January and May 2012 and hard copies were sent to informants in all Arab countries, to private and public universities in the region. Emails were sent once to students and professors in the social sciences that were identified through previous contacts with us (Hanafi is an editor of an Arab journal), who were asked to complete the survey questionnaire. The questionnaire was filled out by 165 people; 87 obtained a Masters degree (56 percent) and 68 are PhD holders (43 percent). Among the target pool, 66 percent earned their degrees from universities in the Arab world, and the rest earned their degrees, primarily PhDs, from foreign countries with topics concerning the Arab world. We received responses mainly from Arab public universities (47 percent of responses), 17 percent from private non-profit universities, 2 percent from private for-profit universities, and the remaining 44 percent from foreign universities. This reflects probably rather fairly the actual distribution of young social scientists doing research. Most of them are located in large, public or some older and larger private non-profit universities, or are doing their studies in a foreign country.

We had more answers from the Arab East (53.4 percent) and fewer (12.3 percent) from the Western Arab Francophone countries like Tunisia, Algeria and Morocco, while European and American universities comprised 23.3 percent and 10.4 percent of the answers, respectively. Our bias against French-speaking Maghreb countries is a sign in itself: the survey was posted in Arabic and English and we know that many social scientists in the Maghreb countries do not feel comfortable in either of these two languages.

The questionnaire reached recent graduates (85.3 percent of our responses) and also some people who graduated in the 1980s (4.9 percent) and 1990s (9.8 percent). We wanted to do some comparative analysis to see whether the situation was evolving. Unfortunately the low numbers make conjecture difficult; nonetheless, our own experience might be of some help. Also, our bias was largely in favor of the social sciences and humanities (85.7 percent), in comparison to business administration (5 percent), natural sciences (3.7 percent) and applied sciences, mainly engineering (5.6 percent). This second bias was rather useful, since we have had no precedent for this kind of analysis in the social sciences.

As mentioned in the introduction, this sample cannot be considered in any way representative of the Arab social sciences, but points to some structural aspects concerning the use of languages as sources of research. The figures indicating the magnitude in the use of specific language in scientific references gathered in this survey are unique, and draw attention to the use of English, French and Arabic comparatively by the same sample of people. Absolute figures are probably of less significance, although the results of the quasi-exhaustive coverage of the social sciences production in the Maghreb countries of Waast *et al.* (2010) lead us to believe that we have a view that reflects the actual distribution of language use in the social sciences.

4.1 Using references in Arabic and foreign languages

According to the responses (Table 7.2), 31 percent of references were in Arabic — 29 percent for Masters holders and 34 percent for PhD holders. That is significantly lower than references in English (nearly half of the references). French occupies nearly one-fifth of the references; other languages account for only 1.8 percent.

The databases mentioned in order to access foreign-language academic journals where JSTOR, followed by Google Scholar; the more recent Francophone graduates used Cairn and revues.org. Arabic sources that were mentioned were the UN reports and Google, which are actually not academic databases. To the question of what Arab journals they used in their research, answers covered both academic journals (e.g., *Journal of the Social Sciences* or *Idafat: The Arab Journal of Sociology*) or more general content journals addressed to a wider audience (e.g., *al-mustakbal al-'arabi*) or newspapers (*al-safir*, *an-nahar*, etc.).

The sample in Table 7.3 (by country of graduation) shows that respondents used about 30 percent of references in Arabic and 48 percent in English. As can be seen, the use of Arabic references is the same whether they graduated in the

Table 7.2 Distribution of bibliographic references used in the Masters or PhD thesis, by language of reference

Degree	Number of respondents	Percentage of Arabic references	Percentage of English references	Percentage of French references	Percentage of other languages references
Masters	87	29.3	50.5	18.3	1.9
PhD	68	34.1	44.3	19.8	1.7
Total	155	31.4	47.8	18.9	1.8

Source: authors' own survey, 2012.

Table 7.3 Distribution of bibliographic references by language and country of graduation

Region	Number of respondents	Percentage of Arabic references	Percentage of English references	Percentage of French references	Percentage of other languages references
Arab East	84	39.9	50.3	8.8	0.9
North Africa	19	39.8	7.6	45.6	6.9
Europe	36	11.1	53.9	33.1	1.9
North America	17	17.3	73.3	8.4	0.9
Other countries	1	0	100	0	0
Total	157	30.6	48.8	18.7	1.9

Source: authors' own survey, 2012.

Arab East or West, but French references are a bit higher in the Maghreb countries (about 33 percent). Those graduates from foreign universities use significantly fewer references in Arabic: 11 percent in Europe and 17 percent in North America. Although we have a small number of respondents, the fact that Arabic references are fewer in Europe as compared to the United States/Canada is challenging, but is most probably explained by the fact that French-speaking Arab graduates tend to more easily use French-language references than Arabic ones, something we know from our Lebanese or Maghrabi colleagues.

It is worth noting that among the respondents, graduates from the social sciences use references in Arabic (34 percent) in greater proportions than those from other fields (close to 20 percent) (Table 7.4). Graduates from business administration cite only 18 percent of their references in Arabic, similar to the political sciences (17 percent). English is twice as frequently used in other disciplines than the social sciences and humanities. This distribution is confirmed by the MIRA Survey in Mediterranean Arab countries, mentioned above (Gaillard *et al.* 2013) and by the Maghreb social sciences literature analysis (Waast *et al.* 2010).

Interestingly, there is a close connection between the use of references in Arabic with the types of universities, which certainly resides in the universities' language of instruction (Table 7.5). The percentage of references in Arabic

Table 7.4 Distribution of bibliographic references by language and fields of science

Field	Number of respondents	Percentage of Arabic references	Percentage of English references	Percentage of French references	Percentage of other languages references
SSH	135	34.2	44.4	19.5	1.8
Business	8	18.4	63.0	16.3	2.4
Basic sciences	6	16.7	83.3	0.0	0.0
Applied sciences	8	0.0	75.6	21.9	2.5
Total	157	31.0	48.5	18.7	1.9

Source: authors' own survey, 2012.

Table 7.5 Distribution of bibliographic references by language and type of university

	Number of respondents	Percentage of Arabic references	Percentage of English references	Percentage of French references	Percentage of other languages references
National	74	48.8	31.9	16.7	2.6
Private not-for-profit	27	17.1	66.2	16.7	0.0
Private for profit	3	35.3	64.7	0.0	0.0
Foreign countries	54	12.9	62.0	23.1	1.9
Total	158	30.9	48.7	18.6	1.9

Source: authors' own survey, 2012.

decreases from 49 percent for graduates of national universities to 17 percent for graduates of private non-profit universities (Table 7.5). These are mainly the universities that use English or French as the main teaching language. The same applies to universities in foreign countries: studying in a foreign country greatly influences the language of references, as we stated above, but, rather by increasing the proportion of foreign-language references than by diminishing the Arabic references. Thus, around 85 percent of references are in a foreign language in foreign-language universities as well as universities in foreign countries, whereas in national universities the percentage falls to around 50 percent. This proportion is thus affected by the country and type of university of instruction. Respondents also mentioned that the number of references used in Arabic increased when their supervisor encouraged the students to use them.

The weak use of references in Arabic cannot be linked to one's proficiency in the language – only 6 percent declared being beginner-level Arabic-speakers and only 3 percent cannot read Arabic language. However, the language of instruction while studying is a very important factor in the choice of the language of references. Nearly 90 percent of references are in a foreign language when the language of instruction is foreign in high school, at the undergraduate or graduate levels of university. We only present the results for graduate studies here, but percentages are very close for all three levels (Table 7.6). The percentage of foreign references, however, is much lower (around 60 percent) when the

Table 7.6 Distribution of bibliographic references by language, and language of teaching at the university

Language of teaching in graduate studies	Number of respondents	Percentage of Arabic references	Percentage of English references	Percentage of French references	Percentage of other languages references
Arabic	38	54.2	33.3	10.0	2.5
Foreign language	63	9.0	69.3	20.3	1.5
Both	42	40.9	35.5	23.2	0.4
Total	143	30.4	49.8	18.4	1.4

Source: authors' own survey, 2012.

language of instruction is both Arabic and English, but still higher than when teaching was in Arabic only.

As we mentioned before, private universities such as USJ, LAU and AUB don't teach Arabic textbooks. It comes as no surprise that the graduates from these universities that teach in English and French cite so few Arabic references in their own academic work.

Although only 5 percent of the surveyed persons reported that they are unfamiliar with the English language, we suspect this percentage to be much higher. In looking at the actual references the respondents claimed they used in their Masters and PhD theses, we noticed that many authors did not seem to have a good understanding of the foreign sources they used. Moreover, as we show in the following pages, one of the reasons for using relatively more Arabic references is a mediocre proficiency in reading in a foreign language.

4.2 Using references: options and constraints

The respondents' reasons for not using a lot of references in Arabic were varied and attributed to the difficulty of access and, to a lesser extent, to issues related to content (Table 7.7). The first complaint expressed by almost half of the respondents was that references in Arabic are not available and they do not find them easily at university or in public libraries. A graduate from the Lebanese University expressed further:

> I looked in the following Arab Universities – University of Cairo, University of Jordan, most libraries of universities in Lebanon and Asad library [Damascus] – for sources and literature that could help me in my research and I found a minimal number.

The same importance of access is given as a main reason for not using foreign references: libraries do not give satisfactory access to books and/or journals in foreign languages, except some universities known for the high quality of their libraries, such as American Universities of Beirut or Cairo and USJ.

Another researcher from Egypt who graduated in 2004, before the internet became widespread, stated:

> It was difficult to get sources in English that had direct relation to my main topic, if I was going to rely solely on the library of Aïn Shams University [Cairo] or the public libraries like that of Alexandria. But, I had a subscription to the American University in Cairo's library; if it wasn't for that, I really would not have been able to find the appropriate references.

The problem becomes much more acute for those who studied in foreign countries where the libraries rarely procure references in Arabic.

The second reason, also related to access difficulties, as reported by 43 percent of the respondents, was that the university library or public library do

Table 7.7 Reasons for difficulty of using sources in Arabic

Reasons	Answers concerning Arabic references		Answers concerning foreign references	
	N	Percentage	N	Percentage
I had difficulty finding them in public/university library	51	49.5	31	55.4
There were no databases from which I could get articles (only for Arabic references)	44	42.7	–	–
Public/university libraries do not have subscription for article databases (only for foreign references)	–	–	21	37.5
Arabic references (or foreign references) were irrelevant to my topic	43	41.7	17	30.4
I couldn't find references in Arabic when I used search engines (Google, Yahoo, etc.)	41	39.8	–	–
I didn't find the Arab (or foreign) scholarship particularly interesting	36	35.0	6	10.7
My reading proficiency in Arabic (or foreign language) is not adequate	18	17.5	25	44.6
I couldn't afford to buy Arab (or foreign) books	7	6.8	11	19.6

Source: authors' own survey, 2012.

not subscribe to databases and academic journals in Arabic. Those who graduated before 2000 claim to be unaware of these databases. Many recent graduates complained about the unavailability of that service in their university libraries. A graduate in sociology from the University of Baghdad explains:

> I researched for the sources painfully inside and outside the university. Till this day, the university library does not have serious scientific international journals. Subscription to international journals has been restricted in Baghdad University since 1989. Many instructors are not concerned whether students get references or not. The university libraries are not qualified to offer books or journals for graduate students.

More importantly, many respondents claim the content of the references in Arabic (rather than access) is irrelevant to their topics (44 percent) and 35 percent of the respondents claimed they do not resort to sources in Arabic because they do not find them of interest. Accordingly, one of the respondents explained:

> most of the time, the sources in Arabic are either weak or poorly translated from rich sources or they don't provide in-depth and varying information as the sources in foreign languages.... Sociological and ethnographic texts and studies concerning migration in the Southern Maghreb are very limited.

This claim is probably the one that needs some more investigation. This is striking because foreign-language references are considered less relevant.

A study by Sari Hanafi, currently in preparation, reveals the weakness in usage of references in Arabic in migration studies that concern the Arab world. We found only 37 percent of the Arab references in Arab journals and 11 percent in foreign journals, respectively. A graduate from Canada further attributes this to the fact that "there is a reputation that what is written in Arabic are not refereed articles."

More than five researchers also mentioned the problem of translation, claiming that translation to Arabic is so poorly done that the texts are very difficult to read, and there is an absence of standardization of the scientific concepts. This is a severe problem: the absence of discussion – and thus the absence of legitimization – of new concepts generate translated work that is not only difficult to read, but that also leaves plenty of concepts in a foreign language without translation. Maher Charif, the translator of a fundamental (and difficult) sociological work of Castoriadis (*L'institution imaginaire de la société*) told us the translation was long and complex because of so few discussions and references to basic sociological analysis in Arabic. Translators need thus to invent words on their own, or transliterate them.

Respondents also had several reasons for not using sources in foreign languages. The access is again the main reason: 55 percent of them claimed that they do not easily find sources in foreign languages in university or public libraries. Second, 45 percent of the respondents' abilities in foreign languages are weak and 37 percent of them stated that the university or public library did not have membership to databases that hold scientific journals (Table 7.7). Some of the details the respondents presented reveal that the sources in foreign languages are primarily used for establishing the theoretical framework of the research.

The databases mentioned in order to access foreign-language academic journals where JSTOR, *Journal of the Social Sciences* or *Arab Journal of Sociology*, or more general-content journals addressed to a wider audience (e.g., *al-mustakbal al-'arabi*) or newspapers (e.g., *al-safir, al-nahar*).

There was a low percentage of respondents who wanted to buy books and journals in Arabic (7 percent) or English (11 percent) as they did not find them in public libraries. While this might be due to a resource problem, it is primarily caused by censorship, as described by Frank Mermier (2005), which hinders the circulation between Arab countries. Some could not afford it due to their high costs. This could be related to the scarce scholarship funds for graduate studies in the Arab world.

Those who can afford to pay for access to their own sources in foreign languages have difficulty finding those sources. In the same vein, one of the respondents further explains:

> The most difficult issue I encountered in completing my research was the scarce availability of sources and their lack of relevance to my topic. Consequently, I was forced to frequently visit the national library of Algeria, the international book fair and request references from my friends that live abroad. Pierre Bourdieu's book, "Ce que parler veut dire," for instance, I got hold of it after having paid a Moroccan publisher in a book fair on the spot and he sent it to me later on. But these tricks for procuring academic references take time and affect one's thesis and stalls the date of its completion.

Our study clearly shows that graduate students face a fundamental structural problem which relates to access to foreign sources of knowledge, as well as to an evaluation of the usefulness or relevance of sources. Students who learned English through a program that teaches in both English and Arabic in high school or university can use the academic references in a more balanced manner than those who learned only in one language, be it Arabic or English. As such, the Arabic language does not lose its value and the students benefit from foreign references that are recognized for their richness in theories, open to global debates. Of course, there is another mechanism for reaching the global debate without proficiency in foreign languages, but this requires a serious process of translation of books and articles into Arabic, as well as from Arabic to other languages. This will be the object of the following section, which assesses the situation of translation in the Arab world.

5 The case for translations

The increase in publishing translations in Arab countries is quite recent and comforts our analysis concerning overcoming the intellectual connection between the local and the global. Recent studies of Transeuropéennes (2013: 38) and Hasna Dessa and Mohamed-Saghir Janjar (2010) show an increasing awareness of the importance of translation of social sciences and humanities (SSH) books into Arabic. More specifically, 2,670 books were translated and published by Arab publishers over the course of the decade 2000–2009 (268 per year, on average), representing a 38 percent increase on the previous decade. This increase reflects a new policy of some Arab public institutions and foundations (such as the Arab Organization for Translation and Alexandria Trust), but also the extraordinary growth of private publishing in Arab countries since the 1990s (Mermier 2005). However, this translation effort is still very far from meeting the needs of transfer of new knowledge, the appropriation of great classical works or the popularization and dissemination of modern culture originating from SSH.

There is a concentration of editorial activity in this area among a small group of 34 publishers, who together published a total of 1,315 books, representing 49 percent of the entire collection studied. The remaining translations are spread between around 300 publishers (Mermier 2005: 9). Translation has mobilized not only private publishers but also public agencies. Among the 34 major publishers of translations in the field of HSS, 25 are private establishments, with 65.5 percent of the translated books. The most dynamic of these private publishers are in Lebanon (ten publishers, 428 books), Syria (six publishers, 168 books) and Morocco (four publishers, 140 books). The public sector in Egypt (mainly the Supreme Council of Culture and the National Center for Translation) and the Gulf countries[1] have almost complete monopoly of the market (Mermier 2005: 11). Recently the Arab Center for Research and Policy Studies in Doha launched a very ambitious translation program.

The good news is that translation is not only from the hegemonic English language (fewer than half of the translated books), but also from French (one-third) and others (Table 7.8). Furthermore, there is a relative growth in Arab translations of Iranian intellectual production, owing to Shiite Arab intellectuals in Lebanon, and to a lesser extent Iraq, who made known the work of contemporary Iranian philosophers and theologians, along with thinkers of the so-called reformist current. For instance, the Center of Civilization for Islamic Thought Development has translated tens of Iranian books in SSH and religious studies.

Who is translated? Publishers are interested in celebrities such as Noam Chomsky and Edward Saïd, but also classical Western work (Spinoza, Descartes, Leibniz, Kant, Hegel). French philosophers get a good position, including Paul Ricœur, Jacques Derrida, Tzvetan Todorov, Gilles Deleuze, Michel Foucault, Jean Baudrillard, Edgar Morin, Marcel Gauchet and René Girard. What is also interesting is the translation of authors who are interested in reforming Islam (Henry Corbin, Malek Cherbel). Of course, translation includes the work of Arab diasporic scholars (Wael Hallaq, Samir Amin, Hisham Sharabi) (Table 7.9).

Table 7.8 Distribution of translations by original language

Original	Language	Percentage
English	1,298	48.50
French	894	33.50
Persian	158	6.00
German	112	4.00
Spanish	63	2.36
Russian	35	1.31
Hebrew	34	1.27
Other languages	76	3.06
Total	2,670	100

Source: based on Dessa and Janjar (2010: 12).

Table 7.9 The most translated authors

Author	Original language	Language from which the translation was done	No. of titles
Noam Chomsky	English	English	18
Edward Said	English	English	14
Friedrich Nietzsche	German	German, French, English	12
Paul Ricœur	French	French	12
Pierre Bourdieu	French	French	8
Bernard Lewis	English	English	8
Malek Bennabi	French	French	7
Jacques Derrida	French	French	7
Umberto Eco	Italian	French and English	7
Bertrand Russell	English	English	7
Jürgen Habermas	German	German, French, English	6
AbdolKarim Sourouch	Persian	Persian	6
Tzvetan Todorov	French	French	6
Robert Blanché	French	French	6
Anthony Giddens	English	French	6
Mohamed Arkoun	French	French	6
Said Nursi	Turkish	Turkish	6

Source: based on Dessa and Janjar (2010: 12).

6 Discussion

We did not want to refer to cultural "imperialism" or some neo-colonial effect in order to explain the predominance of the English language in research and, consequently, the marginalization of the Arabic language. Our limited data unfortunately confirm a limited use of Arabic references in the academic work written by young Arab scholars. We found also that the use of references is affected by the language of instruction in the university, and by access issues. We saw that a proportion of nearly 30 percent mention foreign-language references as irrelevant, whereas 40 percent mention Arabic references as irrelevant. There is a gap in understanding and this makes us believe a much deeper process is at work in choosing/using references in one or another language: we believe there is a coexistence of different – and competing – legitimization processes at work in the social sciences in the Arabic-speaking countries.

Many mechanisms are playing against any social science produced in the periphery and developed in a language other than English: access to scientific knowledge and sources in local and foreign publications, exposure to debate – which should be the main function of a scientific community – relevance of topics to a given social reality and the ability to enter into public debate outside the academic arena.

Out of the interviews we conducted, funding sources and promotion mechanisms seem to be the two main mechanisms that influence the pressure toward publication in English and in core (that is mainly American and European) journals. Although not surprising, this does not explain alone the domination of Western sociologies over the national ones.

Against the trend, there have been repeated calls for the indigenization of social theory by Sayed Farid Alatas (2001; 2003). Before him, famous sociologists from the periphery had also made similar calls, such as Ziad Gökalp in Turkey or Ali Shariati in Iran. They insist on thinking a local sociology against what Lander (2003) named the "coloniality of knowledge." Foreign influence can be sufficiently strong to create a new discipline, as was the case of ethnology in Greece produced against German anthropology in the late nineteenth and early twentieth centuries (Herzfeld 1982).

Moreover, social scientists might also be profoundly influenced by a tradition of public debate where the academic journal has no relevance. Public social science is a way of writing and a form of intellectual engagement that cannot be accommodated in an international refereed journal, especially if one takes into account the delay (sometimes two years) in publication. Moreover, the debate will be in the local language, and probably what happened in the Arab countries is that they published locally, in newspapers or spaces that are not recognized internationally, and were "dying" internationally. Their institutions, especially those teaching in a foreign language, push for academics to publish exclusively globally, which would lead inevitably for them to perish locally. What is the point of being a researcher who enjoys considerable international recognition from one's peers for the high quality and impact of their recent research outputs while she or he is unknown locally? Many social scientists in Lebanon and the Arab world fall into this category.

The reverse is also true: many Lebanese professors in an elite and English-speaking university, when asked, were not certain whether a local journal existed in their field or not, and even fewer had written in one of them. Neither the *Lebanese Science Journal* nor any other journals published locally for science was taken seriously in natural, medical and exact sciences. In no case was this feeling made more explicit than with examples that would sustain the simple idea that local journals, when they exist, are bad, as opposed to the idea that foreign journals were of a higher standard. All this is obvious and seems not to need explaining. What is really being discussed in not the quality of the local publications; what is at stake is its impact on promotion. By a halo effect, social sciences are expected to do the same.

The marginality of the Arab-language production in the global arena is accompanied by invisibility in international scientific fora. Few scholars coming from the Arab world attend international conferences. National universities rarely provide scholarships to attend them. For instance, there were only five, seven and ten Arab participants, respectively, in the World Congress of the International Sociology Association in Madrid (1990), Bielefeld (1994) and Montreal (1998).

Finally, these issues in the Arab world are accentuated by the ongoing policies of promotion of foreign-language teaching institutions, and the existence of elite universities that teach in foreign languages. The language issue is a serious one.

The French linguist Louis-Jean Calvet (1987) reminds us that conflict over languages tells the story of social conflicts; and the wars of languages often signal an underlying educational or economic war. Linguistic struggles tell us a story of societal struggles. The advocates of *teaching in English* (like Mohamed Al-Sayid Salim 2009) put forth three main arguments that can be summarized as follows: first, in the era of globalization, knowledge cannot be accumulated without academic cooperation, which occurs in most cases in Western centers. Therefore, it is requested from the student to master a foreign language and be able to attend international conferences. It is not sufficient to merely learn the language as a language; one must also be able to fully process and absorb its content. The second argument revolves around the necessities of the market, whereby international and civil organizations' activities have increased, and these organizations are sponsored and funded by foreigners. In addition, there are several foreign companies and banks in the Arab world. The third argument is about the instruction in the English language, which isn't considered a threat to the Arab identity because this identity is firmly attached to structural cultural factors. Studying in foreign countries did not affect the national identity of Arab students abroad. People read in English because they don't have a lot of choice. The numbers of translated books are scarce; one cannot wait until textbooks are translated into Arabic.

The supporters of Arabization point out that most of the students are not sufficiently fluent in foreign language to easily understand foreign references. Also, teaching in a foreign language may create a split personality, consequently leading him/her to be isolated from his/her primary culture. Furthermore, these advocates argue that teaching in the mother tongue is time efficient and saves the effort usually wasted in understanding foreign texts. The energy could be directed toward understanding the academic subject itself. The Arabic language is capable of absorbing the current sciences, and advocates draw on the example of the Syrian universities. The basic scientific concepts in Arabic match better with the Arab culture and yet this does not mean that one should neglect the necessity of learning foreign languages to have better access to the new research.

The two camps' opinions can be summarized as follows: the supporters of instruction in foreign languages consider language a tool for communication, while the supporters of instruction in the Arabic language consider it a system of thought and carrier of culture.[2] In our opinion, a human can carry more than one cultural and intellectual system, as long as she or he organizes and prioritizes them. In this transitional period, teaching in universities should depend primarily on the Arabic language along with some courses in foreign languages in order to make sure the student is capable of using references in both languages. Advancing research will never be achieved if the student does not become proficient in at least one foreign language. His or her proficiency at a foreign language will introduce the student to foreign cultures, will allow him/her to explore all realms of human thought and knowledge and to enrich their country's knowledge and add to the overall human knowledge. By doing so, a student is involved in a give-and-take relationship; benefiting from foreign languages and contributing to the local and global spheres. Translating from and to Arabic allows the Arab researchers' efforts to be read by local Arab and global audiences.

This reciprocal relationship between cultures does not obligate an instruction in the English language, yet the weak level of the Arab students in foreign languages complicates interaction with such languages. The Israeli educational experience is a case study worthy of investigation. Three of their universities were ranked within the 500 top universities in the world, while the Arab universities are below such a ranking. Although the universities in Israel teach exclusively in Hebrew, some Arab researchers there that we interviewed assured us that Israeli students' status allows them to easily access and use foreign references if they need to. Unfortunately, to strengthen the instruction in the English language, some of the Gulf countries requested foreign companies to choose their curriculum and academic books. Moreover, the Middle Eastern upper class send their children to schools and universities that do not teach Arabic. In brief, we shouldn't engage in a zero-sum game entangled with either–or extremes. The key is to strategically combine two languages, while not undermining the Arab national identity or creating walls of isolation between elites living in the same society in the Arab region.

The situation becomes more complicated when we examine instruction not only as a policy put forth by leaders who design and plan linguistic policies, but also as an issue of compromise where we have to take into account the opinions of students. It would be beneficial if one traces back to previous research, such as that conducted in 2000 by Sally Findlow, which included 350 students in Emirati University in the United Arab Emirates (UAE). The research revealed that 50 percent of the target pool expressed that they prefer the English language as the language of instruction, whereas 22 percent preferred the Arabic language and 28 percent preferred both Arabic and English as languages of instruction. There are two reasons why some students preferred Arabic: 79 percent said the Arab identity was their motivator; the remainder declared being motivated to enable them to move into specific professions or academic disciplines.

According to the author of this study, the group has competing values represented in the service of society (those who prefer Arabic) and in individualism (those who prefer English) (Findlow 2005: 26). She also expands the argument by proposing that there could be a modern collective identity in the UAE that manages these apparently contradictory values. In case this is not an exaggerated claim, it contradicts the usual national educational precepts, for example, the modern Saudi Arabian collective identity. As another survey revealed, the majority of students and teachers support the instruction of all subjects in Arabic; according to them, this makes it easier for teachers to transfer the information to students and for the students to better understand the subject, and this will make the application to the science more relevant to the local society and reduce the "infiltration" of foreign cultures. We might remember, after El-Kenz and Waast (1997), that modernity in Algeria gave birth to two competing sets of values that were continuously fighting around education and research. Language was an important ingredient: the technocratic rationality was better expressed in French while the Arab identity was based on Arabic. Until today, this competing rationality has not been resolved peacefully.

To sum up our discussion, the use of foreign languages as the language of instruction or research is driven not only by a state policy but also by the compartmentalization of the national society (by social classes, among other things). Thus, it is not an either–or situation and the required solution is not a matter of either studying only in Arabic at the graduate level or only in English. The focus should be on how to rely on both languages in a transitional phase, while giving the Arabic language priority in all departments and programs and not just in social sciences. Here the translation will play a major role and will need some development.

7 Conclusion: does globalization equal hegemony?

We have been witnessing a rapid expansion of higher education in the Arab world, and a rapid expansion of scientific research in all fields, including social sciences. At the same time, however, Arab scholars seem to face difficulties in getting recognized when publishing in their own language or from their home institutions. The situation is complex because of the existence of famous universities that teach in foreign languages, but also because of practical and political issues in their own countries.

They also have to face the pressures of globalization, which legitimizes research published in English and funded internationally. This has contributed to the silent spread of evaluation based on WoS/Scopus and other indicators, because of pressure to publish in high-impact journals coming from academic institutions, in particular those teaching in English. The move has enforced a management bias, and a neoliberal ideological background that puts an emphasis on individual merit and market-like circulation of ideas (Gingras 2008; Abakumov *et al.* 2010).

In short, the promotion system effectively internalizes the hegemony of "central" social sciences, thereby deepening the divide among Arab social scientists. The dominating countries in this international division of scientific work thus produce *peripheral science* (Losego and Arvanitis 2008) and *peripheral visions* (Connell 2009), reinforcing "academic dependency" (Alatas 2003). This rating system inhibits the emergence of autonomous sociological production, marginalizing it and not supporting work that is "more consequential" (Appadurai 2000: 3). Wiebke Keim (2010) concludes that social scientists in peripheral countries should have the courage to refuse the worldwide rankings completely.[3] Her call was followed by some scholars advocating for this radical solution. However, interesting new research (Keim *et al.* 2014; Rodriguez Medina 2013; Beigel 2011) refuses to fall to the temptation of a simple one-way domination that the center–periphery approach may suggest. Instead, a more complex view was adopted to put an emphasis on the importance of local relevance and debate in social science despite its internationalization.

What remains defines precisely what Losego and Arvanitis (2008) have called hegemony in science: the capacity to influence the choice of topics in the worldwide agenda. The agencies and organizations that evaluate projects are asking for international networking and, under the pretext of multidisciplinarity, transdisciplinarity and benefits of international comparison, they have been asking for larger and more extended project teams. English is always said to be the language of the response to calls for proposals, under the pretext that evaluators are "international peers" and that English is the only common language. No effort is ever made to accommodate foreign language or persons that would be of great value but have little or poor understanding of English. Given our experience as editors of academic journals, both authors of this book believe we have to be very cautious as to the degree of real understanding of English by foreign-speaking academics. Although language is maybe not exclusively an instrument of domination, its unconditional use really is.

The idea of language-based marginalization has already been brought up in different settings; the most important finding we highlight here is that universities that use both local and foreign languages for instruction train better in the use of references in different languages, in a balanced way.

Notes

1 We could also point to the project undergone by the Saudi Ministry of Education in collaboration with the King Fahd University and Obaikan Library, whereby they are translating the most important scientific sources (100 books for phase 1).
2 See the comment of George Dorlian and Fadia Kiwan representing the first position. See, for instance, their comments to Abdel Elah Balqaziz's paper, which represents the other position (Balqaziz 2011).
3 See the section on ranking universities in Chapter 2 of this book.

8 The politics of citation

Who frames the debate on the Arab uprisings?

1 Introduction[1]

The definition of knowledge is often equated to fact or truth. The implication of this definition is that knowledge possesses a static nature, in that anything you "know" is also true, wherein the determining characteristics of truth are universality and eternality. The nature of knowledge, however, is essentially dynamic. What we knew 200 years ago differs greatly from what we know today, both qualitatively and quantitatively.

Knowledge has been historically transmitted through schools, which have gone through, and continue to go through, secular transitions, which take the form of (broadly defined) Western academic institutions. These transitions, which invariably differ across histories and geographies, play a determinant role in the qualities and capacities of these schools as producers of knowledge.

In addition, the impact of geography and language, as well as the impact of the political economy on the institutionalization and internationalization of knowledge production and research practice, is beginning to emerge.

This chapter is focused on the way the scientific literature has perceived the Arab uprisings and the ways in which they are portrayed in scientific discourse, taking into account the social forces that come into play in the production of knowledge. In line with Latour and Fabbri (1977), this study analyzes both the content of academic journal articles on the Arab revolutions, as well as who produces and who frames the debate about such scholarship through an analysis of the network of authors who are considered influential. In addition to analyzing citations, we also analyze the content and style of the articles by applying semiotic analysis, and using quantitative measures of "sociological markers," such as discipline, language and institutional affiliation. We do not assume that academic journal articles solely shape public debate or policy debates on the Arab uprisings, but they definitely are very important.

1.1 Methodology

In order to yield the best results, a keyword search was conducted in Arabic, English and French for Arab Revolution; Arab Spring; Arab Uprising; Arab

Awakening; and Arab Upheaval. This yielded 519 results (published between December 2010 and December 2012). English articles were primarily derived from Web of Science (WoS) and Scopus.[2] Arabic articles were scarcer, primarily due to the limited availability of Arabic databases – E-Marefa, the only Arabic database available yielded only 15 results,[3] while the rest of the articles were only available in hard copies.[4] The French articles were derived from the Cairn. info platform.[5] Table 8.1 indicates the relative disparity in the quantity of production between English- and Arabic-language articles: 14 percent of the sample is composed of Arabic articles derived from the available nine peer-reviewed Arabic journals, while the majority (71 percent) is composed of English articles derived from 165 peer-reviewed journals. This stark difference in the number of peer-reviewed journals within the sample size reflects the relative disparity in the overall production of knowledge in the Arab world. In addition, even though the topic is "local," the number of articles written in French is still greater than the number of articles on the revolutions written in Arabic. There are two major limitations of this study: first, the nine Arabic journals covered by our research are the main regular journals that have regional coverage rather than a local one. Local journals are very locally cited and not accessible except locally. We do believe, thus, that the sources analyzed here are quite a reliable output, despite these limitations. Second, we did not deal with other texts that are written by scholars, such as blogs, newspapers or books.

2 Sociological markers of the articles

This section introduces some of the main findings by quantifying the sociological markers of each article.

2.1 Geography of production of articles

The majority (75 percent) of articles on the Arab uprisings is produced outside the Arab world; only 25 percent are produced within the region. If we remove the 20 articles included from *Contemporary Arab Affairs*, a journal published by the Center for Arab Unity Studies (CAUS), this rate shrinks to 7.5 percent. As indicated in Figure 8.1, four countries account for 62 percent of the articles written from within the Arab world, namely Egypt, Lebanon, Tunisia and Morocco – these are the Arab countries that usually produce most of the social

Table 8.1 Number and percentage of production by language

	No.	Percentage
Arabic	72	13.9
English	367	70.7
French	80	15.4
Total	519	100.0

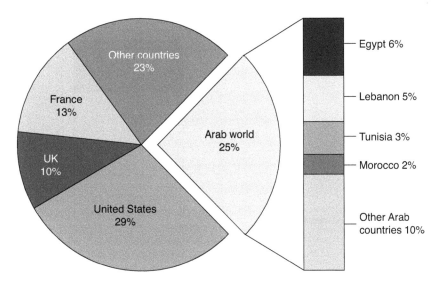

Figure 8.1 Percentage of publications per country.

science research. Notably, authors writing from the United States contribute nearly 30 percent of the entire sample collected in the three different languages.

Concerning the language of production, Figure 8.2 indicates most articles are written in English and that articles written in Arabic from within the Arab world only slightly outnumber those written in English.

The findings in this section indicate two main issues: first, the majority of articles on the Arab revolutions are being produced outside the region; second, what little knowledge is being produced within the region is being produced in Arabic, constraining it to the local community and isolating it from potential global debates.

While there is a move toward encouraging translations, only 2 percent of the articles in the sample are translated from their original language. The journal *Contemporary Arab Affairs* accounts for most of these articles, the majority of which are originally written in Arabic and translated to English. As illustrated in Figure 8.3, authors from Egypt, Tunisia, Morocco and Lebanon are the most frequent producers in the Arab world. In terms of language, those in Tunisia write mainly in Arabic, while Egypt has a frequency of two-fifth in English and three-fifths in Arabic. Lebanon produces more than double the number of Arabic articles than those published in English, while the majority of publications in French come from Morocco.

As Figure 8.4 shows, the majority of articles on the uprisings are being produced within universities (70 percent), while research centers[6] contribute around 20 percent. Figure 8.5 indicates the distribution of institutional affiliations by language of publication. University publications slightly outnumber publications by research centers in Arabic, both of which are relatively low compared to English publications affiliated with universities.

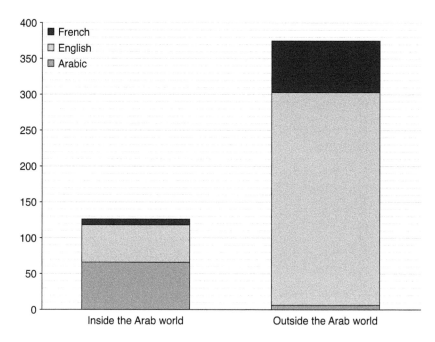

Figure 8.2 Language of publication by region.

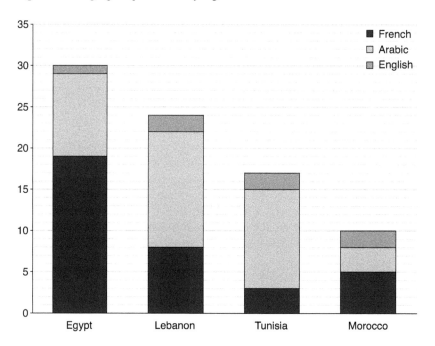

Figure 8.3 Language of publication among Arab countries.

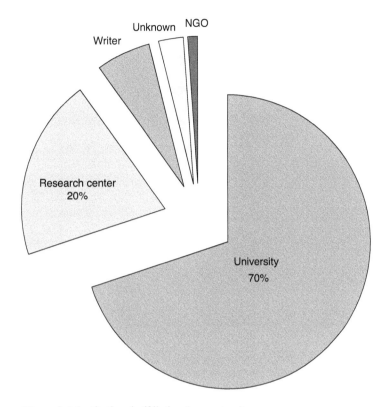

Figure 8.4 Institutional affiliation (percentage).

Most strikingly, university professors produce 84 percent of English articles against only 54 percent of Arabic articles. We have shown that writing in English within Arab universities is mostly related to the university promotion system, in addition to the fact that there are limited Arabic outlets where one could publish. Among the 80 authors publishing in French, 59 are affiliated to French institutions, 30 to a university (that is 50 percent of French institutions) and 18 with a public research organization (30 percent of French institutions).

2.2 Authorship

At this point, the findings indicate that most of the knowledge on the Arab revolutions is being produced outside the Arab world (predominantly in the United States) by university affiliates who are most likely to publish in English. Figure 8.6 indicates that 56 percent of articles are being produced by non-Arabs, 24 percent by Arabs and 20 percent by the Arab diaspora, 57 percent of whom are writing from the United States.

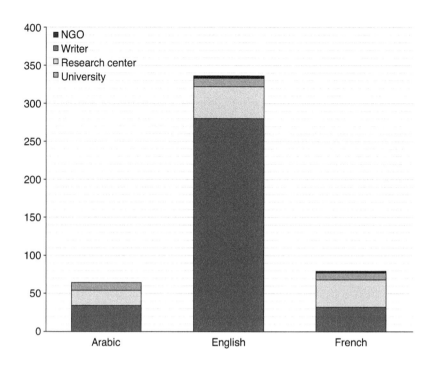

Figure 8.5 Institutional affiliation by language of publication.

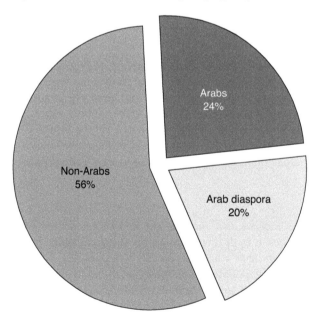

Figure 8.6 Percentage of publications by ethnicity.

2.3 Content as illustrated by disciplines and keywords

Figure 8.7 illustrates the authors' distribution by discipline. Almost half (47 percent) of the authors are from political science and international relations (IR). This predominance is unchallenged by any other discipline: sociology accounts only for 8 percent, while anthropology is 2 percent; Middle Eastern studies (MES) account for only 6 percent. This does not reflect at all the disciplinary distribution of the social sciences among Arab authors (Arvanitis *et al.* 2010), where political science is far from being a dominant discipline.

The predominance of political sciences is the same in all languages, as illustrated by Figure 8.8 which shows the distribution of disciplines by language of publication. In Arabic, a small disparity in the range of disciplines engaged in the topic can be observed as compared to English publications. English publications contain the largest range of disciplines and include MES, sociology, economics, media and law. In French, political sciences, economics, law, anthropology and geography are prevalent. These figures should be read with caution as the numbers are very small. It is interesting to note that very few mainstream economic articles were identified: most economists on the topic are rather unorthodox economists or write on institutional economics.

We distinguish between three types of articles: (1) articles based on fieldwork and articles without fieldwork that could be either (2) in the form of an essay (no

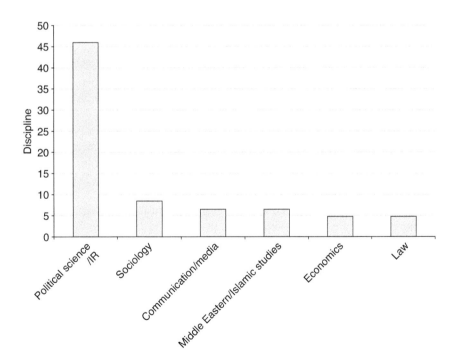

Figure 8.7 Percentage of publications by discipline.

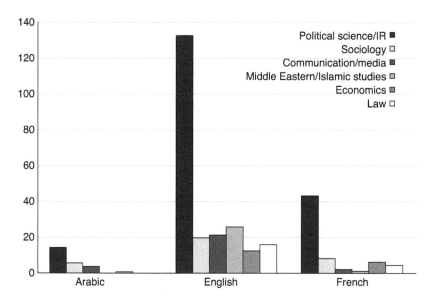

Figure 8.8 Distribution of disciplines by language of publication.

citation at all) or (3) in the form of a critique of existing literature. As indicated in Figure 8.9, the most common type of articles are critical of existing literature, while only 14 percent of research is based on fieldwork, predominantly in English (19 percent vs. 3 percent in Arabic and 1 percent in French), conducted by those who are affiliated outside of the Arab region. Fifty percent of the articles written in Arabic are essays, while essays constitute only 20 percent of the entire sample.

When researchers use fieldwork for their papers, they tend to prefer qualitative research methods (45 percent vs. 29 percent), as expected since the nature of the research topic (the Arab uprisings) makes it difficult to conduct quantitative field research based on surveys. The remaining percentage (26 percent) is articles that used both methods.

Most articles discuss the Arab world in general; of the remainder that does not, the majority are single-country cases that focus on Egypt and Tunisia. We use keywords to indicate the focus of the articles, such as social/political/economic factors, or general themes such as youth or class. The Arab revolutions, according to our sample, are observed mainly through the lens of political factors (45 percent of articles), followed closely by social factors (around 40 percent). Islamism, Islamic culture and/or secularism are mentioned in nearly 37 percent of the articles. Foreign intervention and geopolitics follows by a frequency of 35 percent, while economic factors account for only about 17 percent of the keywords – the same percentage for media and communication. Social factors and social class are around three times more likely to appear in Arabic than those

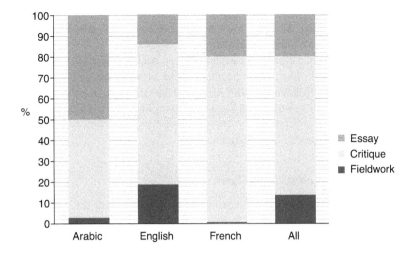

Figure 8.9 Type of article by language of publication.

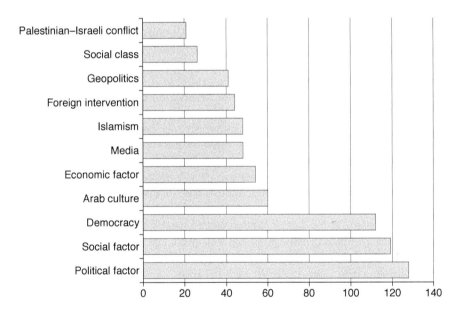

Figure 8.10 Frequency of keywords.

written in English (23:7). Ethnicity is a theme predominantly explored in English and French articles (12 articles) and only once in Arabic. Islamism is also more predominant in articles written in English and French (39 articles) than in Arabic (6 articles).

Overall, English articles contain larger lists of references than French or Arabic: the average number of citations per article is 21 for English language, 12 for French and 8 for Arabic. This will affect the network analysis and tend to bias a proper view of the material with fewer citations.

In addition, only 10 percent of citations are Arabic (most of which are cited in Arabic articles), while 75 percent of cited articles are written in English. Authors who are affiliated with the Arab world tend to cite more Arabic articles. Arabs writing from Lebanon and Egypt are more likely to use English articles in addition to Arabic articles, while Arabs writing from Morocco and Tunisia tend, obviously, to cite more French articles.

3 Network and citation analysis

Table 8.2 is a list of the 25 most cited authors on the topic of the Arab uprisings. Ten of these authors are American political scientists who are affiliated to think-tanks. Only four sociologists are on the list, followed closely by three journalists, suggesting a remarkable shift in the legitimation of knowledge producers. Twenty-one authors are from the United States, two authors are French, along-side two Arab diasporic authors. Only four theorists are among the most cited authors. They are Samuel Huntington (political science; democratization), Edward Said (literature; orientalism), Manuel Castells (sociology; social networks) and Charles Tilly (sociology; social movements). These authors are seen as pioneers in their respective fields, whom most authors often cite to pay homage to, and not necessarily critique.

In order to study the collective process involved in knowledge production, a closer look at the references used, as well as their modalities, will be explored in the next section. Concurrently, a co-citation network analysis was conducted to elucidate the dynamics between these references across different languages of publication. The resulting network is presented in Figure 8.11. Each node corresponds to cited authors, links correspond to closely linked authors and each circle corresponds to a cluster of names of authors that are cited simultaneously in the whole set of articles.

Before looking at the data, it is necessary to specify the metrics we used. We mapped the co-citation network of the 120 most cited authors in our dataset (Figure 8.11). Co-citation networks are ubiquitous in bibliometric studies (White and McCain 1998; Chen 1999). In such networks, nodes are linked when they are jointly cited in publication reference list. In our case, we focus on cited authors to produce a co-citation map, a method which was first introduced by White and Griffith (1982). We only consider the authors who have been cited more than five times in total in our corpus, resulting in a network of 120 nodes. We enumerate every occurrence of pairs of cited authors to build a co-occurrence matrix from which we obtain a proximity network using a statistical semantic measure primarily introduced by Weeds (2003: 82).[7] The Louvain community detection algorithm (Blondel *et al.* 2008) is then applied to the resulting proximity network to retrieve clusters of cohesive subgroups of authors that are then

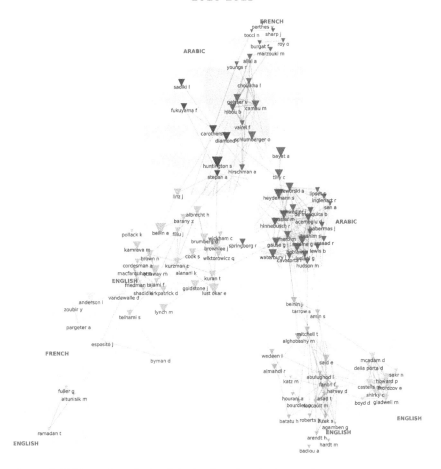

Figure 8.11 Network analysis of cited authors (co-citation map).

colored accordingly on the final map. Additionally each cluster is also assigned a tag ("English," "Arabic," "French") that represents the most frequently used languages in publications citing these authors in the cluster (chi^2 specificity score). All the computation was performed under the CorText platform.[8]

In this co-citation map of 120 most cited authors, node sizes scale with total number of citations received (from 5 to 32). Authors are grouped according to the cluster they belong to. Each cluster is also associated to a tag (capital letters) indicating the most specific language used in publications citing corresponding authors. In the map, we can see eight clusters of authors.

Table 8.2 Most cited authors

Name of cited author	No. citations	Place of the institution	Type of scholarship	Institutional affiliation
Samuel Huntington	33	USA – NY	T	Political science, Harvard/Columbia
Asef Bayat	22	USA – CH		Sociology/MES, University of Illinois
Edward Said	22	USA – NY	D & T	Literature, critical theory, Columbia University
Eva Bellin	20	USA – MA		Political science, democracy, Brandies University, Harvard, AUC (2007)
Lisa Anderson	20	USA/Egypt		International relations. University of Colombia; President AUC; APSA
Marc Lynch	18	USA – DC		Political science and international affairs, George Washington University
Marina Ottaway	17	USA		Carnegie Endowment for International Peace (Carnegie), foreign affairs, Wilson Center, political reform, taught at AUC
Steven Heydemann	17	USA – DC		Political science/public policy, Georgetown University/special adviser on Middle East Initiatives at the US Institute of Peace
Charles Tilly	16	USA	T	Sociologist, Columbia University, contentious politics
Jason Brownlee	16	USA		Government and MES, University of Texas at Austin, Wilson Center
Philip N. Howard	16	USA		Sociology, communication, impact of ITCs on democracy and social inequality, University of Washington
Vincent Geisser	16	France		Researcher at French CNRS (currently based in Beirut)
Michel Camau	15	France		Political scientist in France (IREMAM) and French Institute in Tunisia (IRMC)
Jack Goldstone	15	USA		Political science and sociology, international relations and public policy at George Mason University, US government consultant (USAID Democracy Program), Brookings Institute senior fellow

Name		Country		Description
David D. Kirkpatrick	14	USA	J	Technology journalist (the Facebook Effect), Forbes Techonomy Media
Larry Diamond	14	USA		Political science and sociology at Stanford University, democracy studies, senior fellow at Hoover Institute
Manuel Castells	14	Spain	T	Sociology, University of Southern California/Open University of Catalonia
Daniel Brumberg	13	USA		Department of Government, Georgetown University, special adviser for US Institute of Peace's Muslim World Initiative
Béatrice Hibou	12	France		Researcher in Center d'Etudes pour les Relations Internationales (CERI) (Paris)
Mehran Kamrava	12	Qatar and USA		Political sciences, Georgetown University, Qatar
Mona Elghobashy	12	USA	D	Political science professor at Bernard College, Carnegie scholar
Ghassan Salamé	11	Paris	D	Lebanese political scientist at Science Po in Paris
Joel Beinin	11	USA		History/ME history, Stanford University, Director of MES at AUC (2008)
Malcolm Gladwell	11	USA	J	The New Yorker
Thomas Carothers	11	USA		Vice president of Carnegie; expert on democratization and US foreign policy
Bernard Lewis	10	USA		Historian, Orientalist, Princeton University, foreign policy advisor for Bush Administration
Clay Shirky	10	US	J	Socio-economic effects of internet technologies

Notes
T = theoretical; J = journalism; D = diaspora.

3.1 Cluster I: new media and the Arab uprisings

Cluster I (the circle on the bottom right corner of the diagram) constitutes a niche of tightly connected technology journalists/scholars who specialize in social media, information technology and globalization. These authors include Clay Shirky, Evgeny Morozov and Malcolm Gladwell. Manuel Castells contributes to this niche with his theoretical contributions to network societies and the effect of social media on contentious politics.

Predominant arguments made by such authors include the role of the new media in the political strategies of state repression, on the one hand, and social media as a new public sphere that transcends the national level, on the other. Gladwell's "The Tipping Point" (2000) is also cited as an argument for how ideas spread like viruses when referring to the Arab uprisings (Alqudsi-ghabra 2012). Cited authors in this niche are particularly closely linked, as evident in Christian Fuchs' article "Some Reflections on Manuel Castells' Book *Networks of Outrage and Hope. Social Movements in the Internet Age*," which argues that Castells' book is situated in an intellectual discourse that focuses on the political implications of social media and that has involved Clay Shirky, Malcolm Gladwell and Evgeny Morozov.

In addition, it is also evident that this niche is very loosely connected to Arabic-language publications, indicating that much of the discussion about the impact of information technology on the Arab uprisings is only happening in English.

3.2 Cluster II: "radical theorists"

Closely connected to this cluster we find cluster II of venerable names of well-known theorists, mainly philosophers and historians. It contains one block of authors that are French or connected to themes that are frequent among "French theory" authors or French-inclined authors, as well as philosophers that have been translated into Arabic and/or are also frequently mentioned worldwide (Agamben, Arendt, Badiou, Fanon, Bourdieu, Samir Amin, Zizek). It is interesting to note that the authors are discussed in English and to a lesser extent French reviewed articles, but rarely in Arabic.

We also find Edward Said, one of the most cited authors. In a similar manner to which Gladwell's "ideas as viruses" is used, Said's notion of "travelling ideas" (Said 1983) is used to describe the spread of revolutionary fervor in Egypt (Abdelrahman 2011). However, it is Said's much contested "Orientalism" (1978) that is most cited in this context. In most cases, orientalism was cast in contrast to the much unanticipated events of the Arab uprisings by the West, which has long since attributed negative values to the otherness of the Orient (Erdem 2012; Shelley 2011). The orientalist notion of the inability of Arabs to govern themselves under democratic regimes is heavily contested, using the revolutions as evidence for political agency and self-determination. Generally, references to Said and others in this niche are set in the context of post-colonial resistance.

3.3 Cluster III: mainly theorists often cited in Arabic

Above, we find in cluster III a group of political scientists, many of which are cited in Arabic articles. We find in this group Habermas and Bernard Lewis, which have become ritual references in political sciences when talking of the Arab world or Arab "public space." Lewis is cited as a reference to the "alieness" of the notion of the secular in Islamic countries (Erdem 2012) and he argues that Islamic societies and cultures are antithetical to democracy (Da'na 2011). Lewis was under heavy attack in many Arabic articles (e.g., by Jacques Kabbanji [2011] and Sari Hanafi) for his essentialist view of the Arab world. Economists are also present in this cluster (Amartya Sen, Daron Acemoglu, etc.). They were cited by Arab authors to put emphasis on the importance of social justice as a key theme in Arab writing much more than English or French articles.

In English articles, and in a similar vein, Heydemann's arguments fall into cluster VI, which includes mainstream IR arguments, mainly as a reference to factors that account for authoritarian resilience in the region (see Bellin 2012), as well as a reference to the ways in which authoritarian regimes try to channel change within the regime in order to be able to prevail at all costs.

Ghassan Salameh is a diasporic author who is the third of the diasporic authors (after Said and Elghobashy) who is well cited and part of this cluster. He is cited in scholarship in all three languages, but mainly in Arabic and English, for his two books: one of them is edited by him and published in three languages: *Democracy Without Democrats? The Renewal of Politics in the Muslim World*, published in the mid-1990s. Kassem (2012), as others Arab writers, reminds us that one of the major historical challenges to democracy in the Arab world consists of a lack of elite commitment in this region to democracy, and the impossibility of using strategic-actor models that grew out of the experiences of Latin America.

3.4 Cluster IV: French-speaking authors

Charles Tilly and Asef Bayat serve as "bridges" to the upper cluster IV constituted by French-speaking authors (Hibou, Geisser, Camau, Burgat as well as the president of Tunisia, Al Marzouki). With the exception of Jean Pierre Fillu, all French-speaking authors specializing on the Arab world are located in this cluster. Among the 25 most cited authors, two are French.

First, Béatrice Hibou is cited 12 times, half of which are in English articles and half in French. In English she is cited as a reference to explain the Tunisian economy (Hibou *et al.* 2011) and the predatory nature of its ruling elite (Hibou 2011), as well as the ways in which the state responded to economic challenges in the past (particularly concerning foreign aid), and the impact this strategy had on society. For instance, Schwarz and Corral (2011) argue that

> In times of fiscal crisis it challenged the foundations of many states: international pressures to enact economic reform and privatization measures, and

cut-off patronage networks left the state apparatus weakened and some privileged private entrepreneurs strengthened, and in some cases exceeded a
particular state's capacity to enact reforms, thus undermining its capacity
even further and encouraging neopatrimonialism to become even more
rampant.

Hibou is also cited in English and French because she set the stage for denouncing the corruption of the Ben Ali regime.

Second, Vincent Geisser is a researcher at the French CNRS, currently based
in Beirut, who has spent many years in Tunisia. Exclusively French authors cite
his scholarship. Geisser is often cited because of his critique of French foreign
policy supporting Arab dictatorships and its stance vis-à-vis the Arab Islamists.

3.5 Cluster V: rather a negative stance toward the Arab world, cited in Arabic

Close to the "French" clusters lies an "American" cluster (cluster V) constituted
by famous authors quite frequently mentioned by Arabic-language articles,
mainstream political US scientists and thinkers. Most of these names take a
similar (negative) stance toward the Arab world: Samuel Huntington, Francis
Fukuyama and Larry Diamond, who are referred to as prominent political scientists who propagated skepticism toward the viability of democracy in the Arab
world.

In Faleh Abdel Jabbar's (2012) Arabic article, Diamond is cited for his
concept of gradual transformation. In English articles, Diamond is cited for his
definition of liberal democracy and his justifications for Arab exceptionalism
with regards to democracy (2010a). Lynch (2011) cites Diamond (2010b) in reference to claims that authoritarian regimes have become more capable of controlling and punishing dissent through the internet. Huntington is cited most
frequently in English for his "the third wave" and "the clash of civilizations,"
either as refutation or approval of his controversial assertions that (political)
modernization (which is perceived by many authors as one of the demands of
the uprisings) without institutional infrastructure leads to political instability.
Huntington is also frequently mentioned (including much in Arabic) in order to
refute his theory of the clash of civilizations, arguing that the Arab Spring is
evidence of global political development and modernization, and that the "third
democratic wave's" failure to reach the Arab world is shaped by an invalid
Western Orientalist view of the region. He is the most central author in the small
cluster of highly cited American authors, and it is striking to see the clear-cut
division of the whole network around this cluster. Huntington is rarely cited
commonly with Albert O. Hirschman. On the contrary, Huntington is the name
that plays the role of pivot between the left and right side of the network.

It is interesting to note the absence of linkages between these two last clusters: the only author in common is Alfred Hirschman, an American liberal economist very frequently read in France and the developing countries.

3.6 Cluster VI: mainstream IR cited in English

One of the most significant findings of this study is that almost half (40 percent) of the most influential authors are American political scientists, predominantly graduates of Ivy League universities, who in addition to holding academic positions in leading universities in the United States, such as Georgetown or George Washington University, usually in the fields of MES, foreign policy or governance, are also research fellows at US-led think-tanks such as the Wilson Center, Carnegie and the Brookings Institute. Many of these authors also serve as foreign policy advisors to the US government. We refer to these authors as the "central authors" (not all of them theorists) due to their evident intellectual hegemony on the topic of the Arab uprisings. They are located mainly in this cluster and in the following one. Of the most cited are Lynch, Goldstone, Bellin, Brumberg, Brownlee, Kirkpatrick and Ottaway. These authors are closely linked and are often cited in the same articles in English. Among them, only one is cited in Arabic in the context of highlighting the weakness of the Arab uprisings.

The predominant theme in this niche is the analysis of the newly emerging political dynamics between the Arab public and authoritarian regimes; however, more focus is placed on the analysis of authoritarian responses and resilience than the dynamics of the movement. For example, Lynch (2011) and Bellin (2012) cite Brownlee (2007) as a reference to the extensive literature written on Arab authoritarianism during the past decade. Weyland (2012) cites Brownlee *et al.* (2012), who argues "in only one Arab country, Tunisia, did the domestic balance of power favor challengers during the transition" (p. 928). Brumberg is predominantly cited for his justifications of the failure of democracy in the region, in his notion of "liberal autocracy" (Brumberg 1990) and his assumptions that these autocracies are unsustainable. For instance, Carothers (cited in Pace and Cavatorta 2012) argues that

> [t]he questioning of the validity of the paradigm of authoritarian resilience has meant that the theoretical assumptions of the democratization paradigm seem to have found a new lease on life after the criticism of the late 1990s and early 2000s.

What is most notable here is the extent to which these authors are presented as leading authorities on the dynamics of the Arab uprisings, particularly in terms of the way in which the discussion of the uprisings is framed, namely in terms of challenges to democratization. One gets little sense of the internal dynamics of the revolutions and the ways in which they relate to the local populations.

3.7 Cluster VII: mainstream IR cited in French

This cluster has few references cited in English and in French. Only two authors are frequently cited: Lisa Anderson and John Esposito. They are among the rare

Americans cited by French scholarship. Michel Camau (2012), for instance, is cited to demystify the sweeping optimism of journalists and scholars regarding the homogenizing use of the "Arab Spring." In English articles, Anderson is also cited in contexts where the democratic potential of Arab countries is discussed (Blaydes and Lo 2012; Pace and Cavatorta 2012). Esposito is more interested in political Islam and cited for the fact that the youth is claiming democracy and thus some of them claim a form of political Islam that fits with this concept.

3.8 Cluster VIII: Turkey as a model

At the bottom left we find cluster VIII, with three names (Tarek Ramadan, Graham Fuller, Meliha Altunışık) that relate to English articles on the future of Arab regimes and whether the Turkish model led by the moderate Islamic party, the Justice and Development Party (AKP), can fit the current process of democratization, and it's supposed exemplarity concerning modernization and Islamic rule.

3.9 Bridges

Beyond these clusters, there are four well-cited authors that don't belong to any of these clusters and are often cited by all languages. They are interesting because they offer a sort of "alternative" view without being peripheral authors. They are, by order of the frequency of the citations, Bayat, Tilly, Elghobashy and Beinin (respectively 22, 16, 12, 11).

Asef Bayat is a professor of sociology at the University of Illinois. Two aspects qualify Bayat as a "theoretically" alternative author. First, his work is often based on deep, longstanding, empirical knowledge of some Middle Eastern societies (Egypt and Iran). His work on youth everyday politics, for instance, demonstrates his sensitivity to the interplay between their social conditions and the changes in the cultural scripts that influence their world vision and inspirations (see Bayat 2013a; 2013b; Herrera and Bayat 2010). Second, the level of complexity in his arguments reflects the entanglements of the Arab uprising and connects the political to the social and economic with historical depth. For instance, he argues that the contrasting reactions of authors of the revolution – lauding and lamenting – reflect the paradoxical reality of the Arab "revolutions." While they are appraised as "movements," which has been the predominant narrative in most knowledge produced on the Arab revolutions, their capacity to bring about "change" is narrated as less than commendable, although little, according to him, has been written about how to deal with these challenges (Bayat 2013a: 48). Bayat argues: "a world in need of revolutions does not mean that it has the capacity to generate them, if it lacks the means and vision necessary for a fundamental transformation" (Bayat 2013a: 49). Indeed, what happened was that "few Arab activists (and I would add, intellectuals or scholars) had really strategized for a revolution.... In general, the desire was for reform, or meaningful change within the existing political arrangements" (Bayat 2013a:

58). This is evident in how little knowledge has been produced outside of the "normative" ideology of reform. In other words, although many authors are positive about the revolutions, none of them approach the issue with any truly "revolutionary" approach.

In light of this, Bayat refers to the Arab revolutions as "refolutions," which he describes as "revolutions that aim to push for reforms in, and through, the institutions of the existing regimes" (Bayat 2013a: 53). He argues that this is occurring in light of an intellectual climate dominated by the global advance of neoliberal ideology informed by the spirit of individual self-interest and accumulation. Bayat saw, up until the 1990s, the predominance of three major ideological traditions that offered strategies for fundamental change in the Arab world: anti-colonial nationalism, Marxism and Islamism (Bayat 2013a: 54). His study was confirmed by other studies in the Arab world.[9] What is obvious here is a significant finding: that social change in local contexts is invariably influenced by global ideological shifts. Former anti-colonial revolutionaries

> turned into administrators of the post-colonial order, they largely failed to deliver on their promises; in many instances nationalist governments devolved into autocracies, were saddled with debt, then pushed into neoliberal structural adjustment programs, if they had not already been overthrown by military coups or undermined by imperialist intrigues.
>
> (Bayat 2013a: 55)

Post-1990s saw the advent of what he calls the "post-Islamist" trends (e.g., Tunisia's Ennahda Party), which "aim to transcend Islamist politics by promoting a pious society and a secular state, combining religiosity with rights, to varying degrees" (Bayat 2013a: 57). Bayat, like François Burgat (2010), witnessed the demise of the Arab Left and the predominance of two political ideologies, neoliberal on the one hand (being the most influential international ideology) and post-Islamist on the other, both of which share the narrative of reform. In brief, the connection between politics and the social was rarely well articulated by influential figures of social science. Hanafi (2012) demonstrated that many think-tanks (Freedom House, Economist Intelligence Unit, Arab Reform Initiative, etc.) investigate formal indices that prove helpful in tracking the micro-transformations of the Arab world, and in determining which state has undergone governance change and moved toward the rule of law; however, they fail, as Hanafi argues, to examine the potential for real political restructuring.

Among the 22 times that Bayat is cited, two are by Arabic authors. Both Saad-aldine Ibrahim (2012) and Hanafi (2011) cited his concept of "social non-movements" as a way of understanding the latent preparation for Arab uprisings. Along with Mohamed Bamyeh (2012), Bayat was one of the rare scholars that noticed longstanding Arab civic traditions of self-organization that are ignored by social movement organizations and scholars.

Charles Tilly is an influential sociologist on the subjects of contentious politics and social movements, and also, after Huntington and Edward Said, the most cited theorist on the topic of the Arab uprisings. Most of the citations are in English and only one is in Arabic. Tilly is often cited in English articles to support the claim that "revolutions are not distinct occurrences, in a category apart, but almost always develop out of other forms of political conflict" (Harsch 2012: 49). Overall, Tilly is cited to support and explain the theoretical foundations behind political contention and social mobilization.

Mona El-Ghobashy is one of the three Arab diasporic authors (besides Said and Salamé) in the top 25 most cited authors list. El-Ghobashy, a political science professor at Columbia University, did extensive fieldwork on the Egyptian revolution, and is also a Carnegie scholar. Her research focuses on political mobilization in contemporary Egypt, and she has published articles in American academic journals. In this sample, she is cited in English only, 16 times across 14 articles by authors writing from outside the Arab world. El-Ghobashy (2011) is most cited for her great detailed description of the Egyptian protests. Pace and Cavatorta (2012) cite an earlier publication to support their claim that Islamism is a broad field, and movements such as the Egyptian Muslim Brotherhood have gone through considerable ideological and structural transformations. Overall, El-Ghobashy is cited as a reference to the socio-political conditions that both accompanied and preceded the Egyptian protests.

Finally, *Joel Beinin* is professor of Middle Eastern history at Stanford University. He was also director of MES at American University in Cairo (AUC) (left 2008). Beinin is significant as he is the most leftist scholar among the top 25 most cited authors. Beinin is cited 16 times across 12 English articles and two articles written in French. He is also the author of some articles where he discusses social class, union organization in Egypt and the strengths and weaknesses of the workers' movement as the largest and best-mobilized leftist revolutionary coalition. Beinin is most cited as a reference to details regarding labor strikes and workers' movements in Egypt both before and after the 2011 uprising.

4 Qualitative analysis of Arab scholarship

In this section we highlight some features of the scholarship written in Arabic, and identify sources of its weakness in framing the debate and in reaching international audiences. As indicated above, only 25 percent of the articles on the Arab uprisings are produced from within the region, out of which around 50 percent are produced in Arabic, 45 percent in English and 5 percent in French, with the majority of those contributing being Arabs. Although no Arab authors are present in the list of the top 25 most cited authors, Samir Amin is cited ten times, most commonly for his contributions to post-colonial analysis of the impact of capitalist imperialism in Egypt and North Africa, by both Arab and non-Arab authors alike. Most Arabs writing from within the Arab world in English tend to cite both Arabic and English references. In addition, around 40 percent of the articles are based on fieldwork, which results in an abundance of detailed descriptions in many of these articles.

However, there is very little evidence of any of these authors engaging each other in debate. In exceptional cases when authors do engage, they are not explicit in their critique. For instance, after some authors replied to Altahir Labib's editorial in *Idafat* (issue 18) in an implicit manner, *Idafat* editor, Sari Hanafi, asked them to criticize him or any other authors more overtly, to generate a debate. They were reluctant to do so.

Eighty percent of Arabs who produce articles in English are affiliated to universities, both public (Qatar, Egypt, Jordan, Oman, among others) and private (predominantly from AUC and AUB). The rest are either writers or affiliated to local or regional research institutions (such as CAUS). Since many of these authors base their studies on fieldwork, they tend to lay out a structured plan organized around an introduction, methodology, findings section and a discussion and conclusion (also called the "IMRAD" structure),[10] and tend to adhere to this American academic standard of publication. Qualitative analysis conducted on the sample of Arabic publications seems to suggest that the opposite is true: most Arab authors who publish in Arabic tend not to lay out a structured plan for the article in the introduction; a common feature has been to use numbered sub-headings to indicate a thread through the article. This has implications in making it difficult for Arab authors to write for international outlets and this can reinforce their marginalization.

When theory is used, it is generally a foreign theoretical framework. This is true for both Arabic- and English-language publications. One hypothesis is that this is due to the scarcity of Arabic "theoretical frameworks." Arab authors publishing in Arabic also seem to rely more heavily on media (News, Facebook pages, etc.) in their citations, as opposed to Arabs who write in English who tend to cite academic journal articles and books. In general, Arabic references are less likely to be academic references, and in many cases include blogs, newspaper articles, interviews and other first-hand accounts. In addition, much of the fieldwork is conducted in Arabic for reasons of accessibility, which is why it is striking to find that few authors who publish in Arabic rely on fieldwork. The two cases that do include fieldwork rely on secondary statistical data to explain the situation rather than getting first-hand observations produced by local, grassroots actors.

The paradigmatic position of many Arab authors is that they use the revolutions as an indication of a legitimate struggle for social justice against oppressive autocracies. They also tend to a retrospective view of the historical socio-political conditions that led to the uprisings, usually framing the events as a necessary outcome of long-term systemic oppression. As we show in cluster III, many Arab authors place more emphasis on the importance of social justice than English or French authors.

5 Conclusion

The network analysis we conducted demonstrates clearly that there is an evident hierarchy between three levels of knowledge production, indicating the different levels of influence of those who will frame the debate about the Arab uprisings. At the first level, knowledge producers who have the highest level of legitimacy (and the highest citation factor) are often from US foreign policy Ivy Leaguers,[11] who create the theoretical, informational and/or analytical center. These authors are cited by all levels of knowledge producers and publish often in high-impact factor journals. Their legitimacy comes from their status as "experts" on authoritarianism in the Middle East, democratization and political reform. "Expert" in this context has little to do with local knowledge, since few of these producers reference local authors when studying the region. Instead, some of their expertise is confined to understanding the costs and benefits of US foreign policies in the ME, while some is critical to the longstanding US administration's support for Arab authoritarian regimes. Titles like "Common Interests, Closer Allies, How Democracy in Arab States Can Benefit the West," and "Authoritarian Learning and Authoritarian Resilience: Regime Responses to the 'Arab Awakening'" are pertinent examples of the ways in which these producers perceive the problems they are studying. In addition, their status as both academics and researchers at prominent US think-tanks is particularly problematic when it comes to scientific ethos, where their research imperatives are necessarily inclined toward US private interests. The Brookings Institute, Carnegie Endowment for International Peace, the Wilson Center and other US think-tanks are funders of political/social scientific research in the Middle East, a factor that has undoubtedly affected the production of knowledge. Their legitimacy is further solidified through their public appearances on international news networks like CNN, and regular publications in journals such as *Foreign Affairs* and *Foreign Policy*. Unfortunately this chapter cannot further examine the differing influence of publication outlets.[12]

At the second level we find scholars who do not have a pronounced level of intellectual authority. Here, we are not talking about the local scholars who are sometimes used as "informants" to first-level knowledge producers. Mona Abaza (2011) complains strongly that local academics have often been reduced to "service providers for Western 'experts' who jet in and jet out." Rather, we are referring to scholars who are less cited in spite of the significance of their work. The best example is El-Ghobashy, who has followed the Egyptian revolutions very closely on the ground. However, what we noticed is that her writings were subsequently used as a reference to factual events that occurred during the time and not as a theoretical reference. Other authors in this category might include Arab authors writing from within the Arab world in English or French. We also find many French-speaking authors that belong to this level, clearly identified in the network analysis and disconnected from the American networks. As we showed in the clusters, those who bridge between different clusters often provide alternative voices to the mainstream analysis.

Third-level producers are peripheral knowledge producers and include Arabs writing from within the region, in Arabic. As the names within the cluster showed, these voices are seldom heard on the international level, and are only referenced by second-level knowledge producers. These voices privilege social justice over geopolitics (very debated by American and French scholarships). What is particularly problematic is the one-way relationship between first- and third-level producers, which creates the hierarchal structure of legitimacy; while third-level producers cite first-level producers (thus legitimizing them), first-level producers do not cite third-level producers, thereby delegitimizing their positions as knowledge producers at the international level. The collective nature of knowledge production is broken, and a hierarchical structure based on the legitimacy of hegemonic Western-institutionalized standards of political and ideological normativity is set in place.

This hierarchy of legitimacy in knowledge is due in part to where the articles are produced. The majority of articles are indeed produced outside the Arab world and in English. This is primarily due to the hegemony of the English language (Mosbah-Natanson and Gingras 2014; Hanafi and Arvanitis 2014) in social science research, facilitated by the dominance of Western academic institutions and think-tanks, as well as the standards of publication in international journals, which give little to no effort to accommodating foreign languages. Furthermore, what little knowledge is being produced within the Arab world is produced in Arabic and not being translated. In fact, scarcely any authors who write in English or French reference in Arabic. To a large extent, authors who write in a particular language, cite in that particular language. Houssay-Holzschuch and Milhaud (2013) find that French authors tend to quote mostly French references and this is confirmed by our work. The issue of language compartmentalization becomes significantly poignant here. Some authors see translation as an opportunity for increased reflexivity (Hanafi 2011), which might lead to new ways of conceptualizing and articulating concepts. New ways of thinking can indeed be *found* in translation, as long as translation is understood and practiced as a process that is never-ending, dialogical, and fraught with heuristic tensions (Houssay-Holzschuch and Milhaud 2013).

The hegemony of political science is significantly problematic as well, in addition to the weakness of peripheral authors (both geographical and theoretical), which greatly impoverishes the international debate. Karim Makdisi in *Reflections on the State of IR in the Arab Region* provides an overview of influential IR journals and demonstrates that voices and research from the Arab region are notably absent, and moreover that those IR "conversations" dealing with the Arab region routinely eschew Arabic sources, let alone oppositional Arab voices.

Given Arab scholars' lack of resources, language barriers and poor publication record in mainstream journals, it is clear that many Arab scholars working in Arabic and within national institutions are virtually invisible internationally. The challenge today is the disengagement of social science research from its local context, which is amplified by the hegemony of neoliberal interests and concurrent narratives for change, as well as the marginalization of local knowledge by many Arab scholars who suffer from both local and global constraints on knowledge production.

Notes

1 The early version of this chapter was written with Nada AlMaghlouth (American University of Beirut) and Jean-Philippe Cointet (National Agronomic Research Institute and Institut Francilien Recherche, Innovation et Société [IFRIS]).
2 Fifteen references were added out of 11 different journals not included in the two platforms.
3 It is a small number as the e-Marefa needs time to enter new issues of Arab journals.
4 In the following journals: *Idafat, Al-Mustaqbal Al-Arabi, Majalet al-Dirasat al-Falastiniya, Majalat el "Ouloum el Siyasiya*, and *Omran.*
5 Created in September 2005 by four Belgian and French publishers, today Cairn offers the most comprehensive collection of full-text publications in the French language in the humanities and social sciences available online. See www.cairn.info.
6 These research centers are not affiliated to universities and often have either the form of NGOs in the Arab world or private think-tanks outside the region. However, there are in the Arab world foreign research centers, like the American Research Center in Cairo and French research centers in the Middle East (CEDEJ, IFPO, etc.).
7 More precisely, the measure we use is called "difference-weighted mutual information-based co-occurrence retrieval models." The similarity between two authors results from the comparison of their respective profile of mutual information they share with every other author in the network.
8 CorText is the digital platform of Institut Francilien Recherche, Innovation, Société which includes direct access to network computing tools named the CorText Manager.
9 Two studies conducted in Lebanon in the 1970s and 1993 examining the ideological orientations of Lebanese youth reveal that there was a drastic paradigm shift in political identification and ideological orientation. While emphasis on Arab nationalism was more predominant in the 1970s, with 42 percent of youth identifying as Arab nationalists, this figure significantly declines in 1993 to 16 percent, to be replaced by Lebanese nationalism accounting for 68 percent of the youth's orientations. In the 1970s, 25 percent identified as Lebanese nationalists, only 5 percent more than those who identified as internationalist (communist). This figure also declined in 1993 to 8 percent, where internationalism is defined as Islamism (Faour 1998).
10 The classic IMRAD structure, as Pontille (2003) has shown, is rarely used in sociology; it is more frequent in American articles and more so when exposing formal research (modelization, mathematical and statistical analysis) and quantitative and survey analysis.
11 The universities are Brown, Columbia, Cornell, Dartmouth, Harvard, Pennsylvania, Princeton and Yale.
12 Not only because of the lack of space, but also because we consider the impact factor provides thin evidence of how influential a journal is.

9 The demise of public social science

Writing op-eds in Lebanese newspapers

> True understanding does not tire of interminable dialogue and "vicious circles" because it trusts that imagination eventually will catch at least a glimpse of the always frightening light of truth.
>
> (Hannah Arendt 1953: 392)

1 Introduction

The opinion pages worldwide are among the most read sections of any newspaper and of any publication. They allow the non-professional writer to place an issue in the view of decision-makers and the public eye or to bring his or her perspective and expertise to the news. Six basic kinds of items appear in opinion pages: (1) editorials written by newspaper staff; (2) letters to the editor written by readers; (3) op-eds (*op*posite the *edi*torials on the page) generally written by people with special expertise or credibility in a certain field; (4) statements, declarations or petitions published in newspapers with their signature; (5) long interviews; and finally (6) a new form that consists of asking an expert to reply to the questions raised by readers on specific topics.

The aim of this chapter is to investigate the contribution of academics (mainly in Lebanon) on writing op-eds in Lebanese newspapers. This dimension of public social sciences is in accordance with Michael Burawoy's four-pronged typology (2005). As we mentioned in Chapter 5, Burawoy distinguishes between four types of sociologies: *professional* and *critical* sociology are relevant to academic audiences, and *public* and *policy* sociology relate to a wider audience. Public research activity enters the researcher into dialogue with different publics through direct talks, media and newspapers. It entails a double conversation and reciprocal relationships, in which meaningful dialogue fosters mutual education that not only strengthens such publics but also enriches sociological work itself and helps it in setting research agendas.

This chapter raises many questions: Why do academics write op-eds? What is the importance of academics' contribution? Does their opinion reinforce the newspaper's worldview or constitute a counterbalance to the worldview of the newspaper? What kind of issues do they choose to write about? What is the role of the "gatekeepers" (editors in charge) of the op-ed pages?

Academic contribution to the public arena of course is not limited to writing op-eds. Interviews are another important way to contribute to the debates. For instance, browsing the Lebanon *Daily Star* we find two articles, in the September 13, 2013 issue, from contributors affiliated to the American University of Beirut (AUB). Journalist Lysandra Ohrstrom interviewed three academics at the AUB school of medicine for her article "Bat's blood: Hair removal potion or old wives' tale?"[1] Kareem Shaheen interviewed an academic from the faculty of public health about "The dark side of gambling."[2] But in general, long interviews or expert advice to a public issue (not only related to political and social life) are almost absent from newspapers.

1.1 Lebanon: a politically divided media milieu

Since the early 1960s, Lebanon has had a good margin of freedom to operate newspapers covering Lebanese issues and beyond. Lebanon has been the epicenter of Arab intellectual life since the late nineteenth century (Favier 2004: 8).[3] It was the country *par excellence* where discussions in *Al-Safeer* and *Al-Nahar* ranged around decolonization, Arab–Israeli conflict, pan-Arabism and the Third World, as well as other important political and social issues. *Al-Hayat*, a London-based newspaper owned by a Saudi businessman, can be considered the only pan-Arab newspaper that tackled a similar range of issues.

However, Lebanese media have become increasingly complex and the media milieu is highly fragmented. Although they still are among the freest in the Arab region, they are highly partisan and anything but fair and balanced (Dabbous 2010: 721). Media outlets (newspapers, television and radio), even those published in non-Arabic language, reflect power divisions along political and confessional lines, very unique to Lebanon, that reflect their major shareholders, and thus serve as extensions of political affiliations (Dabbous-Sensenig 2000); thus, they have become "viewspapers," to cite an acute observer of Arab media, Nabil Dajani (1992: 11). Mainly funded by businesspeople and political actors, media in general and newspapers don't even claim to seek objectivity (Sakr 2008). In fact, some scholars suggest that they have become part of specific political forces according to their partisan support and representation in Lebanon (Dabbous 2010; Dabbous-Sensenig 2000). As a consequence, there exists a "double, unwritten social contract" whereby journalists are bound to media owners – and tied to their political affiliations – while, similarly, the journalists are beholden to citizens, in which the former serve as political opinion indicators, rather than as a source for new developments and potential opinion leaders (Dabbous 2010: 724). In other words, we find that a high degree of partiality for media outlets in a deeply divided country effectively transforms the media into a political messaging tool.

1.2 Methodology

The methodology consisted of two stages. First, we selected a systematic random sample to determine the importance of the contribution of academics to editorials, compared to other categories of authors.

Three Lebanese newspapers were chosen based on a combination of high circulation rates and robust national and regional coverage. The Arabic newspapers *Al-Akbar* and *Al-Nahar* hold the title of the second and third highest circulations in Lebanon, respectively.[4] The *Daily Star*, an English newspaper, was also included. *Al-Akbar* is usually considered ideologically as representing "the left" (very close to Hizbullah) while Al-*Nahar* and *The Daily Star* offer conservative (rather liberal) opinions. Nonetheless, ideological orientation was of little importance for this research. By selecting only these three newspapers, we excluded two other important newspapers: *Assafir* and the French-language *L'Orient-Le Jour*. To mitigate the effect of this exclusion, we asked the two journalists in charge of the editorial pages of the op-eds about the contribution of academics to their op-eds pages and they confirmed the result we have from the other newspapers.

In addition, these two newspapers, along with *Al-Hayat*, will be included in the second stage, i.e., constituting a list we created which will be the most important body for the analysis in this chapter.

The collection of the material was sampled in the following way: the newspaper op-eds were collected once every four weeks over a period of one year, from 1 August 2010 to 1 August 2011. In this way, we built the first sample, statistically representative, which covers a large diversity of topics over the year (see Table 9.1).[5]

For the second stage, which is important for this chapter since it will serve the qualitative analysis, we increased the number of analyzed op-eds published in Lebanese newspapers by targeting academics appearing in the last three years (2011–2013) in the same three newspapers, as well as four additional newspapers. We collected in this manner a larger list of 147 articles authored between 2011 and 2013 by active (90 articles) or retired (57 articles) academics (Table 9.2). We will call it the *Academic list*. For the purpose of this research, we excluded some rare authors who somehow are affiliated to a university but with a rather loose connection: former academics who usually write for the newspapers (e.g., Dalal al-Bizri), journalists that indicate they have a PhD (e.g., Omar Nashabeh) or journalists and part-time teachers in universities (e.g., Rami Khouri).[6]

Table 9.1 Distribution of editorials in the sample

	Number	*Percentage*
Al-Nahar	53	23.6
Al-Akbar	120	53.3
Daily Star	52	23.1
Total	225	100.0

Table 9.2 Distribution of editorials in the academic list

	Number	Percentage
Al-Nahar	12	8.2
Al-Akhbar	27	18.4
Assafir	31	21.1
Daily Star	8	5.4
L'Orient Le jour	8	5.4
Al-Hayat	14	9.5
Al-Modon	47	32.0
Total	147	100.0

2 Who writes in newspapers?

Authors of op-eds were typologized into seven categories: journalists, university academics, retired academics, practitioners,[7] affiliates to independent study centers,[8] politicians (non-academic) and writers.[9] As indicated by Table 9.3, only a very small portion of op-eds (17 percent) is written by academics in the representatively sampled newspapers. In addition, 10 percent were authored by affiliates to independent research centers, which are often private think-tanks. Not all of these authors are conducting research: many keep this affiliation but work rather as political analysts.

The importance of the academic contribution to op-eds is even smaller, if one considers not the number of published op-eds but the number of academic authors. As we will see in detail, only 18 academics are identified over a Lebanese community estimated at 2,200 full-time university academics. Our estimate, although based on a partial identification of authors, is that no more than 35 Lebanese academics actually contribute to the op-ed pages of newspapers.

As we will see later, the level of involvement of university academics is much less than it is in other countries, especially in the Western world. In Canada, a study done by Jean-Pierre Robitaille and Yves Gingras at Université du Québec

Table 9.3 Distribution of editorials by types of author in the sample

	Number	Percentage
Journalist	74	33.3
Writer	41	18.5
Academic (university)	38	17.1
Politician non-academic	28	12.6
Affiliates to independent center	23	10.4
Practitioner	17	7.7
Retired academic	1	0.5
Total	222	100.0
N/A	3	
Total	225	

(Drouin 1998) used a methodology that is different from ours, by looking not only at op-eds but also the news coverage to identify the usage of scientific research by some Québec newspapers in 1996. They demonstrate the importance of academic research cited in these newspapers. Benoît Godin also reveals (Drouin 1998) that half of the most active research professors have engaged in the dissemination of scientific knowledge to the general public (writing books or articles, participation in radio and television, conducting exhibitions, etc.).[10]

Women's voices are few in the op-eds of our sample and even fewer in the academic list (Table 9.4). Op-eds written by academics are almost all written by men (97 percent). Carol Jenkins (2008) confirms a similar trend in her study of the *Washington Post*, *New York Times*, and *Newark Star-Ledger*.

As indicated in Table 9.5, 25 academics wrote 147 op-eds, out of which 18 are Lebanese, four live abroad and three are from Palestine.

Thus, rather few academics in Lebanon are interested in writing op-eds in newspapers. All Lebanese, except Nadim Mansoury, are residing in Beirut, where the symbolic and cultural resources are concentrated. Some are retired (Fawaz Trabulsi, Ahmad Beydoun and Ahmad Baalbaki). It is interesting to note that there is only one woman: Mona Fayyad. In terms of generations, it seems that a significant majority is from an older generation, and that the younger generation is more reluctant to engage with that form of public intervention. It also appears that mainly Lebanese write op-eds. Foreign academics that we interviewed have no interest, or believe they have no credibility for participating in the local debates.

Of those who live in a foreign country, some are academics but also prolific writers in op-eds such as Asaad Abou Khalil, Joseph Massaad or Khaled Hroub.[11] The fact that many newspapers are now available online in English has increased online readership among people outside the Arab region but mainly in the Arab diaspora.[12] *Jadaliyya* is one of these online publications that attract a lot of Arabic diasporaic writers.[13]

Some of the op-eds are research-based, while others are not. But what is interesting is that, when looking at the CVs of these op-ed authors, some are recognized professional researchers: good researchers can thus spend time in doing "public social science." The op-ed is thus to be considered by some authors as a necessary conversation with the public. For those who also publish in refereed journals and books in English or French, they find the op-eds to an opportunity

Table 9.4 Distribution of editorials by sex

	Sample		Academic list	
	Frequency	*Percentage*	*Frequency*	*Percentage*
Male	207	92	144	98
Female	18	8	3	2
Total	225	100	147	100

Table 9.5 Academics list contributing to op-eds: residents of Lebanon or from the Lebanese diaspora

Authors	Affiliation	Discipline	Living abroad	Number of op-eds
Fawwaz Traboulsi	Retired – Ex-LAU	History/sociology		26
Ahmad Beydoun	Retired – Ex-UL	Sociology/history		23
Jad Chaaban	AUB	Economics		19
Assaad Abou Khalil	University of California	Political science	Living abroad	8
Massoud Daher	LU	History		7
Bashar Haydar	AUB	Philosophy		6
Fadi Bardawil	University of Chicago	Anthropology	Living abroad	5
Ahmad Baalbaki	Retired – LU	Sociology		4
Samer Frangieh	AUB	Political science		4
Mona Fayad	AUB	Social psychology		3
Sari Hanafi	AUB	Sociology		3
Daoud Khairallah	Georgetown University	Middle Eastern studies	Living abroad	2
Albert Dagher	LU	Economics		1
Antoine Fleyfel	Université catholique de Lille	Philosophy/theology		1
Faysal J. Mohammad	LU	Political science		1
Gilbert Achcar	SOAS, University of London	Middle Eastern studies	Living abroad	1
Hareth Sleiman	LU	Political science		1
Hussein Alzein	LU	Law		1
Kamal Wehbe	University of Montreal	Political science	Living abroad	1
Nadim Mansoury	LU	Sociology		1
Nawaf Kabbara	Balamand University	Political science		1
Kamal Deeb	Ottawa University	Economics	Living abroad	1
Total				120

to write in Arabic and spread their message to their local community and beyond. Finally, concerning the disciplines, all these academics, as we can see in Table 9.5, are social scientists.

It is interesting to note that rare are the Lebanese academics who write for the *Daily Star*. Most of them are non-Arabs that have been commissioned by Project Syndicate.[14] The result is that few op-eds in this newspaper are concerned with local affairs.

2.1 Recruiting writers: editors as gatekeepers

Opinion section editors face limitations on space, time and public interest. They have to identify opinion articles – both editorial and op-ed – that they will consider as more newsworthy than others. Their choices will influence the nature of the opinion pages of the newspaper, as well as the calendar or the choice of topics.[15] A first stance of these gatekeepers is the one described by Golan (2010), who defends the idea that opinion editors reinforce the newspaper's worldview by using the op-ed section. Such an editorial strategy would entail abandoning a self-designated role of counterbalance to the newspaper's worldview, which is accepted from newspapers with a wide audience. Moreover, it offers the readers a one-sided perspective regarding controversial political issues, but this goes beyond the objective of this chapter.[16]

Academics writing opinion articles might choose the strategy of not "preaching to the choir," by selecting newspapers that can reach audiences supposedly against the argument used by that author. In this way, they might open up the debate and introduce new ideas to the public. But this strategy might also prove dangerous, as these academics would put themselves in the line of fire by selecting an audience of opposing ideology. It might be that the risks associated with debating with audiences of differing opinion accounts for the lack of academics participating in the media. Another strategy might be that of choosing to target audiences of like-minded opinions, in agreement with the view expressed by Michel Wieviorka (2014: 103) that public sociologists are more effective when they address well-targeted audiences that express a desire for debate.

By interviewing three editors of op-ed pages in Lebanon, we found that they rarely invite people to write for their newspapers. More often than not, it is the other way round. Additionally, editors complained that some pieces they received were not publishable, as they "didn't provide arguments but political positioning and insults," as expressed by one of the op-eds editors. He complained that he received pieces from academics that are too partisan, in which inherent and unredeemable evilness is attributed to the party that one opposes without bringing information to readers. Academics, for this editor, are just organic citizens, in the sense of Gramsci, linked to political parties.

Generally speaking, the newspaper editors we met didn't seem to appreciate the necessity of inviting academic scholars to write in their pages, nor the importance it might have to include academics in debates appearing in their pages.

3 Styles of expression: the reflective, the provocative and the citizen

Three styles of expression are identifiable when glancing into the content of the whole academic list: a reflective style, a provocative style and a "citizen" style. These styles may help provide an explanation on the type of contributions that academics use in the op-eds.

The reflective style is both *analytical* and *reflexive*. Analytical, in the sense that it is bringing complex arguments to understand/explain a social phenomenon or a political event, using information from history and geography. Reflexive, in the sense of self-criticism beyond the ideological entrenchment and of revising questions and even re-framing the way we read a social phenomenon or a political event. Having said that, we don't want to idealize what is analytical as neutral: being analytical can embody a utopia and a will to help a social movement in the making. The relationships between the scientific, journalistic and political fields are complex and the risk of co-option is there (Mauger 2011).

For instance, in his piece "Syrian Revolution in 2012: 'Good and Evil' or 'in Favor and Against,'" Samer Frangieh, associate professor of political science at AUB, captures the reader's attention with new information and fresh analysis, comparing for instance the Syrian uprising with the French revolution, showing the ambivalent relationship between ethics and politics. "Those who don't want to take position from the Syrian uprising choose to hide behind a moralistic stance of 'good vs. evil' arguing that the Syrian opposition is also violating human rights." He is also reflective by starting his article by pointing out the violation of human rights by the Syrian opposition. His writing is analytical and occasionally uses anecdotes, helping readers to enhance their understanding of complex issues. There is always an educational side without preaching. In "Kamel al-Assad and the Identity in Crisis," Kamal Wahbeh (2010), professor at the Lebanese University (LU), contested an op-ed written by Talal Atrissi that the Lebanese Shia get their conscience as a community thanks to the Sader movement in the early 1980s. He used the work of historian Philippe Hitti and treats the notions of community and class consciousness, using Karl Marx and other social scientists. In the same vein, we find a very analytical article in *Assafir* newspaper (17 August 2013) by Ahmad Balbaki, a sociology professor retired from the LU, about a crime caused by a mixed marriage between a Druze and a Sunni.

The second style of expression is not only analytical but also *goes against the mainstream common sense and opens new venues for the debates*. As an example, one can mention some articles of Mona Fayyad, professor of social psychology in the LU ("To be a Shia Today" or "Are the Arab Shia 'Enemy Collaborators' in their Countries?") or those of Bashar Haydar, professor of philosophy at AUB ("Syrian Revolution is a Moral Act but not Gaza Rockets" or "Supporting the Occupation is a Moral Duty," both in *Al-Hayat*). These articles are provocative and full of passionate, strong opinions. They open discussion through the online section of media and also through replies to other op-eds. Regardless of whether one agrees or disagrees with these authors, academics here bring about new paths of reflection and creative imagination to the public.

A third style is when academics *write as citizens*, and one cannot find a disciplinary reference, or any theory or empirical research mentioned. It is sometimes difficult to differentiate when an author writes as a citizen or as a researcher, as is the case, for example, of many articles by Asaad Abu Khalil in *al-Akhbar*, or one article by Samer Frangieh in *Al-Hayat*. This style is frequent in op-eds and is usually expressed by academics that are politicized. The major characteristic of this style is their expression of emotion or opinion without factual backing. Some of these articles can be considered as advocacy and denunciations.

4 Topics: the predominance of politics

The sweeping majority of the op-eds are political in nature. Academics write mainly on politics: 69 percent of articles vs. 18 percent in social issues (see Table 9.6). The predominance of politics is not due only to the fact that there are more political sciences and related fields (Middle Eastern studies and international relations), but also to the fact that Arab newspapers are more interested in politics. Hazem Saghieh, the editor of op-ed pages in *Al-Hayat*, points out that "since ages the Arab world is burning by the fact that it has dysfunctional political systems and lagging social issues."[17]

Op-eds are mainly concerned with local or regional debates and rarely with international debates.[18] Moreover, it is practically impossible to find a full debate with different opinions. In each issue, op-eds are juxtaposed without connection. Usually the orientation of the newspaper will determine who will be published. There are some exceptions. *Al-Nahar* presented two debates in the last few years to which different opinions contributed: one about the Palestinian presence in Lebanon and another about the legacy of Kamel al-Assad, who was a leading Lebanese Shia figure. The outcome is a sort of mini-forum that is used sometimes in readings in university classes.

In order to see how topics are dealt with, let us focus on one particular and very hot topic, the case of the Special Tribunal of Lebanon (STL).[19]

Table 9.6 Distribution of topics of op-eds in the academics list

	Number of op-eds	*Percentage*
Politics	100	70.4
Social issues	26	18.3
Economic issues	9	6.3
Cultural issues	7	4.9
Total	142	100
Other	5	

4.1 Case of the Special Tribunal of Lebanon

We conducted a study about newspaper coverage in Lebanon dealing with the STL in order to examine the extent to which the Lebanese media facilitated or stifled "rational" debate about the STL. We covered 234 articles (March–December 2009), from which almost 75 percent are news coverage and 25 percent are editorials. Journalists and editors were responsible for more than 89 percent of all coverage in the sample. While one may consider this an asset, and indeed, in an "objective" news milieu it may be, the significant fissures in the media and political spheres in Lebanon meant the coverage merely reflected the two-sided unwritten social contract. Journalists, bound to media owners, served as conduits for their political stance on the STL, yet journalists were simultaneously beholden to citizens, and thus served as political opinion leader indicators.

The question of how this was manifest in the coverage and its impact remains to be understood. Certainly the marginal op-ed contributions by law practitioners (2.1 percent) and academics (1.3 percent) suggest an overwhelming role of editors and journalists in shaping the debate.

One academic, Chibli Mallat, appeared in the coverage with four editorials. He was by then a professor of law at USJ, but also an outspoken human rights advocate,[20] editor of the law page of the *Daily Star* and a former presidential candidate in Lebanon. Mallat represents a bridge between the public and academic spheres, or the nexus between *professional* and *public* research. In Mallat's own words, he seeks an active role in the construction of what he terms "consensus-forming common discourse" within society, or in other words, an authoritative statement – whether academic or legal in nature – which will have an impact on society (Mallat 2009: 92). He writes in the *Daily Star*:

> We need to keep the pressure on the STL, Bellemare and now President Cassese, to deliver justice. A dispute with Sayyed[21] is useful only to the extent that it forces justice to be done, and seen to be done, by justice acting globally. So let us team up on the need to get justice for our fellow Lebanese victims, and see their assassins in jail – without a single exception – from those who killed Kamal Jumblatt and kidnapped Musa al-Sadr to the murderers of Hariri and Samir Kassir.
>
> (Mallat 2009)

Mallat is keenly aware also of the importance of a "rational" scholarly community voice in the media. He published a text co-signed with Alan Dershowitz on a new vision for the Palestinian–Israeli peace process in English in *The National* (Emirati newspaper and one of the three main English-language papers in the Arab Middle East) and in Arabic in two main pan-Arab newspapers, *as-Sharq al-Awsat* and *al-Hayat*.

Yet for all of his expertise, advocacy and perspective, Mallat's voice appeared in four articles, one of which was subject to a response through the "right of reply" from General Jamil el Sayyed, a key security official at the time of the assassination of Hariri. In one of the three articles as part of an ongoing debate between figures, he wrote:

> Does Mallat not see that unveiling the truth and arresting the perpetrators would have been easier for Lebanon had the former chiefs of security continued their investigations and had they not been targets of political arrest through Siddiq[22] and other false witnesses?[23]

Mallat countered that "The Lebanese victims, and those who are working for international justice, need to get to the bottom of this murky affair," but he stresses the importance of the international community toward this aim.[24]

This exchange was one of the rare instances of exchange, yet the debate did not stray far from the major talking points of the increasingly entrenched factions. Indeed, "international justice" and "false witnesses" permeated the discussion, in what was effectively a discussion between the two competing factions. As a result, while healthy debate enriched perspectives on the STL, the inability to stray away from a particular position ended up with little more than an exchange of political party representatives. Now, whether this was unconscious or intentional is a matter beyond the scope of this chapter, but a strong case could be made that the only debate in the newspaper media was a reflection of political stances.

As we observe from the above exchange, as well as the type of coverage and authors, the political parties either instrumentalize or influence the debate over the STL. As a result, while the media could serve as a very public forum for constructive and rational debate, the marginalization or simple absence of seemingly unaffiliated actors translated to the stifling of debate beyond those advanced by political affiliations.

5 Writing op-eds: importance and challenges

Op-eds and interviews are examples of "agile formats" that combine literary journalism with academic research, as César Rodríguez-Garavito (2014) suggested in his call for new ways to disseminate academic work. Many authors have highlighted the importance of such activity, and without seeking to broaden the discussion, we would like to examine, based on our results, some of the many reasons, challenges and difficulties on why academics may write op-eds.

We first want to reject a rather evident motivation, the economic benefit. Some interviewees mentioned the financial gain from writing in newspapers. But after verification, most of the authors who do not write on a regular basis do not receive money when they publish in newspapers. It might be the case for those publishing a regular column, but again they are more attentive to their political and moral standing than the financial benefits. In a similar way, it could be argued that writing newspaper articles is a way to enhance their prestige and enhance their "social capital." Nonetheless, most authors we reviewed here are already well known personalities, at least in Lebanon and often well beyond the frontiers of the country.[25] Most are known academics before being authors in newspapers, and more often for reasons that are more related to their political past rather than their academic position.

Publishing in the opinion pages is a way for scholars to be exposed to social realities from distinct perspectives and can be a way to express opposition to mainstream opinions that the author considers as not based on empirical facts. A nice example, in France, is provided by Michel Wievorka's interviews for *Le Monde*, based on his research about anti-Semitism in France, which was published after the shooting of three Jewish children at a school in Toulouse. Wievorka influenced the public discussion by easing fears about the return of anti-Semitism (Wievorka 2014: 100). Similar examples can be found where the academic contributions may foster constructive debates that challenge some of the false arguments used for political purposes, or reveal the injustice of the current global power balance. The small amount of academic writing in the newspapers in Lebanon is insufficient to attain this objective.

Another reason that can be a strong motivation is that by contributing to public debate, academics become part of the public they address. This could be the case if the public perceives academic knowledge as being essentially Western-oriented and foreign to the local situation (Rodríguez-Garavito 2014: 23). In the Arab world, social sciences are often delegitimized because their emergence coincides with the presence of the colonial power (Selmi 2001). The same happens within other scientific fields, and the constitution of scientific communities have often been in the hands of powerful elites linked to the colonial power (Gaillard *et al.* 1997b; Raj 2006). Social sciences can be particularly affected by this past, and their presence in the media can provide an opportunity to challenge the theories that are "forged in the historical crucible of Western modernity" (Von Holdt 2014: 51). It may also be a way to challenge "the imbalances of academic power between the global North and South" (Sundar 2014: 36). Specifically for Lebanon, we do not feel that this is exactly the case. As we said, Lebanese newspapers have a history of rather free and autonomous writing and academic life is vivid and relies on an important historical tradition. Thus, social scientists do not feel they represent any foreign body of knowledge even when they write in foreign languages.

Another possible strong motivation for academics to contribute to op-eds is that research, in this way, is not confined to a highly isolated work environment (Rodríguez-Garavito 2014: 24). In the same way, by engaging in a dialogue with the public (either in the pages of the newspapers or after the publication of the articles), the academics can examine social realities they are interested in from a different perspective, contributing to a thick analysis. Of course, this holds only when the authors are also particularly interested in receiving the opinions expressed outside academia. And this can be a matter of choice, as we already mentioned above, in selection, i.e., selecting newspapers that reach like-minded or opposed audiences.

Nonetheless, we still can argue that in many cases Lebanese academics choose to write in the newspapers to express a political position rather than to bring research to the public. The comparison with France is enlightening. While writing this chapter, we monitored *Libération* and *Le Monde*, two leading newspapers in France, during the month of September 2013 and could observe the importance of the intellectual contributions in op-eds, as well as in short and long interviews. When the headlines of the newspapers on the Syrian crisis are normative (*La ruse Russe, L'offensive médiatique de Bachar Al-Assad*, etc.) normativity is often justified by an extensive use of facts and analysis delivered by journalists and academics. During the five days from 25 to 30 September, *Le Monde* and *Libération* published 15 op-eds about the tax system and the lack of reform in the political economy, out of which 12 are either professors at French universities or researchers at CNRS. In addition, *Le Monde* on 25 September interviewed the economist Elie Cohen on taxation advice.[26] *Le Monde* uses academic experts in an even more interactive way. When the 2013 report of the IPCC – Intergovernmental Panel on Climate Change – appeared, *Le Monde* of 27 September 2013 interviewed the climatologist Hervé Le Treut. The objective of this brief comparison is not to set the bar so high (French model) and judge the Lebanese scholars, but to bring an example of how the scholarly community can directly be involved in the topics of its own interest.

Returning to our Lebanese case, even expressing political issues may have an extraordinary effect. Either being conservative or critical toward the hegemony of the ruling classes, academics, by addressing a larger public, can also indicate that there are differences inside academia itself. *Al-Nahar* newspaper, for instance, provided the public, in 2005, with conflicting views of scholars concerning the presence and living conditions of the Palestinian refugees in Lebanon. Since political subjects are so often the topics of op-eds, the presentation of lively differing points of view could enrich the public debate.

Among the risks involved in writing in newspapers, it is necessary not to underestimate the risk of *burn-out*, associated with engaging in active public debate. Presenting opinions and research to public debate, although satisfying a moral commitment to contribute to society, puts the academics in a direct line of fire. Once under public scrutiny, academics are no longer protected by their institutions. By sharing their research or opinions with the public they take the risk of public criticism, an experience that can be emotionally draining, especially when considering the political nature of their contributions. Additionally, speaking "inconvenient truths" to the powerless or acting as a "counter-power" can be even harder than protesting against the powerful, because "it alienates us from the people that in other situations we most admire" (Sundar 2014: 39).

A second challenge, with the university becoming increasingly commodified, is that academics compete for funding and awards within the walls of institutions, and the university is pushing them to publish globally mainly in academic journals, even if at the expense of connection with the local community. Some academics do not mention their pieces published in newspapers in their CVs. The American Psychological Association and the Kennedy School of Government have taken up the banner, encouraging their members to write (Bishara 2004). Interviews with academics in Lebanon show that for some scholars, involvement in the media is a dangerous use of time and energy that may jeopardize their "academic capital," à la Bourdieu, as defined by US/European standards (Hanafi *et al.* 2013). Some believe that as soon as one secures a position at the university, they would have no time to spend with the public. Those who are against academics being involved in public life consider that the energy and commitment required by academics who assume multiple roles (researcher, professor, activist, public expert) can lead to a sacrifice in the quality of professional work. For them, this concession of time can lead to compromising academic responsibility to teaching and research. Involving oneself in the fast-paced media is seen by some scholars as contradictory to the isolated, patient and concentrated environment of the academic world that many might say is needed to produce quality work. This argument indeed has some truth. However, one can see this as a dilemma that one should always strike a balance.

A third challenge is related to the newspapers themselves, since, as we mention above, the Lebanese media are politically differentiated and even lack the seriousness that would be required to rationalize public debates over societal issues (rather than reporting one's views in supporting specific political parties or groups). In contributing to political debate, academics take the risk of losing the neutrality that enables research. Again, this is another dilemma: although Nandini Sundar's idea of a "public role" involves much more than writing in newspapers, her involvement in defending indigenous groups compromised the neutrality necessary to conduct research (Sundar 2014: 38). The difficulty of "remain[ing] objective while not being neutral" might be an impossible challenge in the Lebanese political atmosphere and therefore a risk not worth taking.

The final challenge is that at times an academic's contribution to the media can work against the initial intention of involvement. The experience of Elena Zdravomyslova and Anna Temkina (2014: 110) in the field of gender studies in Russia and their participation in the media was a frustrating one marked by disingenuous journalists that often misinterpreted statements presented by the researchers. In Russia, where the ideas about gender presented by the academics were unfamiliar, the public statements were criticized as imperialist and contradictory to Russian tradition. In Lebanon, academics might shy away from associating with newspapers out of fear of misinterpretation or playing into the hands of the political organizations and businesspeople with specific agendas. A lack of control in what is published certainly affects the willingness of academics to give interviews to journalists.

6   Newspapers and academics in the public space

If we rely on some historical precedent, we can maybe find another important reason that explains the lack of use of op eds by the academics.

Agnès Favier (2004) provides us a very interesting historiography of the role of the intellectuals in Lebanon that played a major role to become either *militant intellectuals* or *intellectual militants*. Since 1990 a group of intellectuals constituted an oppositional group of the ruling political class that divided authority along sectarian lines into three competing authorities. They were supporting the social claims of the workers' unions, especially the General Confederation of Lebanese Workers (CGTL) that were conducting strikes.[27] Intellectuals signed statements and petitions as a mode of political action. The "petition of the 55," signed by 55 intellectuals on 12 December 1994, (composed by 32 academics, ten journalists, seven economists, seven writers, five researchers, two editors, two lawyers and one worker; the total exceeds 55 as some have more than one profession) led by the editorial of Ghassan Tueini in *Al-Nahar* newspaper, was followed by another editorial in *l'Orient-le Jour* on 14 December 1994 and then by a statement of the parliamentary bloc of Salim Hoss. At the time, newspapers already having prominent intellectual figures in charge of the op-eds (Fawaz Trabulsi, Rudwan Al-Sayyed, Samir Kassir, Jihad Al-Zein, etc.) encouraged intellectuals to express their opinions. More radical intellectuals expressed themselves in the literary supplement of *Al-Nahar* under the direction of Elias Khoury. This statement was followed by other statements, denouncing issues like political corruption, the lack of independence for the judicial system and urbanism. The following statements were signed by more scholars (150, 445) (Favier 2004). These statements do not only criticize political decisions but also propose some solutions. The petitioning intellectuals understood that the political realm is no realm for saints, as Max Weber suggested, in the sense that politicians should marry the ethic of ultimate ends with an ethic of responsibility.

What distinguishes them from the current academic authors of the op-eds is that they were involved in collective action and mixing academic action with activism. They were a group of closely connected intellectuals that knew their role was to affect social and political change. A clear echo of this view is expressed in the lecture of Edward Said on the "Representations of the Intellectual" in Beirut on 5 January 1995. Favier identifies what she calls a "permanent" circle of 52 persons that signed between three and five statements during the year 1995. The circle was made up of journalists or academics mainly from Beirut. Some became political entrepreneurs by entering the political realm and others restrict themselves to moral entrepreneurship. The latter had no interest in becoming politicians, but rather in working toward a utopia rationalized and moralized through public discourse. Ahmad Beydoun, in a sort of auto-ethnography (2013), enlightens us about 50 intellectuals, the majority of whom were academics that had a major impact on Lebanese debate in the 1960s. Most of them were involved in a semi-political, semi-intellectual group called "the circle of Socialist Lebanese" constituting a kind of a "new left." Again this is an example of how connected academics involved in societal debate were helped by the fact that they belonged to a corps of intellectual activists. This strengthened and disseminated their message beyond the academic world.

This intellectual debate in Lebanon is often tinted by an ideological tone but it does not only concern the leftists. Take, for instance, Wajih Kawtharani.[28] His research interests focus on social history and political sociology with a specific focus on Bilad-Al-sham, methodology of history and Islamic thought. He published his PhD thesis, *The Social and Political Trends in Mount Lebanon and*

Arab Mashreq: 1860–1920) (Kawtharani 1976). This thesis generated a vivid debate between 1977 and 1988. Academics have rather negative criticism: Issam Khalifeh considers it as "a thesis that used middle age approach," Mahdi Amel as "right wing and sectarian ideology," Ahmad Beydoun as "war culture" and Ghassan Salameh as "Western breakthrough" and Suhail al-Qash as "Orientialist-Islamist text." Mainly journalists (Joseph Samaha, Hazem Saghiyeh, Jihad al-Zein) have positively criticized the book (Kawtharani 1996: 184).

This academic-activist corps needs a space, as one component of the Habermasian public sphere. Nicolas Pouillard (2013) provides us with a very beautiful portrait of Hamra Street in West Beirut. This street constituted from the 1960s to 1980s a vanguard space for Lebanese and even Arab intellectuals with its cafés, bar and the proximity to AUB. For instance, Café-restaurant Faisal, in front of the AUB gate, was the bastion of intellectual debate of Arab nationalists. When Sari Hanafi had his job talk at AUB, he was invited by the department for a lunch and was asked to select the restaurant; he asked about Faisal. The young university faculty ignored the name and an older faculty member said: "Alas! Now it is McDonald." Hamra then was a Habermasian public sphere; it is now a shopping area where all the usual multinational outlets are to be found, depriving the main Hamra Street of its old intellectual life and symbolism. The fact that Beirut does not offer the same lively political public space might explain a certain disengagement on the side of academics. Again, we are not nostalgic for this model of the academic-activist, à la Jean-Paul Sartre, but we do believe that it was very efficient in that time and the bulk of Lebanese academics did not find the reason to engage in the public debate.

Beyond the Arab world, one can find numerous examples of the active dialogue that academics can have with the public (Turkey, China,[29] Egypt). Turkey provides as well an excellent example where the academics' contribution to the public life is through not only newspapers but also television. This is rare in the Arab world, maybe with the exception of Egypt. The Al-Ahram Center for Strategic Studies provides excellent experts whose expertise is based not only on academic research but also on journalism. Their experts are present in Egyptian (*Nile TV*, newspapers) and Arab media (*Al-Jazira* and *Al-Arabiyya*). The participation of academics in Egypt and Turkey reminds us of Rodriguez-Garavito's "intermediate genres," which he recommends use of in order to fill the gap between conventional academic production and what is accessible to the public (Rodriguez-Garavito 2014: 28) Of course, this implies an increased emphasis on television and radio that challenges the written form usual to academics. But, by opening issues to a larger portion of the public, academics make room for the kind of social engagement that can lead to reconsidering well-established theories and practices.

7 Conclusion

We have showed that only a few academics are interested in writing in the newspapers, although it appears to be a rather straightforward way to participate in the public debate. Many arguments can be formulated to explain this reluctance: the promotion system of universities does not recognize these forms of public involvement; the difficulty finding an appropriate newspaper;[30] the fear of public criticism; the distrust of academics about the media in their capacity to present research without sacrificing academic quality; and the fear of compromising one's professional work through a time-consuming and risky public activity.

It is important to consider that some of these fears are not felt in the same way by all academics; probably the younger ones, more under pressure from the academic evaluation mechanisms, are more reluctant than the retired or older generation, as our analysis exemplifies. Authors writing op-eds in Lebanon are, in most cases, recognized professional academics, but do not count on these publications to get recognition. This is probably a general rule: those becoming famous academics to the non-academic public, such as Edward Said and Noam Chomsky, were good scholars in their scientific field. But it is difficult to talk of an interconnection between the public fame and the academic recognition since it works in only one way, the author uses his/her moral authority as a recognized academic but cannot use the public fame as an additional value in a professional career. Moreover, there is a running idea, mainly among social scientists, that publishing in newspapers is as important as publishing in academic outlets (El-Kenz 2005b).[31] Data do not, unfortunately, support this argument.

Finally, while we noticed that academics have used the three styles to voice their ideas (reflective, provocative and as citizens) and all are important styles, we noticed that the last style is more pronounced. On the last style, academics in the op-eds usually talk about Lebanese politics, and they do so by expressing opinions, not keeping a neutral, purely analytic position. This should not be seen as a default of any kind, but it certainly gives an advantage to social scientists who can rely on their knowledge of history and political sciences. The relative demise in expressing views on other topics (social issues, environmental concerns, other policy issues) is rather disappointing. It might also be the direct consequence of the extreme politicization and fragmentation of the newspapers in Lebanon.

No matter what the style of expression used by academics, the historical and current debates about these styles are not over. For Michel Wieviorka (2014), the French intellectual debate is embodied by the figure of the expert which is different from the classical figure of the intellectual, à la Jean-Paul Sartre, i.e., they do not wish to voice an opinion in areas in which they have no particular expertise. Enzo Traverso (2013), however, is very nostalgic for the Sartian figure. We are not.[32] We believe that the figure of the expert and the Sartian figure can have their respective forms of commitment and of criticism of power. Being political and critical can be expressed in different ways. The importance is to express that, and here is where we have our major conclusion, this relative disconnection of the academic and non-academic publication worlds should be questioned.

As Hanna Arendt's exergue at the outset of this chapter indicates, one cannot separate the knowledge production process from the "interminable dialogue" with the public. Op-eds are not a collection of polished articles, following the protocol of an academic article, nor are they supposed to be documents that solely function emotionally; they are interventions in a possible debate, be it an actual debate or the designation of an important issue that should be put to public enquiry. In all cases, academics could use the public forum that is offered by the newspapers to rationalize an issue or a debate. Although infrequent, op-eds written by academics, especially when they write reflectively or provocatively, do play an important role. Not publishing more academic voices has important consequences that go beyond Lebanon, since they impoverish the public debates in all Arab countries. In effect, academics could utilize the op-ed pages as a laboratory to test their ideas and to enter into direct conversation with different audiences. This could be the case for all kinds of positions, either when contesting the social and political order, an activity that requires direct interaction with the public, or by exploring public policy issues. Moreover, this rather thin flow of articles from academics is expressing distrust toward universities and more generally knowledge production. This is a complex and yet understudied aspect of social and political life.

To finalize, we consider that the rarity of contributions by academics in the newspapers is a double failure: failure on the side of Lebanese newspapers to incorporate academics' voices in the information and the analysis they provide for the public; and failure on the part of the academics to engage in the public sphere.

Notes

1 www.dailystar.com.lb/Culture/Lifestyle/2013/Sep-13/231063-bats-blood-hair-removal-potion-or-old-wives-tale.ashx#ixzz2f2GhaXR9.
2 www.dailystar.com.lb/News/Lebanon-News/2013/Sep-13/231091-the-dark-side-of-gambling.ashx#ixzz2f2HH8goK.
3 This cultural mission of Lebanon can be echoed in the vision of the late prominent Lebanese philosopher Michel Chiha, who wrote: "L'intérêt du monde arabe tout entier est que nous lisions tous les livres pour lui, et que, pour lui, nous assimilions toutes les connaissances.... Notre mission éternelle est là. Notre richesse est là" (Chiha 1980: 45; cited by Favier 2004).
4 The author thanks Anastacia Hajj and Julia Kristina Daley for their contribution to data collection and revision for this study.
5 The newspaper archives were found as microfilms in the AUB libraries for the following newspapers: *Al-Nahar* and *Daily Star*. *Al-Akhbar* archives were found online on the *Al-Akhbar* website (www.al-akhbar.com/archive).
6 Here the boundaries between these profiles are blurred. One should admit that journalism has become more academic and academics are taking on more journalistic techniques (Rodríguez-Garavito 2014: 23).
7 Often leaders of NGOs.
8 These are independent consultancy companies, study or research centers, usually producing reports on social, economic and political matters. Very active in the Arab region, they are mostly policy-oriented (Issam Fares Institute 2011). We have studied the importance of these NGOs' status for these centers (Hanafi 2010).
9 Writers are often former journalists or professionals who write for the public.

10 In order to encourage the dissemination of scientific research on newspapers, some American universities, such as Duke University, host a special center on op-ed writing.

11 Masaad and Hroub are not in the table as they are not Lebanese.

12 Publications online are not limited in terms of length and can be published almost immediately, allowing the academic more freedom in presenting their research or opinion.

13 We may also mention *e-intifada* or other foreign newspapers. However, rare are the Lebanese academics who contribute. One exception is Charles Harb, who wrote three times for the *Guardian* in the last eight years.

14 Project Syndicate presents itself as a project that

> brings ... commentaries by esteemed leaders and thinkers from around the world to readers everywhere. By offering incisive perspectives on our changing world from those who are shaping its economics, politics, science, and culture, Project Syndicate has created an unrivaled venue for informed public debate.

> It provides articles to 491 newspapers in 154 countries. Project Syndicate commentaries are translated into "nine languages, and reach more than 76 million readers in 151 countries" (www.project-syndicate.org).

15 For example, Russian media are interested in discussing gender issues on particular calendar dates that relate to women's events or in relation to certain situations (criminality, deviance, etc.) (Zdravomyslova and Temkina 2014: 110).

16 Marwan Bishara (2004) goes further in explaining that

> Mass-circulated newspapers produce masses out of citizens. They are corporations whose first task is to generate revenue for their shareholders by reproducing the status quo of power relations, and thus often op-ed writers are best at generic writing that tap-dances around controversial issues, doing no more than flirting with power. These writers skillfully adapt their perspective to the revolving door of the powerful with all its complex dynamics.

17 The predominance of purely political debates rather than social debates is exemplified in the trajectories of engaged citizens and academics, examined by Pénélope Larzillière in Jordan (Larzillière 2012; 2013).

18 One of the exceptions is the article of Massoud Daher, professor of history at LU and expert in Asian affairs, on the 2013 crisis between North and South Koreas. It was published in *Assafir* on 26 April 2013.

19 The following section concerning STL was written with Are Knudsen and Robert Flavis.

20 In his law practice he received international attention for bringing the case of *Victims of Sabra and Shatila* vs. *Ariel Sharon et al.*, to a court in Belgium, under the law of universal jurisdiction.

21 This article, "Saving the Special Tribunal for Lebanon from Failure: A Response to Jamil al-Sayyed and Antonio Cassese" was a Right of Reply to Mr. al-Sayyed.

22 Zuhair al-Siddiq was one of the accused "false witnesses."

23 Jamil al-Sayyed, "Exercising the Right of Reply: General Sayyed's response to Chibli Mallat." *Daily Star*, 22 October 2009.

24 Chibli Mallat, "Saving the Special Tribunal for Lebanon From Failure: A Response to Jamil al-Sayyed and Antonio Cassese," *Daily Star*, 8 October 2009.

25 Lebanon has always been a strong publishing location and publishing companies are usually widely circulated into the Arab world, as is well documented, for example by Franck Mermier (2005).

26 In an article entitled "La France ne saisit pas l'urgence d'une réforme." See more at: http://boulesteix.blog.lemonde.fr/2013/09/25/fiscalite-le-discours-dominant-est-infonde/ #sthash.dgavdoII.dpuf.

27 Favier writes about a context characterized by the

> (re)prise de parole plethorique au sein du milieu intellectuel beyrouthin: tables-rondes, conferences et debats politiques se multiplient en effet dans quelques hauts lieux publics de la "colloquerie" beyrouthine, et leurs contenus sont ample-ment repris dans les pages culturelles et d'opinions des quotidiens libanais.
>
> (Favier 2004)

28 He is professor emeritus of the Faculty of Humanities at the LU, as well as the current Beirut branch director of the Arab Center for Research and Policy Studies. He got a PhD in history (Sorbonne University – Paris, France) and Doctorat ès lettres from USJ.

29 The investigation of working conditions at Foxconn sites in China, a manufacturing company of electronics that provides Apple, and the proceeding international campaign was buttressed by the group efforts of academics and students. The group, composed of individuals from Taiwan, Hong Kong and mainland China, not only worked together to develop a report based on empirical research, but also published a joint report sent to multiple government and corporate entities. By working collectively they were able to combine research power and knowledge on how to most effectively share their findings (Ngai *et al.* 2014: 74).

30 Newspapers might be less important nowadays as online publication offers a lot of choices for academics (online newspapers, websites, blogs, etc.).

31 Ali El-Kenz, in his review of Arab social sciences, also exposes this argument, mainly from the Algerian case and the case of Al-Ahram in Egypt (El-Kenz 2005a).

32 For a detailed criticism of Traverso's book, see Arvanitis (2014).

10 Conclusion

> Research freedom and the free exercise of critical thinking in the social sciences suppose to admit diversity as a pre-requisite of knowledge and to pose alterity as constitutional of social relations, against all authoritarian temptations of a closed world where one sees recognition effects.
>
> (Hannoyer 1996: 402; authors' translation)

We talk about research, about our colleagues, and about us. We can't limit it to radical criticism, a simple temptation, since we will get downhearted and risk disempowering the research community to which we belong. We have sought to criticize the situation of research, acknowledging the dramatic transformation of our societies, without nostalgia for the old times when the state took care of the little research that was being done and the universities where we were studying.

We tried to analyze research practices and research institutions as complex social activities that are fragmented, and to a large extent still not recognized socially and politically. They are mirrors of the research systems elsewhere, they are created in close relation to the global world and are the ferment of an intense international activity; but they also reflect the social and political problems in the Arab world. The policies devised by international organizations, mainly the World Bank as we have shown, have been organized around the idea that it might be necessary to promote "knowledge economies," to transform the Arab economies into knowledge economies. We have defended the argument that this might not necessarily be the best and only possible way to go, in that it is an impossible promise delivered to the Arab world that will not be attained, generating a lot of frustration. Some of this knowledge economy already exists, some fragments are already there (enterprises, labs, incubators, etc.), and the question is how these fragments will mirror specific willingness and creativity of social actors, but very little will rely – if the "knowledge economy" agenda is pursued – on the scientific community itself.

This knowledge economy appears more as an impossible promise to fulfill but it sounds agreeable to the ears of the Arabs that have become increasingly aware of their chronic state of underdevelopment in science and technology. Thanks to the Arab uprisings, this acute sense of unequal status has been highly

enhanced, and its remains to be understood how this rare mix of cultural proud-
ness and voluntary action will end. The bell was rung before in recent history,
when the Arab renaissance (*nahda*) occurred, another unfulfilled promise. But
more recently, the three *Arab Human Development* reports under the protective
name of the UNDP advocated for a stronger role for education, greater freedom
and the improvement of the living and social status of women in the Arab region.
The controversy raised by the criticism these reports contained on the backward-
ness of the education systems and the lack of research triggered intense reflection, which partially found its way into the 2009, 2010–2011 and 2014 *Arab
Knowledge Reports* produced by the Al Maktoum Foundation and UNDP. What
survived in the process was a politically innocuous policy orientation toward
more research. This happened because of the political risk that the former exercise had entailed, and due to the fact that Arab governments had taken into their
hands the intellectual exercise of describing the state of research. Nonetheless,
inside society, the initial call for greater freedom was accompanied by another
one: over the last ten years, in every Arab country, scientists and policy-makers
involved in education and research (very often former scientists themselves)
have been trying very hard to transform their research systems. They have tried
to do this by creating a space for science inside the political arena and inside
their administrations and institutions. They have worked diligently at a very slow
pace and have secured, finally, a few small and fragile commitments. Governments usually discovered for themselves that when scientists began working, all
sorts of unpredicted benefits appeared. However, many of these Arab governments have not yet taken the political risks entailed by the scientific activity:
they discouraged, if not prevented, any intermediary scientific association that
might have significant inputs. The engagement with science policy in recent
years differs greatly from one country to another, and is interpreted diversely by
different social groups. Research policies are not all geared toward promoting
the independence and prestige of Arab governments; there are many other
reasons why research has been needed, requested and carried out in the region.

In all cases, it was a movement originating from the institutions, universities,
schools, research institutes, and some policy-makers, which sought to secure
resources for research. In the process, governments (sometimes) discovered that
science is no longer simply a fashionable, cultural and entertaining "social"
activity; it is now professionalized worldwide and, more importantly, quite
expensive. Some countries outside the Arab region, such as Brazil, Chile, Malaysia, Tunisia, Turkey and South Africa, have shown that in a very short time there
can be a spectacular increase in the level of spending on and benefits accruing
from research. The question is whether the Arab region is ready for such a major
overhaul.

No policy can engineer society, despite claims of "evidence-based policies"
or, before them, technocratic projects that had the objective to modernize, even
without the people's consent. We have given some examples of recommendations based on the kind of analysis proposed here (see especially the conclusion
in Chapter 3). In the concluding sections, we would like to remind what would

be the conditions for this major overhaul that Arab societies have to undertake. We insist on four major socio-cognitive elements that deeply affect research in the Arab region and which will necessarily be part of any substantial change: the model of development the Arab region wants to adopt, the trust it will put in science, the conduciveness of the social environment to the development of science, and finally the link between research and society, especially in the case of social science.

1 Models of development in the Arab region

Most Arab countries are rentier economies, i.e., they rely on income from natural resources (for instance the oil economies, or phosphates for Jordan and Morocco), or from the development of services (tourism in Lebanon and Tunisia) and remittances from émigrés (in Lebanon as well as the Maghreb). These income sources do not rely on science and research – at least not in their actual form. The commitment to research needs to be based on a certain vision of the future. More generally, science has been viewed as a sort of prestigious cultural activity. Research is less understood, being a new form of organization. Many universities were maintained to serve a purpose for the elite, inviting top-flight professors and supporting research for the sake of prestige, but the commitment is unclear.

Historically, there has been a strong link between the development of science and industrialization. The nationalist governments that tried to develop import substitution, even when they failed, generally established a scientific base which has remained a national asset in countries like Egypt, Morocco and Algeria. Industrialization may be a greater or lesser priority in some countries, notably those with service economies, but productive activities in information and communication technologies, as well as in traditional industries, require a technological base. Today, this base is much more important than it was 50 years ago: the science that goes into equipment and modern technology relies on skilled labor and a far higher degree of integration between the productive and technological sectors. Using a productive process can no longer be a closed black-box of some imported technology. Moreover, the technologies themselves get close to the research in that the type of knowledge needed today is at the molecular (or nano) level. Even simple automatization of productive tasks relies on sophisticated knowledge. Additionally, the management of natural resources for food, agriculture and water resources require greater knowledge input. Thus, even if the industrialization project seems out of date compared to the more fashionable knowledge economy, one should recall that production is indispensable: countries without a local productive base will be swept away in a global competition based on highly skilled knowledge and "dynamic" competitive advantages. This competition is, until now, deeply unequal, more than the industrialization model ever was. The knowledge gap will widen if there are no local productive activities and if skilled locals depart in search of better employment and living conditions.

It must be stressed that (re)building a scientific base is slower and more difficult than destroying one; moreover, waffling between support and suppression of science leaves deep scars. However, under the hammer of the market and neo-liberalism, the "national" mode of knowledge production fell into disgrace, and more linkages were established with the market economy. This shift, more often than not, resulted in a withdrawal of state support, and in some cases local scientists found themselves disparaged as parasites or "cultural curiosities," but not active members of the national productive project. Reclaiming a space for research is one of the steps necessary to achieving a productive development model.

2 Trust in science

> While the discourse on science has always been legitimate, the practice of science has not.
>
> (Jean-Jacques Salomon, preface in Khelfaoui 2000: 5; authors' translation)

It is necessary to build a relation, at least an implicit one, between science and society. Roland Waast has called this a pact with society. However, as the above citation from Jean-Jacques Salomon suggests, the discourse on science is easily formulated and legitimized, but the practice of research is more difficult to pursue, given the lack of professionalization of the scientific community and its lack of institutionalization.

Since World War II, science has been viewed as benefiting the people and generating new, salutary technologies. The degree of acceptance in science is still known to be very high in Europe. Among the main results of the Mouton and Waast's *Comparative Study on National Research Systems* is that some countries with a reasonably strong science base were found to treat research as a source of progress for humankind; its support was understood to be the duty of the state; and its results were considered public goods. This applied to the developing world, too, and in the post-colonial era, when governments began building higher education and research centers, with international cooperation and funding, and with great ambitions. Until the 1970s, scientists organized professionally, but the promised benefits of education and research seemed to be a long time in coming. In the 1980s, as market economics (that is, market deregulation and a certain disdain of public policy) became the new norm, well-being was no longer sought from the state but from private enterprise, and curiously this progress was not particularly favorable to research. Perhaps this was because it changed the status of science itself, from an activity for the benefit of the state to a specific activity with many different potential beneficiaries. In the new model, well-being was supposed to come from innovation, but innovation relies on technology, and technology, more often than not, is based upon research. Moreover, countries confident in research have also been better off developing a sound innovation system – or at least good conditions for innovation to take place. Even if scientific research does not seem directly translatable into commercial products, it increases the capacity of the country to promote innovation. None-theless, the "demand for research," whether from the public sector or, occasion-ally, from the private sector, is not only low but also directed preferably to "applied" objectives. There is a certain perplexity toward basic research, and policy measures usually forget that all research, even when applied or technolo-gical, relies on fundamental research. Research is a practice, not a theory; it is not very different as a practice from one area to the other, it is different in the objects it mobilizes and the actors involved. Knowledge production is the product of this practice, it needs not only financial resources and a "critical mass" of researchers: it also needs some more intangible elements such as trust and circulation of ideas.

Trust in science, research and technology does not mean to be uncritical toward some of its trends. In many Western countries, thanks to the political ecology, some activists formulated a critique of the very notion of industrial development, denouncing the impact of industrialization on both society and nature. Technology more than research and science have been the aim of critics. In South Korea, for example, activists and researchers questioned science that focused mainly on means, rather than impact. They insisted on the need for technological independence and for industrial development serving the interests of the nation (Quet and Noel 2014). So far, rare are the individual researchers who were interested in the critique either of science or of technology in the Arab world; one cannot mention any such "movement" in favor of a debate on research. Our worry is rather that the knowledge economy framework might blur this need by just promoting entrepreneurship, new enterprises in new sectors, and more competitiveness.

3 The social environment

The social environment of research is an important component of the motivation of scientists. It is composed of the direct work environment, but also the larger social environment. The job environment of researchers should be scrutinized with some care: trust comes from the scientists' employer (often the government or "autonomous" public universities). Since most researchers are also in univer-sities, and since universities have been primarily geared toward teaching, research has not been identified as a key priority in their job description. Until very recently, the terms of reference for a university professor in the Arab region did not include research. The latter was an ill-defined activity which could serve the purpose of securing a promotion, at best. However, the most salient issue that is discussed nowadays is the career patterns and whether professors should be tenured based on their merit or not and whether the research activity is simply publication or more than that (public engagement and dissemination of research to the larger public).

Societal and political values are another component of the social environment within which researchers operate, in particular with reference to the role science is given in conceptualizing and planning for the future. Some countries have traditionally held science in high regard, but have failed to give researchers the social standing and means corresponding to this more abstract respect for the discipline. There is a distance between the professed glorification of science and the almost infamous condition for the research practice: knowledge has certainly been prized, but the locations where knowledge has been cultivated were neither cared for nor championed by concrete policies.

Understanding the value of knowledge is also part of this double recognition as an aspiration, both as part of the nation-building project and as a practical endeavor. Knowledge production depends upon its everyday practice, not as a discourse but as an activity. Political power or material wealth may supersede all other aspirations. Religious beliefs, values related to aristocratic ancestry or to the family may exercise similar force. All these factors may well interfere with a commitment to science and its standards. In some Arab countries, among others, we have documented examples of self-censorship for religious or political reasons, as well as because of family duties superseding professional obligations. In many places, this has reached the point where practicing research has no other meaning than fulfilling the formal requirements of building one's career. If the research itself is not valued, then science will not prosper.

4 Connection to society and the role of the social sciences

We observed the difficulty of structuring research in social sciences; we found a highly fragmented sector, with segments of the academic community that are strongly involved either in favor or against strong political power, seeking funding opportunities outside the academic frontiers, linking actively to foreign sources of funding and international research collaborations. Academic institutions put strong pressure on publication in high-impact journals, increasing the marginalization of Arabic language but also pushing toward a formulation of social issues in terms that may not be relevant locally.

The reflection on research and science has no sense without thinking *for whom* and *for what*. In other words, professional and critical research should have public and policy moments. Research should find its way between being autonomous as a field and creative as individual and team activities, but also at a service to the society and its economy. As a service that is part of the society. This tension we formulated as opposing the internationalization of research and its relevance to societal needs. Tension does not mean contradiction. Some of our colleagues (Keim *et al.* 2014; Kuhn and Okamoto 2013) are very sensitive to the cognitive and epistemological content of the internationalization of the social science. For us, the internationalization raises fewer problems in terms of incompatibility of the Western concepts that have been forged in specific contexts of the European nation states, than in terms of sociological and institutional environments and challenges influencing researchers in the global south.

The compartmentalization of the research activities, the high degree of fragmentation highlighted in Chapter 5, is directly linked to this tension. For instance, there is an inflation for policy research, especially in the Arab East, at the expense of professional and critical research. Foreign funding promotes a specific type of research that yields direct recommendations to "resolve" some social problem. At the same time, we noticed a weak "public" research, that is research that is directly engaged in debates and exchanges with the wider society, to the point that we suggested in Chapter 9 the demise of public social science. The paradox is that we found a "healthier" situation in the Arab Francophone countries, where we noted a more balanced distribution of social sciences among these four types of social research. Moreover, the importance of "professional" research is a good indicator of a buoyant situation. Nothing being perfect, our Moroccan, Tunisian and Algerian colleagues will probably reject this view. The debate for us is open, it's part of our professional activity to question reflexively the status of our disciplines.

Chapters 6–8 raised the question of language used by researchers in its relationship specifically to social research, but not only this. Authors writing in English refer mainly to English-language literature, and authors writing in Arabic adhere to Arabic literature. Among the reasons explaining this situation we have to mention: lack of proficiency in the respective languages and lack of availability of research literature, mainly among the authors from an Arab institutional background writing in Arabic language. Moreover, some researchers considered Arabic references of little relevance to their subjects of study, or despised their quality. These factors were aggravated by the fact that private institutions "force" Arab academics to write in English and to publish in international journals with a high-impact factor. This circumstance disconnected them from the academic and public debates that were going on in local publications, because they seldom afford the time to write immediate contributions to ongoing debates in the Arab language.

Arab readers demand publication in Arabic not only for empirical research, but also for theory and methodology. This would break from the famous division of labor between peripheral researchers dealing only with the first domain while Western scholars theorize in the social science. To break with this division, two conditions are needed: first, a group of scientists to demand it, as this requires a lot of peer reviewing work; and second, to create such knowledge for the sake of it and not for the sake of professors' promotion.

However, the main difficulty here is that academic institutions, for reasons that are purely institutional, have a tendency to promote departmental journals. These are strongly "endogamic" journals, publishing articles only from the personnel who belong to the university. In very large universities that might make sense, while it is an absolute waste of time in smaller ones. Journals are better defended when they belong to a specific disciplinary group (as scientific associations), focused on some very precise topics or on broader disciplinary areas. Moreover, universities and science councils should defend the popularization of science. A massive effort should be made to create a wider audience for science and innovation by creating lively journals, websites, newspapers, documentaries and other dissemination tools for scientific activities. Citizens should not be kept ignorant of what happens in their own countries in their laboratories, schools and universities.

5 A vision of the future

Finally, in this book we tried to show that the research and innovation activities could only prosper when certain sets of political and general orientations are realized (for more details, see the conclusions of Chapter 3).

First, there is a major need for fixing the broken cycle between research, universities and society. The results of this disconnect have varied depending on the domain of economic, political or social life under consideration. This requires real reform in higher education, recognizing the status of researchers within their universities (the major site of research production in the Arab world) and changing the promotion systems of the academics.

Second, there is a crucial role of the state, making innovation a clearly stated objective of public policy. Additionally, the private sector should invest in R&D. The best strategy, which we found in many spots in the Arab world, would be collaborative work between technical entities (labs, centers, research teams) and companies that wish to develop internal R&D activities.

Third, there is a real need to make research a political topic. The Arab world, through its institutions (League of Arab States and Arab League Educational, Cultural and Scientific Organization – ALECSO) should go beyond a simple discourse into practice to develop a science and technology strategy for the entire Arab region, in coordination with specialized Arab and international bodies.

Fourth, as we cannot really talk about a science "system" in many of the Arab countries, it is perhaps a more apt metaphor to describe the situation of research in most of the Arab countries by the phrasing of *research arrangements*. The image of an "assemblage" of fragile, somewhat disconnected and constantly under-resourced institutions fit better to the reality. Here, we should accept a more diversified model in which multiple national and international actors will enter into play. The most important activity will be to *identify research* within universities and allocate budgets to *stabilize and consolidate teams* as funding should go mainly to teams, not individuals. This should be the result of a publicly recognized mechanism that is accepted by all as a legitimate way to recognize the research units, as the example of Tunisia shows us. Building teams takes time, and it needs to have a certain stability over time. Very short-term research assignments can kill teams, which have to adapt quickly and respond to the offer. Consultancies do bring funding but do not favor team building.

Fifth, research prospers through "linking" strategies and establishing different levels of collaboration in local, regional and international arenas. Alas! Joint projects between Arab scientific research institutions working in similar fields remain extremely rare, particularly within the same country. Sometimes, even the local networking is missing, as in the case of Lebanon (compartmentalization by the use of different languages). Concerning the international collaboration, we may highlight the role the diaspora could play in fostering connection between the place of origin and the place of residence. Outstanding scientific expatriates in developing countries can be temporarily recruited to work or volunteer in their countries of origin, although the experiences do not necessarily have to end. More importantly, we have shown that the research population is quite good at identifying the right resources available internationally. They should be given freedom to manage funds, which is practically impossible today in nearly all Arab universities.

Sixth, there is a real need for more academic journals in the Arab world in all disciplines, but above all in the social sciences as they are culturally situated more than the other sciences. This may facilitate a new profile of researchers who are different from those who *publish globally and perish locally*. However, we have another profile of those who *publish locally and perish globally* and this leads us to a major issue related to the languages used for research and instruction in the universities in the Arab world. Our research clearly reveals that students who learned English through a program that teaches in both English and Arabic in high school or university have published in international and local journals and use the academic references in a more balanced manner than those who learned only in one language, be it Arabic or English. As such, Arabic does not lose its value and the students benefit from foreign references that are characterized for their richness in theories and openness to global debates (see Chapter 7).

Thus, it is not an either–or situation where one language should be chosen for teaching. The focus should be on how to rely on both languages in a transitional phase, giving the Arabic language priority in all departments and programs, not just in social sciences. We stress this phase of transition because if the process of translation of books and journals into Arabic is accelerated and they are made available in public and university libraries and information centers, perhaps there will be no need to teach in any language besides Arabic, while maintaining the necessity for Arab students to learn at least one foreign language.

Finally, let us reiterate that the Arab world has more problems in knowledge use than in knowledge production. Without translating academic research into policy and public awareness, research will be read by few people who constitute an elite that is disconnected from the society and thus does not have an impact on it. Research needs also to be critical of the state, society and microphysics of power, including some religious authorities. In the time when we are concluding our manuscript, the Arab region is going into two different forms of totalitarianism: that of many Arab regimes and that of ISIS. In this context, some Arab academics pay a heavy price. The last one is Emad Shahin, an Egyptian professor of public policy at the American University in Cairo, who was sentenced by a very politicized tribunal (according to many human rights organizations) to death. Many academics signed petitions in his favor, yet his case is so revealing of the lack of the scientific community in the Arab world. No institution has condemned this sentence except for the American Policy Studies Association.

Let us reiterate our initial claim: there will be no important research in the Arab countries without freedom to think, speak and write. As far as research is concerned, it means institutionalizing research, consolidating the scientific community. And this is true whatever the knowledge area, in the natural sciences as well as the social sciences. It includes, of course, opinions on the polity, but it also includes freedom to manage research funds and research teams. Otherwise, the fragments of knowledge will remain just that: fragments of an impossible promise. And important research will be done elsewhere, and far from the actual needs and desires of the Arab population.

Appendices

Total production and international co-authorship

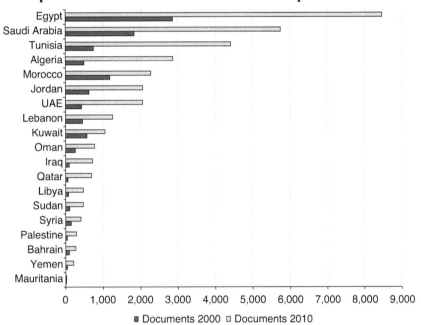

International co-authorship of Arab countries 2000–2010

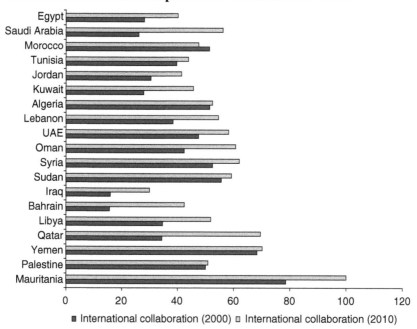

■ International collaboration (2000) □ International collaboration (2010)

Shares by discipline of the whole of Arab region 2000–2010

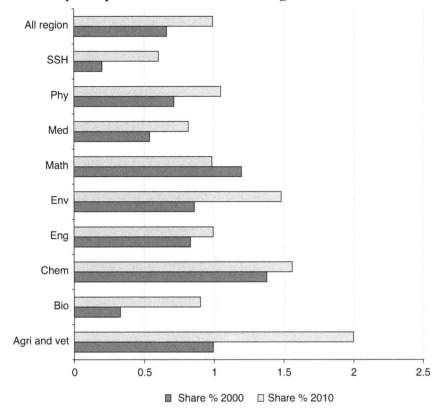

Specialization index of the whole Arab region (2000–2010)

Specialization index = 1 when activity in the domain is similar as the country's activity in the world production; above 1 there is a specialization in the specific domain; below 1 there is less specialization.

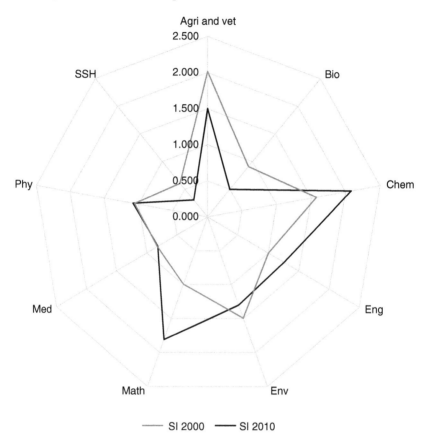

Country shares in each scientific domain (per thousand publications in the discipline)

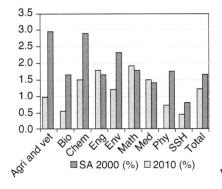

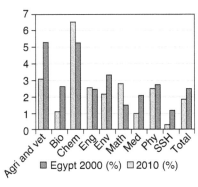

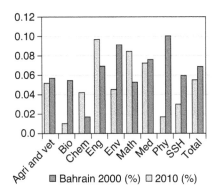

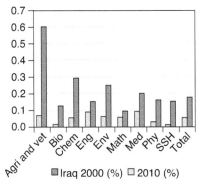

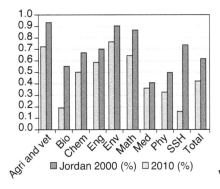

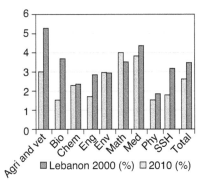

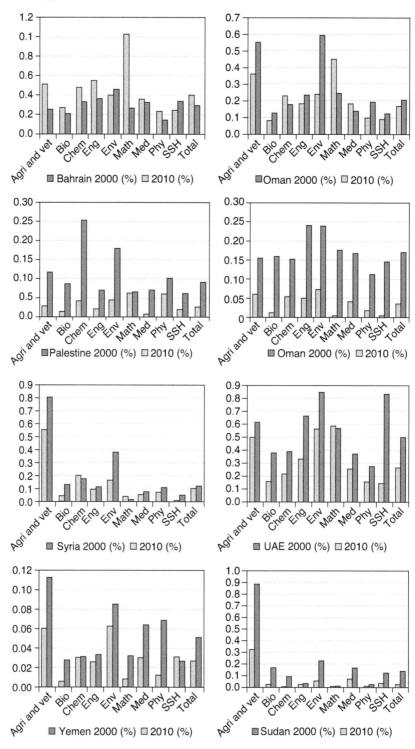

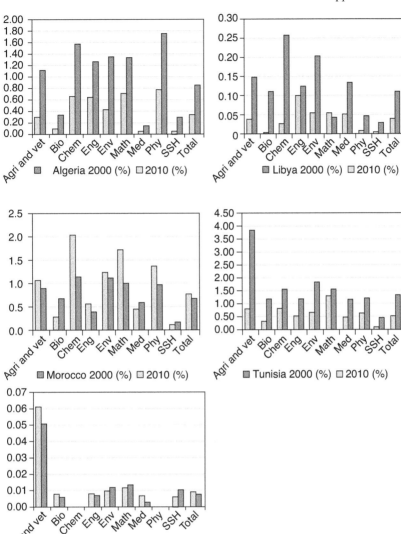

Specialization Index of Arab Countries (2000–2010)

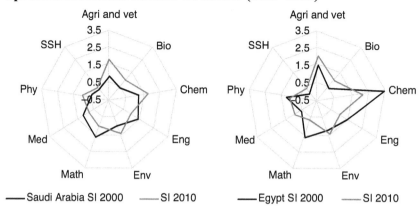

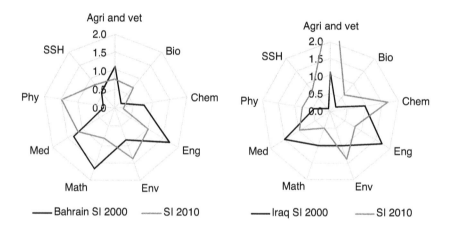

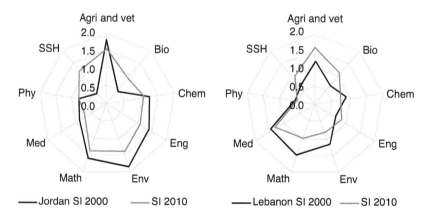

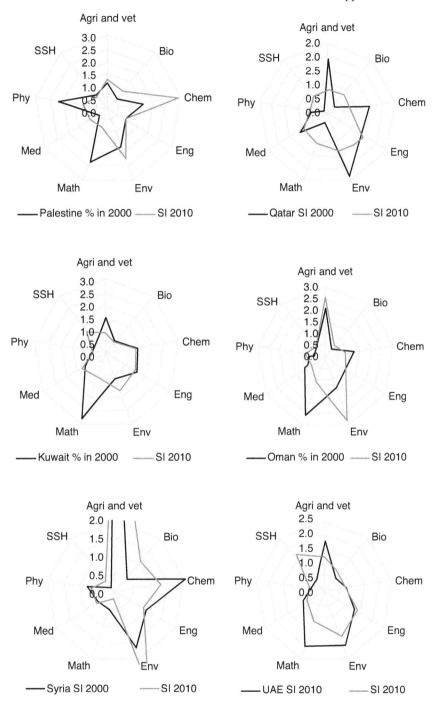

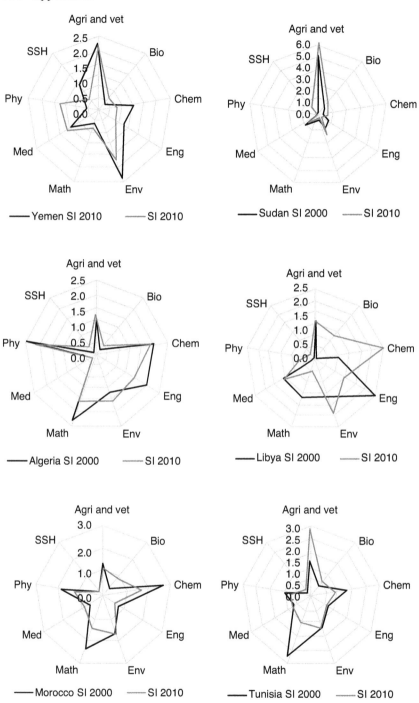

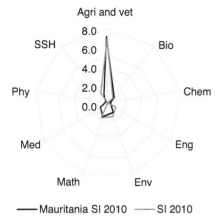

- Mauritania SI 2010 — SI 2010

Bibliography

Abakumov, E., A. Beaulieu, F. Blanchard, *et al.* 2010. "Compter et Mesurer. Le Souci du Nombre dans L'évaluation de la Production Scientifique." http://hal.archives-ouvertes.fr/hal-00533570/fr/.

Abaza, Mona. 2011. "Academic Tourists Sight-Seeing the Arab Spring." *Ahram Weekly*, September. http://english.ahram.org.eg/News/22373.aspx.

Abdel Jabbar, Faleh. 2012. "The Impact of Social Integration in the Process of Revolution And Its Consequences." *Almustaqbal Alarabi*, 398 (in Arabic).

Abdelrahman, M. 2011. "The Transnational and the Local: Egyptian Activists and Transnational Protest Networks." *British Journal of Middle Eastern Studies*, 38 (3): 407–424.

Abou-Rjeily, K. and B. Labaki. 1993. *Review of Wars in Lebanon*. L'Harmattan.

Afandi, Mohammed Ahmed. 2012. "The Impact of Research Centers and Research in Government Decision-Makers: A Special Reference to Yemen." Arab Center for Research and Policy Studies (in Arabic).

Akkari, Abdeljalil. 2009. "Privatising Education in the Maghreb: A Path for Two-Tier Education." In *World Yearbook of Education 2010: Education in the Arab World. Political Projects, Struggles, and Geometries of Power*, André Mazawi and Ronald Sultana, eds., 43–58. New York: Routledge.

Akl, E., *et al.* 2012. "Effects of Assessing the Productivity of Faculty in Academic Medical Centres: A Systematic Review." *Canadian Medical Association Journal*, 184 (11): 602–612.

Al Maktoum Foundation and UNDP. 2009. *Arab Knowledge Report 2009: Towards Productive Intercommunication for Knowledge*. Dubai: Dar al-Gharir.

Al-Adi, Hawari. 2014. "Cognitive Gaps in the Arab Social Science." In *Future of the Sociology in the Arab World*. Beirut: Center for Arab Unity Studies (in Arabic).

Alatas, S.F. 2003. "Academic Dependency and the Global Division of Labour in the Social Sciences." *Current Sociology*, 51 (6): 599–613.

Albion, Small. 2001. *The Cameralists: The Pioneers of German Social Polity*. Canada: Batoche Books.

Al-Khatib, Hayat. 2014. "Towards a Paradigm Shift in Higher Education in the MENA Region." In *Handbook of Research on Higher Education in the MENA Region: Policy and Practice*, Neeta Baporikar ed., 8–29. Hershey, PA: IGI Global.

al-Khazendar, Sami. 2012. "Role of the Research Centers in Decision Making and Policy Orientation in the Arab World." Arab Center for Research and Policy Studies.

al-Lahibi, F.S.M. 2013. *Postion of the Islamic Though Concerning the Western Ideas: The Case of "The End of History"*. Riyad: Taaseel Center.

Alqudsi-ghabra, Taghreed. 2012. "Creative Use of Social Media in the Revolutions of Tunisia, Egypt and Libya." *The International Journal of Interdisciplinary Social Sciences*, 6 (6): 147–158.

Ammon, U. 2010. "The Hegemony of English." In *World Social Sciences Report*, 149–153. Paris: UNESCO.

Ammon, U. 2014. *Arab Knowledge Report 2014: Youth and Localisation of Knowledge*. Dubai: Dar al-Gharir.

Amsden, A.H. 2001. *The Rise of "the Rest": Challenges to the West from Late-Industrializing Economies*. Oxford: Oxford University Press.

Andersson, Thomas and Abdelkader Djeflat, eds. 2013. *The Real Issues of the Middle East and the Arab Spring: Addressing Research, Innovation and Entrepreneurship*. Berlin: Springer.

Antonorsi-Blanco, Marcel, and Ignacio Avalos. 1980. *La Planificación Ilusoria. Ensayo Sobre la Experiencia Venezolana en Política Científica Y Tecnológica*. Caracas: CENDES/Ateneo de Caracas.

Appadurai, A. 2000. "Grassroots Globalization and the Research Imagination." *Public Culture*, 12 (1): 1–19.

Arab Thought Foundation. 2009. *The Second Arab Report for Cultural Development*. Beirut: Arab Thought Foundation.

Arellano Hernández, Antonio, Rigas Arvanitis and Dominique Vinck. 2012. "Global Connexity and Circulation of Knowledge: Aspects of Anthropology of Knowledge in Latin America." *Revue d'Anthropologie des Connaissances*, 6 (2): a–aa.

Arendt, Hannah. 1953. "Understanding and Politics." *Partisan Review*, 20: 377–392.

Arvanitis, Rigas. 2007. *Towards Science and Technology Evaluation in the Mediterranean Countries (ESTIME Final Report)*. Paris: IRD.

Arvanitis, Rigas. 2011a. "La division internationale du travail scientifique: Compte-Rendu d'un dossier édité par Terry Shinn, Dominique Vellard et Roland Waast, Cahiers de la Recherche sur l'Éducation et les Savoirs." *Revue d'Anthropologie des Connaissances*, 5 (3): 635–637.

Arvanitis, Rigas. 2011b. "Que de réseaux! A propos du livre de Caroline Wagner: The New Invisible College." *Revue d'Anthropologie des Connaissances*, 5 (1): 177–184.

Arvanitis, Rigas. 2012. "Euro-Med Cooperation on Research and Innovation." In *Mediterranean Yearbook*, 259–268. Barcelona: IEMED.

Arvanitis, Rigas. 2013. *Industrial Innovation in Lebanon*. Beirut: LCNRS.

Arvanitis, Rigas. 2014. "Où Sont Passés les Intellectuels? Ailleurs que là où Enzo Traverso Regarde." http://rigas.ouvaton.org/spip.php?article534.

Arvanitis, Rigas and Yvon Chatelin. 1988. "National Scientific Strategies in Tropical Soil Sciences." *Social Studies of Science*, 18(1): 113–146.

Arvanitis, Rigas and Jacques Gaillard. 1992. *Science Indicators in Developing Countries: Proceedings of the International Conference on Science Indicators in Developing Countries*. Paris: ORSTOM/CNRS, UNESCO. http://horizon.documentation.ird.fr/.

Arvanitis, Rigas and Hatem M'henni. 2010. "Monitoring Research and Innovation Policies in the Mediterranean Region." *Science Technology & Society*, 15 (2): 233–269.

Arvanitis, Rigas, Roland Waast, and Abeld Hamid Al Husban. 2010. "Les Sciences Sociales dans le Monde Arabe." In *World Social Science Report*. Paris: UNESCO.

Arvanitis, Rigas *et al.* 2012. "La Science au Service de la Puissance." In *L'Atlas du Monde Diplomatique*, 70–73. Paris: Le Monde Diplomatique/Vuibert.

Arvanitis, Rigas, Alain Gallochat and Arturo Menéndez. 2012. *Mécanismes incitatifs pour encourager le secteur privé à investir dans la R&D au Maroc (rapports de mission mai 2012, septembre 2012 et synthèse)*. Paris & Rabat: Jumelage institutionnel Maroc & France-Espagne.

Arvanitis, Rigas, Rafael Rodriguez, and A. Hamid Zoheiry. 2013a. "The Policy Framework of Euro-Med Cooperation on Research and Innovation; Effects on Research Collaborations." In *Moving to the Future in the Euro-Mediterranean Research and Innovation Partnership: The Experience of the MIRA Project*, Ch. Morini, R. Rodriguez, R. Arvanitis and R. Chaabouni, eds. Paris: CIHEAM. http://om.ciheam.org/option.php?IDOM=1009.

Arvanitis, Rigas, Rula Atweh and Hatem M'henni. 2013b. "Assessing International Scientific Cooperation in the Mediterranean Region: An International Challenge Ahead." In *Moving to the Future in the Euro-Mediterranean Research and Innovation Partnership: The Experience of the MIRA Project*, Chiara Morini, Rafael Rodriguez, Rigas Arvanitis and Refaat Chaabouni, eds. Paris: CIHEAM. http://om.ciheam.org/option.php?IDOM=1009.

Arvanitis, R., S. Hanafi and A. Pancera. 2014. *Funding Research: Research Granting Councils and Funds in the Middle East and North Africa (MENA). Scoping Study*. Beirut: Report for IDRC, American University of Beirut and Institut de Recherche pour le Développement.

Assad, Jamal. 2007. La recherche: développement et l'innovation dans les entreprises marocaines – déterminants et impact à partir de l'enquête nationale sur la R&D et l'Innovation. Mémoire. DESA Econométrie, Université Hassan II, Casablanca.

Badran, Adnan, and Moneef R. Zou'bi. 2010. "UNESCO World Science Report: Arab States." In *UNESCO World Science Report*. Paris: UNESCO

Balqziz, A. 1999. *The End of the Advocator*. Beirut: Markaz al-Thaqafi al-Arabi (in Arabic).

Balqaziz, A. 2011. *The Francophone Ideology: Challenging Cultural-Linguistic Policies*. Beirut: Center for the Study of Arab Unity (in Arabic).

Bamyeh, M. 2012. "Anarchist Philosophy, Civic Traditions and the Culture of Arab Revolutions." *Middle East Journal of Culture and Communication*, 5: 32–41.

Baqader, Abu-Baker and Hassan Rachiq. 2012. *Anthropology in the Arab World*. Amman: Dar al-Fiker (in Arabic).

Barré, Rémi. 2001. "Policy Making Making Processes and Evaluation Tools : S&T Indicators." In *Science and Technology Policy*, Rigas Arvanitis, ed. Oxford: EOLSS Publishers and UNESCO. www.eolss.net

Bashshur, Mounir. 2006. "Standards of Quality of Higher Education in Lebanon." In *L'enseignement Supérieur dans le Monde Arabe : une Question de Niveau?*, Mounir Bashshur, Youssef Courbage and Joseph Labaki, eds. Beyrouth: Institut Français du Proche-Orient.

Bayat, Asef. 2010. *Life as Politics: How Ordinary People Change the Middle East*. Stanford, CA: Stanford University Press.

Bayat, Asef. 2013a. "The Arab Spring and Its Surprises." *Development and Change*, 44 (3): 587–601.

Bayat, Asef. 2013b. *Post-Islamism: The Changing Faces of Political Islam*. Oxford: Oxford University Press.

Bechara, Joseph and Jacques Kabbanji. 2006. "Rapport sur l'état des sciences exactes au Liban." Background report for ESTIME.

Beigel, Fernanda. 2011. *The Politics of Academic Autonomy in Latin America: Public Intellectuals and the Sociology of Knowledge*. Farnham: Ashgate.

Beigel, Fernanda and Hanan Sabea, eds. 2014. *Dependencia académica y profesionalización en el sur: Perspectivas desde la periferia*. Mendoza, Argentina: Editorial Universidad Nacional del Cuyo.

Bellin, E. 2012. "Reconsidering the Robustness of Authoritarianism in the Middle East." *Comparative Politics*, 44(2): 127–149.

Benguerna, M. 2011. *Les sciences sociales en Algérie: genèse et pratique*. Alger: CREAD.

Beydoun, Ahmad. 2013. "Socialist Lebanon: The Emergence of a Group of the 'New Left' Youth and Its Trajectory in the Sixties." *Kalamon*, 8.

Binder, Leonard. 1976. "Area Studies: A Critical Reassessment." In *The Study of the Middle East: Research and Scholarship in the Humanities and the Social Sciences*, Leonard Binder, ed. New York: Wiley.

Bironneau. R. 2012. *China Innovation Inc. Des politiques industrielles aux entreprises innovantes*. Paris: Presses de Sciences Po.

Bishara, Marwan. 2004. "Writing International Development: The Op-Ed Page." *Signs*, 29: 564–569.

Blaydes, L. and J. Lo. 2012. "One Man, One Vote, One Time? A Model of Democratization in the Middle East." *Journal of Theoretical Politics*, 24 (1): 110–146.

Blondel, V.D., J.L. Guillaume, R. Lambiotte and E. Lefebvre. 2008. "Fast Unfolding of Communities in Large Networks." *Journal of Statistical Mechanics: Theory and Experiment*, 10..

Boekholt, Patries, Jakob Edler, Paul Cunningham and Kieron Flanagan, eds. 2009. *Drivers of International Collaboration in Research: Final Report*. Luxembourg: European Commission, DG Research, International Cooperation.

Bond, Michael, Heba Maram, Asmaa Soliman, and Riham Khattab. 2012. *Science and Innovation in Egypt*. London: The Royal Society.

Bouhdiba, Abdelwahab. 1970. "La sociologie du développement africain." *Current Sociology*, 16 (2).

Bourdieu, P. 1984. *Homo Academicus*. Paris: Minuit.

Bourdieu, Pierre, *et al.* 1973. *Le métier de sociologue: préalables épistémologique*. Paris and The Hague: Mouton.

Bowker, Geoffrey C. 1992. "What's in a Patent ?" In *Shaping Society/Building Technology*, W.E. Bijker and J. Law, eds., 53–74. Cambridge, MA: MIT Press.

Bowker, Geoffrey C. 2001. "The New Knowledge Economy and Science and Technology Policy." In *Science and Technology Policy: A Section of the Encyclopedia of Life Support Systems (online)*, Rigas Arvanitis, ed. Oxford: EOLSS Publishers and UNESCO. www.eolss.net.

Brandt, E. and Pope, A.M., eds. 1997. *Enabling America: Assessing the Role of Rehabilitation Science and Engineering*. Washington, DC: National Academy Press.

Bristol-Rhys, Jane. 2008. "The Dilemna of Gender-Separated Higher Education in the United Arab Emirates." In *Higher Education in the Gulf States*, C. Davidson and P. Mackenzie Smith, eds. London: London Middle East Institute at SOAS.

Brownlee, J. 2007. *Authoritarianism in an Age of Democratization*. New York: Cambridge University Press.

Brownlee, J., Masoud, T. and Reynolds, A. 2012. *After the Awakening: Revolt, Reform, and Renewal in the Arab World*. Oxford: Oxford University Press.

Brumberg, D. 1990. "An Arab Path to Democracy?" *Journal of Democracy*, 1 (4): 120–125.

Burawoy, Michael. 2005. "For Public Sociology." *American Sociological Review*, 70 (1): 4–28.

Burawoy, Michael. 2014. "Preface." In *Global Knowledge Production in the Social Sciences: Made in Circulation*, W. Keim, E. Çelik and V. Wöhrer, eds. Farnham: Ashgate.

Burgat, François. 2010. "Un changement Islamiste dans la continuité: salafistes contre Frères Musulmans." *Le Monde Diplomatique*, June.

Callon, M., P. Laredo and P. Mustar, eds. 1997. *The Strategic Management of Research and Technology. The Evaluation of Research Programmes*. Paris: Economica.

Calvet, J.L. 1987. *La guerre des langues et les politiques linguistiques*. Paris: Payot

Camau, Michel. 2012. "Un printemps arabe ? L'émulation protestataire et ses limites." *L'Année du Maghreb*, 8: 23–43.

Campbell, D., M. Picard-Aitken, G. Côté, *et al.* 2010. "Bibliometrics as a Performance Measurement Tool for Research Evaluation: The Case of Research Funded by the National Cancer Institute of Canada." *American Journal of Evaluation*, 31 (1): 66–83.

Caswill, C. 2005. "Whose Agency? Looking Forward to the Virtual Research Council." *Information, Communication & Society*, 8 (1): 1–29.

Center for Mediterranean Integration. 2013. *Transforming Arab Economies: Traveling the Knowledge and Innovation Road*. Marseille: CMI, World Bank, EIB and ISESCO. www.cmimarseille.org/ke.

Chen, C. 1999. "Visualising Semantic Spaces and Author Co-citation Networks in Digital Libraries." *Information Processing & Management*, 35 (3): 401–420.

Chen, Derek H.C. and Carl J. Dahlman. 2005. "The Knowledge Economy, the KAM Methodology and World Bank Operations." World Bank. http://siteresources.world-bank.org/KFDLP/Resources/KAM_Paper_WP.pdf.

Cherkaoui, Mohammed. 2008. M. Cherkaoui: Les décideurs sont dans le flou. *"Economia."* www.economia.ma/fr/numero-02/e-revue/m-cherkaoui-les-decideurs-sont-dans-le-flou.

Chiha, Michel. 1980. *Politique intérieure*. Beirut: Editions du Trident.

Chikhani Nacouz, Léla. 1996. "L'entre-Deux Fascinant Propos Sur Une Pratique." *Bahithat*, 153–175.

Cohen, Shana. 2014. "Neoliberalism and Academia in Morocco." *British Journal of Middle Eastern Studies*, 41 (1): 28–42.

Connell, R. 2009. "Peripheral Visions: Beyond the Metropole." In *Globalizing the Research Imagination*, Jane Kenway and Johannah Fahey, eds., 53–72. London: Routledge.

Cordero, Cynthia, R. Delino, L. Jeyaseelan, *et al.* 2008. "Funding Agencies in Low- and Middle-Income Countries: Support for Knowledge Translation." *Bulletin of the World Health Organization*, 86 (7): 524–534.

Crane, D. 1972. *Invisible Colleges: Diffusion of Knowledge in Scientific Communities*. Chicago, IL and London: University of Chicago Press.

Dabbous, Yasmine T. 2010. "Media with a Mission: Why Fairness and Balance are Not Priorities in Lebanon's Journalistic Codes." *International Journal of Communication*, 4: 719–737.

Dabbous-Sensenig, Dima. 2000. "Media Versus Society in Lebanon: Schizophrenia in an Age of Globalization." *Media Development*, 47 (3): 14–17.

Dajani, Nabil. 1992. *Disoriented Media in a Fragmented Society: The Lebanese Experience*. Beirut: American University of Beirut Press.

Da'na, S. 2011. "The Mismeasure of Arabs: Culture and Revolution." *The Arab World Geographer/Le Géographe du Monde Arab*, 14(2): 145–152.

Debailly, R. 2010. *Les classements et les indicateurs dans la gouvernance de l'enseignement supérieur et de la Recherche*. Paris: Université Paris Est, France.

Debailly, R. and C. Pin. 2012. "Quels impacts des dispositifs d'évaluation sur la recherche universitaire ?" *Cahiers de la Recherche sur l'éducation et les Savoirs*, 11: 11–32.

Dennis, M. Aaron. 1987. "Accounting for Research: New Histories of Corporate Laboratories and the Social History of American Science." *Social Studies of Science*, 17 (3): 479–518.

Dessa, Hasnaa, and Mohamed-Sghir Janjar. 2010. *A Study of the Current State of Arabic Translation of Human and Social Sciences (2000–2009)*. Paris and Casablanca: Transeuropéennes and Fondation du Roi Abdul Aziz. www.transeuropeennes.eu/ressources/pdfs/TiM2010_HSS_Arab_world_Hasnaa_DESSA_Mohamed_Sghir_JANJAR_38.pdf.

Diamond, L. 2010a. "Why are there no Arab Democracies?" *Journal of Democracy*, 21 (1): 93–112.

Diamond, L. 2010b. "Liberation Technology." *Journal of Democracy*, 21(3): 71–83.

Dreher, A. 2006. "Does Globalization Affect Growth? Evidence from a New Index of Globalization." *Applied Economics*, 38 (10): 1091–1110.

Dreher, A., G. Gaston and P. Martens. 2008. *Measuring Globalisation: Gauging Its Consequences*. New York: Springer.

Drouin, Gilles. 1998. "Science et médias: un mariage réussi." *Le Magazine de l'Université du Québec*, 30 (2). www.uquebec.ca/mag/mag98_10/report.html.

Dubar, Claude. 2006. *Faire de la sociologie: un parcours d'enquêtes*. Paris: Belin.

Dumont, J and G. Lemaître. 2005. *Counting Immigrants and Expatriates: A New Perspective*. Paris: OECD, Direction du travail, de l'emploi et des affaires sociales.

Dumortier, Brigitte. 2008. "La société de la connaissance dans une perspective arabe." *Maghreb-Machrek* Printemps 2008, n°195: 13–20

Dutta, S., ed. 2012. *The Global Innovation Index 2012. Stronger Innovation Linkages for Global Growth*. New Delhi: INSEAD and World Intellectual Property Organization.

Economist, The. 2015. "Top of the Class." 28 March. www.economist.com/news/special-report/21646987-competition-among-universities-has-become-intense-and-international-top-class?frsc=dg%7Ca.

El-Amine, Adnan. 1998. "Lebanese University in the Shadow of Acute Sectarianism." *Al-Muraqib*, 2 (in Arabic).

El-Ghobashy, M. 2011. "The Praxis of the Egyptian Revolution." *Middle East Report* 41(258): 2–13.

El-Jardali, F., J.N. Lavis, N. Ataya and D. Jamal. 2012. "Use of Health System and Policy Research Evidence in the Health Policy-Making in Eastern Mediterranean Countries: Views and Practices of Researchers." *Implementation Science*, 7 (1): 2.

El-Kenz, Ali. 2005a. *Les Sciences Sociales dans les Pays Arabes*. Bondy: IRD – Projet ESTIME. www.estime.ird.fr/article50.html.

El-Kenz, Ali. 2005b. "Al-Ulum Al-Ijtimayaa Fi Al-'alam Al-Arabi (Social Sciences in the Arab World)." *Idafat: The Arab Journal of Sociology*, special: 17–48.

El-Kenz, Ali and Roland Waast. 1997. "Sisyphus or the Scientific Communities in Algeria." In *Scientific Communities in the Developing World*, J. Gaillard, V.V. Krishna, and R. Waast, eds., 53–80. London and New Delhi: Sage.

El-Kenz, Ali and Roland Waast, eds. 2013. *Sciences, techniques et sociétés (Actes de la rencontre d'Annaba, 25–30/5/91)*. Alger: ENAC Editeur.

Enzo Traverso. 2013. *Où sont passés les intellectuels?*. Paris: Textuel.

Erdem, B.K. 2012. "Adjustment of the Secular Islamist Role Model (Turkey) to the 'Arab Spring': The Relationship Between the Arab Uprisings and Turkey in the Turkish and World Press." *Islam and Christian Muslim Relations*, 23 (4): 435–452.

Ernst, Richard. 2010. "The Follies of Citation Indices and Academic Ranking Lists." *CHIMIA International Journal for Chemistry*, 64: 90.

ESCWA. 1998. *Research and Development Systems in the Arab States: Development of Science and Technology Indicators*. Cairo: UNESCO.

ESCWA. 2014. *Arab Integration: A 21st Century Development Imperative*. Beirut: ESCWA.

ESTIME. 2007. *Towards Science and Technology Evaluation in the Mediterranean Countries (Final Report by R. Arvanitis)*. Paris: IRD and ESTIME. www.estime.ird.fr/article242.html.

European Commission. 2010. *Assessing Europe's University-Based Research*. Luxembourg: Expert Group on Assessment of University-Based Research.

Faour, M. 1998. *The Silent Revolution in Lebanon: Changing Values of the Youth*. Beirut: American University of Beirut.

Favier, Agnès. 2004. *Logiques de l'engagement et modes de contestation au Liban. Genèse et éclatement d'une génération de militants intellectuels (1958–1975)*. Aix-en-Provence: Université Paul Cézanne Aix-Marseille III.

Findlow, Sally. 2005. "International Networking in the United Arab Emirates Higher Education System: Global–Local Tensions." *Compare*, 35 (3): 285–302.

Florida, Richard. 2014. *The Rise of the Creative Class–Revisited: Revised and Expanded*. New York: Basic Books.

Frenken, Koen, Jarno Hoekman and Sjoerd Hardeman. 2010. "The Globalization of Research Collaboration." In *World Social Sciences Report*, 144–148. Paris: UNESCO. http://unesdoc.unesco.org/images/0018/001883/188333e.pdf.

Friedman, Thomas. 2005. *The World is Flat: A Brief History of the Twenty-First Century*. New York: Farrar, Straus and Giroux.

Gabsi, Foued, Hatem M'henni and Karim Koouba. 2008. "Innovation Determinants in Emerging Countries: An Empirical Study at the Tunisian Firms Level." *International Journal of Technological Learning, Innovation and Development*, 3 (3): 205–225.

Gaillard, Anne-Marie, Jacques Gaillard, Jane M. Russell, *et al.* 2013. "Drivers and Outcomes of S&T International Collaboration Activities: A Case Study of Biologists from Argentina, Chile, Costa Rica, Mexico and Uruguay." In *Research Collaborations between Europe and Latin America: Mapping and Understanding Partnership*, Jacques Gaillard and Rigas Arvanitis, eds., 151–186. Paris: Editions des Archives Contemporaines.

Gaillard, Jacques. 1994. "The Behaviour of Scientists and Scientific Communities." In *The Uncertain Quest: Science, Technology, and Development*, Jean-Jacques Salomon, Francisco Sagasti and Céline Sachs-Jeantet, eds., 213–249. Tokyo, New York and Paris: UNU Press. http://unu.edu/unupress/unupbooks/uu09ue/uu09ue00.htm#Contents.

Gaillard, Jacques. 2007. *Evaluation of Scientific, Technology and Innovation Capabilities in Lebanon*. Paris: IRD. www.estime.ird.fr/IMG/pdf/JGLebanonFinal28Sept_ar7.pdf.

Gaillard, Jacques. 2010a. "Measuring Research and Development in Developing Countries: Main Characteristics and Implications for the Frascati Manual." *Science, Technology & Society*, 15 (1): 77–111.

Gaillard, Jacques. 2010b. "Science and Technology in Lebanon: A University-Driven Activity." *Science, Technology & Society*, 15 (2): 271–307.

Gaillard, Jacques. 2014. "Research Granting Councils and Funds in Morocco." Submitted to IDRC.

Gaillard, Jacques and Rigas Arvanitis, eds. 2013. *Research Collaborations between Europe and Latin America: Mapping and Understanding Partnership*. Paris: Editions des Archives Contemporaines.

Gaillard, Jacques and Anne Marie Gaillard. 2003. "Can the Scientific Diaspora Save African Science?" *SciDev.Net*. www.scidev.net/index.cfm?originalUrl=global/migra-tion/opinion/can-the-scientific-diaspora-save-african-science.html.

Gaillard, Jacques and Bernard Schlemmer. 1996. "Chercheurs du Nord, chercheurs du Sud: itinéraires, pratiques, modèles." In *Les Sciences au Sud. Etat des lieux*, Roland Waast, ed., 113–135. Paris: ORSTOM.

Gaillard, Jacques, V.V. Krishna and Roland Waast, eds. 1997a. *Scientific Communities in the Developing World*. New Delhi & London: Sage.

Gaillard, Jacques, V.V. Krishna and Roland Waast. 1997b. "Scientific Communities in the Developing World." In *Scientific Communities in the Developing World*, Jacques Gaillard, V.V. Krishna and Roland Waast, eds., 11–49. London and New Delhi: Sage.

Garfield, Eugene. 1996. "The Significant Literature Appears in a Small Core of Journals." *The Scientist* 10 (September). www.the-scientist.com/?articles.view/articleNo/18038/title/The-Significant-Scientific-Literature-Appears-In-A-Small-Core-Of-Journals.

Gérard, Etienne. 2008. *Mobilités étudiantes Sud-Nord: trajectoires scolaires de Maro-cains en France et insertion professionnelle au Maroc*. Paris: Publisud.

Gérard, Etienne and Mina Kleiche. 2002. *Les sciences humaines et sociales au Maroc: repères sur leur composition et production*. Rabat: Centre Jacques Berque & Institut de Recherche pour le Développement.

Gérard, Etienne and Mina Kleiche-Dray. 2009. "La revue scientifique : un élément d'analyse des sciences humaines et sociales." *African Sociological Review* 13 (1). www.ajol.info/index.php/asr/article/view/57757/46126.

Ghafoor, Abdul, Humam Abdul Khaliq and Abdel Halim alhajaj, eds. 2009. *Strategic Nuclear Program in Iraq as Part of Science and Technology Policy*. Center for Arab Unity Studies (in Arabic).

Ghattas, Kim. 1999. *Expatriates on the Move Home, Sweet Home* (Report for Tokten pro-gramme). Retrieved from www.tokten.com/employ.htm.

Gieryn, Thomas. 1995. "Boundaries of Science." In *Handbook of Science and Techno-logy Studies*, Sheila Jasanoff, Gerald E. Markle, James C. Petersen and Trevor Pinch, eds., 398–443. London and New Delhi: Sage.

Gingras, Yves. 2008. "La fièvre de l'évaluation de la recherche. Du mauvais usage de faux indicateurs." CIRST. Retrieved from www.cirst.uqam.ca.

Gingras, Yves and Sébastien Mosbah-Natanson. 2010. "Where are Social Sciences Pro-duced?" In *World Social Sciences Report*, 149–153. Paris: UNESCO. http://unesdoc.unesco.org/images/0018/001883/188333e.pdf.

Gladwell, Malcolm. 2006. *The Tipping Point: How Little Things Can Make a Big Differ-ence*. Boston, MA: Little, Brown.

Glänzel, Wolfgang. 1996. "A Bibliometric Approach to Social Sciences: National Research Performance in 6 Selected Social Science Areas, 1990–1992." *Scientomet-rics*, 35 (3): 291–307.

Godin, Benoît. 2005. *Measurement and Statistics on Science and Technology: 1920 to the Present*. London and New York: Routledge.

Golan, Guy J. 2010. "Op-Ed Columns Frame Medical Marijuana Debate." *Newspaper Research Newspaper*, 31 (3): 50–61.

Goudineau, Yves. 1990. "Etre excellent sans être pur: potentiel technologique et pouvoir technocratique à Singapour." *Cahier des Sciences Humaines*, 26 (3): 379–405.

Grossetti, Michel, Denis Eckert, Laurent Jégou, Marion Maisonobe, Yves Gingras and Vincent Larivière. 2013. "La diversification des espaces de production du savoir."

CERISCOPE Puissance, 2013, [en Ligne], consulté le 18/03/2015, http://ceriscope.sciences-po.fr/puissance/content/part2/la-diversification-des-espaces-de-production-du-savoir.

Guedjali, Assia. 2011. "L'enseignement des sciences économiques en Algérie: entre croyances et réalités." In *Les sciences sociales en Algérie: genèse et pratique*, Mohamed Benguerna, ed., 27–46. Alger: CREAD.

Hage, Ghassan. 2013. "The Social Sciences and the Two Critiques." *Bidayyat*, 6: 12–24 (in Arabic).

Hammam, Abdul Khaliq and Abdel Halim alhajaj, eds. 2014. *Higher Education Strategy in Iraq as Part of Science and Technology Policy*. Baghdad: Al-ayyam (in Arabic).

Hanafi, Sari. 2007. "Impact of Western Funding System on Social Sciences' Research in the Arab East: The Dilemma of the Research Centers External to Universities." Background report presented to the project ESTIME, 13 July.

Hanafi, Sari. 2008. "Virtual and Real Returns." In *Crossing Borders, Shifting Boundaries: Palestinian Dilemmas*, Sari Hanafi, ed. Cairo: American University in Cairo Press.

Hanafi, Sari. 2009. "Palestinian Sociological Production: Funding and National Considerations." In *International Handbook of Diverse Sociological Traditions*, Sujata Patel, ed. London: Sage.

Hanafi, Sari. 2010. "Donor Community and the Market of Research Production: Framing and De-Framing the Social Sciences." In *Facing an Unequal World: Challenges from Sociology*, Michael Burawoy, Mau-Kuei Chang, and Michelle Fei-Yu Hsieh, eds., 3–35. Taipei: International Association of Sociology.

Hanafi, Sari. 2011. "University Systems in the Arab East: Publish Globally and Perish Locally Vs. Publish Locally and Perish Globally." *Current Sociology*, 59 (3): 291–309.

Hanafi, S. 2012. "The Arab Revolutions: The Emergence of a New Political Subjectivity." *Contemporary Arab Affairs*, 5 (2): 198–213.

Hanafi, Sari and Rigas Arvanitis. 2013a. *The Broken Cycle between Research, University and Society in Arab Countries: Proposals for Change*. Beirut: ESCWA, CNRS, and IRD. http://etc-un.org/PR/Default.aspx?ln=1&pid=4860&pvr=0.

Hanafi, Sari and Rigas Arvanitis. 2013b. *Strengths and Weaknesses of Science and Technology Institutions in the Arab Countries (SWOT Analysis)*. Beirut: AUB & IRD, http://etc-un.org/PR/Default.aspx?ln=1&pid=4864&pvr=0.

Hanafi, S. and R. Arvanitis. 2014. "The Marginalization of the Arab Language in Social Science: Structural Constraints and Dependency by Choice." *Current Sociology*, 62 (5): 723–742.

Hanafi, Sari, Rigas Arvanitis and Justine Baer. 2013. "Internationalization of Research in Lebanon: The Case of the American University of Beirut." In *Spatial Social Thoughts in Global Knowledge Encounters*, Michael Kuhn, ed., 167–197. Stuttgart: IBIDEM.

Hannoyer, Jean. 1996. "De la recherche en général, au CERMOC en particulier." *Bahithat*, 3: 394–405.

Harb, A. 1996. *Illusions of the Elite or Criticism of the Intellectuals*. Beirut: Markaz al-Thaqafi al-Arabi (in Arabic).

Harsch, E. 2012. "An African Spring in the Making: Protest and Voice Across a Continent." *The Whitehead Journal of Diplomacy and International Relations*, 12 (1): 45–61.

Henriques, L. and P. Larédo. 2013. "Policy-making in Science Policy: The 'OECD Model' Unveiled." *Research Policy*, 42 (3): 801–816.

Herrera, Amilcar O. 1971. *Ciencia y política en América latina*. México: Siglo XXI.

Herrera, Linda, and Asef Bayat. 2010. *Being Young and Muslim: New Cultural Politics in the Global South and North*. Oxford: Oxford University Press.

Herzfeld, Michael. 1982. *Ours Once More: Folklore, Ideology and the Making of Modern Greece*. Austin, TX: University of Texas Press.

Hibou, B. 2011. *The Force of Obedience*. Cambridge, MA: Polity Press.

Hibou, B., H. Meddeb and M. Hamdi. 2011. *Tunisia after 14 January and its Social and Political Economy*. Copenhagen: Euro-Mediterranean Human Rights Network.

Hicks, Diana M. and Sylvan J. Katz. 1996. "Where is Science Going?" *Science, Technology & Human Values*, 21 (4): 379–406.

Hicks, Diana, Paul Wouters, Ludo Waltman, Sarah de Rijcke and Ismael Rafols. 2015. "The Leiden Manifesto for Research Metrics." *Nature* 520: 429–431.

Hitti, J. 2011. "Arabic and the Politics of Language, Language, Culture, and the Role of the Interpreter," 15th Annual Conference of the New England Translators Association, May 7, 2011, Boston. http://sslinguafranca.wordpress.com/2011/12/08/arabic-and-the-politics-of-language/

Hotayt, Fadia. 1996. "The Guidelines of Research Governing University Theses in Psychology." *Bahithat*, 3: 24–41.

Houssay-Holzschuch, M. and O. Milhaud. 2013. "Geography after Babel: A View from the French Province." *Geographica Helvetica*, 1: 1–5.

Hsaini, Abderraouf. 2007. *Le système national d'innovation et de recherche en Tunisie: Un essai de caractérisation et d'évaluation du rôle des centres techniques*. Grenoble: Background research documents, ESTIME project.

Ibrahim, Saadaldine. 2012. "Factors in the Rise of the Arab Revolutions." *Almustaqbal Alarabi*, 399 (in Arabic).

IFI. 2011. *Public Policy & Research in the Arab World: Pre & Post Uprising. Report of the First Meeting of the CAPRI (Consortium of Arab Policy Research Institutes)*. Beirut: Issam Fares Institute.

IFI-CAPRI. 2014. "A Preliminary Overview of Policy Research Institutes in the Arab World: A Compilation and Synthesis Report." www.aub.edu.lb/ifi/public_policy/rapp/Documents/20140331ifi_RAPP_monograph.pdf.

IFPO. 2007. *Répertoire des chercheurs et répertoire des centres de recherche Liban/Syrie/Jordanie. Projet ESTIME*. Beyrouth: Institut Français du Proche-Orient.

Inkster, Ian. 1991. *Science and Technology in History: An Approach to Indusrial Development*. London: Macmillan.

INSEAD and S. Dutta, eds., 2012. *The Global Innovation Index 2012: Stronger Innovation Linkages for Global Growth*. Paris: INSEAD

INSEAD, S. Duta, B. Lanvin and S. Wunsch-Vincent, eds., 2014. *The Global Innovation Index 2014: The Human Factor in Innovation*. Paris: INSEAD

Jacques, Jean. 1990. *L'imprévu ou la science des objets trouvés*. Paris: Editions Odile Jacob.

Jenkins, Carol. 2008. "Voices Too Often Missing in Op-Ed Land: Women's." *The Christian Science Monitor*, July.

Ju'eit, Hisham. 2001. *Crisis of Islamic Culture*. Beirut: Dar al-Tali'a.

Juma, Calestous and Yee-Cheong Lee, eds., 2005. *Innovation: Applying Knowledge in Development*. London: Earthscan, UN Millenium Project, Task Force on Science, Technology and Innovation.

Kabbanji, Jacques. 2005. "kiyfa Taqra' Al-Intaj Al-Sociologi Al-Arabi (How to Read the Arab Sociological Production)." *Idafat: The Arab Journal of Sociology*, special issue: 59–88.

Kabbanji, Jacques. 2007. *L'innovation au Liban: structures, institutions, apports et limites*. Beirut: ESTIME.

Kabbanji, Jacques. 2010. *Rechercher au Liban: communautés scientifiques, chercheurs et innovation.* Beyrouth: Publications du Centre de Recherche de l'Institut des sciences sociales de l'université libanaise.

Kabbanji, Jacques. 2011. "Why Do the Arab Uprisings in Tunisia and Egypt Surprise Us?" *Idafat: The Arab Journal of Sociology,* 14 (in Arabic).

Kabbanji, Jacques. 2012. "Heurs et malheurs du système universitaire libanais à l'heure de l'homogénéisation et de la marchandisation de l'enseignement supérieur." *Revue des Mondes Musulmans et de la Méditerranée,* 131: 127–145.

Kabbanji, Jacques. 2014. "The 'Internationalization' of Social Sciences as an 'Obstacle' to Understanding the Ongoing Arab Revolts." *Contemporary Arab Affairs,* 7 (1): 115–124

Kabbanji, J. and A. Moussaoui. 2007. *Rapport sur l'état des sciences sociales et sciences exactes au Liban.* Beirut: ESTIME.

KACST. 2012. *Annual Report of King Abdulaziz City for Science and Technology (2012).* Retrieved from www.kacst.edu.sa/en/about/Pages/default.aspx

Kadri, Ali. 2014. *Arab Development Denied: Dynamics of Accumulation by Wars of Encroachment.* London and New York: Anthem Press.

Kamal Wahbeh. 2010. "Kamel Assad and the Identity in Crisis." *Alnahar,* March (in Arabic).

Kasparian, Choghig. 2006. *Le devenir des diplômés de l'Université Saint-Joseph 2000–2004: Enquête réalisée en 2005.* Beyrouth: Observatoire universitaire de la réalité socio-économique, Presses de l'USJ.

Kasparian, Chohig. 2003. *L'entrée des jeunes dans la vie active et l'émigration des Libanais, depuis 1975.* Beyrouth: Observatoire universitaire de la réalité socio-économique, Université St-Joseph.

Kassem, Abdel Hai. 2012. "Common Features of the Arab Systems and Dealing with the Variable of Revolution." *Almustaqbal Alarabi,* 399 (in Arabic).

Kassir, Samir. 2004. *Considérations sur le malheur arabe.* Paris: Actes Sud.

Katz, J. Sylvan and Ben R. Martin. 1997. "What is Research Collaboration?" *Research Policy,* 26 (1): 1–18.

Kawtharani, Wajih. 1976. *The Social and Political Trends in Mount Lebanon and Arab Mashreq: 1860–1920 (Al-Ittijihat al-ijtima'iyya al-siyasiyya fi Jabal Lubnan wa al-mashriq al-'arabi, 1860–1920).* Beirut: Beirut Arab Development Institute.

Kawtharani, Wajih. 1996. "The Historian within the University and Outside." *Bahithat,* 3.

Keim, Wiebke. 2008. "Social Sciences Internationally: The Problem of Marginalisation and Its Consequences for the Discipline of Sociology." *African Sociological Review,* 12 (2): 22–48.

Keim, Wiebke. 2010. "Pour un modèle centre-périphérie dans les sciences sociales. Aspects problématiques des relations internationales en sciences sociales." *Revue d'Anthropologie Des Connaissances,* 4 (3): 570–598.

Keim, Wiebke. 2011. "Counterhegemonic Currents and Internationalization of Sociology: Theoretical Reflections and an Empirical Example." *International Sociology,* 26 (1): 123–145.

Keim, Wiebke, Ercümen Çelik, Christian Ersche and Veronika Wöhrer, eds. 2014. *Global Knowledge Production in the Social Sciences: Made in Circulation.* Farnham: Ashgate.

Kerrou, Mohamed. 1991. "Etre sociologue dans le monde arabe ou comment le savant épouse le politique." *Peuples Mediterraneens,* 54–55: 247–268.

Khatabi, Abdelkébir. 1975. "Sociologie du monde arabe: Positions." BESM, 126: 13–26.

Khelfaoui, H. 2000. *Les ingénieurs dans le système éducatif: l'aventure des instituts technologiques algériens*. Paris: Publisud.

Khelfaoui, H. 2004. "Scientific Research in Algeria: Institutionalisation versus Professionalisation." *Science, Technology & Society*, 9 (1): 75–101.

Khelfaoui, H. 2006. "La recherche scientifique en Algérie, otage de la médiation politique." In *Savoirs, insertion et globalisation: vu du Maghreb*, E. Gérard, ed., 189–216. Paris: Publisud.

Khodr, Hiba. 2011. "The Dynamics of Policy Innovation and Diffusion in the Gulf Cooperation Council: A Case Study of Three Specialized Cities." Beirut: IFI, American University of Beirut.

Kleiche, Mina and Roland Waast, eds. 2008. *Le Maroc scientifique*. Paris: Publisud.

Kreimer, Pablo and Juan Pablo Zabala. 2008. "Quelle connaissance et pour qui? Problèmes sociaux, production et usage social de connaissances scientifiques sur la maladie de Chagas en Argentine." *Revue d'Anthropologie Des Connaissances*, 2 (3): 413–440.

Kriener, Jonathan. 2014. "Lebanese Social Scientists at Lebanese University and Lebanese American University in their Scientific Community." Paper presented at the Orient Intitute, Beirut.

Kuhn, Michael and Kazumi Okamoto, eds. 2013. *Spatial Social Thoughts in Global Knowledge Encounters*. Stuttgart: IBIDEM.

Kumar, Krishna and Desiree van Welsum. 2013. "Knowledge-Based Economies and Basing Economies on Knowledge Skills: A Missing Link in GCC Countries." RAND. www.rand.org/pubs/research_reports/RR188.html.

Lablaoui, H. 2010. "Return of Algerian Qualified Expatriates: End of an Experience in Diaspora or A New Cycle in International Mobility?" *Idafat: The Arab Journal of Sociology*, 10: 75–97.

Lander, Edgardo, ed. 2003. *La colonialidad del saber: eurocentrismo y ciencias sociales – perspectivas latinoamericanas*. Buenos Aires : CLACSO.

Larédo, Philippe. 2003. "Six Major Challenges Facing Public Intervention in Higher Education, Science, Technology and Innovation." *Science and Public Policy*, 30 (1): 4–12.

Larzillière, P. 2010. "Research in Context: Scientific Production and Researchers' Experience in Jordan." *Science, Technology & Society*, 15 (2): 309–338.

Larzillière, Pénélope. 2012. "Sociologie de l'engagement à partir du Proche-Orient." In *Les Palestiniens entre etat et diaspora: le temps des incertitudes*, Jalal Al Husseine and Aude Signoles, eds., 179–188; 299–301. Paris: Karthala, IISMM-EHESS.

Larzillière, Pénélope. 2013. *La Jordanie contestataire: militants islamistes, nationalistes et communistes*. Arles: Actes Sud.

Latour, Bruno. 1987. *Science in Action*. Cambridge, MA: Harvard University Press.

Latour, B. and S. Woolgar. 1979. *Laboratory Life: The Social Construction of Scientific Facts*. Beverly Hills, CA: Sage.

Latour, Bruno and Paolo Fabbri. 1977. "La rhétorique de la science: pouvoir et devoir dans un article de science exacte." *Actes de la recherche en Sciences Sociales*, February: 81–95.

Latrache, Abdelkader. 2010. "Domains of Contribution of the Arab Diasporic Social Scientists." *Idafat: The Arab Journal of Sociology*, 10: 64–74.

Laurens, Patricia, Christian le Bas, Antoine Schoen, Lionel Villard, and Philippe Larédo. 2014. "The Rate and Motives of the Internationalisation of Large Firm R&D (1994–2005): Toward a Turning Point?" *Research Policy*, 44: 765–776.

Lavis J.N., J. Lomas and M. Hamid. 2006. "Sewankambo NK: Assessing Country-Level Efforts to Link Research to Action." *Bulletin of the World Health Organization*, 84: 620–628.

Lee, Richard, *et al.* 2005. *From National Dilemmas to Global Opportunities*. Paris: MOST Papers, Social Science and Social Policy.

Lepori, Benedetto, Rémi Barré, and Ghislaine Filliatreau. 2008. "New Perspectives and Challenges for the Design and Production of S&T Indicators." *Research Evaluation*, 17 (1): 33–44.

Leresche, Jean-Philippe, Philippe Larédo and Karl Weber, eds. 2009. *Recherche et enseignement supérieur face à l'internationalisation: France, Suisse et Union européenne*. Lausanne: Presses polytechniques et universitaires romandes.

Leydesdorff, Loet and Caroline Wagner. 2008. "International Collaboration in Science and the Formation of a Core Group." *Journal of Infometrics*, 2 (4): 317–325.

Lightman, Alan. 2008. "The Role of the Public Intellectual." Retrieved from http://web.mit.edu/comm-forum/papers/lightman.html.

Lopez-Martinez, Roberto. 2006. "A Systems Approach to Innovation Policy." PhD thesis, Manchester University.

Lord, Kristin 2008. *A New Millennium of Knowledge? The Arab Human Development Report on Building a Knowledge Society, Five Years On*. Washington, DC: Saban Centre at Brookings Institution.

Losego, P. and R. Arvanitis. 2008. "Science in Non-Hegemonic Countries." *Revue d'Anthropologie des Connaissances* 2 (3).

Louvel, Séverine and Annick Valette. 2014. "Les carrieres a l'université: Une approche par les modes d'engagement." *Revue d'anthropologie des connaissances*, 8 (3): 523–546.

Lynch, M. 2011. "After Egypt: The Limits and Promise of Online Challenges to the Authoritarian Arab State." *Perspectives on Politics*, 9 (2): 301–310.

Mallat, Chibli. 2009. "Saving the Special Tribunal for Lebanon from Failure: A Response to Jamil Al-Sayyed and Antonio Cassese." *Daily Star*, October.

Makdisi, Karim. 2009. "Reflections on the State of IR in the Arab Region." In *International Relations Scholarship around the World*, Arlene B. Tickner and Ole Wæver, eds., 181–190. New York: Routledge.

Marezouki, N. 2004. "Théorie et engagement chez Edward Saïd." *La Revue Mouvements*. www.cairn.info/revue-mouvements-2004-3-page-162.htm.

Martin, Eloísa. 2012a. "Making Sociology Current Through International Publication: A Collective Task." *Current Sociology*, 60 (6): 832–837.

Martin, Eloísa. 2012b. "Report on Current Sociology." Unpublished report.

Mattsson, Pauline, Patrice Laget, Anna Nilsson and Carl-Johan Sundberg. 2008. "Intra-EU vs. extra-EU Scientific Co-publication Patterns in EU." *Scientometrics*, 75 (3): 555–574.

Mauger Gérard, "La participation des sociologues au débat public sur l'insécurité." Histoire@Politique 2/2011 (n°14): 112–121

Mazzucato, Mariana. 2013. *The Entrepreneurial State: Debunking Public vs Private Sector Myths*. London: Anthem Press.

McLaughlin, Neil and Kerry Turcotte. 2007. "The Trouble with Burawoy: An Analytic, Synthetic Alternative." *Sociology*, 41 (5): 813–828.

Meadows, A.J. 1974. *Communication in Science*. London: Butterworths.

Melki, Jad. 2009. "Journalism and Media Studies in Lebanon." *Journalism Studies*, 10 (5): 672–690.

Mellakh, Kamal. *2007. Rapport de l'enquête qualitative sur le dispositif institutionnel et les dynamiques de l'innovation dans les entreprises au Maroc.* Casablanca: Background Report for ESTIME.

Mermier, Franck. 2005. *Le livre et la ville. Beyrouth et l'édition Arabe.* Arles: Sindbad/Actes Sud.

Meyer, Jean-Baptiste, J. Charum, D. Bernal, *et al.* 1997. "Turning Brain Drain into Brain Gain: The Colombian Experience of the Diaspora Option." *Science Technology and Society*, 2 (2): 285–315.

Mezouaghi, Mihoub, ed. 2006. *Les territoires productifs en questions.* Tunis: Institut de recherche sur le Maghreb contemporain.

M'henni, Hatem. 2007, (with the collaboration of Ben Othman, Arbia, Ghozzi, Chiraz, Ben Salah, Najeh, M'henni, Sami and Trabelsi, Mhenni). 2007. *Le système de recherche en Tunisie. Background reports* (three volumes). Tunis: ESTIME.

M'henni, H. and R. Arvanitis. 2012. "La résilience des systèmes d'innovation en période de transition: la Tunisie après le 14 Janvier 2011." *Revue Tiers Monde*, 212 (October): 57–81.

MIRA. 2011. "Assessment of International Scientific Cooperation in the Mediterranean Region: An International Challenge Ahead." White paper. www.cnrs.edu.lb/LORDI&MIRA-Workshop/White%20Paper-Feb2011.pdf.

Mitchell, Timothy, 2002. "The Middle East in the Past and Future Social Science." In *The Politics of Knowledge: Area Studies and the Disciplines*, David L. Szanton, ed., Vol. 3. Berkeley, CA: University of California Press. http://escholarship.org/uc/item/59n2d2n1#page-1.

Mofleh, Ahmad. 2015. "The Image of the Arab Intellectuals: Sociological Study of the Journal of Al-Mustabal Al-Arabi." *Idafat: The Arab Journal of Sociology*, 27: 43–67.

Moisseron, Jean-Yves. 2005. *Le partenariat Euroméditerranéen: L'échec d'une ambition régionale.* Grenoble: Presses Universitaires de Grenoble.

Molinié, Antoinette and Geoffrey Bodenhausen. 2010. "Bibliometrics as Weapons of Mass Citation: la Bibliométrie Comme Arme de Citation Massive." *Chimia*, 64: 78–89.

Monastersky, R. 2005. "The Number that's Devouring Science." *Chronicle of Higher Education*, 25 (8). http://chronicle.com/free/v52/i08/08a01201.htm.

Morini, Chiara, Rafael Rodriguez, Rigas Arvanitis, and Refaat Chaabouni. 2013. *Moving to the Future in the Euro-Mediterranean Research and Innovation Partnership: The Experience of the MIRA Project.* Bari and Paris: Options Méditerranéennes, CIHEAM. http://om.ciheam.org/option.php?IDOM=1009.

Mosbah-Natanson, S. and Y. Gingras. 2014. "The Globalization of Social Sciences? Evidence from a Quantitative Analysis of 30 Years of Production, Collaboration and Citations in the Social Sciences (1980–2009)." *Current Sociology*, 62 (5): 626–646.

Moulin, Anne Marie. 2015. "A la recherche de la science Arabe." In *Les ancrages nationaux de la science mondiale*, Mina Kleiche-Dray, ed. Paris: IRD.

Mouton, Johan and Roland Waast. 2009. "Comparative Study on National Research Systems: Findings and Lessons." In *Higher Education, Research and Innovation: Changing Dynamics*, V. Lynn Meek, Ulrich Teicher and Marie-Louise Kearney, eds., 147–169. Paris: UNESCO. http://firgoa.usc.es/drupal/files/UNESCO_Research_and_Innovation.pdf#page=152.

Mouton, Johann, Jacques Gaillard, Milandré van Lill 2014. "Science Granting Councils in Sub-Saharan Africa." Centre for Research on Evaluation, Science and Technology.

Mrad, F. 2011. *RDI for Knowledge Economy.* Beirut: ESCWA.

Musa Badawi, Ahmed. 2010. "Competitiveness of the Arab Social Research: Comparative Analysis of Research Published in Scientific Journals." *Idafat: The Arab Journal of Sociology*, 12 (in Arabic).

Nahas, Charbel. 2009. *Financing and Political Economy of Higher Education in Lebanon.* Beirut: Economic Research Forum.

Naim, S. Tanveer and Atta-ur Rahman. 2009. *Mapping Scientific Research in Member States of the Organization of Islamic Conference (OIC)*. Paris: UNESCO.

Nasser, Ramzi. 2014. "Educational Reform in Qatar." Paper presented at the Lecture in Lebanese Center for Educational Studies, Beirut.

Ngai, P., S. Yuan, G. Yuhua, L. Huilin, J. Chan and M. Selden. 2014. "Trans-Border Sociological Intervention in Foxconn." In *Precarious Engagements: Tackling the Dilemmas of Public Sociology*, Michael Burawoy, ed. London: Sage.

Nour, S.S. 2005. "Science and Technology Development Indicators in the Arab Region." *Science, Technology and Society*, 10 (2): 249–275.

Oliveira, João Batista Araujo. 1984. *Ilhas de competência: carreiras científicas no Brasil.* São Paulo: Editora Melhoramentos.

Ortiz, Renato. 2008. *La supremacía del Inglés en las ciencias sociales*. México: Siglo XXI.

Oulion, Marina and Rigas Arvanitis. 2014. "Le Système de Recherche Chinois: Entre la Politique Planifiée du développement et le marché." In *Les ancrages nationaux de la science mondiale*, Mina Kleiche, ed. Paris: TBC.

Pace, M. and Cavatorta, F. 2012. "The Arab Uprisings in Theoretical Perspective: An Introduction." *Mediterranean Politics*, 17(2): 125–138.

Pancera, Aurélie, Kyriaki Papageorgiou, S. Boutros, Latifa Bousselmi, S. Abdelhak, and A. Al-Bawab. 2013. "First Lessons Learnt from the Mediterranean ERA-WIDE Projects." In *Moving to the Future in the Euro-Mediterranean Research and Innovation Partnership: The Experience of the MIRA Project*, Chiara Morini, Rafael Rodriguez, Rigas Arvanitis and Refaat Chaabouni, eds., 63–78. Bari and Paris: CIHEAM. http://om.ciheam.org/option.php?IDOM=1009.

Papageorgiou, Kyriaki. 2007. "Seeds of Doubt: Genetic Narratives and Ethnographic Sequences in Contemporary Egypt." PhD anthropology thesis, University of California, Irvine.

Pasimeni, Paolo. 2011. "The Europe 2020 Index." *Social Indicators Research*, no. 110: 613–35.

Pasimeni, Paolo. 2012. "Measuring Europe 2020: A New Tool to Assess the Strategy." *International Journal of Innovation and Regional Development*, 4 (5): 365–383.

Pasimeni, P., A.S. Boisard, R. Arvanitis, *et al.* 2007. "Towards a Euro-Mediterranean Innovation Space: Some Lessons and Policy Queries." The CONCORD seminar ITPS.

Piron, Sylvain. 2010. "La bibliométrie comme arme de citation massive." *Évaluation de la recherche en SHS*. 26 April. http://evaluation.hypotheses.org/884.

Pontille, David. 2003. "Authorship Practices and Institutional Contexts in Sociology: Elements for a Comparison of the United States and France." *Science, Technology & Human Values*, 28: 217–243.

Pontille, David. 2004. *La signature scientifique: une sociologie pragmatique de l'attribution*. Paris: CNRS Éditions.

Pouillard, Nicolas. 2013. "Boire à Hamra. Une jeunesse nostalgique à Beyrouth ?" In *Jeunesses arabes du Maroc au Yémen: loisirs, cultures et politiques*, Laurent Bonnefoy and Myriam Catusse, eds. Paris: La Découverte.

Price, Dereck de Solla. 1963. *Little Science, Big Science*. New York: Columbia University Press.

Qi, Xiaoying. 2012. "A Case Study of Globalized Knowledge Flows: Guanxi in Social Science and Management Theory." *International Sociology*, 27: 707.

Quet, Mathieu, and Marianne Noel. 2014. "From Politics to Academics: Political Activism and the Emergence of Science and Technology Studies in South Korea." *East Asian Science, Technology and Society*, 8: 175–193.

Rachik, Hassan and Rahma Bourqia. 2011. "La sociologie au Maroc." *Sociologies*, October. http://sociologies.revues.org/3719?lang=en.

Raj, Kapil. 2006. *Relocating Modern Science: Circulation and the Construction of Scientific Knowledge in South Asia and Europe, Seventeenth to Nineteenth Century*. Delhi: Permanent Black.

Raymond, Candice. 2013. *Réécrire l'histoire au Liban. Une génération d'historiens face à la période ottomane, de la fin des années 1960 à nos jours*. Thèse pour le doctorat Histoire et civilisations. Paris: EHESS.

Reiffers, Jean-Louis, and Jean-Eric Aubert. 2002. *Le Développement des Économies Fondées sur la Connaissance dans la Région Moyen-Orient et Afrique du Nord: Facteurs Clés*. Marseille: World Bank. www.femise.org/PDF/KBE-0209-FR.pdf.

Ringer, K.F. 1991. *Fields of Knowledge: French Academic Culture in Comparative Perspective*. Cambridge: Cambridge University Press.

Rodriguez Medina, Leandro. 2013. *Centers and Peripheries in Knowledge Production*. New York and London: Routledge.

Rodríguez-Garavito, Cesar. 2014. "Amphibious Sociology: Dilemmas and Possibilities of Public Sociology in a Multimedia World." In *Precarious Engagements: Tackling the Dilemmas of Public Sociology*, Michael Burawoy, ed. London: Sage.

Romani, Vincent. 2001. "Universités et universitaires palestiniens d'une Intifada à l'autre, entre crise et routine." Revue *Egypte/Monde Arabe* (CEDEJ), 6: 55–80.

Romani, Vincent. 2008. "Sciences sociales et lutte nationale dans les territoires occupés palestiniens: La coercition comme contrainte et comme ressource scientifique." *Revue d'anthropologie des connaissances*, 2 (3): 487–504.

Romani, Vincent. 2012. "Internationalisation des Politiques Universitaires et Contournement de Leurs Publics ?" *Revue des Mondes Musulmans et de la Méditerranée*, 131. http://remmm.revues.org/7578.

Rosenberg, Nathan. 1982. *Inside the Blackbox: Technology and Economics*. Cambridge: Cambridge University Press.

Rossano, Marinela, José Bonfim, Refaat Chaabouni and Georges Bonas. 2013. "The Monitoring Committe for RTD." In *Moving to the Future in the Euro-Mediterranean Research and Innovation Partnership: The Experience of the MIRA Project*, Chiara Morini, Rafael Rodriguez, Rigas Arvanitis and Refaat Chaabouni, eds. Bari and Paris: CIHEAM. http://om.ciheam.org/option.php?IDOM=1009.

Roussillon, Alain. 2002. "Sociologie et identité en Égypte et au Maroc: le travail de deuil de la colonisation." *Revue d'Histoire des Sciences Humaines*, 2 (7): 193–221.

Ruffier, Jean. 1991. "El debate sobre la transferencia de tecnología ha llegado a un estancamiento." *Sociología del trabajo, Nueva época (Madrid)*, 12 (91): 105–122.

Russell, Jane M., Rigas Arvanitis and Angelica Maria Rosas. 1995. Institutional production cutting across disciplinary boundaries: An assessment of chemical research in Mexico. *Proceedings of the Fifth International Conference on Scientometrics and Infometrics*, River Forest, Illinois, June 1995.

Sabour, M. 1988. *Homo Academicus Arabicus*. Joensuu: University of Joensuu.

Said, Edward. 1978. *Orientalism: Western Representations of the Orient*. New York: Pantheon.

Said, Edward. 1983. Travelling theory. In: *The Word, the Text and the Critic*, E. Said, ed. Cambridge, MA: Harvard University Press.

Saint Laurent, B. 2005. *Innovation, pôles technologiques et attraction d'investissement en Méditerranée*. Marseille: ANIMA.

Sakr, Elias. 2008. "Experts Lament Bias of Lebanese Media." *The Daily Star*, June.

Salih, Nabil Abd al-Majid. 2008. *Science and Technology Indicators in the Arab Countries 2006*. Cairo: UNESCO.

Salim, Mohamed Al-Sayid. 2009. "Foreign Languages Instruction in the Egyptian Universities." Egyptian Community Club. www.egyptclub.de/Studium-in-Fremdsprache.htm.

Salomon, Jean-Jacques. 2001. "Social Sciences, Science Policy Studies, Science Policy-making." In *Science and Technology Policy*, Rigas Arvanitis, ed. London and Paris: Encyclopedia of Life Support Systems and UNESCO.

Sassen, Saskia. 2007. *A Sociology of Globalization*. New York: Norton.

Schmoch, Ulrich and Torben Schubert. 2008. "Are International Co-publications an Indicator for Quality of Scientific Research?" *Scientometrics*, 74 (3): 361–377.

Schwab, Klaus and Xavier Sala-i-Martín, eds. 2012. *The Global Competitiveness Report 2012–2013*. Geneva: World Economic Forum. www.weforum.org/issues/global-competitiveness.

Schwarz, R. and M. de Corral. 2011. "States Do Not Just Fail and Collapse: Rethinking States in the Middle East." *Democracy and Security*, 7 (3): 209–226.

Selmi, Adel. 2001. "L'émergence d'un champ scientifique: l'ethnosociologie et la sociologie en Tunisie (1881–1970)." *Gradhiva*, 29: 43–57.

Shami, Seteney and Nefissa Naguib. 2013. "Occluding Difference: Ethnic Identity and the Shifting Zones of Theory on the Middle East and North Africa." In *Anthropology of the Middle East and North Africa: Into the New Millennium*, Sherine Hafez and Susan Slyomovics, eds. Bloomington, IN: Indiana University Press.

Shehadeh, Mahdi and Saleh Tayyara. 1999. *Role of the Research Centers in Policy Making*. Beirut: Center for Arab European Studies.

Shelley, F.M. 2011. "Forum on the 2011 'Arab Spring' Orientalism, Idealism, and Realism: The United States and the 'Arab Spring.'" *The Arab World Geographer/Le Géographe du Monde Arab*, 14 (2): 169–173.

Siino, François. 2004. *Science et pouvoir dans la Tunisie contemporaine*. Paris: Karthala.

Sivertsen, Gunnar. 2014. *European Trends in Performance-Based Funding of Research Institutions*. Oslo: Nordic Institute for Studies in Innovation, Research and Education. www.etag.ee/wp-content/uploads/2014/10/Sivertsen-Tartu-Nov-2014.pdf.

Stanton, Richard. 2009. "On Mayhew: The Demonization of Soft Power and Validation of the New Citizen." In *Public Relations and Social Theory: Key Figures and Concepts*, Øyvind Ihlen and Betteke Van Ruler, eds. London: Routledge.

Stehr, Nico. 1994. *Knowledge Societies*. London: Sage.

Stephan Hachem, Maud. 1996. "Research and Communication." *Bahithat*, 3: 76–96.

Sufiani, Abdullah. 2014. *Veiling the Vision: Reading in the Hidden Effects on the Fiqh Discourse*. Riyyad: Namaa Center for Research and Studies (in Arabic).

Suleiman, Yasir. 2003. *The Arabic Language and National Identity: A Study in Ideology*. Baltimore, MD: Georgetown University Press.

Sultana, Ronald G. 1999. "The Euro-Mediterranean Region and its Universities: An Overview of Trends, Challenges and Prospects." *Mediterranean Journal of Educational Studies*, 4 (2): 7–49.

Sundar, Nandini. 2014. "In Times of Civil War: On Being a Schizophrenic (Public) Sociologist." In *Precarious Engagements: Tackling the Dilemmas of Public Sociology*, Michael Burawoy, ed. London: Sage.

Touraine, A. 1981. *The Voice and the Eye: An Analysis of Social Movements*. Cambridge: Cambridge University Press.

Traboulsi, Fawwaz. 2014. *Social Classes and Political Power in Lebanon*. Beirut: Heinrich Boell Foundation – Middle East. http://lb.boell.org/en/2014/05/04/social-classes-and-political-power-lebanon.

Transeuropéennes. 2013. *Mapping of Translation in the Euro-Mediterranean Region*. Paris: Transeuropéennes. Retrieved from www.poliglotti4.eu/docs/Publis/A_Mapping_of_Translation_in_the_Euro-Mediterranean_Region.pdf.

Traverso, Enzo. 2013. *Où Sont Passés Les Intellectuels?* Paris: Textuel.

Tremblay, André. 2011. *Les classements internationaux sont-ils la clef d'accès à l'économie de la connaissance? Analyse des universités du Liban et Dubaï*. Lebanon: Université Saint-Joseph de Beyrouth.

TTCSP. 2014. *2013 Global Go To Think Tank Index Report*. The Think Tanks and Civil Societies Program (TTCSP) at the University of Pennsylvania. http://gotothinktank.com/dev1/wp-content/uploads/2014/01/GoToReport2013.pdf.

UNDP. 2000. *The Four Year Brain Gain*. Jerusalem: UNDP.

UNDP. 2003. "Human Development Reports Indicators Lebanon." http://hdr.undp.org/statistics/data/cty/cty_f_LBN.html.

UNDP. 2004. "Le Rapport du développement humain dans le monde arabe 2003." www.undp.org/rbas/ahdr/frenchpresskit2003.html.

UNDP. 2005. *Arab Human Development Report 2004: Towards Freedom in the Arab World*. Amman: UNDP Regional Bureau for Arab States.

UNDP. 2009. *Arab Human Development Report 2009*. New York: UNDP. www.arab-hdr.org/publications/other/ahdr/ahdr2009e.pdf.

UNESCO. 2010a. "Measuring R&D: Challenges Faced by Developing Countries." UNESCO. www.uis.unesco.org/Library/Documents/tech%205-eng.pdf.

UNESCO. 2010b. "Science Report: The Current Status of Science Around the World." UNESCO. www.unesco.org/new/en/natural-sciences/science-technology/prospective-studies/unesco-science-report/unesco-science-report-2010.

Valenti, G., M. Casalet, R. Casas, *et al.*, eds. 2008. *Instituciones, sociedad del conocimiento y mundo del trabajo*. Mexico: FLACSO Mexico, Plaza y Valdés Editores.

Vessuri, Hebe. 1994. "The Institutionalization Process." In *The Uncertain Quest: Science, Technology, and Development*, Jean-Jacques Salomon, Francisco Sagasti, and Céline Sachs-Jeantet, eds., 177–212. Tokyo, New York and Paris: UNU Press.

Vessuri, Hebe, Michael Kuhn and Kazumi Okamoto. 2013. "The Transformation Processes in Global Social Knowledge." In *Spatial Social Thought: Local Knowledge in Global Science Encounters*, M. Kuhn, ed. Stuttgart: IBIDEM.

Von Holdt, Karl. 2014. "Critical Engagement in Fields of Power: Cycles of Sociological Activism in Post-Apartheid South Africa." In *Precarious Engagements: Tackling the Dilemmas of Public Sociology*, Michael Burawoy, ed. London: Sage.

Waast, Roland. 2006. "Savoir et société: Un nouveau pacte à sceller." In *Savoirs, insertion et globalisation: vu du Maghreb*, Etienne Gérard, ed., 373–403. Paris: Publisud.

Waast, Roland. 2008. *National Research Systems in the Developing World. Arab States Regional Report*. Paris: UNESCO Forum for Higher Education, Research and Knowledge.

Waast, R. 2010. "Research in Arab Countries (North Africa and West Asia)." *Science, Technology & Society*, 15 (2): 187–231.

Waast, Roland and Mina Kleiche-Dray, eds. 2009. *Evaluation of a National Research System : Morocco.* Luxembourg: European Commission. http://ec.europa.eu/research/iscp/pdf/morocco_evaluation.pdf.

Waast, Roland, and P.L. Rossi. 2009. "A Scoreboard and Beyond: The Experience of ESTIME for Morocco and Other Mediterranean Countries." www.estime.ird.fr.

Waast, R. and P.L. Rossi. 2010. "Scientific Production in Arab Countries." *Science Technology & Society*, 15 (2): 339–370.

Waast, Roland, Rigas Arvanitis, Claire Richard-Waast and P.L. Rossi. 2010. "What do Social Sciences in North African Countries Focus On?" In *World Social Science Report*, 176–180. Paris: UNESCO. http://unesdoc.unesco.org/images/0018/001883/188333e.pdf.

Wagner, Caroline. 2006. "International Collaboration in Science and Technology: Promises and Pitfalls." In *Science and Technology Policy for Development. Dialogues at the Interfaces*, L. Box and R. Engelhard, eds., 165–176. New York: Anthem.

Wagner, Caroline. 2008. *The New Invisible College: Science for Development.* Washington, DC: Brookings Institute Press.

Wahbeh, Kamal. 2010. "Kamel Assad and the Identity in Crisis." *Alnahar*, March (in Arabic).

Wahishi, Khalid. 2010. "Introduction." *Idafat: The Arab Journal of Sociology*, 11: 7–12.

Weeds, Julie Elizabeth. 2003. "Measures and Applications of Lexical Distributional Similarity." PhD thesis, University of Sussex.

Weyland, K. 2012. "The Arab Spring: Why the Surprising Similarities with the Revolutionary Wave of 1848?" *Perspectives on Politics*, 10 (4): 917–934.

White, H.D. and B.C. Griffith. 1982. "Authors as Markers of Intellectual Space: Cocitation in Studies of Science, Technology and Society." *Journal of Documentation*, 38 (4): 255–272.

White, H.D. and K.W. McCain. 1998. "Visualizing a Discipline: An Author Co-citation Analysis of Information Science, 1972–1995." *Journal of the American Society for Information Science*, 49 (4): 327–355.

Wieviorka, M. 2000. "Sociologie Postclassique ou Déclin de la Sociologie?" *Cahiers Internationaux de Sociologie*, 108 (January): 5–35.

Wieviorka, M. 2014. "Sociology's Interventions: Engaging the Media and Politics while Remaining a Social Scientist." In *Precarious Engagements: Tackling the Dilemmas of Public Sociology*, Michael Burawoy, ed. London: Sage Publications.

Willson, M. 1997. "Community in the Abstract: A Political and Ethical Dilemma?" in *Virtual Politics: Identity and Community in Cyberspace*, D. Holmes, ed., 121–159. London: Sage.

World Bank. 1999. *Knowledge for Development.* Washington, DC: World Bank.

World Bank. 2012. *Knowledge Assessment Methodology. Knowledge Economy Index 2012 Rankings.* Washington, DC: World Bank. http://go.worldbank.org/JGAO5XE940.

World Economic Forum. 2002. *The Global Competitiveness Report 2002–2003.* Oxford: Oxford University Press.

World Economic Forum. 2005. *The Global Competitiveness Report 2005–2006.* Basingstoke: Palgrave Macmillan.

Wu, X. 2009. "Between Public and Professional: Chinese Sociology and the Construction of a Harmonious Society." *ASA Footnotes*, 37 (5). www.asanet.org/footnotes/mayjun09/intl_0509.html.

Yahya, Abbad. 2014. "Statistics and Social Research in the Occupied Territory: The Impact of Colonial Fragmentation of the Palestinian Society." *Omran*, 7 February.

Yılmaz, Ferruh. 2012. "Right-Wing Hegemony and Immigration: How the Populist Far-Right Achieved Hegemony through the Immigration Debate in Europe." *Current Sociology*, 60 (3): 368–381.

Zahlan, A.B. 2012. *Science, Development, and Sovereignty in the Arab World*. New York: Palgrave Macmillan.

Zakhia, Elsa. 2007. *Répertoire des chercheurs; Répertoire des centres de recherche: Liban/Syrie/Jordanie*. Beyrouth: ESTIME. www.estime.ird.fr/article255.html.

Zaouadi, Mahmoud. 2011. "The Legitimization of the Revolution and the Struggle of Language in the Tunisian Personality." *Al-Mustaqbal Al-Arabi* (in Arabic).

Zdravomyslova, Elena and Anna Temkina. 2014. "Gender's Crooked Path: Feminism Confronts Russian Patriarchy." In *Precarious Engagements: Tackling the Dilemmas of Public Sociology*, Michael Burawoy, ed. London: Sage.

Zughoul, M. 2000. "The Language of Higher Education in Jordan: Conflict, Challenges and Innovative Accommodation." In *Challenge and Change in the Euro-Mediterranean Region: Case Studies in Educational Innovation*, R. Sultana, ed. New York: Peter Lang.

Index

Page numbers in *italics* denote tables, those in **bold** denote figures.

For Product Safety Concerns and Information please contact our EU
representative GPSR@taylorandfrancis.com
Taylor & Francis Verlag GmbH, Kaufingerstraße 24, 80331 München, Germany